NICARAGUA
without ILLUSIONS

NICARAGUA
without ILLUSIONS

Regime Transition and
Structural Adjustment
in the 1990s

edited by
THOMAS W. WALKER

A Scholarly Resources Inc. Imprint
Wilmington, Delaware

Scholarly Resources Inc.
104 Greenhill Avenue
Wilmington, DE 19805-1897

Cover: The drawing, "Nicaragua sin ilusiones: Régimen de transisión en los 1990s," was created especially for this book by Leoncio Sáenz of Managua. During the revolutionary period, Sáenz was a frequent artistic contributor to *Nicaráuac*, *Pensamiento Própio*, and other Nicaraguan publications. In addition, his works hung in President Daniel Ortega's outer office and were featured in exhibitions around the world.

Library of Congress Cataloging-in-Publication Data

Nicaragua without illusions : regime transition and structural adjustment
  in the 1990s / edited by Thomas W. Walker.
        p.   cm.
    Includes index.
    ISBN 0-8420-2578-2 (cloth : alk. paper). — ISBN 0-8420-2579-0
(paper : alk. paper)
    1. Nicaragua—Politics and government—1990–   . 2. Democracy—
Nicaragua. 3. Political participation—Nicaragua. I. Walker, Thomas W.
F1528.N51785   1997
972.8505'4—dc21   96-45590
                                                                                       CIP

⊗The paper used in this publication meets the minimum requirements of the American National Standard for permanence of paper for printed library materials, Z39.48, 1984.

About the Editor

THOMAS W. WALKER is professor of political science and director of Latin American studies at Ohio University, Athens, Ohio. He is the author of *The Christian Democratic Movement in Nicaragua* (1970) and *Nicaragua: The Land of Sandino* (3d ed., 1991); the coauthor, with John Booth, of *Understanding Central America* (2d ed., 1993); and the editor/coauthor of four other books on Nicaragua, including *Reagan versus the Sandinistas: The Undeclared War on Nicaragua*, which appeared on *Choice* Magazine's 1987 list of Outstanding Academic Books.

Professor Walker began his field research in Nicaragua in 1967. In 1982 he was part of the Central America Task Force of the United Presbyterian Church's Council on Church and Society. In 1983–84 he was founding co-chair of the Latin American Studies Association's (LASA) Task Force on Scholarly Relations with Nicaragua. In 1984, Professor Walker served as co-coordinator of a LASA delegation sent to observe the Nicaraguan elections of November 4, in 1989–90 he was a member of the LASA team that observed the 1990 elections, and in 1996 he observed Nicaragua's elections as part of a Hemisphere Initiatives/Washington Office on Latin America team.

1

Introduction
Historical Setting and Important Issues

Thomas W. Walker*

Background

It would be impossible to understand the Nicaragua of the 1990s without at least looking briefly at that country's evolution over the nearly five hundred years following the arrival of the Spaniards.[1] The fact that Nicaragua, like El Salvador and Guatemala, experienced social upheaval in the late twentieth century, whereas neighboring Costa Rica and Honduras were relatively peaceful, is no accident but rather the product of very different pathways in their social and political formation.[2]

The first conquistadors to come to Costa Rica had difficulty in pacifying local Indians and thus eventually either killed them off or drove them out of the fertile mountain valleys where they had chosen to settle. As a result, since there was no racially distinct underclass to exploit, a relatively egalitarian society eventually came into being. By the late nineteenth century, programs for universal education were implemented, and a half century later a functioning democracy emerged. On the other hand, Honduras was such an economic backwater that a propertied elite never developed to the point that they felt confident in ruthlessly exploiting the impoverished majority. Although democracy there would be practiced only sporadically, human rights were much less frequently violated in twentieth-century Honduras than in any of the three adjoining states.

*I am indebted to the Latin American Studies Association for accommodating our three-session panel on "Nicaragua in the 1990s" at LASA's XIX International Congress in Washington, DC, on September 29, 1995. These sessions gave almost all of the authors a chance to present their findings and receive scholarly comment prior to sending their manuscripts to me. In addition, I would like to thank my department for giving me a course reduction at the time of peak editing activity.

What sets Nicaragua, El Salvador, and Guatemala apart is the fact that, in these three colonies, relatively large Indian populations were subdued by the conquistadors and thence turned into an exploited underclass, and there were sufficient natural resources to motivate and stimulate the growth of exploitative propertied elites. Thus, in the late nineteenth century, as Costa Rica was beginning to lay the foundations for twentieth-century democracy and as Honduras still languished as a forgotten economic backwater, the other three countries were entering a phase of "modernizing" economic activity that would accentuate already severe class polarization and exploitation.[3] A set of policies—called the "liberal reforms" in Mexico and elsewhere in Latin America but actually introduced by Conservative governments in Nicaragua—were carried out to help the local elites take advantage of the new international demand for certain primary products, notably coffee in the case of Nicaragua. In 1877 all forms of rural propertyholding in Nicaragua were banned by law except for individual rights recognized by legal title. Communal indigenous properties as well as plots held previously under common law by the illiterate mestizo peasantry instantly became "unoccupied" national territory that could be purchased by the agricultural elite. To add insult to injury, the cultivation of plantain, the banana-like staple food of the peasantry, was outlawed and "vagrancy" was made punishable by forced labor in productive enterprises (often the coffee plantations that quickly replaced peasant and Indian communal farms). The Liberal governments that came to power in 1893 and ruled the country off and on until 1979 simply accentuated this cruel and exploitative agroexport system.

Understandably, Nicaragua's rural poor often rebelled against their oppressors. Several thousand Indians lost their lives in 1881 in the tragic War of the Comuneros. Peasants and Indians assisted Augusto César Sandino in his guerrilla war against the Nicaraguan government and U.S. troops in the late 1920s and early 1930s. The same groups were also instrumental in the 1979 triumph of the Sandinista revolution over Liberal dictator Anastasio Somoza Debayle.

Meanwhile, an equally important theme in Nicaragua's historical formation was recurrent foreign interference.[4] First came the Spaniards who, in turn, were raided by buccaneers and challenged by the British, especially on the Atlantic Coast. After formal independence, England and the United States quarreled over control of the region. In the mid-1850s a Yankee filibusterer, William Walker, assisted local Liberals in seizing power but soon declared himself president. Although Walker was quickly overthrown and eventually executed, the United States would become increasingly involved in Nicaraguan affairs. Tensions mounted in the late nineteenth century between the nationalist Liberal dictator José Santos Zelaya and a United States that was experiencing a growing sense of manifest destiny and an urge toward imperialism. Zelaya had the audacity to refuse to yield canal-building rights that would have included U.S. sovereignty over certain Nicaraguan territory. In 1909, a few years after the United States had helped engineer the independence of the Colombian province of Panama in order to obtain canal rights through that region, the Taft administration became alarmed at rumors that Zelaya was negotiating with the British and the Japanese to build a second, potentially competitive canal through Nicaragua. U.S. agents then encouraged an uprising by the minority Conservative Party and sent a military force to Bluefields on the Atlantic Coast to see to it that the rebels were not defeated. By 1910, Zelaya and his hand-picked Liberal successor had been forced out of office and replaced by a Conservative government more pliant to the wishes of Washington.

In 1912, when Liberal patriot Benjamín Zeledón rebelled against the Conservative government, U.S. Marines occupied the country and apparently winked and looked the other way as the captured Zeledón was executed and publicly mutilated by government forces.[5] From then until the end of 1932, with the exception of a short interval in the mid-1920s, Nicaragua was occupied by the Marines. Treaties injurious to its interests were signed under U.S. pressure, and a National Guard was created to maintain internal order. It was against this background that another patriot, Augusto César Sandino, waged a long guerrilla war that ended in the withdrawal of U.S. forces in 1932.

The Somoza Period

As the United States withdrew, command of the National Guard, for the first time, was turned over to a Nicaraguan. A bright, congenial young man who spoke fluent English, Anastasio Somoza García had ingratiated himself with the occupying Americans.[6] Once in command of the military, he quickly consolidated his power. Sandino was assassinated in 1934, a coup and rigged election took place in 1936, and the caudillo was formally inaugurated as president on January 1, 1937. Thus began the longest-lived dynastic dictatorship in Latin American history. Somoza himself would run the country until his assassination in 1956. His eldest son, Luis Somoza Debayle, would then rule directly or through puppet presidents until 1967. And Luis's younger brother, Anastasio Somoza Debayle, would then take up the reins of power until overthrown by mass-based insurrection in 1979.

The personalities and governing style of the three Somozas differed one from the other. The father was a sort of populist dictator; Luis liked the appearance of "democracy" and 1960s developmentalism; and Anastasio, Jr., was an intemperate, greedy man more prone to the use of force. Nevertheless, the Somoza formula for governing was simple and fairly constant during most of the forty-three years of family rule. It rested on three pillars: 1) co-optation of key domestic elites; 2) direct control of the National Guard; and 3) the support of the United States.

The co-optation of elites was extremely important. Key to this strategy was a continuing effort to get a fraction of the "opposition" Conservative Party to participate in rigged elections or cogoverning schemes. As a reward for thus legitimizing regimes that they could not hope to defeat in elections, certain Conservative elites achieved status and occasional minority participation in Somoza-run governments. In addition, the Somozas usually refrained from killing members of high-status families and saw to it that the monied elite had considerable freedom to pursue their business interests.

The National Guard was controlled through two devices. First, the family never allowed the direct command of the military to slip from its hands. Anastasio Somoza García and then, upon his death, Anastasio Somoza Debayle directly commanded the Guard, initially during the presidency of his elder brother and two puppets, and then while acting as president in his own right. Second, and equally important, the family encouraged officers and men alike to be very corrupt. The Guard was a sort of mafia in uniform that controlled prostitution and gambling, engaged in smuggling, ran protection rackets, and took bribes and kickbacks. Thoroughly hated by civilians of all political stripes and social classes, the Guardsmen knew that their survival depended on that of the Somozas. Finally, American support was carefully cultivated. All three of the Somoza dictators had been educated in the United States, spoke fluent English, and could relate well to (frequently ethnocentric) U.S. diplomats and visiting congressmen and businessmen. But, more important, the Somozas deliberately and consistently subordinated the foreign policy of Managua to that of Washington. Nicaragua provided military bases during World War II, offered to send troops to both Korea and Vietnam, and allowed its territory to be used as one of the bases for CIA operations against Guatemala in 1954 and as the launching place for the CIA-organized Bay of Pigs invasion of Cuba in 1961. In return, though it occasionally tried to step back from its embarrassing ally,[7] Washington was usually very supportive. Indeed, by the time the last Somoza was overthrown in 1979, the corrupt National Guard was the most heavily U.S.-trained military establishment in all of Latin America.[8]

The Somoza system accentuated class differences and social problems. The socially regressive agro-export economy, developed in the nineteenth century, was made even more exploitative as a new wave of peasant farmers was displaced in order to make way for the production of cotton in the 1950s. As more and more land was cultivated to produce export crops, less and less food was produced for consumption by an ever-expanding population. Per capita income remained below average even for impoverished Latin America, with the lower 50 percent of the population in the late 1970s probably having access to under $300 per person per year. Social conditions, as seen in high infant mortality and illiteracy rates and very low average life expectancy, were simply horrendous. Meanwhile, the Somoza family fortune, which had consisted of a small, run-down coffee farm in the early 1930s, had risen to at least $500 million by the time the last Somoza was toppled. Corruption and abuse of power rather than unusual business acumen clearly accounted for most of that sum.

The Overthrow of Somoza

In the early 1970s the Somoza system began to unravel and, on July 19, 1979, was finally toppled by a mass-based insurrection. A number of alternative single-factor explanations have been offered as to why this insurrection, unlike so many others in Latin America, succeeded—Somoza was corrupt, the system was exploitative, the revolutionaries had the right strategy, the United States had not intervened to stop the revolutionaries, and so forth. But as Timothy P. Wickham-Crowley shows, none of these single-factor explanations is adequate in itself.[9] Instead, he claims that four broad conditions were met in Nicaragua (and in Cuba in 1959) that were not present (at least not all four) in any of the many other Latin American countries that had experienced insurrection since the late 1950s. Basically, Nicaragua had the right social conditions; a target regime so despicable that it had managed to alienate most of its political base; temporarily, the right international environment; and an intelligent and flexible guerrilla movement.

That the social conditions in Nicaragua in the 1970s were ripe for revolution hardly needs elaboration. Much of the rural population consisted of extremely impoverished people living in very precarious circumstances. Some were part-time, poorly paid rural migrants who drifted around the country following work at harvesttime and squatted in urban slums or on small remote plots during the rest of the year. Others were highly exploited sharecroppers or small peasants often squatting on plots to which they had no title. In addition, the harsh and exploitative character of agro-export had driven many poor people into urban areas in search of a better life. There, most ended up in slums with few employment opportunities and little access to social services. In Managua, their situation was made even more desperate following an earthquake in 1972 that destroyed most of the city. Although the dictatorship received over $100 million in international aid, very little ever went to relieving the suffering of the city's poor majority. In all, by the late 1970s, most Nicaraguans were impoverished, desperate, and owed little to the existing system.

The second factor that contributed to the success of the revolution was that it faced the ideal type of foe: in Wickham-Crowley's words, a "mafiacracy." The last of the Somozas was a self-centered tyrant who lacked the political skills of his father or older brother. His behavior following the 1972 earthquake alienated one of the important pillars of the Somoza system, the domestic elite. He saw the influx of international aid and the spending programs created in the demolition and reconstruction of Managua as an opportunity to enrich himself and his cronies. Accordingly, he bullied his way into key sectors of the economy (demolition, cement, concrete, and construction, among others) and had the government award his enterprises lucrative contracts. He also allowed the Guard to misappropriate and sell food and material relief supplies. In so doing, he lost the support of most civilian elites. Thus, by 1977, when the Carter administration pressured the dictator to reinstate freedom of the press, Pedro Joaquín Chamorro's Conservative opposition daily *La Prensa* had a field day detailing the corruption and greed of the regime.[10] Chamorro's assassination in the following January made any rapprochement between the elites and the regime impossible.

The third important factor that contributed (unwittingly) to the success of the insurrection was a temporary moderation in U.S. Cold War policy. Unlike administrations immediately before or after it, the Carter administration placed considerable rhetorical emphasis on human rights. Accordingly, although the Somoza regime tried to accommodate Washington in certain cosmetic ways, the United States eventually cut off military aid and cut back on nonmilitary assistance. Even though Israel (the biggest U.S. foreign aid recipient in the world) immediately replaced the United States as Somoza's arms supplier with no audible objection from Washington, the symbolic significance of the change in aid policy was profound. The dictator and his cronies were demoralized and the insurgents and their backers were energized. In the end, though the Carter administration abhorred the idea of a rebel victory and even made a last-minute plea for the Organization of American States to send a "peace keeping" force (to block such an outcome),[11] the United States at least refrained from direct military intervention.

The final factor was the nature of the insurgency itself. The Sandinista National Liberation Front (Frente Sandinista de Liberación Nacional, or FSLN) was formed in 1961 by a small group of Marxist students who had left the Nicaraguan Socialist Party, which they saw to be too closely controlled by the Soviet Union. Inspired by Sandino and the Cuban revolution, they adopted a rural guerrilla focus (*foco*) approach to insurgency. Never numbering more than a few dozen in the 1960s, most Sandinista cadre were killed in a rural confrontation with government forces at Pancasán in August 1967. The surviving Sandinistas then adopted a strategy of "the accumulation of force in silence,"[12] according to which, for seven years, they worked quietly among university students and the urban and rural poor.

Meanwhile, in 1968 the Latin American bishops held a historic conference in Medellín, Colombia. In their final document they called on all religious personnel to make a "preferential option for the poor" and to spread what they saw as Christ's liberating message to the masses by training Lay Delegates of the Word who, together with priests and nuns, would create

"Christian base communities" (CEBs) in which small groups of ordinary people would discuss the "social gospel." When the bishops' directives were implemented in Nicaragua in the late 1960s and early 1970s, the regime, seeing the resultant grass-roots activity as subversive, reacted with violence that sometimes resulted in deaths. Ironically, this violence helped the rebel cause by convincing many Catholics that there was no way to bring justice to Nicaragua except through armed struggle. From then on, the insurgent effort would blend both nationalist Marxist and progressive Catholic elements and thus considerably broaden its appeal.[13]

Although the Sandinistas would stage one spectacularly successful hostage/ransom operation in 1974 and a flurry of attacks on urban areas in 1977, the insurgency did not really catch fire until late 1978. In August of that year the FSLN staged another successful hostage/ransom operation, this time holding the National Legislative Palace in the heart of Managua for several days until the regime agreed to several humiliating concessions. The following month, inspired by this event, groups of young people in several important cities set up barricades and fought off the National Guard for up to two weeks. The Guard defeated the poorly armed insurgents at the cost of several thousand civilian lives, but, from then on, both the regime and the people knew that the overthrow of the system was imminent. The FSLN, whose leadership had been squabbling for several years over insurrectionary tactics, finally came together around an effective multiclass strategy that combined both rural and urban tactics, and a big influx of recruits quickly swelled the FSLN's formal army from a few hundred to several thousand. The demoralized Somoza elite and officer corps began transferring assets out of the country. Early the following summer, the FSLN declared its "final offensive" as well-coordinated fighting broke out on six "fronts" in various parts of the country. As the National Guard imploded, the FSLN announced the liberation of one city after another. On July 17, 1979, Somoza fled to Miami. Two days later, the FSLN marched into Managua and accepted the surrender of what remained of the Guard.

In all, the FSLN had shown considerable skill and flexibility in its struggle against the dictatorship. It had changed strategies and tactics until it finally found a formula that worked. It had integrated new groups, such as progressive Catholics, into its ranks and had sought multiclass support. And it had demonstrated great skill in public relations by sending spokespersons around the world to gain international backing, and by running a rebel radio station that not only reached Nicaraguans but also could be heard as far away as the United States.

The revolutionary victory had come at a considerable cost. Around 50,000 people, or about 2 percent of the population, had died. An equivalent loss in the United States would be 4.5 million, or well over seventy-five times the U.S. death toll in the entire Vietnam War. Nevertheless, on a

visit to Nicaragua during the first week following the victory, I was struck
by the joy and optimism expressed by people of all classes.[14] A "new dawn,"
they believed, had come to their country.

The Sandinista Period

The Sandinista leadership that came to power in 1979, though revolutionary, was well aware that there were important constraints on what it could
and should do. The Latin American Catholic Church had recently made its
"preferential option for the poor" and thus could not simply be dismissed as
a reactionary enemy of the people. Socialism in the Soviet Union and the
Eastern Bloc was beginning to lose its glow. Fidel Castro, while in many
ways a genuine hero for most Sandinistas, had been in power long enough
to make a number of mistakes (for example, the cult of personality, an
oversocializing of the economy, restrictions on political freedoms,
overbureaucratization, and a tendency on occasion to unnecessarily twist
the U.S. tiger's tail) that the Sandinistas wanted to avoid.

The FSLN was determined to carry out a revolution responding to
Nicaragua's own domestic and international reality at that point in time
(*coyuntura*). Not only would the Sandinistas immediately issue decrees to
prevent the emergence of the veneration of a strongman but, throughout
their administration, they would also be far more respectful of civil and
political rights than other revolutionary regimes and, indeed, than most Latin
American governments. They would pursue a mixed economy that, though
perhaps overregulated by the state, would allow the bulk of production to
remain in private hands. And they would embark on a foreign policy intended to maintain cordial relations with all countries, regardless of the
form of government, desiring to have relations with Nicaragua.

It is useful to divide the ten and one-half years of Sandinista rule into
two roughly equal segments: the transitional Government of National Reconstruction (July 1979 to January 1985) and the Constitutional Period
(January 1985 to April 1990).[15] The first was a time of innovation, experimentation, and some excesses yet considerable success in a number of categories. In the second period, the U.S.-organized Contra war, although never
a military threat, inflicted such heavy economic, fiscal, and human damage
that the revolution began to unravel and the system lost credibility to the
point that it was eventually voted out of office.

THE GOVERNMENT OF NATIONAL RECONSTRUCTION, 1979–1985. The most
convenient way to discuss the first subperiod of Sandinista rule is to examine it under four categories: economic, social, political, and international.
Though Marxist-Leninists in some respects, most Sandinistas realized from
the start that it would be foolish for a small nation such as theirs, in the
heart of the Western Hemisphere, to try to move to a socialist command
economy. Instead, they opted for a "mixed economy" in which the bulk of

production would remain in the hands of a now more heavily regulated private sector. True, the properties of the Somozas and their cronies were quickly nationalized as were those assets that appeared abandoned by wealthy people who had panicked and emigrated to other countries. But the public sector never accounted for more than 40 percent of the productive capacity of the country. Indeed, though this policy tended to become a casualty of escalating mutual suspicion, the government actually used loans, favorable exchange rates, and other means to try to encourage those entrepreneurs who remained in the country to behave as a productive "patriotic bourgeoisie."[16]

Confiscated properties were turned into state farms, peasant cooperatives, and, to a lesser extent, individual plots. Although the initially heavy emphasis on state farms and cooperatives disappointed many peasants, it is clear that far more peasants had access to land—cooperative or individual— than in the past and that, as a result, for those few years until the Contra war disrupted production, Nicaragua became much more self-sufficient in domestic food production than time in recent memory. Sandinista policymakers also attempted during these years to avoid international economic isolation. Accordingly, the new government immediately announced its willingness to service the huge and onerous foreign debt left behind by the Somozas. It also sought to maintain or establish trade and aid relations with all countries regardless of regime type.

The results of these policies were generally positive, if measured in terms of growth in gross domestic product (GDP) per capita. Indeed, from 1979 through 1983, Nicaragua experienced an overall growth in GDP per capita of 7 percent while Central America as a whole suffered a decline of 14.7 percent.[17] It was only in the wake of the full impact of the Contra war and the U.S.-orchestrated cutoff of World Bank and Inter-American Development Bank loans that the Nicaraguan economy first stagnated (1984) and then began a sharp decline (1985).

These years were also a time of innovative and effective social policies aimed at reducing the extreme suffering of the poor majority. Social security and social welfare were radically expanded. Agrarian reform gave many thousands of peasants access to land. But perhaps most impressive were the programs in health and education. Here, the enthusiastic voluntary efforts of tens of thousands of young people were harnessed to carry out one of the world's most ambitious and successful literacy crusades (1980) and an equally impressive grass-roots program of preventive medicine (beginning in 1981). Even the report issued by the Kissinger Commission, appointed by President Ronald Reagan with the obvious purpose of justifying U.S. policy in Central America, admitted that "Nicaragua's government has made significant gains against illiteracy and disease."[18]

The first half-decade of Sandinista rule also featured experimentation, innovation, and some significant successes in the area of politics and government. One of the most striking phenomena of these years was an explosion in grass-roots organizational activity. Although some Sandinista leaders believed in a top-down Leninist approach to politics and government, many were very enthusiastic about what they saw as true participatory democracy. Accordingly, they encouraged the growth of organizations representing neighborhoods, women, youth, urban and rural workers, and peasants. They allowed them significant autonomy, channeled resources through them to the people, and gave them formal representation in governmental decision-making bodies and on the Council of State—the corporative structure that served as the country's legislature until 1985. In turn, these organizations played a central role in the implementation of social programs and boosted production.[19] By late 1984 an in-house U.S. embassy report placed membership in grass-roots organizations at seven to eight hundred thousand, the equivalent of about half of the country's population age 16 or over.[20]

The revolution also moved during this time from transitional government, through elections, to constitutional government. The first institutions of government consisted of a multiperson executive (junta), a corporative legislature or Council of State (appointed in 1980), and a judiciary branch comprised of the usual lower and higher courts plus People's Anti-Somocista Tribunals set up to process charges against Somoza-era war criminals and later to deal with captured or suspected Contras. Although these branches were staffed by persons having a variety of political orientations and class backgrounds, all were appointed by the nine-person Sandinista Directorate.

Meanwhile, in the early 1980s, the Council of State debated and ultimately passed a Parties Law and an Electoral Law that would make possible national elections. Modeled on West European practices, these laws were drafted in close consultation with the Swedish Electoral Commission. The elections themselves were moved forward from an original nonspecific target date in 1985 to November 4, 1984, in order to preempt the perceived possibility that the United States might use an alleged lack of democracy in Nicaragua as a pretext for possible invasion during Reagan's second political "honeymoon" following his expected reelection two days later. In the most internationally observed election in Latin America to that point in time, one in which 75 percent of the electorate participated, FSLN presidential candidate Daniel Ortega Saavedra and Sandinista Constituent Assembly candidates won 63 percent of the votes (or 67 percent, if only valid votes are counted) in an open contest against six parties: three to the right of the Sandinistas and three to their left.[21]

A final political aspect of this period is human rights. Although the Sandinista record in this respect was not perfect, it was certainly better than that of most other contemporary Latin American governments, including heavily U.S.-backed ones such as those of El Salvador and Guatemala. There were no government-backed death squads and, indeed, very few apparently ad hoc violations of the right to life. Most of the infringements that occurred involved civil and political rights and took place during states of emergency occasioned by the U.S.-sponsored Contra war. International law recognizes the right of states to restrict liberties on such occasions, and most states do so (for example, the U.S. censorship of the press and internment of Japanese Americans during World War II).[22]

The worst problems encountered by Nicaragua in the early 1980s were in foreign affairs. The Sandinistas had wanted to preserve or promote good relations with all governments willing to have relations with theirs. In some respects, they were successful. Within a year, they had doubled the number of nations with which Nicaragua had diplomatic involvement. Their country quickly joined the Nonaligned Movement and in October 1982 won a nonpermanent seat on the UN Security Council. Nevertheless, relations with the United States, the hemisphere's major power, went sour almost immediately. While the Sandinista victory was accepted with frigid resignation by the Carter administration, it was treated as a threatening extension of Soviet-backed communism by the Reagan administration, which took office eighteen months later. Although there was little objective reality to this frightening specter, it played to an important political constituency in the United States and therefore would motivate Washington's policy toward Managua until the Sandinistas left office.[23]

The Reagan administration's assault on Nicaragua was multifaceted.[24] Among other activities, it involved training, equipping, and directing an exile counterrevolutionary (Contra) army to fight against its own government; using U.S. influence in the World Bank and the Inter-American Development Bank to cut off all normal lending to the upstart republic; and orchestrating a massive anti-Sandinista propaganda campaign typified by frequent distortion and outright fabrication.

U.S. behavior vis-à-vis the Nicaraguan election of 1984 gives a good glimpse of the use of propaganda as a weapon. Apparently fearing that the still very popular FSLN would win and be legitimized by free elections, the Reagan administration denounced the 1984 elections as a "Soviet-style farce" as soon as they were announced late in 1983. Then "teaser" candidate Arturo Cruz, at the time a highly paid CIA asset with connections to the Contras, was employed to show apparent interest in running, campaign without formally registering, and then withdraw with great fanfare claiming that conditions for a free election did not exist. Later, one of the six registered opposition candidates was persuaded by the U.S. embassy to withdraw at the last moment, again with great drama. Finally, immediately after the election, when it became obvious that reports from observers such as Willy Brandt, representing the Socialist International, and from credible delegations such as the British Parliament and Irish Parliament were likely to find them clean and valid, Director of the CIA William Casey arranged government "leaks" of a wholly fabricated story that Soviet-built MiG jet fighters were en route to Nicaragua aboard Socialist-bloc freighters. As surely intended, this rumor caused a great alarm in the U.S. media reminiscent of that of the Cuban missile crisis of 1962 and prevented less dramatic news about Nicaragua, such as the favorable international election observer reports, from even being mentioned.[25]

THE CONSTITUTIONAL PERIOD, 1985–1990. The second half of the Sandinista period was a time of significant achievement as well as serious economic, social, and political setbacks for the revolution. First, in spite of the fact that the country was fighting a war against the Contras, the Sandinistas continued to show a relatively high level of respect for human rights—certainly in comparison to the three Central American countries to the north.[26] In addition, the new governmental system was formally institutionalized. The Constituent Assembly, elected in 1984, wrote a constitution that, after considerable debate, national and international consultation, and modification, was promulgated in 1987.[27] That same year, the Assembly also formalized an innovative Autonomy Law for the peoples of the Atlantic Coast. Later, new laws related to parties and elections were passed (1988) and amended (1989) in order to honor the constitutional mandate for an election in 1990. The election itself took place that February 25 under unprecedentedly heavy international observation and was universally certified as clean and valid. Two months later, the losing FSLN turned over power to the victorious opposition.

However, this was also a time of setbacks that ultimately led to the Sandinista defeat at the polls. For one, the economy went into a freefall from the mid-1980s onward, largely due to the direct and indirect cost of the Contra war and related U.S. programs of economic strangulation. But Sandinista economic policy, which became ever more erratic in the face of the hopelessness of the situation, did not help. The wild printing of unbacked currency to finance the war led to hyperinflation that passed 33,000 percent in 1988. And, though the Sandinistas themselves implemented structural reforms in that year and the next that brought inflation down to 1,690 percent for 1989,[28] the unemployment and social pain that those policies caused were enormous.

This period also saw real decay in the innovative social programs first implemented in the early 1980s, partly due to the result of a shift in budgetary priorities from social programs to the war. But it also reflected the success of Contra strategy that deliberately targeted government social services and personnel. In various trips into the war zone, I personally saw numerous rural clinics, schools, food-storage facilities, and such, which had been destroyed by the Contras. And detailed war casualty statistics compiled by the government for its internal use indicate that 130 teachers, 40 doctors and nurses, 152 technicians, and 41 other professionals were among the 30,865 Nicaraguans killed in the war.[29] In practical terms, these losses meant that large sectors of rural Nicaragua were deprived of the government services they had come to expect in the early 1980s.

Finally, grass-roots participatory democracy, a vibrant feature of the early 1980s, suffered a serious decline in the second half of the decade.[30] One reason may have been the fact that the deliberately corporatist Council of State, which had given formal representation to mass organizations early in the revolution, was replaced in 1985 by a Constituent Assembly based on traditional geographic representation. Then, too, the worsening economic situation in the late 1980s meant that ordinary people were now so busy trying to survive that they had less time for grass-roots activity and that the government now had far fewer resources to channel to the people via such organizations. Finally, the Sandinistas themselves, desperate to win the war and revive production, increasingly used the grass-roots organizations for their own ends. This "tasking" from above tended to deprive the organizations of their autonomy and, hence, their legitimacy in the eyes of ordinary people. Accordingly, by 1990 the neighborhood committee movement and the women's organization had virtually collapsed. Only the farmers' organization, which had maintained much of its autonomy, was still doing well.

This deteriorating situation provided an incentive for Washington to modify its posture vis-à-vis elections in Nicaragua. In 1984 the Reagan administration had worked to discredit and encourage abstention from a clean election that it knew the opposition could not possibly win. In the late 1980s, however, the Bush administration would adopt a two-track policy. On the one hand, with an eye to the possibility that opinion polls might be right and that the Sandinistas would win, it frequently criticized the elections as unfair.[31] On the other, sensing that a Sandinista defeat was at least a possibility, it encouraged the opposition to participate and to unify as a coalition. Leaving nothing to chance, Washington, in the words of one State Department official, decided to "micromanage the opposition."[32]

U.S. diplomats barraged the opposition with tactical advice, and tens of millions of dollars in covert (CIA) and overt (National Endowment for Democracy) funds were provided or promised. Because this money would be available only to parties and politicians who joined the National Opposition Union (UNO) or to "nonpartisan" civic organizations that in fact shared overlapping directorates with UNO, an extremely fractious and diverse collection of microparties and politicians stayed more or less unified throughout the campaign period.[33] In addition, in an apparent effort to warn Nicaraguan voters of the consequences of retaining the Sandinistas in power, the Contra war itself was dramatically escalated.[34] These strategies worked. On February 25, 1990, UNO and its presidential candidate, Violeta Barrios de Chamorro, won an impressive 55 percent of the valid vote. Two months later, outgoing President Ortega Saavedra placed the sash of office on the shoulders of Violeta Chamorro.

The Sandinista revolution was formally over. However, many of the institutional, political, and societal changes that the FSLN had brought to Nicaragua would live on, thus making that country's ongoing experience in regime transition and structural adjustment unique, in many ways, from that of other Latin American countries.

Some Important Issues

The main focus of this volume is Nicaragua in the 1990s. This subject is important not only intrinsically—in that it is the epilogue to a subject that dominated U.S. media and foreign policy attention in the 1980s—but also because it provides a singular and interesting vantage point from which to view various issues and subjects crucial to an understanding of Latin American reality in general. These issues include: 1) the aftermath of hegemonic intervention/manipulation; 2) regime transition and democratization; and 3) structural adjustment/economic neoliberalism in a postrevolutionary society.

The Aftermath of Hegemonic Intervention/Manipulation

In 1990, Nicaragua joined a growing list of countries in the Western Hemisphere whose political systems had been abruptly altered by direct U.S. intervention or manipulation. In just the four and one-half decades of the Cold War, these countries included Guatemala (1954), the Dominican Republic (1965), Chile (1973), Grenada (1983), and Panama (1989). The devices used by the United States had varied. Propaganda, diplomatic pressure, and a surrogate invasion by CIA-trained exiles had effected the change in Guatemala. Direct U.S. military intervention had been the dominant device in the Dominican Republic, Grenada, and Panama. A CIA-orchestrated program of destabilization had triggered the military coup that brought an end to Chile's experiment in democratic socialism. The change in Nicaragua had been brought about by a combination of tactics, many of them refined from those used in these earlier interventions.

What is important here is not so much the nature of the interventions but rather their short- and long-term impact on the target countries and polities. Although some attention has been paid in the literature to the history of individual countries in the aftermath of U.S. intervention, comparative study of such cases is still a virgin field. Perhaps it would be useful to consider, through broad comparative analysis, how the political cultures of such countries are affected by decisive political intervention or manipulation by the regional hegemon. While this volume does not attempt to fill that gap, it is designed to offer a comprehensive overview of the Nicaraguan case that could be used by future scholars desiring to examine this broad, if untapped, subject.

Regime Transition and Democratization

The comparative study of regime transition and democratization, on the other hand, has resulted in a rich and extensive literature.[35] In fact, it was the "hot" topic in the study of Latin American politics in the 1980s and 1990s, at least as important as "revolution" and "dependency" in earlier decades. The Nicaraguan experience had much in common with that of many other Latin American countries, including pact making, establishing ground rules, and depoliticizing the military. But, as Philip J. Williams noted in 1994, it was also unique.[36] He argues that Nicaragua went through a two-step transition from authoritarian rule. Unlike Argentina, Brazil, and Chile, for instance, which passed directly from right-wing authoritarian regimes to liberal democracies, Nicaragua in 1979 had gone from authoritarian rule under the Somozas to a revolutionary system which, at first, promoted participatory democracy expressed through the grass-roots organizations, the Council of State, the literacy crusade, and so forth. From 1984 onward, an emphasis on electoral representative democracy would partly eclipse, but not completely obliterate, the participatory aspects of the system.

In all, the democratic legacy of a decade of Sandinista rule was not just the peaceful transfer of government to the opposition in 1990, or even the holding of clean elections in both 1984 and 1990. It was also reflected in the existence of a highly mobilized population with experience in grass-roots participation and little reticence about making demands. Accordingly, and ironically, civilian rule in Nicaragua in the 1990s would be much more difficult than in other countries. Elsewhere, outgoing dictatorships and incoming opposition elites could negotiate transitions without being overly concerned with the interests of disadvantaged classes, the latter having been politically demobilized through years of government-sponsored terror.[37] In Nicaragua, however, the poor majority could not be ignored. Thus, though the case of Nicaragua may be "messy," it is precisely that messiness which should make it an obligatory object of attention for "transitologists."[38]

Structural Adjustment/Economic Neoliberalism

Nicaragua in the 1990s also gives us an interesting vantage point from which to view structural adjustment/neoliberalism because, in this case, the "reforms" involved were being implemented in a country emerging from a socially progressive revolution rather than a right-wing dictatorship. Lest some readers be confused, we should explain that the word "neoliberalism" plays off of the term "liberalism" as used to describe the economic philosophy that dominated Latin America from early in the second half of the nineteenth century well into the twentieth century. Not to be confused with U.S. liberalism, with its government regulation of the economy and its social programs designed to protect the disadvantaged, the Latin American brand of liberalism promoted free enterprise, free trade, and a very restricted role for government. Although Latin American liberalism was associated with economic growth, it also accentuated income inequality and was eventually replaced in most countries by systems in which the state played a more active role in both the economy and the social sector. By the midtwentieth century, many countries were implementing "import substitution" policies designed to promote local industrial production through the erection of trade barriers to foreign imports. Many states nationalized key industries in order to protect labor, increase national revenue, and block foreign encroachment. Finally, especially with the encouragement of the U.S.-organized Alliance for Progress in the early 1960s, most countries invested increasingly large sums in health, education, housing, and welfare.

"Neoliberalism" came into existence in the 1970s and 1980s as a response to various economic problems generated by these state-dominated systems, including high inflation, low productivity, and heavy foreign indebtedness. Implemented with much fanfare and apparent success in Chile during the dictatorship of Augusto Pinochet (1973–1990), it had been adopted by virtually every other country in the region by the 1990s. Even Cuba, after the collapse of the Soviet Union, eventually implemented tentative "market reforms."[39] In principle, neoliberals advocate certain basic changes: 1) downsizing of government and the balancing of budgets; 2) privatization of state-owned enterprises; 3) deregulation of private enterprise; and 4) sharp reduction in or elimination of tariff barriers to foreign trade. All these, it was believed, would eliminate inflation, strengthen local currency, increase productivity, stimulate international trade, and result in rapid economic growth. Although many people would be dislocated and suffer in the short run, long-term economic growth would eventually be to the benefit of all.

In Nicaragua, structural reforms actually began under the Sandinistas. A program of sharp government downsizing (*compactación*) was implemented in 1988 and 1989 in order to combat world record levels of hyperinflation. In the 1990s the Chamorro government, ideologically dedicated to neoliberalism, continued the process. To be sure, neither Nicaragua nor any other Latin American country, including Chile under Pinochet,[40] ever implemented neoliberalism in an absolutely "pure" form. Even so, Nicaragua in the 1990s provides an interesting case study of the initial effects of this economic model, at least in modified form.

The overall objective of this volume is not so much to generate new theory about the three issue areas mentioned above (the impact of intervention, regime transition and democratic consolidation, and neoliberal adjustment) as it is to shine a spotlight on an unusual case against which those issues can be examined. The main body of the book is divided into three parts. The first examines the international setting in which developments in Nicaragua were taking place. The second looks at the "new order" encompassing not only institutional changes in government, the constitution, and the armed forces but also continuity and change in economic, agrarian, social, and environmental policy. The third part features chapters on groups and institutions and considers how these entities and actors were impacting and being impacted by the new system. These three sections are followed by two short chapters by the editor—"Reflections," in which he relates preceding chapters to the issue areas identified above, and "Epilogue," in which he discusses the October 1996 general election.

Notes

1. For more detail about the history of Nicaragua, see Thomas W. Walker, *Nicaragua: The Land of Sandino*, 3d ed. (Boulder, CO: Westview Press, 1991).

2. For a more extensive discussion of the role of history in shaping the distinct characteristics of the five Central American republics, see John A. Booth and Thomas W. Walker, *Understanding Central America* (Boulder, CO: Westview Press, 1993 [3d ed. forthcoming in 1997]).

3. For an examination of early class formation in Nicaragua, see E. Bradford Burns, *Patriarch and Folk: The Emergence of Nicaragua, 1798–1958* (Cambridge: Harvard University Press, 1991).

4. For a history of U.S. involvement in Nicaragua, see Karl Bermann, *Under the Big Stick: Nicaragua and the United States since 1848* (Boston: South End Press, 1986).

5. Richard Millett, *The Guardians of the Dynasty: A History of the U.S.-Created Guardia Nacional de Nicaragua and the Somoza Family* (Maryknoll, NY: Orbis Books, 1977), 32.

6. For a study of the life and reign of the first of the Somoza dictators, see Knut Walter, *The Regime of Anastasio Somoza, 1936–1956* (Chapel Hill: University of North Carolina Press, 1993).

7. For a defense of U.S. policy toward the first Somoza, see Paul Coe Clark, Jr., *The United States and Somoza, 1933–1956* (Westport, CT: Praeger, 1992).

8. Millett, *Guardians of the Dynasty*, 252.

9. Timothy P. Wickham-Crowley, *Guerrillas and Revolution in Latin America: A Comparative Study of Insurgents and Regimes since 1956* (Princeton, NJ: Princeton University Press, 1992).

10. Chamorro was distantly related to the nineteenth-century president of the same name.

11. For an examination of U.S. policy toward Nicaragua in this period, see Morris H. Morley, *Washington, Somoza, and the Sandinistas: State and Regime in U.S. Policy toward Nicaragua, 1969–1981* (New York: Cambridge University Press, 1994).

12. Ricardo E. Chavarria, "The Nicaraguan Insurrection: An Appraisal of Its Originality," in *Nicaragua in Revolution*, ed. Thomas W. Walker (New York: Praeger, 1982), 28.

13. For more on the role of Catholics in the revolution, see Michael Dodson and T. S. Montgomery, "The Churches in the Nicaraguan Revolution," in *Nicaragua in Revolution*, 161–80.

14. For my impressions during that visit, see Thomas W. Walker, "Images of the Nicaraguan Revolution," in *Nicaragua in Revolution*, 81–91.

15. Although a formal constitution did not come into being until 1987, I choose to call this the "Constitutional Period" because, during all of these five years, the country was ruled by an elected president and the Constituent Assembly.

16. See Rose Spalding, *Capitalists and Revolution in Nicaragua: Opposition and Accommodation, 1979–1993* (Chapel Hill: University of North Carolina Press, 1994).

17. For the sources behind these statistics and discussion of the Sandinista economic model, see Michael E. Conroy, "Economic Legacy and Policies: Performance and Critique," in *Nicaragua: The First Five Years*, ed. Thomas W. Walker (New York: Praeger, 1985), 219–44.

18. Kissinger Commission, *Report of the National Bipartisan Commission on Central America* (Washington, DC: Government Printing Office, 1984), 30.

19. See Luis Hector Serra, "The Grass-Roots Organizations," in *Nicaragua: The First Five Years*, 65–89; and Gary Ruchwarger, *People in Power: Forging a Grass-Roots Democracy in Nicaragua* (Granby, MA: Bergin and Garvey, 1987).

20. This information was revealed by an official of the U.S. embassy on June 25, 1985, to a group of which I was a part.

21. For a description of that election and citation of observer delegation reports, see *Nicaragua: The Land of Sandino*, 50.

22. For more information, see Michael Linfield, "Human Rights," in *Revolution and Counterrevolution in Nicaragua*, ed. Thomas W. Walker (Boulder, CO: Westview Press, 1991), 275–94.

23. For a discussion of these matters, see Mary B. Vanderlaan, *Revolution and Foreign Policy in Nicaragua* (Boulder, CO: Westview Press, 1986).

24. See *Reagan versus the Sandinistas: The Undeclared War on Nicaragua*, ed. Thomas W. Walker (Boulder, CO: Westview Press, 1987).

25. For documentation of the assertions in this paragraph, see Walker, *Nicaragua: The Land of Sandino*, 50–51, and accompanying endnotes.

26. Again, see Linfield, "Human Rights."

27. See Kenneth J. Mijeski, ed., *The Nicaraguan Constitution of 1987: English Translation and Commentary* (Athens: Ohio University Monographs in International Studies, 1991).

28. Both inflation figures are from the UN's Comisión Económica para América Latina y el Caribe, "Balance preliminar de la economía de la América Latina y el Caribe, 1990," *Notas sobre la Economía y el Desarrollo* 500/501 (December 1990): 27.

29. These statistics are from eight pages of charts provided to me by the Ministry of the Presidency in January 1990.

30. Luis Hector Serra, "The Grass-Roots Organizations," in *Revolution and Counterrevolution in Nicaragua*, 49–76.

31. For example, "Quayle Calls Nicaragua's Plans for Elections in 1990 Just a 'Sham,' " *New York Times*, June 13, 1989.

32. An unidentified State Department official as quoted in "Chamorro Takes a Chance," *Time* (May 7, 1990).

33. For a well-documented discussion of the role of the United States in this election, see William I. Robinson, *A Faustian Bargain: U.S. Intervention in the Nicaraguan Elections and American Foreign Policy in the Post-Cold War Era* (Boulder, CO: Westview Press, 1992).

34. My individual assignment, as part of the Latin American Studies Association's observer delegation in 1989–90, was to monitor the campaign in the northern war zones. My impression that Contra presence and activity in Nicaragua had been significantly increased during the campaign period was confirmed by John

Boardman, acting deputy chief of mission and political officer at the U.S. embassy in Managua, in an interview with the LASA observers on November 22, 1989. While avoiding any mention of U.S. responsibility, he noted that several thousand additional Contra troops had crossed into Nicaragua after the electoral campaign had begun.

35. Some important books in this vast literature are John Higley and Richard Gunther, eds., *Elites and Democratic Consolidation in Latin America and Southern Europe* (Cambridge, Eng.: Cambridge University Press, 1992); Scott Mainwaring, Guillermo O'Donnell, and J. Samuel Valenzuela, eds., *Issues in Democratic Consolidation: The New South American Democracies in Comparative Perspective* (Notre Dame, IN: University of Notre Dame Press, 1992); Guillermo O'Donnell, Philippe C. Schmitter, and Lawrence Whitehead, eds., *Transitions from Authoritarian Rule: Tentative Conclusions about Uncertain Democracies* (Baltimore: Johns Hopkins University Press, 1986); Dietrich Rueschemeyer, Evelyne Huber Stephens, and John D. Stephens, *Capitalist Development and Democracy* (Chicago: University of Chicago Press, 1992); and Mitchell A. Seligson and John A. Booth, eds., *Elections and Democracy in Central America* (Chapel Hill: University of North Carolina Press, 1995). Two useful articles are Juan J. Linz, "Transition to Democracy," *Washington Quarterly* (Summer 1990): 143–64; and Terry Lynn Karl, "Dilemmas of Democratization in Latin America," *Comparative Politics* 23, no. 1 (October 1990): 1–21. As of the mid-1990s, numerous other good articles on that subject were appearing in *Journal of Democracy*.

36. Philip J. Williams, "Dual Transitions from Authoritarian Rule: Popular and Electoral Democracy in Nicaragua," *Comparative Politics* 26, no. 2 (January 1994): 169–85.

37. When I visited Chile in November 1991 and Argentina and Brazil in the summer of 1995, I was struck by the paucity of grass-roots activity in those countries, certainly as compared with Nicaragua in the same period. In Argentina, the most notable exception was a vibrant grass-roots program encouraged by the governor of the province of Córdoba. Even so, Lic. Hector Rolando Vélez, the governor's subsecretary for community and family development, told our group that it was not until the early 1990s—long after the 1983 transition to "democracy"—that community development promoters there had been able to persuade the region's numerous slum dwellers to overcome their fear and form community organizations to express their interests. Similarly, Pat Breslin quotes Graciela Palomeque, a Córdoba grassroots activist whom he interviewed in February 1995, as saying: "Before the military dictatorship, the social movement, the *gremios*, were strong. With the military, many of these people disappeared and this left a great fear. People were afraid of trying to organize. When you started talking about organizing, you could see that people were afraid. And that still exists to some degree." Pat Breslin, *Each Grain of Sand* (Washington, DC: Inter-American Foundation, forthcoming).

38. For a half-humorous discussion of that term and that "science," see Philippe C. Schmitter, "Transitology: The Science or the Art of Democratization," in *The Consolidation of Democracy in Latin America*, ed. Joseph S. Tulchin with Bernice Romero (Boulder, CO: Lynne Rienner, 1995), 11–41.

39. On a visit to Cuba in March 1995, the author was impressed by an increase in private enterprise, as exemplified by numerous flourishing farmers' markets, and foreign investment.

40. See Eduardo Silva, "Capitalist Regime Loyalties and Redemocratization in Chile," *Journal of Inter-American Studies and World Affairs* 34, no. 4 (Winter 1993): 77–117.

I

The International Setting

In the lone chapter in this section, William Robinson contends that Nicaragua in the 1990s found itself in a virtual straitjacket dictated by its reinsertion into the global capitalist economy. The constraints imposed by this process would not only affect the country's economic options but, equally important, would also shape its social and political evolution. He argues that any discussion of "transition to democracy," including that of Philip Williams, simply misses the point: Nicaragua from the late 1980s onward was undergoing a forced transition to nonparticipatory elite "polyarchy," the political form most compatible with economic neoliberalism. He documents how the U.S. Agency for International Development in Managua—suddenly the largest USAID program in the world—and the international lending agencies dominated by Washington were serving as enforcers of this new order. Although many observers, including some of the other authors in this volume, would argue with the overall pessimism of this piece, Robinson makes it very difficult for anyone to view what was happening in Nicaragua as occurring in a vacuum.

2

Nicaragua and the World
A Globalization Perspective

*William I. Robinson**

The goal of this chapter is not to describe any "trees" in Nicaragua, nor even to step back and paint a picture of the "forest." Rather, it is to focus on the even larger ecosystem in which the Nicaraguan reality—and behind it, the Central American and the hemispheric reality—was unfolding in the 1990s. In this perspective, the country's recent history is properly seen through the lens of the macrosocial dynamic of our epoch: globalization, which is the world-historic context of national developments in the late twentieth century.

This chapter does not share conventional notions of "transitions to democracy" in the Third World, conceived as changes in sets of state managers and political systems separate from historic movement in social structure. Conventional "democratization" paradigms such as those put forward by Guillermo O'Donnell et al. disaggregate social totalities and obscure, rather than elucidate, historic movement.[1] What is referred to as "democracy" in Latin America is in fact *polyarchy*, a term first coined by Robert Dahl,[2] which refers to a system in which a small group actually rules and mass participation in decision making is confined to leadership choice in elections carefully managed by competing elites. Polyarchy, as distinct from authoritarian systems based on coercive domination, is a form of political organization based on consensual domination, or a Gramscian hegemony. "Regime transitions" in the Third World are properly seen as transitions from coercive (authoritarian) to consensual (polyarchic) forms of political organization. These national transitions are linked to new forms of

*I would like to thank Kent Norsworthy, David Dye, and Nina Serafino for critical comments on earlier drafts of this chapter, and David Dye for assistance in obtaining several documents. The usual caveats apply.

transnational social control under global capitalism. National political systems are no longer autonomous units. Globalizing pressures have been undermining previously embedded forms of political authority. An emergent transnational polyarchic political system in the Western Hemisphere reflects an emergent global political "superstructure" of the global economy. The "democratic consensus" in the hemisphere is a consensus among an increasingly cohesive hemispheric elite on the type of political system most propitious to the reproduction of social order in Latin America in the new global environment.

Philip Williams has noted that the Nicaraguan transition to "democracy" does not fit comfortably with dominant democratization paradigms, for which reason it has been largely neglected or relegated to passing discussion. But Williams remains within the conceptual and theoretical parameters of those paradigms. He demonstrates how the development of "democracy" among elites operating in the institutional arena in the 1980s strengthened dominant groups who were able structurally to block popular socioeconomic change and popular class participation. But this contradiction is attributed to two different "levels of democracy" (popular/participatory in civil society, and electoral/institutional in the political arena), even though he has shown these levels to be internally antagonistic—that is, the existence of one negated the other. Williams's argument demonstrates the underlying normative orientation of dominant paradigms, with their assumption that a process of democratization was actually under way in Nicaragua in the 1990s.[3] In contrast, I am arguing that dominant paradigms have largely ignored that country precisely because Nicaragua demonstrates the antinomies of dominant paradigms.

When I use the term "transition," therefore, I do not mean a transition to democracy, since Nicaragua is not in the process of becoming a democratic society, in any meaningful sense of the concept of democracy. The transition does not involve any authentic democratization based on rule (*kratia*) by the people (*demos*). Rather, when I refer to a transition in Nicaragua, I mean an ongoing, fundamental change in the social order, involving a complex restructuring of society at all levels. This transition began in the 1960s and continued into the 1990s. The structural backdrop to this transition was Nicaragua's ongoing, gradual, and highly contradictory entrance into the emergent global economy and society, in which globalization exercised structural causality. What was taking place in the late twentieth century was a far-reaching restructuring of the nature of power and the class structure itself in Nicaragua, inextricably bound up with external linkages and broader global dynamics. At the political level, change in Nicaragua involved the breakup of an authoritarian political system, an attempt to construct a popular democracy that collapsed owing to a host of internal and external as well as subjective and objective factors, followed by a transition from 1990 onward, unconsolidated and far from complete, to polyarchy.

But these should be seen as phases in a single historic process. There is a paradox of underlying continuity, explained by globalization, despite dramatic surface disjunctures between the mid-1960s to 1979, then from 1979 to 1990, and then after 1990, as discussed below. The United States as the dominant external actor at the behavioral level facilitated the disaggregation of Nicaragua's external linkages between 1979 and 1990. After 1990 the country's reinsertion into the global economy and new transnational class alignments and international political relations therein transpired under the tutelage of the United States, conceived as the dominant world power playing a leadership role on behalf of an emergent hegemonic transnational configuration. Nicaragua's relations with the world "passed through" its relations with the United States, and Managua-Washington relations form the backdrop to this chapter.

Globalization and the Nicaraguan Transition

The defining feature of our epoch is the emergence of a capitalist global economy, which brings with it the material basis for the emergence of a singular global society. Nations are no longer linked externally to a broader system but internally to a singular global social formation. In sum, the world has been moving in the past several decades to a situation in which nations have been linked via capital flows and exchange in an integrated international market to the globalization of the process of production itself. This move involves the restructuring of the international division of labor and the reorganization of productive structures in each nation, with major consequences for the social and political texture of each society. Technological and organizational changes have facilitated the decentralization across the globe of complex production processes simultaneous to the centralization of decision making and management of global production. Capital now moves unrestricted around the world, searching for the cheapest labor and most congenial conditions without regard for national borders.

This integration of national economies erodes boundaries and brings with it a tendency toward uniformity, not only in the conditions of production but also in the civil and political superstructure in which social relations of production unfold, including the externalization of states, the restructuring of national classes, and political regime change. Seen from the broadest structural level, authoritarianism and dictatorship had become a fetter to the emergent patterns of international capital accumulation corresponding to the global economy. Transnational capital has become sufficiently disruptive and intrusive so as to break down all the old barriers that separated and compartmentalized groups in and between societies. The globalization of social life has brought new social movements and revolutions in civil society around the world, pushing people into new roles as economic and social agents and stirring masses to rebel against authoritarian arrangements, which are unable to manage the expansive social intercourse associated with the global economy.

The agent of the global economy is transnational capital, which has become the hegemonic fraction of capital on a global scale and is managed by a class-conscious transnational elite based in the center countries and led by the United States. The concentration of capital and economic power around this transnational elite has profound effects on arrangements between existing social groups, class constellations, and political systems in every country of the world system. Political and economic power tends to gravitate toward new groups linked to transnational capital and the global economy, either directly or through location in reorganized local state apparatuses. In every region of the world, from Eastern Europe to Latin America, states, economies, and political processes are becoming transnationalized and integrated under the guidance of this new elite. This transnational elite has local contingents in each nation of the South, in a new breed of New Right "technocratic" elites in Latin America, Africa, and Asia. These transnational kernels or fractions, sometimes called a "modernizing bourgeoisie," are overseeing sweeping processes of social and economic restructuring in the Third World.

The transnational elite has an economic project and a political counterpart to that project. The economic project is neoliberalism, a model which seeks to achieve the conditions for the total mobility of capital. This model includes the elimination of state intervention in the economy and the regulation by individual nationstates over the activity of capital in their territories. The neoliberal "structural adjustment" programs sweeping the South seek macroeconomic stability (price and exchange-rate stability, for example) as an essential requisite for the activity of transnational capital, which must harmonize a wide range of fiscal, monetary, and industrial policies among multiple nations if it is to be able to function simultaneously, and often instantaneously, across national borders. This economic project is being imposed worldwide by the transnational elite through core states and their specialized branches, such as the U.S. Agency for International Development (USAID), and through supranational institutions such as the International Monetary Fund (IMF) and the World Bank, in coordination with New Right technocratic fractions in the South as "in-country" counterparts who have gained (or vie for) control over peripheral states. The goal is to construct *neoliberal states* that exhibit three functions: assure macroeconomic stability and juridical conditions for the operation of capital, provide the human and physical infrastructure necessary for capital accumulation, and maintain social order.

In turn, the political project is the consolidation of political systems that function through consensual mechanisms of social control—that is, of polyarchic systems. Polyarchy is better equipped than authoritarianism to contain popular-sector demands as each nation enters the global economy.

Polyarchic political systems lend themselves to more durable forms of social control, and therefore to stability. While mediating interclass relations, polyarchy is also a more propitious institutional arrangement for the resolution of conflicts among dominant groups. Under the fluid conditions of an integrated global society, a polyarchic system is seen as more disposed to defusing the sharpest social tensions and to incorporating sufficient social bases with which to sustain stable environments.[4]

The United States has taken the lead in pushing the political side of the transnational elite project, through the shift in its post-World War II policy of developing strategic alliances with authoritarian regimes in the Third World, such as the alliance with the Somoza dictatorship, to its emergent policy of "promoting democracy." This new policy orientation is an effort to develop consensual mechanisms of transnational social control, at containing demands placed on states by newly mobilized majorities in the Third World, and at preempting more radical political and socioeconomic change by attempting to steer national democratization movements and the breakup of authoritarianism into nonthreatening outcomes. As is well documented elsewhere, promoting polyarchy as a new modality of U.S. intervention is conducted through a transnationalized "democracy promotion" apparatus which includes the AID's Center for Democracy and Governance, the National Endowment for Democracy (NED), and new agencies in the Departments of Justice and Defense, among others. It involves the use of "political aid" in conjunction with the panoply of established U.S. foreign policy instruments, including economic and military aid, traditional diplomacy, and so forth. The policy seeks to foment functioning polyarchic political systems in peripheral countries and targets civil societies as the locus of hegemonic order and social control, in tandem with efforts to influence states.[5]

Globalization involves new forms of economic and political articulation between center and periphery. It involves the penetration of peripheral states by the transnational elite through diverse direct and indirect mechanisms made possible by the structural power that global capital exercises over nation-states, particularly small peripheral ones. It involves as well penetration of the organs of civil society through diverse "political aid" and "democracy promotion" operations and the development of state-civil society nexuses. Transnational nuclei develop in peripheral countries in liaison with the transnational elite as in-country counterparts. These nuclei act as "transmission belts" of the transnational agenda by capturing key state apparatuses and ministries, by the hegemony they are expected to achieve in civil society, and by the power they wield through their preponderance in the local economy and the material and ideological resources accrued through external linkages. As the new international division of labor reorganizes national productive structures, neoliberalism gives an immanent class bias to agents of the external sector. These agents tend to fuse with political managers of the neoliberal state and to coalesce gradually (in a process checkered with contradictions and conflict) into a transnationalized fraction of the elite. Classes are thus restructured by the globalization process. Precapitalist classes and autonomous domestic producers, such as the peasantry, small-scale artisans, and capitalist fractions oriented toward domestic markets, tend to disappear.

We can see all this unfolding in Nicaragua from the late 1960s to the 1990s. Support for the Somoza family dictatorship for nearly five decades reflected the preglobalization "elective affinity" between authoritarianism and U.S. domination in the Western Hemisphere. Foreign capital poured into Central America in the 1960s and 1970s as part of the U.S.-promoted Central American Common Market, integrating the region into the emergent global economy, displacing the peasantry and local artisans, and creating new capitalist fractions opposed to the type of "crony capitalism" that traditional autocrats such as the Somozas (or the Marcos, or the Duvaliers) tended to practice.[6] All this laid the structural basis for the social upheavals of the 1970s and 1980s. Authoritarianism could not manage the social dislocations and reorganization generated by capitalist penetration and the insertion of Nicaragua into the nascent global economy from the 1960s onward, which engendered pressures for its breakup.

The U.S. government had attempted to facilitate a transition from authoritarianism to polyarchy (from Anastasio Somoza to the anti-Somoza elite) between 1978 and 1979, but this effort failed owing to a host of country-specific reasons and historic timing. The Sandinista revolutionary forces constructed a viable counterhegemony to the dictatorship and seized state power in the 1979 revolution, taking advantage of a momentary political "opening" in the world system. But the structural constraints of globalization, combined with U.S. policy, made impossible a viable basis for consolidating and sustaining a social revolution out of the initial political opening, independent of behavioral factors such as Sandinista state conduct. Apart from its internal weaknesses and contradictions, including top-down vanguardism and its characteristic subordination of civil society to the state, the Sandinista model of popular democracy was not viable due to global structural factors. This structural power of transnational capital conjoined with the vastly superior direct power of the U.S. government, applied through a massive destabilization campaign, to make unworkable a popular alternative to polyarchy and free-market capitalism.[7]

The links are complex and multifarious between structural pressures bound up with globalization and changes in internal Nicaraguan economic, social, political, and other variables from the 1960s to the 1990s. Beyond behavioral factors (for example, concrete Sandinista policy decisions), the global structural context faced by Nicaragua in the 1980s pushed the revolutionary government into class alliances with capitalist fractions that had emerged in the 1960s and 1970s. These fractions remained linked to the international capitalist market, increasingly replaced the state as the principal intermediary between Nicaragua and those markets, and developed ties to emergent U.S.-led transnational fractions. They acted as points of access for U.S.-transnational penetration, including a structural capacity to impose policies on the Sandinista state, such as private agri-business and industrial subsidies, which undermined the classes that constituted the revolution's social base and reoriented internal power away from these classes and toward an elite in the process of reconstitution.

From the mid-1980s the objective of the United States changed from a military overthrow of the Sandinistas by an externally based counterrevolution seeking an authoritarian restoration to new forms of political intervention under the rubric of "democracy promotion," in support of an internal "moderate" opposition. This opposition, organized and trained through large-scale political aid programs, operated through peaceful means in civil society to undermine Sandinista hegemony, culminating in the 1990 electoral defeat of the Sandinistas and the installation of the elite through a nascent polyarchic political system. After the elections, a coalition led by an embryonic transnationalized nucleus (known early on as the "Las Palmas" group) took over the state, particularly such key ministries as Finances, the Economy and Development, the Central Bank, and Foreign Affairs, and the highly centralized executive itself, through the powerful Ministry of the Presidency, headed by Violeta Chamorro's son-in-law, Antonio Lacayo. A program of reinsertion of Nicaragua into the global economy and a far-reaching neoliberal restructuring ensued.

The global economy from the 1960s to the mid-1990s squeezed, in general, domestic market producers and, in particular, the Nicaraguan peasantry, which became semiproletarianized in the post-World War II period. The Sandinista agrarian reform prolonged the life of this class and other domestic economic agents, but the reconstitution and preservation of a peasantry was not viable structurally. To give one example, it required state subsidizing of peasant production for export and of internal consumption (the attempt at national autonomy) to align internal prices with world market prices (the global structural factor beyond national control). In turn, price supports and other subsidies fed macroeconomic disequilibrium, which further undermined the viability of a revolutionary project trying to survive in an integrated global economy and society. To give another example, the need for labor in the agro-export sector (whose continued existence was dictated by extranational forces), largely in the hands of a rural bourgeoisie, limited the scope and pace of agrarian reform and strengthened the Sandinista alliance with objectively counterrevolutionary forces.[8] The push and pull of rural class transformation became linked with a U.S.-led counterrevolution whose social base became the peasantry, whose resistance to Somoza and the Sandinistas responded to the incursion of socioeconomic forces that undermined their status yet also made impossible a new equilibrium for the peasantry as a class. The neoliberal program in place in the 1990s, including the restoration and modernization of agri-business and credit and price structures that closely tie the domestic economy to the world market, constituted the consummation of globalizing pressures in the Nicaraguan countryside and threatened to do away, possibly for good, with a peasantry.

The global capitalist economy was the causal macrostructural factor in this highly complex scenario spanning several decades. The U.S. government has acted as the point of external linkage with the transnational pool. Neoliberalism and polyarchy became the dominant project in Nicaragua since 1990 but faced numerous difficulties and contradictions in its stabilization, which raised major questions regarding its consolidation and long-term viability.

Constructing Polyarchy and a Neoliberal State: U.S. Intervention after the Sandinistas

The 1990 electoral defeat of the Sandinistas was as much a stunning success for new U.S. doctrines of low-intensity warfare and the strategy of promoting polyarchy as it was a dramatic statement to the limits of change in any one country in the age of globalization. Following the formal change of government, U.S. intervention entered a new stage, that of advancing the transnational agenda under Nicaragua's unique conditions of an unraveling revolution, an uncertain regime change, and shaky, war-torn economic and social structures. Washington's goals became: 1) to dismantle what remained of the revolution, including the partial transformation of property relations in favor of the popular classes that had taken place, the revolution's juridical structure, and its military apparatus; 2) to reconstitute a propertied class and a political elite under the leadership of New Right technocrats tied to the international capitalist order and attuned to the transnational agenda; 3) to construct a neoliberal state; 4) to deepen the process, begun in the 1980s, of penetrating Nicaraguan civil society and constructing a counter-hegemony to that won by the Sandinistas therein; and 5) to oversee the reinsertion of Nicaragua into the global economy and tie internal social order to transnational order.

After a year-long study, the newly opened AID mission in Nicaragua (the AID had withdrawn from the country in 1981) stated in a report laying out overall policy for 1991 to 1996, the year in which the next elections were scheduled: "The strategy presented in this document is an extremely ambitious one. It is difficult to overemphasize the degree of change in the Nicaraguan economy and Nicaraguan society which it envisions."[9] The *Strategy Statement*, a remarkable blueprint for the construction of a neoliberal republic, laid out a comprehensive program of restructuring every aspect of

Nicaraguan society on the basis of the economic power that the United States and the international financial agencies would be able to wield over the shattered country. The strategy involved what Nicaraguan economist Angel Saldomando termed "counterreform" in every institutional and policy arena.[10] Such massive economic and institutional restructuring would logically lead to change in the correlation of internal political and social forces.

The Sandinistas surrendered the formal executive apparatus. But this transition unfolded within a constitutional framework developed under the revolution, whose social, economic, political, and ideological structures were still in place. The electoral defeat plunged the Sandinista party, its social base and legitimacy already seriously eroded during the long years of war, into a sharp internal crisis over programs, ideological orientation, and strategy. But the FSLN in 1990 was still the largest and best organized party in the country. The popular classes remained politicized and mobilized in the old mass organizations and, even more so, in new social movements that flourished after the elections. The vote for UNO was not a vote of support for its antipopular program. And neither old and new fractions of the Nicaraguan elite nor the United States could count, in 1990, on a repressive military apparatus to impose their agenda, since the Sandinista People's Army (EPS) remained largely intact following the change in government.

The difficulties in the transnational project became evident in the months following Chamorro's April 1990 inauguration. The new government announced sweeping neoliberal measures, including massive public-sector layoffs, privatizations, rate increases in public services, a sharp reduction in social spending, and the elimination of subsidies on basic consumption. The measures triggered two consecutive national strikes, in May and in July, both of which paralyzed the country and demonstrated the popular classes' willingness and ability to mount resistance. The new government was forced to compromise. The program would have to be implemented gradually, through a strategy of "slow-motion counterrevolution." Nicaragua entered a period of endemic social conflict in which cycles of standoff, negotiation, and compromise alternated with peaceful and violent strikes, demonstrations, and clashes in the countryside and the cities. Chronic instability and social conflict provided the backdrop to ongoing realignments of the country's political forces and a creeping implementation of the neoliberal program.

Following the elections, Washington approved a two-year, $541-million package for Nicaragua, including $25 million in political assistance channeled through the AID and the NED.[11] The AID program in Nicaragua became the largest in the world, and the U.S. embassy in Managua became the most heavily staffed in Central America. Personnel increased from seventy-eight accredited diplomats in 1989 to over three hundred by mid-1990. Penetration of the Nicaraguan state following the vote was immediate. The AID sent a team of legal advisers to the Chamorro transition team and provided the Center for Democracy, a quasi-private group tied to the U.S. government's "democracy promotion" apparatus that had handled several million dollars in anti-Sandinista political aid in the 1980s, with new funds to set up a permanent office in Managua to advise and train National Assembly legislators.[12] The AID sent advisers and funds to the National Assembly "to improve its internal operations in resolving conflict and forging consensus on national policy" and to implement "constitutional reforms"; to the Electoral Commission, "to prepare for and monitor the 1996 national elections"; to judicial institutions and to the Comptroller General, "to install financial controls in government institutions"; and to municipal governments, to help in "implementing overall strategy."[13]

The ideological dimensions of slow-motion counterrevolution involved two objectives. One was rooting out any vestige of Sandinista influence and incorporating into a new historic bloc the masses, whose consciousness and "daily practices" had been transformed in ten years of revolution. As Nicaraguan sociologist Oscar René Vargas noted, the difficult task of reviving a latent fatalism and submissiveness of the popular classes would have to rely heavily on cultural and ideological mechanisms.[14] The other objective, which proved even more difficult and elusive, was to try to inculcate a polyarchic political culture among the elite as an important component of reconfiguring a domestic bourgeoisie. Ten years of revolution had further disfigured a bourgeoisie that, as a class, had remained historically truncated as a result of Nicaragua's particular history, external dependency, and decades of dictatorship. Political aid played an important role in these endeavors.

The development of a polyarchic political culture and the legitimization of a neoliberal social order was the crucial counterpart to eroding the revolution's value system. The manipulation of religious values, patriarchal and traditional cultural patterns, and economic insecurities was central to this endeavor. One of the first steps was the penetration and restructuring of the educational system as a key institution of ideological reproduction. The AID allocated $12.5 million to replace textbooks that the Sandinista government had developed for public schools. The old texts were ordered burned by the new Education minister, Humberto Belli. The new "depoliticized" textbooks began with the Ten Commandments, referred to divorce as a "disgrace" and to abortion as "murder," and stressed the importance of "order in the family" as well as "obedience to parents and legitimate authorities." The AID director in Nicaragua, Janet Ballantyne, stated that the textbooks would help "reestablish the civics and morals lacking in the last eleven years."[15]

Parallel to the penetration of the Nicaraguan state, U.S. officials continued to fund political aid programs with anti-Sandinista groups in civil society that had begun in the mid-1980s. They also introduced new ones, including programs to fund such key sectors as trade unions, professional associations, and youth, women's, and civic and community groups. The objective of these postelectoral programs was no longer to develop anti-Sandinista constituencies in civil society that could contribute to the effort at displacing the Sandinista government from state power. Rather, it was to contribute to a depoliticization of the population, to eclipse the more militant grass-roots social movements, and to incorporate key sectors into an emergent historic bloc under the hegemony of a reconstituted private sector. Funding for the Permanent Workers' Congress, for instance, was intended to "offer alternatives to radicalized Sandinista unions."[16] The Nicaraguan Women's Movement was to focus its work on trying to "rescue religion and the family from the libertine philosophy of the Sandinistas." And a national youth organization was to concentrate on "the transmission of a moral and Christian orientation" to overcome the "great decadence in values" brought on by the Sandinista revolution.[17]

While U.S. political aid poured into the country along with economic aid, military aid to the EPS was out of the question. The preservation of a popular army born out of revolution deprived the Nicaraguan propertied classes of a repressive instrument. "The military and the police currently are dominated by Sandinista supporters," stated the AID *Strategy Statement.* "Loyalty of these institutions and its members to the current government is questionable and their actions in response to public disturbances over the last year have raised doubts about whether they respond to the dictates of the party or the mandate of the government." It concluded: "These institutions must be 'professionalized' so they can perform their proper function in society as guarantors of security and justice."[18] The Bush and the Clinton administrations applied enormous pressure following the elections, including diplomatic threats and the temporary suspension of aid disbursements on several occasions, to purge the EPS leadership and to "de-Sandinistize" both the army and the police, as part of broader pressures to push forward slow-motion counterrevolution. In mid-1992 the Bush administration froze aid disbursements altogether, a decision that the incoming Clinton administration ratified. In April 1993, following negotiations with Nicaraguan officials, the Clinton administration finally released the frozen funds, but with numerous conditions attached. Among them were a purging of Sandinistas from the government, the dismissal of army chief Humberto Ortega (a Sandinista) and other high-level EPS officers, further progress in returning properties to their prerevolutionary owners and/or privatizing them to national and foreign investors, and constitutional reforms and other overhauls of the government structure.[19]

By late 1993 these pressures had registered some success. A combination of defunding, restructuring, and the recruitment of new officers from the ranks of the former Contras and right-wing political activists had gone a long way in turning the police into a typical Latin American repressive force, routinely breaking up strikes, dispersing popular protests, and so forth. More important, the EPS leadership itself came to develop a corporate identity of its own once it was no longer tied to a revolutionary state. The EPS leadership came to view the army's institutional integrity as dependent on achieving legitimacy in the eyes of the local elite, Washington, and the international community. Achieving legitimacy meant adopting a doctrine of "constitutionality" and demonstrating its ability to repress protests by popular sectors when such protest transgressed legal or institutional channels. In the 1990 general strikes, the EPS ignored government orders to violently repress the protesters, arguing that its constitutional mandate was limited to defending the country's sovereignty from foreign aggression, not to use force in internal political events. But over the next several years the EPS began more and more to violently dislodge peasants who had taken over land in the countryside, to attack striking workers who occupied factories or government offices, and to break up often-peaceful street demonstrations.

Reinsertion into the Global Economy

Parallel to this political aid, and with a more long-term focus, U.S. economic aid went to bolster the debilitated private sector, to fund balance-of-payments assistance, and to pay debt arrears to the World Bank and the IMF. The AID made disbursal of all assistance contingent on stringent conditions with regard to the Chamorro government's social and economic policies. The AID *Strategy Statement* stipulated across-the-board conditionality. The largest portion of U.S. aid never even entered the country, since it went to pay Nicaragua's arrears to private foreign lenders and international agencies, which reestablished its credit standing and opened the spigot for new lending from the World Bank and the IMF. Representatives from these two institutions, together with AID officials, designed a comprehensive neoliberal structural adjustment program and made all credits, disbursements, and debt restructuring contingent on compliance with this program.[20] After 1992, Washington began to phase out bilateral aid and replace it with funding from the international agencies.[21] U.S. aid was a transitional mechanism for Nicaragua's insertion into international financial structures representing transnational capital and thus inexorably into the global economy. By 1992, Nicaragua's foreign debt stood at nearly $11 billion, one of the highest per capita debts in the world. Of a total of $1.2 billion in foreign bi- and multilateral aid allocated for the country in 1991, over $500 million—or 43 percent—went for debt servicing. Another 26 percent went for imports, mostly of consumer goods.

Figures for 1992 and 1993 showed an almost identical pattern. Nicaragua paid out $495 million in 1992 *in interest alone* on this debt and, according to government projections, was scheduled to pay in debt servicing (principal and interest) $508 million in 1993, $629.8 million in 1994, $654 million in 1995, and $733 million in 1996. (In comparison, export earnings stood at $217 million in 1991.[22]) Debt servicing would clearly be a powerful mechanism for many years to come in compelling a thorough restructuring of Nicaragua's productive structure in accordance with a changing world market and the new international division of labor. With its distinct class bias, it placed the burden of adjustment on public- and formal-sector wage earners and the domestic market and favored exporters, large-scale producers, and commercial and financial conglomerates tied to transnational capital.

The international economic straitjacket imposed on Nicaragua was accomplishing what direct repression might have accomplished under authoritarian arrangements in an earlier period, or elsewhere, such as in the counterreform program in Chile following the 1973 coup. For instance, the AID's "agricultural reform" did not propose the forcible return of lands to their prior owners. Rather, it called for privatization, the promotion of agro-exports, and property ownership determined by free-market forces. As is discussed by Jon Jonakin in this volume in Chapter 6, these purely "economic" criteria applied under the banner of efficiency and macroeconomic stability acted as noncoercive mechanisms that alienated peasant smallholders, undermined the peasantry as a class, reconcentrated land, and fomented a new, modernized capitalist agri-business sector. These same credit and related adjustment policies also undermined urban workers and smallholders.

Trade liberalization was also a powerful instrument of internal social recomposition and economic reorganization. It strengthened some agents, particularly those linked to external constituencies, and weakened others, with concomitant implications for the relative political influence of different sectors. In 1991 public consumption dropped 35 percent and private consumption rose 33 percent, indicating a converse relation between the drop in government spending on social services for the popular sectors and an increase in private consumption among the tiny upper and middle classes. As a result of the sudden opening of the market to imports, Nicaragua experienced an import boom that forced thousands of small-scale industrial and agricultural producers into bankruptcy. The majority of new imports were not inputs for production but consumer goods, especially luxury items, benefiting a new high-income sector as well as large-scale importers who began to use newly accumulated capital to purchase properties and establish financial concerns, thus contributing to the process of a reconcentration of wealth and a restoration, under new conditions, of prerevolutionary property relations. Commercial reactivation was a calculated element in U.S. strat-egy, conducted through a Commodity Import Program (CIP) whose stated purpose was to strengthen the private sector.[23] The CIP was tied to a program to create ten private banks, for which purpose the AID spent $60 million in 1991 and 1992 alone in capitalization funds and in commodity imports by large-scale private importers financed by these private financial institutions. The importers and the members of the new banks' boards of directors often overlapped, fomenting the development of powerful new economic groups.[24] In this way, private banks rather than the Nicaraguan state channeled external resources, including balance-of-payments support that flowed into the private banks from the AID and the IMF.

A private banking system was to act as a direct link between emergent Nicaraguan entrepreneurs and transnational finance capital. The AID *Strategy Statement* noted that a key purpose of these banks would be to mobilize internal resources for the activities of domestic and foreign investors. Another purpose was to transfer the money supply, credits, credit policy-setting, and the financial levers of the economy from the state to the private sector, thereby giving a powerful boost to the reconstitution of a hegemonic propertied class linked to transnational capital, with the capacity and resources to foment a new economic model for Nicaragua. In this model, Nicaragua's reinsertion into the global economy was to be based on a modernized agro-export sector emphasizing nontraditional exports and on *maquiladora* assembling activities in urban-based duty-free export zones, as part of Central America's position as the southern rump of the emergent North American free-trade zone.[25] *Maquiladora* plants are generally dedicated to the labor-intensive final assembly phase of transnationalized industrial production and contribute little to the development of the host country. In 1990 the government set up on the outskirts of Managua the first of what was to be a series of tax-free *zonas francas* for transnational companies. By 1993 a dozen companies were operating—mostly textile plants, paying wages of $30 per month to mostly female workers under state regulations prohibiting unionization.[26] Export-oriented agri-business and *maquiladora* assemblage required abundant cheap labor drawn from a huge pool of propertyless laborers and the unemployed, alongside a reserve army of the unemployed, keeping wages down. The neoliberal program was creating just such a labor force through privatization, mass public-sector layoffs, the reconcentration of rural and urban property holdings, and so forth.

All this was part of the far-reaching process of class restructuring, including atomization of the formerly well-organized working class, proletarianization of the peasantry, and the development of a New Right elite composed of a modernized private sector and administrative technocrats. The transnational agenda could not be realized without national actors strong enough to serve as mediators and attuned to the agenda. Direct U.S. support for a reorganized private sector through the CIP, the private banks, the privatization process, and so forth sought to build up these national actors. The goal was to foment a "modernizing" elite with the capacity to: 1) influence state policies; 2) influence civil society through predominance in the economy; 3) serve as local links to transnational capital; and 4) develop its own economic power and give it the ability to promote and manage capital accumulation within the new economic model. U.S. programs intended to build ties to local elites and challenge popular sectors sought to penetrate the state and civil society, to form a network of institutions in civil society as structures parallel to the state and able to instrumentalize it, and to develop a nexus of state-civil society linkages displaying an interpenetration of interests and personnel between the government and "private" spheres. These linkages were to be developed through close coordination among, and institutional interpenetration between, the government (managing the state) and a private-sector elite hegemonic in civil society. For example, U.S. aid was used to finance several elite universities and technical institutes, including a new AID $3.1-million program in the Central American Institute of Business Administration (INCAE) to "train consultants" and place them in different government ministries as "technical and economic advisers."[27] Although the appointment of numerous U.S. advisers in key economic, social, and policy-planning ministries was a requirement of aid disbursals in the first years after the elections, a more important activity funded by the United States was the creation of a core of New Right technocrats thoroughly trained and ideologically steeped in the worldview and logic of the transnational elite—people who, in Washington's long-term strategy, would eventually go on to assume the reins of the Nicaraguan state and establish internal hegemonic order linked to transnational hegemony.

Changing International Political Alignments and Internal-External Articulation

Foreign policy as the pursuit of the interests of states in the international arena is an expression of a particular socioeconomic structure and the resultant class character of a state. Nicaragua's international political alignments went through three distinct stages from the 1970s to the mid-1990s, reflecting the prolonged period of integration into global society under different internal political regimes and social structures. Under Somoza, foreign policy was a subservient and dependent appendage of Washington's Cold War considerations in Latin America and reflected a preglobalization external dependency that was almost strictly bilateral with the United States. The Sandinistas pursued a dynamic worldwide foreign policy aimed at establishing diplomatic networks in support of their attempt to weaken dependency on Washington and diversify economic relations and strategic alliances with a variety of international forces. This included the Nonaligned Movement and other forums in the South, the former Soviet bloc, Latin America, Third World nationalist and revolutionary regimes, and other core regions in the world system, especially the European Community (EC). This foreign policy registered a certain conjunctural political success, but it ran up against a globalization process unfolding under terms dictated by U.S.

leadership among Northern core powers and their transnational economic and political instruments. In this way, Nicaragua's international alignments under the Sandinistas ultimately "came back to roost" on the conflict with the United States. The Chamorro government's foreign policy was largely "economistic," seeking to link the Nicaraguan state to multilateral agencies, identify new markets and sources of bilateral aid and reestablish those markets and credit sources lost under the Sandinistas, attract foreign investment, and secure preferential debt and trade treatment.

This economistic foreign policy in the 1990s focused concretely on normalization of relations with the United States; Central American economic and political integration initiatives; active diplomacy in the Western Hemisphere within the dynamics of inter-American relations and hemispheric free-trade integration; reconstituting relations with the EC, especially those countries with whom relations deteriorated under the Sandinistas (for example, Germany, the United Kingdom); opening new relations with Taiwan and South Korea; and expanding relations with Japan, the Gulf countries, and the member states of the Association of South East Asian Nations. In addition, Nicaragua signed more than two hundred international agreements between 1990 and 1995, the vast majority intended to delineate the terms for the operation of foreign business in the country and the mechanisms of international economic and concomitant political arbitration under emerging conditions of integration and globalization.[28]

Far from a relation among equals, Washington-Managua relations continued to be ones of domination and subordination, including unilateral U.S. impositions. Most illustrative is Managua's 1991 decision, taken under the Bush administration's threat of suspending bilateral aid and blocking multilateral credits, to withdraw Nicaragua's suit with the International Court of Justice (ICJ) for $12 billion in indemnization for what the ICJ had found in its famous 1986 ruling to be U.S. violations of international law in its policy toward Nicaragua. But the overall framework under which U.S.-Nicaraguan relations unfold had changed, from a world of competition among dominant core powers and their spheres of influence, to one of global integration in which North-South tensions and transnational class conflict constitute the axis of international friction. Post-1990 relations with Washington were less ones of complete bilateral dependence and integration than a close U.S. tutelage in the process of reinsertion into the global system.

Behind formal diplomacy were changes in international political alignments based on new forms of internal-external articulation, the enhanced externalization of the Nicaraguan state, and the integration of the national class structure into patterns of late twentieth-century transnational class formation. In particular, there was the very incipient emergence of a transnationalized kernel vying to become a hegemonic fraction of the elite, and movement to articulate this fraction to the transnational elite. At the risk of simplifying highly complex phenomena, in the postelectoral period the Nicaraguan elite divided roughly into two groups. The first was attuned to the transnational agenda of polyarchy and neoliberalism, with a more long-term vision of capitalist modernization based on the new economic model mentioned above. This group was clustered in the executive inner circle, in key ministries such as Finance and the Central Bank, and in the new universities, think tanks, and financial concerns set up with U.S. and multilateral assistance and economically tied to liberalized external-sector activities. The other was grounded in the old agro-export oligarchy, in the traditional politics of partisan corruption and patronage, and was inclined to restore a Somocista-style authoritarian order.

The struggle between and within these two groups often took the form of highly visible political infighting and personal interests. In part, this struggle is a result of the political culture rooted in Nicaragua's history, but it also reflected a more fundamental conflict over class formation and fractional interests therein intermeshed with the penetration and germination of the transnational project for the country. The coalescing of a transnationalized kernel in Nicaragua has been a highly contradictory and far-from-complete process. Personal ambitions, factional disputes, elite feuds over the spoils of state, and a historically ingrained political culture of authoritarianism and clientelism characterized the political behavior of this kernel and impeded its ability to advance the transnational agenda. This scenario does not lend itself to simplified interpretations, and it has confused observers who analyze conjunctural phenomena or focus on behavioral factors alone.

Conclusion: Contradictions of the Transnational Agenda

This chapter presented an ideal-type theoretical construct and summarized the extent to which a transnational project was advanced in Nicaragua. Although the issue is best left for future research, it is essential to stress in this brief conclusion that this project had registered important successes, as summarized above; but it had also run up against numerous difficulties that indicate a gap between goals and outcome, or intent and ability, and beyond this, deep social and political contradictions in emergent global society, including its dark underside of social apartheid and "poverty amidst plenty." Exuberant over the success of the 1980s campaign against the Sandinistas, U.S. officials originally expected the agenda of the transnational elite to fall smoothly into place in the 1990s. The AID *Strategy Statement* predicted:

> Over the course of the [1991–1996] period, we anticipate a major transformation of the Nicaraguan economy and society. By the end of this period, the economy will be dominated by the private sector, traditional exports will be growing rapidly, and a variety of non-traditional agricultural exports will be well-established. By 1996, enclave manufacturing

will have moved beyond an initial concentration in textiles into a wide variety of manufacturing operations. The United States will once again become Nicaragua's principal trading partner. . . . Civic education efforts and the spread of a wide range of ideas through the media will have helped achieve general acceptance of democratic ideas, attitudes, and values.[29]

Reality proved to be less rosy than this forecast. Social inequalities and consumption differentials, the concentration of wealth and income, and widespread impoverishment, a result of unbridled free-market forces released under the neoliberal program, advanced at an alarming rate in the early 1990s. Relative poverty for much of the population under the Sandinistas became absolute under the new government. For instance, real wages dropped 50 percent in the first year, 69 percent of the population lived in poverty in 1992, and per capita food consumption fell by 31 percent between 1990 and 1992.[30] The health, educational, and other social gains achieved in the 1980s, though they deteriorated late in that decade as a result of the war, suffered a dramatic reversal with the change of government and the application of the neoliberal program.[31] Widespread rural immiseration and the government's policies of squeezing the peasantry spurred renewed military conflict in the countryside. Although the old Sandinista-Contra antagonisms played a part, the new rural conflict, including land invasions, spontaneous violent clashes, and even organized warfare in some areas, reflected the emergence of class polarization and class-based conflict in the countryside. Neoliberalism threw most Nicaraguans into a desperate social and economic situation and excluded and atomized the grass roots by driving people into extreme poverty and despair. Spontaneous outbreaks of individual and collective violence as well as pandemics of street crime, prostitution, and drug addiction unraveled the social fabric and replaced the sense of collective solidarity that had characterized the 1980s revolution with a disturbing social anomie and political apathy.

"Investors will be looking for clear indications that political turmoil will be contained and for evidence of progress toward the establishment of a free-market economy," the AID *Strategy Statement* warned. The government "will need to demonstrate that it has developed a working legal and regulatory structure such that it can guarantee contracts, establish property rights, resolve disputes, and enforce laws which govern business and investment. It must also be able to demonstrate that law enforcement entities have the capability to maintain order in accordance with government directives and policy."[32]

By 1995, however, only the first of the three functions of the neoliberal state—achieving macroeconomic stability—had been met. Nicaragua, seen from the logic of the transnational project, was in a vicious circle. Structural adjustment was to have provided the macroeconomic stability for private capital to enter and operate freely. Private foreign investment was to bring about growth and development. Growth and development were to bring about social peace and political stability. But the twin legacies of a decade of revolution and a historically fractious elite made social stability and the consolidation of polyarchy highly problematic. The popular classes would not allow an antipopular project to stabilize, and the elite remained unable to reach consensus in its own affairs, and thus the economy continued to sink. Transnational capital, literally with "the world to exploit," would hardly chose Nicaragua as a country in which to invest, given chronic instability, less docility among the popular classes than in most countries of the Third World, and the inability of the dominant groups to achieve hegemony.[33] The possibility of consolidating a polyarchic political system and elite social order and renewing externally oriented capital accumulation seemed bleak in 1995. The popular classes resisted being drawn into a renewed elite hegemony and became increasingly restive, putting aside political allegiances as the entire country became polarized into an impoverished mass and an affluent minority. These difficulties in Nicaragua underscored the contradictions internal to global capitalism and the transnational elite's project of "market democracy."

Notes

1. See, for example, Guillermo O'Donnell, Philippe C. Schmitter, and Lawrence Whitehead, eds., *Transitions from Authoritarian Rule*, vols. I–IV (Baltimore: Johns Hopkins University Press, 1986). For a critique of mainstream democratization paradigms, see William I. Robinson, *Promoting Polyarchy: Globalization, U.S. Intervention, and Hegemony* (Cambridge, Eng.: Cambridge University Press, 1996).

2. Robert A. Dahl, *Polyarchy: Participation and Opposition* (New Haven: Yale University Press, 1971).

3. Philip J. Williams, "Dual Transitions from Authoritarian Rule: Popular and Electoral Democracy in Nicaragua," *Comparative Politics* 5, no. 2 (January 1994): 169–85.

4. I must stress that polyarchy is, in my view, normatively preferable to dictatorship, and also opens certain space for popular classes to struggle for their interests and exert influences in ways impossible under dictatorship, even when the essential relations of class domination are reproduced through polyarchic institutional structures and processes. But space constraints preclude discussion.

5. For general discussion and six country case studies, see Robinson, *Promoting Polyarchy*; and for detailed documentation and analysis of this U.S. policy shift as it applies to Nicaragua, see William I. Robinson, *A Faustian Bargain: U.S. Intervention in the Nicaraguan Elections and American Foreign Policy in the Post-Cold War Era* (Boulder, CO: Westview Press, 1992).

6. Among many works on the Central American post-World War II political economy, see Victor Blumer Thomas, *The Political Economy of Central America since 1920* (Cambridge, Eng.: Cambridge University Press, 1987); and Jaime Wheelock, *Imperialismo y dictadura* (Mexico City: Siglo XXI, 1975).

7. Literature on the U.S. war and on the Sandinista attempt at popular democracy is voluminous. For the first, see, for example, Thomas W. Walker, ed., *Reagan versus the Sandinistas: The Undeclared War on Nicaragua* (Boulder, CO: Westview

Press, 1987). For the second, see, for example, Harry E. Vanden and Gary Prevost, *Democracy and Socialism in Sandinista Nicaragua* (Boulder, CO: Lynne Rienner, 1993).

8. See, for example, discussion in Laura Enríquez, *Harvesting Change: Labor and Agrarian Reform in Nicaragua, 1979–1990* (Chapel Hill: University of North Carolina Press, 1991).

9. *Country Development Strategy Statement: USAID/Nicaragua 1991–1996* (Washington, DC: Agency for International Development, June 14, 1991), 62–63.

10. Angel Saldomando, *El retorno de la AID, Caso de Nicaragua: Condicionalidad y reestructuración* (Managua: Ediciones CRIES, 1992).

11. For the $541-million figure, see AID, *Strategy Statement*, "Resource Table," appearing on an unnumbered page following the last numbered page (63). For detailed analysis, see Saldomando, *El retorno de la AID*.

12. Robinson, *A Faustian Bargain*, 163.

13. AID, *Strategy Statement*, 47–48.

14. Oscar René Vargas, *¿Adónde va Nicaragua? Perspectivas de una revolución latinoamericana* (Managua: Ediciones Nicarao, 1991).

15. For details on the AID textbooks, see Midge Quandt, "U.S. Aid to Nicaragua: Funding the Right," *Z Magazine* (November 1991): 478–51.

16. AID, *Strategy Statement*, 46.

17. Quandt, "U.S. Aid to Nicaragua," 49.

18. AID, *Strategy Statement*, 20.

19. See U.S. Department of State, Office of the Assistant Secretary, press release title "Statement by Richard Boucher, Spokesman," dated April 2, 1993.

20. See, for example, Adolfo Acevedo Vogl, *Nicaragua y el FMI: El pozo sin fondo del ajuste* (Managua: Ediciones CRIES, 1993).

21. See Roberto Larios, "Bowing before Financial Organizations," *Barricada Internacional* 13, no. 367–68 (November–December 1993): 8–9; and Nitlapán/CRIES, *De la deuda externa a la búsqueda de alternativas para el desarrollo* (Managua, August 1994).

22. For these details and statistics, see Anne Larson, "Foreign Debt: Where Have All the Dollars Gone?" *Envío* 12, no. 143 (June 1993): 4–10; see also Nitlapán/CRIES, *De la deuda externa*.

23. AID, *Strategy Statement*, 39.

24. See *Strategy Statement*, "Resource Table"; and Saldomando, *El retorno de la AID*, 97, 88–89, for a listing of the new private banks and their principal board members.

25. See, for example, AID, *Strategy Statement*.

26. See "Welcome to the Free Trade Zone," *Envío* 12, no. 150 (January 1994): 27–33.

27. Saldomando, *El retorno de la AID*, 74–78.

28. Nicaragua's 1990–1995 foreign policy is reviewed in detail by Deputy Foreign Minister José Bernard Pallais, in speech to students of the Universidad Autónoma Americana, Managua, May 10, 1995.

29. AID, *Strategy Statement*, 63.

30. "Why Social Conflict?" *Envío* 12, no. 138 (January–March 1993): 18.

31. Ibid.

32. AID, *Strategy Statement*, 8.

33. The London-based *Economic Intelligence Unit* gave Nicaragua a "D" rating for political and policy risk in 1994, for the fourth postelectoral year straight, and forecast an increase in political instability. See "Country Risk Service: Nicaragua," *Economic Intelligence Unit* (London), 4th Quarter, 1994.

II

The New Order

The six chapters in this section deal with the new order in Nicaragua in the first half of the 1990s. To begin, Shelley McConnell and Daniel Premo focus on two of the most important aspects in any regime transition, the establishment of agreed-upon "rules of the game" and the redirection of the military. Both authors describe a long process of political bargaining and pact-making that culminated in the modification of the 1987 Constitution and the issuing of a new Military Code.

The last four chapters look at policy and programs under the new regime. In examining general economic policy, Mario Arana argues that the structural adjustment policies begun by the Sandinistas and accelerated by the Chamorro government were absolutely essential. However, he believes that the way in which they were implemented in the 1990s—favoring big producers and projects over small and medium producers—was not maximally appropriate for the reality and potential of Nicaragua in the 1990s, a country with a large informal sector and numerous small- and medium-sized beneficiaries of Sandinista reforms and Chamorro-era privatization. Jon Jonakin describes the impact of neoliberal policies on the agrarian sector and, in particular, how they were affecting the peasantry, which had acquired access to land in the 1980s. Karen Kampwirth looks at social policy under a conservative administration facing severe fiscal restraints. She states that the character of social policy varied from ministry to ministry, according to the leadership at the top of those institutions and the ability of affected constituencies to articulate their interests. Finally, Desirée Elizondo describes environmental policy in the 1990s, which, though well intended, often encountered indifference or resistance not only from vested economic interests but, equally important, also from ministries concerned with promoting economic growth.

3

Institutional Development

Shelley A. McConnell

President Violeta Chamorro's inauguration in April 1990 did not end political struggle in Nicaragua, much less foster the national reconciliation that she had promised in her campaign. Instead, the transition gave rise to new political actors with a complex array of conflicting interests and reallocated the resources that each of them could bring to bear in deciding policy issues. Although the rules of the game had changed, perceptions of the stakes had changed rather less, leading to hard-fought politics that strained the capacity of the country's young democratic institutions.

Throughout Chamorro's term, many Sandinistas continued to believe their party to be the guardian of a project for social change under assault from counterrevolutionary forces intent upon restoring a prerevolutionary property order. On the right, liberals and conservatives remained persuaded that they were battling for freedom and pluralist democracy against the episodically resurgent forces of violent left-wing authoritarianism. Framed in these zero-sum terms, everyday conflicts of interest around such items as budgets and political appointments took on symbolic value and easily became blown out of proportion. With so much perceived to be at stake, it is not surprising that conflict periodically burst institutional bounds. This turbulent context reflected the fragility of Nicaraguan democracy, underscoring the extent to which political parties and state institutions were unable to channel political participation and address citizens' demands through routine procedures. It also spurred institutional development at the national level as the four branches of state scrambled to expand their capacity for governance and refine their constitutional roles. Rapid institutional evolution culminated in a substantial constitutional reform in 1995 that would shape politics far into the future.

The Sandinista Institutional Inheritance

The institutional structure developed in the wake of the 1979 revolution and inherited by the Chamorro administration reflected the dual transition toward democracy and socialism that the Sandinistas undertook in the 1980s.[1] Initially, the revolutionary government emphasized popular democracy via direct participation in mass organizations affiliated with the FSLN. However, in the face of a counterrevolutionary war that the United States justified as a response to purported Sandinista "totalitarianism," in 1983 the Sandinista government began developing liberal democratic institutions and procedures. Four interdependent branches of state were established—the executive headed by a president, a National Assembly to be elected through a system of proportional representation, a judiciary whose highest organ was the Supreme Court of Justice, and an electoral branch headed by a Supreme Electoral Council (Consejo Supremo Electoral, or CSE). In addition, the Sandinistas permitted the flourishing of a multiparty system. Seven political parties competed for state power in national elections held in 1984. The FSLN won handily, but the six opposition parties gained one-third of the legislative seats.[2]

Three historical facts conditioned the development of a democratic regime in revolutionary Nicaragua. The first was that unlike most Latin American countries attempting to establish a democracy, Nicaragua had never been a democracy. It not only lacked a democratic civic culture, but it also was unable to resurrect any institutional forms from a prior democratic period and thus built its democratic institutions from scratch.[3] Second, the Sandinista revolution had initiated a transition to socialism and established a one-party dominant system. As a vanguard party, the FSLN coordinated policymaking by the state branches through its National Directorate. Party discipline was enforced, and institutional autonomy was restricted, which made conflict between state powers moot.[4] The third factor affecting regime formation was the U.S.-funded counterrevolutionary war designed to destabilize the Sandinista regime. Together with Nicaragua's long history of sultanistic authoritarianism, the wartime context invited the formation of a strong presidential system. It placed the country on a permanent crisis footing, creating pressure for centralization and an exceptionally strong executive branch.[5]

The Constitution was drafted in 1985–86 by the National Assembly in a lengthy public process, and it went into effect in January 1987.[6] It codified the political institutional development achieved in 1984, establishing such liberal elements as the four branches of state, the multiparty system, and national elections as the fundamental institutional matrix governing Nicaragua for the foreseeable future. Sandinista sympathizers praised the Constitution as democratic, but opponents called it totalitarian. Absent the participation of right-wing parties, the constitution-making process had not forged a social contract. Furthermore, the immediate suspension of certain articles via a wartime State of Emergency raised doubts as to whether the Constitution provided citizens with adequate protection against the state. Another difficulty was that the Constitution contained liberal and socialist elements that were not easily compatible in practice.[7] As a result, the rules of the game remained uncertain.

The 1990 elections invested the Constitution with new authority. It had provided the legal framework for Chamorro's election and was thus a touchstone of her government's political legitimacy. For their part, the Sandinistas needed the Constitution as never before to protect their civil rights as an opposition. The elections also changed the substance of complaints concerning the text. In the 1980s opposition elements had voiced concerns about the absence of sufficient guarantees of human rights, civil liberties, and pluralist democracy. Free and fair elections in 1990 silenced most of the critics on that score. Instead, criticism began to focus on the disproportionate strength of the executive and the absence of checks and balances among the branches of state.

As a result of the 1990 elections, the branches of state fell into the hands of distinct interest groups with conflicting political agendas. Chamorro controlled the powerful Presidency, the UNO coalition held sway in the National Assembly, and Sandinista appointees continued to dominate the Supreme Court of Justice and the Supreme Electoral Council. Overnight, the balance of power among these institutions was transformed into a matter of utmost concern. Political battles ensued in which the branches of state sought to increase their power in relation to one another.

Opening Moves: Attempts to Capture the Judiciary

The first move in this institutional chess game was made in July 1990, only two months after Chamorro's inauguration. With UNO voting as a majority bloc in the National Assembly, the governing coalition set out to establish a foothold in the judiciary.[8] Arguing that all seven magistrates were appointed by the Sandinistas and thus loyal to the FSLN, UNO discussed naming eight new members to the Supreme Court to gain a majority. The 1987 Constitution set no limit on the number, leaving the Court open to this packing scheme. Sandinista members of the legislature objected. Although they were a minority, the widespread strikes paralyzing Managua that month underscored the fact that the FSLN had extraparliamentary resources that could be brought to bear in politics. In what had all the marks of an unwritten pact, UNO legislators quietly settled for two additional Court members. At the same time, two Sandinista appointees suddenly resigned, allowing the UNO legislators to name a total of four magistrates to a nine-member Court. Among the remaining Sandinista appointees was Dr. Rafael Chamorro Mora, seen by some as a neutral, so that the new composition of the Supreme Court was relatively balanced.

A measure of independence from the other branches of state, and sufficient institutional capacity to perform its constitutional functions, would also be required for a strong judiciary. As in most other Latin American countries, the Nicaraguan judiciary had historically been dominated by the President of the Republic, and the Chamorro years were no exception. The executive controlled budget-making and gave the judiciary at most 2 percent of the national budget, not nearly enough to handle its caseload. The pay for judges was so low that they were tempted toward corruption. As president, Chamorro was also empowered to name the president of the Supreme Court from among the magistrates and could alter her choice at any time.

Executive dominance was exacerbated by the judicial system's institutional weakness. Operating with an antiquated legal code, the judicial branch adhered to a written, private tradition that placed an insupportable burden of investigation on the courts and particularly on judges. At the top, the Supreme Court accumulated a backlog of cases in which it either simply delayed consideration or could not muster six votes to render a decision. Early in President Chamorro's term there were hopeful signs for judicial independence. Most encouraging was Chamorro's public compliance with a Supreme Court ruling that declared Presidential Decree No. 11-90 unconstitutional. However, since Chamorro had already rescinded her own support for her decree prior to the Court's ruling, the case was not a definitive test. With hindsight, the decision seems to have been an exception to the Court's pattern of rulings coinciding with the executive viewpoint. At best, it was misleading in suggesting the Court's independence; and, at worst, it implied that the president could use the Court to reverse course on policies she had reconsidered.

The failure to rapidly establish the judiciary as a strong and independent branch of state exacted a price in public confidence. By 1995 pollsters reported that 61.7 percent of Nicaraguans believed that Supreme Court magistrates were never fair, and only 12.4 percent thought that they were always fair. Only 7 percent said that the laws applied equally to everyone. Some 37.9 percent thought that justice was only available to the rich, while a mere 8.7 percent believed that the law protected the poor.[9]

The Dysfunctional Legislature

The 1990 elections gave UNO an absolute majority of 51 of the 92 seats in the National Assembly. The FSLN held 39 seats and two opposition parties earned one seat each. The apparent control that these numbers awarded UNO was belied by its volatility as a coalition whose members ran the ideological gamut from communists to socialists, liberals and conservatives. Executive-legislative relations got off to a rough start when, just prior to Chamorro's inauguration, the National Assembly voted in its president, choosing Miriam Argüello. Chamorro had backed Ing. Alfredo César for the job, but he was perceived by many within UNO as an opportunist who had switched camps one too many times. Indeed, in 1989, UNO's Political

Council had ousted César from its ranks. Given their hostility, César was forced to seek support for his election among the Sandinista legislators, a move that only alienated UNO further and resulted in his defeat.

Chamorro definitively lost the support of the right wing of UNO on the day after her April 25 inauguration when she announced that she would retain Gen. Humberto Ortega as chief of the armed forces. This made grace of necessity, as she would need Ortega's help to disarm the Contras and downsize the army. However, the decision infuriated UNO conservatives, who interpreted their electoral victory to mean that they should carry through their campaign program without compromising with the Sandinista minority. Meanwhile, there was no love lost between Chamorro and her vice president, Virgilio Godoy, who preached vengeance against Sandinista leaders. Godoy, not even assigned office space in the executive's building, was ignored. Shortly thereafter, he went into open opposition against Chamorro's government.

César's election to the presidency of the National Assembly in 1991 did nothing to remedy the growing rift between Chamorro's executive and UNO. César rapidly became disillusioned with Chamorro after she rejected the conservative property bill that he had worked hard to pass. In the meantime, the FSLN had grown closer to the Chamorro camp through two years of cooperation on military matters. President Chamorro's veto of the ultraconservative property bill clinched their tacit alliance. Soon even moderates within UNO accused Chamorro of "co-governing" with the Sandinistas.

In 1993 these tensions came to a head in an institutional crisis within the legislature. A progressive legislative alliance formed between the FSLN and a centrist group of eight UNO deputies, whose defection had prevented a legislative override of President Chamorro's veto of the property law. This move left only 45 of the 92 deputies voting with UNO. When two vacancies emerged on the National Assembly's governing directorate, César rightly feared that, when brought to a vote, the seats would be awarded to delegates from the new progressive majority. He delayed filling the positions, and in protest the Sandinistas and their centrist allies staged a walkout. César seized the opportunity to convene a rump parliament of his forty-five faithfuls and repassed the property bill. The Sandinistas challenged the legality of that emerging legislation, arguing that the sitting deputies fell short of a quorum. An appeals court agreed, but the UNO legislators did not desist. In November the issue reached the Supreme Court, which ruled that all actions taken by the National Assembly since September 2, 1992, were null and void for lack of a quorum. The UNO legislators paid the ruling scant attention.

When the legislative leadership came up for reelection, it was expected to be a watershed vote that would restore the Sandinistas to power in the National Assembly. Police protection was provided for the Assembly building to help prevent violence in the tense atmosphere. UNO cried foul, interpreting this display of force as a kind of Fuji-coup (*autogolpe*) designed by Chamorro to intimidate UNO legislators. When Christian Democrat Luis Humberto Guzmán was elected president of the Assembly, heading a directorate composed of Sandinistas and their Center Group allies, UNO deputies rejected the results. For a period of time thereafter they adopted a pro-forma participatory routine, showing up to work so that they could collect their pay but refusing to take part in the proceedings.[10]

Thus, the Assembly went from being a right-wing rump parliament whose decisions were ruled null and void by the Supreme Court to a legally composed and politically progressive body that was nonetheless considered illegitimate by nearly one-half of its members. Smooth operations would not be fully restored until it undertook to reform the Constitution, causing deputies to close ranks in their battle with the executive.

Reforming the Constitution

Right-wing political parties had been demanding constitutional reform from the moment that the Constitution was inaugurated in 1987.[11] The UNO victory generated the expectation that this central plank of its program would receive immediate attention. However, even when the two independent deputies voted with a united UNO bench, the governing coalition could not quite muster the 60 percent of legislative votes needed for reform of single articles of the Constitution, much less the two-thirds majority required for a completely new text.[12]

Many Sandinistas opposed reform, clinging to the Constitution as a bulwark against UNO's counterrevolutionary policy agenda. Constitutional guarantees of agrarian reform, socialized property, state ownership of natural resources, and labor organization were seen as key legal precepts preserving the revolutionary project. When splits within UNO produced a cooperative modus operandi between the FSLN and Chamorro's camp, constitutional reforms designed to limit executive power became impolitic as well.

In 1993 a growing split within the Sandinista party (described in Chapter 9, this volume) paved the way for constitutional reform to reach the legislative floor. Former Vice President Sergio Ramírez emerged as the leader of a Social Democratic current within the party, and he was backed by most Sandinista deputies within the National Assembly. Ramírez's group was soon ousted from the FSLN and formed a separate political party, the Sandinista Renovation Movement (MRS). The fact that the FSLN's ideological split fell along institutional fault lines had important political consequences. Whereas Daniel Ortega's *ortodoxos* supported the executive, Ramírez's *renovadores* sought to empower the legislature, their political stronghold, and thus came to support constitutional reform.[13]

Together with the UNO representatives, Ramírez's camp formed a special constitutional commission to draft a reform proposal, which was introduced into the National Assembly in the fall of 1994. The bill was discussed in public meetings, and the special commission invited comments from fifty-nine political and social groups. Forty-seven groups replied with feedback.[14] After being approved in general form, the bill was returned to the special commission for revision, as is usual under Nicaraguan law-making procedures. On November 7, 1994, the commission introduced the revised and rather more modest reform bill for floor debate. It was approved by the Assembly on November 25. Since the Constitution required that amendments be passed by two consecutive legislatures, the bill was resubmitted to the subsequent National Assembly in early 1995, where it was approved for the final time.[15]

All that remained for the constitutional reform bill (Law No. 192) to enter into effect was its publication by President Chamorro either in the official *Gazette* or, for the sake of expediency given that publication's backlog, in the national newspapers. However, she declined to proclaim the law, in essence refusing to recognize any reform that would substantially reduce her powers. When it became clear that the executive would not relent, National Assembly President Guzmán ordered the law to be published in the national media and proceeded to treat the reformed Constitution as operative. By February 1995, then, the executive and legislature were operating under separate constitutions, inducing a crisis. The Supreme Court of Justice had the power of judicial review and was asked to decide whether the legislature's publication of the law made it valid. However, the Court was paralyzed to act due to three vacancies that left it short of its seven-member quorum.

The National Assembly had not hurried to select new Supreme Court magistrates, preferring to keep the Court out of the political equation. However, on April 6 it moved forward with the appointments in a highly political maneuver. It named six new magistrates using the reformed Constitution's selection procedures, seeking to compose the twelve-member Court envisioned in the reform.[16] The sitting members of the Court were faced with a dilemma: if they recognized the newly appointed magistrates, they were effectively recognizing the reformed Constitution, which would render pointless any ruling against the legislature's publication of the constitutional reform law.

Legislators insisted that the Court must accept all of the appointments or none, but President Chamorro managed to split off one of the six newly selected members by recognizing his election alone as constitutional under the unreformed 1987 Constitution. Dr. Rodolfo Sandino Argüello then agreed to take his seat absent the Court's acceptance of the others. While legislative deputies decried the decision as unprofessional, the Court took advantage of its new quorum to rule that the National Assembly was not empowered to proclaim the constitutional reform. The crisis dragged on. Efforts by a five-nation Group of Friends and the United Nations to foster dialogue failed. Seeking to bring the crisis to a head and force executive compromise, the Assembly increasingly exercised its new privileges contained in the reformed version of the Constitution, passing secondary laws. Still, the executive resisted compromise. Then, in June, the costs of disputing the fundamental rules of governance were made clear to everyone when yet another branch of state was drawn into the political whirlpool.

The Politics of Antipolitics in the Electoral Branch

On June 7, 1995, the terms of office for the Supreme Electoral Council expired. Adhering to separate constitutions, the executive and legislature could not agree on how new members should be named. The top administrative organ for Nicaragua's electoral branch was thrown into political limbo at a moment when the 1996 electoral preparations were already under way.

Nicaragua is among the few democracies with a fourth branch of state, the electoral branch. Perceptions of its power ebb and flow with electoral cycles. In the year preceding the 1990 elections, arguments over the composition of the CSE were among the most divisive political disputes. During the elections the CSE momentarily overshadowed the other branches, yet between elections the electoral branch maintained a low profile.

The electoral branch shared more in common with the judiciary than with the legislative and executive powers. It is not surprising that in the legal realm, some statutes governing the Supreme Court also governed the CSE. Like the Court, the CSE was appointed by the legislature in consultation with the President of the Republic rather than via direct election. Like magistrates, Council members served fixed terms and might be reelected, and statutes covering dismissal of Court magistrates also applied to them. The two institutions shared a structured dependency on the other branches in that neither one had enforcement capacity at its disposal.

By and large, the CSE kept out of the fray of politics in the Chamorro years. Two tense moments were resolved without incident. The first stemmed from the fact that as Nicaragua entered the 1990s, it had neither a recent census nor a permanent electoral register, much less a citizen identification card of the multiple-use sort found in some European countries. President Chamorro set out to remedy that situation by ordering the compilation of a register of citizens. It was not immediately clear whether it was intended to be a census, an electoral register, or a citizen identity-card system. Dr. Mariano Fiallos, president of the CSE, was forced to point out that the compilation of an electoral registry was constitutionally the task of the electoral branch. Here again was a case in which the powers of state were clarifying their roles and establishing boundaries for their functions. In any event, quiet discussion headed off what could have become a major conflict. The executive conducted a census in 1995 separately from the Council's efforts to compile a register of citizens and issue an identity card to be used for voting and other purposes.[17]

The second juncture at which the CSE was forced to tangle with the other branches of state came in June 1995 when its term expired. Showing strategic intuition, Dr. Fiallos played a politics of antipolitics, limiting his role to stating publicly the magnitude of the Council's pressing tasks and leaving hanging the implications of the Council's expiration. It behooved the Council to hold onto the high ground, adopting a legalistic position in which the members ceased work and the positions stood vacant once a term expired. The need to be strictly legalistic was particularly strong given that the Council's authority derives most centrally from its neutral political stance and its strict adherence to the law. Risky as it was to leave the fourth branch without any high-level representative, the vacant posts stood out as a glaring defect in the normal operation of governance, which put pressure on the other branches to settle their constitutional differences.

Resolving the Constitutional Crisis: The Framework Law

Would mounting pressure from the National Assembly have forced the executive to negotiate the constitutional crisis despite the Court's support for Chamorro's position? No doubt, eventually they would have, for elections could not have been held otherwise. In any event, a compromise was reached soon, on June 30, 1995, after a group of bilateral international creditors insisted that the executive settle the constitutional crisis before renegotiating Nicaragua's debt. This compromise was negotiated between representatives of the legislative and executive branches with the aid of Cardinal Miguel Obando y Bravo. The negotiations put into place a Framework Law for the implementation of the constitutional reform. The executive agreed to publish the reform once the legislature passed the law and appointed an agreed-upon list of candidates to the Supreme Electoral Council.

The Framework Law (Law No. 199) stated that the five empty seats on the Supreme Court would be filled by legislative election in which the executive would exercise no influence, but that future vacancies would be filled by executive-legislative accord. The two branches agreed to select a Controller and Subcontroller by common accord. In addition, the Framework Law specified a set of other laws to be passed by consensus with the executive, including a reform of the Electoral Law. They further agreed to form a mixed commission to set a legislative calendar for the remainder of the National Assembly's term.[18] And although the constitutional reform gave the legislature a strong role in developing the budget, the Framework Law insisted that tax laws be formulated jointly with the executive branch and prohibited the legislature from changing the budget ceiling proposed by the

President of the Republic. In short, Chamorro managed to regain some of the lawmaking power that she was losing in the constitutional reform via the back door of the Framework Law, which was approved by the Assembly with the required 60 percent of the vote. Blazing headlines announced the official reform of the Constitution, and President Chamorro spoke of the executive-legislative accord as a compromise for peace and democracy.

Modifying the Balance of Power

The constitutional reform was substantive and broadly supported, and it was expected to be crucial in determining the pace and form of democratic consolidation. Its central accomplishment was to shift power away from the executive branch and into the hands of the legislature, remedying some of the ills of Nicaragua's strong presidential system.

The presidential selection process was altered. In 1986 the FSLN had used its constitutional majority in the legislature to allow presidential re-election even though all the other parties objected. Now, under the reformed Constitution, presidents were not to succeed themselves in office. After waiting an interval of one term, former presidents could run again, but they could serve only a total of two terms. The length of the presidential term was also reduced from six years to five.

Persons working for the executive branch were to resign twelve months in advance of becoming candidates for the presidency or vice presidency. Furthermore, relatives of the president up to the fourth degree and former relatives up to the second degree were prohibited from being candidates. This clause was designed in part to thwart Antonio Lacayo's presidential ambitions. From his office as Minister of Government, Lacayo had become the de facto head of government during his mother-in-law's administration (exercising "efficient" functions), leaving to the politically inexperienced Violeta Chamorro the symbolic activities of head of state (the "dignified" functions).[19]

The selection of the president would also be affected by the introduction of a rule requiring that the winning candidate receive no less than 45 percent of the valid votes cast. If no candidate received that many votes, a second-round run-off election was required between the top two contenders. This clause was drawn up with an eye to the fact that the number of political parties had mushroomed, posing the possibility of a minority president.

Importantly, the constitutional reform placed the National Assembly's informal participation in the budget-making process on a firmer legal footing. During the Sandinista years, President Ortega informed the Assembly of the budget, but it was not until 1989 that the legislature actually undertook to review a budget. Under the 1995 reform, the emergent norm of parliamentary involvement in the budgetary process was made a point of law rather than mere practice. The reform also stripped President Chamorro of the power of decree on fiscal matters, leaving her the decree on administrative matters only. Thus, the president could no longer levy taxes, impose tariffs, or even raise the price of stamps without legislative approval.

The reforms allowed the legislature to approve, modify, or reject an executive decree of a State of Emergency or her suspension of articles of the Constitution. The National Assembly was also required to authorize any use of military troops outside the country. Furthermore, the Assembly's ability to hold state officials accountable was increased because it was empowered to strip them of their political immunity. By and large, the reform shifted power away from the president and toward the National Assembly, restoring a measure of balance to what had been a lopsided system. It also made the two branches more interdependent, particularly on money matters. How well this would work in practice depended on the two branches' ability to open channels of communication and establish new norms of cooperation.

An Independent Judiciary?

The constitutional reform also seemed likely to have important effects on the judicial branch, strengthening it along lines recommended by the Supreme Court itself in 1991.[20] Under the reforms, the Court was expanded to twelve members, who sit on four benches, or *salas* (Civil, Penal, Constitutional, and Administrative), designed to make their work more efficient and thereby eliminate the judicial backlog.

The process for selecting magistrates changed. The National Assembly was no longer constrained to choose someone from a slate presented by the president. She would be invited to submit a list of candidates, but the Assembly could supplement those suggestions with its own list developed through consultation with interested social groups and organizations (for example, the bar association). The Assembly need not choose any of the president's candidates.

Furthermore, the President of the Republic no longer held the authority to select the president of the Supreme Court. Instead, the magistrates would choose the Court's leadership from among their own ranks. Its president was to serve a one-year term, suggesting that leadership would rotate among magistrates far more frequently than in the past. Magistrates' terms of office were extended from six to seven years, ending synchronicity with the presidential and legislative terms and thereby reducing the temptation to appoint a Court whose politics would match fluctuating electoral fortunes.

The Court gained a number of new powers. It could, for example, rule concerning extradition of foreign nationals. Most important of these new functions was the Court's power to resolve jurisdictional or constitutional disputes between the four branches of state, as well as disputes between the central and municipal governments or Autonomous Regions of the Atlantic Coast. The judiciary was also guaranteed 4 percent of the national budget, which was intended to be sufficient to allow judges to earn a dignified salary and thereby end the temptation toward corruption. A career track was authorized, opening the way for development of a profession of judicial administration.

If there was a shadow on the horizon, it was the concern that the judiciary might now be as vulnerable to the legislature as it once was to the executive. The legislature now had a free hand in selecting magistrates. More to the point, it could also fire them. The National Assembly was empowered by Article 138, clause 10 of the 1987 Constitution to "consider and acknowledge the resignations or dismissals of Judges of the Supreme Court of Justice, of Members of the Supreme Electoral Council or the Controller General of the Republic." Article 162 specified that the magistrates of the Supreme Court could be separated from their offices for "reasons determined by law," but under the Sandinista government no legal process was developed for doing so.

When Chamorro came into office, the National Assembly set out to regulate that provision. In April 1995 it specified the reasons for which a magistrate could be dismissed (Law No. 190). They included: 1) being found guilty of a crime; 2) abandonment of the post; 3) incapacity; 4) "conduct that compromises the independence of the judicial or electoral power"; 5) "public conduct contrary to what is moral or good custom"; and, finally, 6) a reduction in the size of the Supreme Court or Supreme Electoral Council.[21] The Assembly could now use the vague conduct clauses to politicize membership of the Court if it was willing to live with the public criticism (not to say questionable judicial practice) that shuffling magistrates would engender.

Interpreting Institutional Evolution

The process of democratic consolidation is much less well understood than either liberalization or democratization.[22] Whereas a decade of research has produced a plethora of hypotheses about how and why authoritarian regimes restore civil liberties and hold "founding" elections, political scientists have often simply taken durability as the measure of consolidation. In reality, however, age is only one characteristic of a consolidated democracy.[23] Democratic consolidation ought to include stabilization of the party system and the system of interest association; rotation of parties in power; regularized, predictable practice of politics; development of a habit of respect for the law; and establishment of institutions that process competing demands without recourse to violence.

Democratic consolidation is by no means a foregone conclusion. The triumphalist rhetoric of liberal democratic ideologues is premature; history has not yet ended. As Philippe Schmitter notes:

> There is no proof that democracy is inevitable, irrevocable, or a historical necessity. It neither fills some indispensable functional requisite of capitalism, nor corresponds to some ineluctable ethical imperative in social evolution. There is every reason to believe that its consolidation demands an extraordinary and continuous effort—one that many countries are unlikely to be able to make.[24]

The most dramatic but least common of the grim alternatives to consolidation is a "sudden death" regression to authoritarian rule by means of a coup d'état (as in Haiti). Alternatively, a hybrid "civilian government with military sovereignty" may develop, dealing the democracy a "slow death" via the "progressive diminution of existing spaces for the exercise of civilian power and the effectiveness of the classic guarantees of liberal constitutionalism" (as in Guatemala). Finally, there is the "lingering demise" of regime persistence without the deepening of democratic practice or beliefs (as in Argentina).[25] In the persistence scenario, "the procedural minima are met with some degree of regularity—but regular, acceptable, and predictable democratic patterns never quite crystallize."[26]

Did the Chamorro years set Nicaragua on one of these paths? Or did institutional development between 1990 and 1996 move it toward a consolidated democracy? Nicaragua's regime remained largely unconsolidated throughout the Chamorro period. Its party system was in flux, due in part to a Political Parties Law and an Electoral Law that fostered splits and favored the founding of microparties (see Chapter 10, this volume). Its system of interest intermediation was pluralist but weak. Political parties, increasingly including the FSLN, had thin organic connections with their social base. Personalist politics gave interest groups access to the state through patron-client relations rather than regularized channels. And although the elections had endowed the regime with legitimacy, a habit of obedience to democratic rules could not be inculcated amid politicized interpretation of the law and rumors of corruption among public officials.

At least until the resolution of the transit strike in 1993, the regime was failing to institutionalize conflict in what remained a highly polarized society. Nicaraguan polarization was political and economic rather than ethnic or religious; such cleavages are more easily mediated. Nonetheless, the depth of the political divisions on such issues as property rights made those divisions qualitative in nature. The stakes of the political game were still largely indivisible, deriving from principle and ideology rather than from interests; actors could not merely split the difference. In short, the failure to rapidly consolidate democracy should be attributed in part to the enormity of the task of social reconciliation in the wake of civil war.

The Chamorro period was above all a time in which Nicaragua's political institutions stabilized their external status—that is, their publicly recognized functions and realms of authority. The constitutional reform shifted power from the executive to the legislative branch, providing balance that seems more conducive to democracy in a country with a tradition of authoritarian presidents. The judiciary also stepped out from under the president's shadow, and it gained crucial resources needed to strengthen its capacity to handle the workload generated in a regime under rule of law. If the legislature learned to exercise its appointment and dismissal powers with care, an independent judiciary might be possible. For its part, the Supreme Electoral Council maintained a comparatively low profile prior to the 1996 elections, but it too stepped forward to clarify the boundaries of its authority through discussion with the executive about establishing an electoral register.

There were many troubling aspects to the reform process. Executive and legislative attempts to manipulate the Supreme Court cast it as a political tool rather than a neutral arbiter. The recklessness with which the National Assembly pitched the country into a constitutional crisis by publishing the reform was matched by the executive's hesitancy in recognizing the legislature's right to reform the Constitution. These problems speak to the difficulty of establishing the rule of law where the fundamental legal framework for the state was contested. It also hinted that even at the constitutional level, politics was still a game of short-term advantage played by temporary coalitions to serve institutional and partisan interests.

The Nicaraguan case allows us to comment on several debates in the consolidation literature. Although the lengthy transition process began in revolution, democratization was achieved by means of a series of elite pacts, after direct mass involvement in politics had been replaced by representative institutions. Evidence from Nicaragua refutes the hypothesis that these transitional pacts will freeze in place undemocratic rules, leaving new-born democracies with "birth defects."[27] The electoral, military, and political pacts forged in 1989 and 1990 held up well, giving the transitional moment a modicum of grace, but this did not prevent their later supercession via piecemeal legal changes. If there was a problem with pacts, it was the absence of an economic accord—that is, the incompleteness of the set of pacts accompanying the transition.

The strident tone and factiousness of politics during the Chamorro years was enough to persuade some Nicaraguans that their country stood on the brink of ungovernability.[28] For although the Chamorro period succeeded in stabilizing the external status of the branches of state, little was accomplished in terms of their internal regulation. It remained to be seen whether and how state institutions would develop patterns of constructive interdependence, including norms of accommodation.

Despite significant accomplishments in defining institutional boundaries, consolidation efforts during the Chamorro years ignored three crucial problems. First, all this institutional wrangling was popularly perceived as *a la cúpula*, a petty dispute among political strongmen with presidential ambitions and of no relevance to the poor majority. Political parties were embroiled in factional quarrels, and the primary institution offering public access—the legislature—was dysfunctional for months at a time. Under these conditions, representation lost meaning. The decline in violence after the resolution of the transit strike in 1993 did not mean that conflict had been institutionalized. Rather, it indicated that resources for open conflict were exceedingly scarce, that Chamorro and the army were comfortable enough with one another to move definitively to end violence, and that new channels for interest articulation had opened up within civil society. As the product of a broad legislative compromise, Nicaragua's constitution had widespread support among political elites, but those elites had few ties to social sectors, and thus the reformed Constitution remained more an elite accord than a social contract.

Second, the Chamorro period was marked by declining faith in democratic governance, as indicated by the poll on the Supreme Court. The vituperative character of the interinstitutional territorial battles pierced the aura of statesmanship that leaders had cultivated for the 1990 elections. Consistent inability to have grievances redressed fostered disappointment in democratic institutions. This state of affairs was predictable. Even in Spain, where consolidation has been comparatively smooth, political scientists have noted a phenomenon of growing disenchantment (*desencanto*) with democracy. Initial expectations about what democratic governance will provide are high; indeed, high hopes may be necessary to spur a transition to democracy beset with risk. Yet it is unlikely that a newly democratic government will be able to fulfill more than a small fraction of the demands made upon it. One reason is that economic crisis is the everyday fare of new democracies.

A third consolidation problem was highlighted by the otherwise welcome resolution of the constitutional crisis. The timing and therefore the content of the executive-legislative negotiations and accord were set by external actors—namely, Nicaragua's creditors. This fact speaks volumes about the country's continued political dependency. Dealings with the International Monetary Fund and World Bank had constrained Chamorro's ability to compromise in the process of economic concertation. Given the Somoza dictatorship's clientalistic relationship with the United States, and the history of U.S. electoral intervention, Nicaraguans had good cause to fear that their government was more responsive to foreign actors than to its citizens.

Elections are a necessary but insufficient condition for democracy, and it is easy to overestimate their value as levers for social change.[29] Dramatic as they were, the 1990 elections did not in themselves settle the political rules of the game. Those rules were set in large part under the Sandinistas and were later refined and codified in a reformed Constitution during the Chamorro period. Institutional development during the Chamorro years paved the way for possible democratic consolidation, but by no means guaranteed it. The minimal requisites of democratic governance were met, but one would have been hard put to identify regular patterns of political interaction. The institutional wrangling in Managua fostered public alienation, disenchantment with democracy, and continued political dependence on foreign actors.

Theorizing beforehand can help in institutional design, but the norms, standards, and operating procedures of newly democratizing regimes will largely be worked out in practice by interested parties in response to conjunctural issues. Nicaragua in the 1990s was engaged in that struggle, with all the prospects for failure that a trial-and-error method entails. The institutional evolution of the Chamorro years was one of an interlocking set of political changes needed for consolidation, but as Violeta's term drew to a close, much more remained to be done.

Notes

1. See Philip J. Williams, "Dual Transitions from Authoritarian Rule: Popular and Electoral Democracy in Nicaragua," *Comparative Politics* 26, no. 2 (January 1994): 169–85.

2. The right-wing Coordinadora Democrática alliance boycotted these elections and joined the United States in dismissing them as fraudulent and noncompetitive. Almost all other observers praised them as clean. See, for example, the Latin American Studies Association, "Report of the Latin American Studies Association Delegation to Observe the Nicaraguan General Election of November 4, 1984," *LASA Forum* 15, no. 4 (1984): 9–43.

3. On the importance of previous experience with democracy, see Larry Diamond, Juan J. Linz, and Seymour Martin Lipset, eds., *Democracy in Developing Countries: Latin America* (Boulder, CO: Lynne Rienner, 1989), especially the introductory chapter by Diamond and Linz, and the chapter on Brazil by Bolívar Lamounier.

4. For information on how the FSLN party functioned and the consequences for democracy, see Harry E. Vanden and Gary Prevost, *Democracy and Socialism in Sandinista Nicaragua* (Boulder, CO: Lynne Rienner, 1993).

5. The effects of the war in shaping Nicaraguan political institutions are explored in Thomas W. Walker, ed., *Revolution and Counterrevolution in Nicaragua* (Boulder, CO: Westview Press, 1991).

6. On the formation of the Constitution and criticism of it, see Kenneth J. Mijeski, ed., *The Nicaraguan Constitution of 1987: English Translation and Commentary* (Athens: Ohio University Monographs in International Studies, 1991).

7. There is an emerging literature on constitution-making as a key element in democratic transitions. The crucial piece treating the problem of incompatible prin-

ciples is Miriam Kornblith, "The Politics of Constitution-making: Constitutions and Democracy in Venezuela," *Journal of Latin American Studies* 23 (February 1991): 80.

8. More detailed discussion of this early reformulation of the Court may be found in "The Constitutional Process in Nicaragua," my contribution to Jacques Zylberberg and François Demers, *America and the Americas* (Sainte-Foy, Canada: Presses de l'Université Laval, 1992), 735–57.

9. These figures are from a nationwide poll of 825 Nicaraguans (400 from Managua) conducted by Fundación Centroamérica 2000 and Consultora M&R and reported in *El Nuevo Diario*, June 27, 1995.

10. This account of events was drawn from David Close, ed., *Legislatures and the New Democracies in Nicaragua and Their Aftermath* (Boulder, CO: Lynne Rienner, 1995), the editor's contribution on Nicaragua. Note that the OAS refused to intervene under the Santiago Declaration provisions, suggesting that it did not view Chamorro's actions as an irregular, undemocratic *autogolpe*.

11. In December of that year, at a National Dialogue held under the auspices of the Esquipulas peace process, opposition parties united around a demand for seventeen constitutional changes, including no reelection of the president, no family succession in government, no right to vote for members of the military, reform of the electoral branch, limitations on presidential power, changes in the nature and function of the armed forces, legalization of conscientious-objector status, independence of the judicial branch, separation of the FSLN from the state and army, suppression of the Preamble to the Constitution, guarantees of property rights, and concrete action toward promised freedom of expression and workers' participation. See the "Pronunciamiento de reformas del Gobierno de la República de Nicaragua sobre la 'Propuesta de reformas constitucionales' presentado por los partidos políticos y agrupaciones políticas participantes en el Diálogo Nacional," December 15, 1987.

12. To this day, many members of the UNO charge that as many as four legislative seats were stolen from the UNO though fraud in the Granada region, supposedly achieved by Sandinista tampering with the null votes. These seats would have allowed the UNO to reform individual articles of the Constitution unilaterally, which would have been opposed by the FSLN and would not have invested the Constitution with anything approaching a social contract. Author's interview with Dr. Hernaldo Zuñiga, Managua, July 8, 1995.

13. One-third of the legislators must back a partial constitutional reform bill for it to be introduced into the legislature; one-half of the deputies plus one are needed for introduction of a bill for total reform (that is, replacement) of the Constitution.

14. These public meetings, called constitutional consultations, were organized by municipality. The 1986 *cabildos abiertos* were organized by social sector— women, urban labor, youth, peasants et al.—in keeping with the Sandinistas' early corporatist tendencies. The account of the reform process given here is taken in large part from "A Month in the Life of the Reforms," *Envío* 13, no. 161 (December 1994): 6–7.

15. In 1993 the legislature passed a one-time-only law that would have allowed the Constitution to be reformed if the amendments were passed in a single legislative session. President Chamorro never signed the bill into law, however, and the idea was abandoned.

16. The new members elected were Drs. Francisco Plata López, Harlan Kent Henríquez Clair, Julio Ramón García Vilchez, Josefina Ramos Mendoza, and Rodolfo Sandino Argüello. Dra. Ramos was to be the second woman on the Court, with

Dra. Alba Luz, who was the only Sandinista appointee to have been reelected. Dr. Henríquez was the first black man and Atlantic Coast citizen ever to be sworn in as a Court magistrate. The appointments were reconfirmed in July, in keeping with the executive-legislative accord.

17. All citizens of voting age (16) were asked to fill out a form supplying information about themselves and family members. The data included names, nicknames, date and place of birth, current residence, nationality, marital status, educational and literacy levels, profession, and the names of each parent. A thumbprint was taken and a photograph attached, and the citizen signed the document. Further forms were available to recognize children, claim parentage, and give sworn testimony to the identity of an adult who had none of the accepted papers (birth certificate, passport). Electoral registration is required by law, although there is no prescribed punishment for not registering. Compliance has been very high, but the process was slow and could not be completed before the 1996 election.

18. Among the laws to be developed cooperatively are the law to privatize the telephone company, the Labor Code, the reforms of the Electoral Law, a new Emergency Law, a law regulating the position of the Vice Presidency, a new pardon law, a law governing the office of Controller General, and the partial veto of the Teaching Career Law. See the Ley Marco (Framework Law), published in *El Nuevo Diario* and all the national newspapers on July 3, 1995.

19. These terms are from Walter Bagehot's classic, *The English Constitution* (London: Fontana, 1967 [1867]). Lacayo's wife Cristiana Chamorro filed suit, challenging the constitutional prohibition, thus circumventing Lacayo's promise not to do so.

20. See the Declaration made at the closing ceremony of the First International Conference on the Protection, Strengthening, and Dignification of the Judicial Power, read at the Olof Palme Convention Center, Managua, September 6, 1991.

21. See Law No. 190, the "Law about removing from office the Controller General of the Republic and the Magistrates of the Supreme Court of Justice and the Supreme Electoral Council," passed in the National Assembly on April 26, 1995. The dismissal law was immediately put into practice by the legislature in an effort to fire the president of the Supreme Court, Dr. Orlando Trejos.

22. Following Guillermo O'Donnell, Philippe C. Schmitter, and Lawrence Whitehead, eds., *Transitions from Authoritarian Rule: Prospects for Democracy* (Baltimore: Johns Hopkins University Press, 1986), I use the term "transition to democracy" to refer to a four-stage process: the breakdown of authoritarian rule, liberalization, democratization, and consolidation. These stages are not perfectly linear and may overlap; and, of course, the transition may be halted at any stage by a military coup.

23. Indeed, certain factors (such as weak accountability procedures) that enhance stability may detract from the democratic quality of the regime. See J. Samuel Valenzuela, "Consolidation in Post-Transitional Settings," in *Issues in Democratic Consolidation: The New South American Democracies in Comparative Perspective,* ed. Scott Mainwaring, Guillermo O'Donnell, and J. Samuel Valenzuela (Notre Dame, IN: University of Notre Dame Press, 1992), 59.

24. Philippe C. Schmitter, "Dangers and Dilemmas of Democracy," *Journal of Democracy* 5, no. 2 (April 1994): 57–74, reference on 58.

25. The descriptive terms here are from Guillermo O'Donnell, "Transitions, Continuities, and Paradoxes," in Mainwaring et al., *Issues in Democratic Consolidation,* 19.

26. Schmitter, "Dangers and Dilemmas of Democracy," 60.

27. This hypothesis is articulated by one of the early theorists on pacted democracy, Terry Lynn Karl, in "Dilemmas of Democratization in Latin America," *Comparative Politics* 23, no. 1 (October 1990): 1–21.

28. Concern about ungovernability was reflected in a public opinion survey conducted by the Institute for Nicaraguan Studies (IEN), commissioned by the United Nations. See Rodolfo Delgado Romero, "La gobernabilidad y el acuerdo nacional en Nicaragua—Investigación desde la opinión pública nacional," Testimony before the UN Support Group concerned with State Powers, Managua, March 14, 1995.

29. A good discussion of the effects and limits of elections may be found in Paul W. Drake and Eduardo Silva, *Elections and Democratization in Latin America, 1980–1985* (La Jolla, CA: Center for Iberian and Latin American Studies, Institute of the Americas, at the University of California, San Diego, 1986), especially the chapters by Drake and Terry Lynn Karl. See also the afterword by Alejandro Bendaña in William I. Robinson, *A Faustian Bargain: U.S. Intervention in the Nicaraguan Elections and American Foreign Policy in the Post-Cold War Era* (Boulder, CO: Westview Press, 1992).

4

The Redirection of the Armed Forces

Daniel Premo

Unlike armies elsewhere in Latin America, the Nicaraguan army was not formed in the independence wars. Before the creation of the National Guard in 1927, Nicaragua had irregular armies or forces that were armed partisans of the Liberal and Conservative parties. After the departure of American troops in 1933, the Guard itself functioned as the personal vehicle of the long-ruling Somoza family. In contrast, the Sandinista People's Army (Ejército Popular Sandinista, or EPS) originated as a military force of popular origins that emerged victorious in 1979. From the beginning, the leadership of the Sandinista Front for National Liberation (FSLN) rejected the presumption that the armed forces should be politically neutral. Instead, the EPS was conceived as an instrument of class control whose principal mission was to defend the revolution.[1]

During the 1980s the EPS played a dominant role in Nicaraguan society as the military arm of the FSLN. From its early reliance on popular militias, the FSLN introduced compulsory military service in late 1983 to meet the increased threat of U.S.-supported Contras operating from bases in Honduras. With arms and training supplied principally by the Soviet Union, Cuba, and the Eastern Bloc countries, the EPS developed sufficient resources, internal cohesiveness, and organizational structure to contain, but not eliminate, the forces of the National Resistance. By 1987–1989 the human and economic costs of the prolonged war had led to a series of negotiations that considered, among other issues, the demobilization of the Contra forces and the reduction of the EPS. Thus, over the course of a decade, the EPS evolved from guerrilla units born out of revolution into a partisan, semiprofessional institution closely identified with the popular sectors.

The Transition Protocol

The Sandinista electoral defeat on February 25, 1990, presented the EPS with the need to guarantee its institutional survival in the face of domestic and international demands ranging from its internal restructuring to its abolition. For UNO's most radical sector, the EPS, as the military arm of the FSLN, represented a threat to its autonomous control. On the other hand, for the outgoing government and the popular forces that had supported the revolution, the EPS was the guarantor of their personal safety. Those in Nicaragua and the United States who identified most closely with the Contras' cause lobbied strongly for the elimination of Sandinista control of the army and the National Police, and in particular for the removal of General Humberto Ortega. In turn, FSLN officials and members of the army's high command made it clear that negotiations with UNO to define new "rules of the game" would have to consider the integrity and institutional interests of the armed forces.

Shortly after the elections, Daniel Ortega demanded "respect for the institutionality and professionalism of the army" based on the national status accorded it in the 1987 Constitution and on Military Organization Law No. 75, decreed two days before the election but antedated to December 27, 1989. The latter broke the link between the FSLN and the army but did not subordinate the military to executive authority. For all practical purposes, it declared the EPS an autonomous body by creating a military council with the authority to name the army chief, determine promotions, and make virtually all important decisions affecting the armed forces.[2]

Transition talks headed by Antonio Lacayo for UNO and General Ortega resulted in an important security framework for both political groups and guaranteed a Sandinista share in power. Under terms of the Transition Protocol signed on March 27, 1990, the government-elect promised to respect the institutional integrity of the armed forces, in return for which it received the military's support and a guarantee that the FSLN would accept an opposition role within the framework established by the 1987 Constitution. Specifically, the Chamorro government agreed to "respect the integrity and professionalism of the EPS and the public order forces, as well as their ranks, personnel registries, and commands, in accordance with the Constitution and the nation's laws."[3]

The decision to retain General Ortega as commander of the armed forces was both the most controversial and the most important concession that Violeta Chamorro made to ensure a peaceful transfer of power. According to Nicaraguan journalist Edwin Saballos, Ortega's presence at the head of the army was the only guarantee of stability in the country's fragile transition.[4] On the other hand, it divided the UNO coalition before Chamorro even took office. Early on, she had indicated that Ortega would not be part of her administration or "remain in the Army in any capacity."[5] Lacayo is believed to have been instrumental in the decision to retain him, which may explain in part the close relationship that subsequently developed between them. Ortega's presence preserved the integrity of the armed forces and guaranteed some degree of Sandinista cooperation in upholding the legitimacy of the Chamorro government. Although Ortega played a key stabilizing role within the EPS in the turbulent early months of the transition, for the domestic right wing and U.S. critics his presence after 1990 was a constant reminder of the partisan origins of the EPS and a symbol of the government's failure to achieve civilian supremacy over the military.[6]

The Transition Protocol assured UNO's immediate objective of a peaceful transfer of power and guaranteed the institutional integrity of the military. The agreement also extracted a commitment from the EPS leadership to undertake an immediate reduction in force and to support the constitutional order in principle. Acceptance of the protocol by the new government, the FSLN, and the EPS made possible the initial consolidation of the democratic process. However, the pact did little to establish limits on the military's political role or to define its institutional role in further efforts at consolidation. The problems of developing a broader social consensus for the transition, how to interpret the pact, and how to fulfill it were left to subsequent negotiation and the good faith of the participants.

The Early Transition, 1990–1992

In societies that have recently experienced a transition from war to peace or are otherwise undergoing a process of democratization, there exist rare opportunities to negotiate fundamental changes in civil-military relationships. "New democracies" such as Nicaragua enjoy, at least temporarily, the advantage of having renounced war and violence as legitimizing factors.[7] When President Chamorro and Lacayo made it clear that national reconciliation and not counterrevolution was to be the overriding goal of the new government, it provided political groups with the opportunity to agree on broad societal goals with respect to the future role of the military.

Realistically, a number of factors limited the Chamorro government's bargaining position in developing a strategy to subordinate the army to effective civilian control. The popularity, size, and relative cohesiveness of the armed forces severely reduced Doña Violeta's options, especially when compared to the tenuous nature of the political coalition that elected her. Moreover, despite its electoral defeat, the FSLN remained the largest single party in the National Assembly, with the best-organized social base of mobilized support.[8]

A wholesale restructuring of the military was out of the question. Any attempt to replace the EPS with a Contra army would have resulted in a bloodbath in view of the former's capacity to resist any such threat to its institutional survival. On the other hand, the government was not in such a position of weakness vis-à-vis the military to make it a mere "client" or "hostage" with no freedom to initiate policies. As seen above, the Transition Protocol provided the basis for a pragmatic strategy of coexistence in the short term, recognizing limits on the government's actions but leaving open the prospect of consolidating civilian rule. Moreover, the compelling needs to decommission the Contras, pacify the countryside, and proceed with downsizing the military deterred the government from any immediate attempt to establish control through a reformation of the military's basic doctrine.

The change in government made it politically possible to achieve the demobilization of the Contras. The Tocontín Accord signed on March 23, 1990, by negotiating teams representing the National Resistance and the government-elect, established conditions for the initial phase of Contra demobilization and committed both groups to work for peace and national reconciliation.[9] Subsequent cease-fire agreements and the mediation of the United Nations' Organization for Central America (ONUCA) and the Organization of American States' International Support and Verification Commission (CIAV-OEA) facilitated the beginning of a pacification process that by June 30 had completed the demobilization and at least partial disarming of 22,413 Contras and family members.[10]

Contra collaboration in the pacification process was predicated on a simultaneous reduction of EPS forces. In June 1990, President Chamorro approved a reduction plan for the army submitted by General Ortega, based on quotas agreed upon at the 1987 Esquipulas Accords. At a joint news conference on June 7, the president announced that during the first reduction phase the EPS would be trimmed from 96,660 soldiers at the beginning of January to 41,000 by July.[11] According to General Ortega, the EPS had planned a downsizing before the Esquipulas agreements. He contended that a "considerable reduction" was necessary before Nicaragua's army could become more professional and improve its organizational structure.[12] To this point, downsizing had affected primarily mobilized segments of the army, not officers. On November 8, Ortega announced the beginning of a process to retire 5,000 officers, 90 percent of them at the ranks of first and second lieutenants, and the remainder at the level of captain or higher.[13]

At the end of 1992, Nicaragua, which once had fielded the largest army in Central America, now had fewer men and women in uniform (15,200) than any country in the region, including Costa Rica.[14] The speed with which the reduction was carried out exacerbated unemployment, poverty, and social unrest. Remarkably, despite the budgetary difficulties that plagued the programs to retire officers, the reduction produced no serious institutional reactions or immediate impact on relations between the EPS and civilian society.[15]

In some respects, budgetary reductions in the early transitional phase generated more open political controversy between military and civilian authorities than troop reduction. The last FSLN military budget for 1990 had been reduced to $103 million in operating expenses, plus an additional $74 million in foreign credit (41.8 percent of the national budget compared to 50 percent at the height of the Contra war). In its first budget negotiations with the new government, the EPS reluctantly accepted a budget ceiling of $78.6 million, a 55 percent reduction in military spending and foreign credit from the previous year, and considerably less than the $131 million it had originally requested. The National Assembly, controlled by a UNO coalition increasingly hostile to the executive, voted to cut the army's budget request from $78.6 to $58.9 million, which President Chamorro vetoed on December 15. The EPS General Command issued a communiqué the same day informing the ranks that it would not allow 10,000 soldiers to be "discharged irresponsibly" because of a reduction in the defense budget. In a not-so-subtle attempt to influence the outcome, the EPS expressed its confidence that "a majority of deputies" would accept the president's veto.[16]

At a news conference defending her decision, Chamorro argued that the country could not immediately absorb more thousands of demobilized soldiers without the risk of producing "profound social conflict as well as unnecessary political tensions."[17] A majority of pro-government legislators sustained the president's veto, and the National Assembly subsequently approved a figure of $70.6 million. In an address to the nation, the president reaffirmed her commitment to strengthen civilian authority and military discipline, "so that in the future the army will not make public pronouncements on matters that pertain to the National Assembly."[18]

Chamorro made an initial attempt to bring the EPS under executive authority in early 1991 with the promulgation of a new Military Organization Law, reforming Sandinista Law No. 75. Known as Decree Law No. 2-91, it designated the president as commander in chief of the armed forces and included among her attributes the authority to designate a civilian defense minister and to appoint the four top military ranks of general, including the army chief from a nominee selected by the Military Council—specifically, the army's highest ranking officer. The reforms established the Defense Ministry as a channel of communication between the president and the army and prohibited active members of the EPS from belonging to any political party directorate or holding civilian public office.[19]

Despite Chamorro's occasional admonitions, the EPS continued to issue periodic communiqués reflecting the military command's own viewpoint or decision on matters of national import. According to General Ortega, the military had a constitutional duty to guarantee order, which gave it a supportive role in diplomatic and political tasks, negotiation efforts, and the search for peace. It had been accustomed to this role during the Sandinista era and fully expected to continue it under the new government.[20] In November 1991, for example, the EPS issued a statement expressing its concern over increased violence in rural and urban areas and called on all sectors of Nicaraguan society to "abandon their confrontational and biased stands."[21]

EPS leaders, especially Ortega, frequently found themselves the targets of criticism both within government circles and the larger society. The small but vocal Civil Movement continued to advocate the abolition of the armed forces, periodically expressing alarm at the military leadership's "flagrant and recurrent meddling in national politics."[22] On October 27, 1992, General Ortega, flanked by the entire high command, read a lengthy communiqué defending the army's institutional status and denouncing those who demanded its abolition. While reaffirming his loyalty to the government and the Constitution, he said that the EPS would not tolerate deeper cuts to its budget or further reduction in its ranks. He reminded the state of its "duty" to provide the military with a budget adequate to fulfill its mission and indicated that officers would continue to voice their opinion on issues of national concern as long as Nicaragua did not achieve "the stability we all desire."[23] Critics accused Ortega of unconstitutionally meddling in politics, and a UNO faction within the National Assembly issued a statement accusing him of a "technical coup d'état." On November 4, after a six-hour meeting between army chiefs of staff and the president, who was accompanied by eight of her ministers, the government issued a terse bulletin reaffirming not only the conclusion of the reduction process and respect for the army but also the government's determination to ensure "the subordination of the military to civilian authority."[24]

The controversy over the communiqué illustrates the struggle during the early years of Chamorro's government to define and establish limits to military autonomy. In this instance, the lack of more decisive presidential action in the face of evident insubordination reinforced the appearance of executive impotence and left unresolved the issue of Ortega's tenure as head of the army. The political realities during the early phase of the democratic transition clearly favored the military. Despite civilian opposition from various quarters, the EPS retained a vital political role for itself by virtue of the coercive means at its disposal, which it committed in support of an increasingly beleaguered government. Ortega had the full backing of the officer corps, despite the drastic reductions in the army's size and budget. On the other hand, President Chamorro, while still personally popular after two years in office, no longer had majority party support in the National Assembly or even a clear conviction in favor of her leadership among the former UNO coalition members.

During the early phase of the transition, Ortega completed the separation of the EPS from the FSLN's control, but without any corresponding subordination of the military to civilian authority. The EPS owed its allegiance primarily to its commanding general, who exercised strong personal control over military policy. By the end of 1992 both civilian and military authorities had come to understand the need to accelerate the drafting of a new organization law that would resolve the vexing problem of the undefined duration of the military command and provide a firmer basis for professionalization.

Establishing Civilian Control, 1993–1995

At a seminar in August 1993 on "The Armed Forces' New Role in Nicaragua," Lacayo said: "We must acknowledge that the military is distrustful of relinquishing the power they derive from their strength, gradually surrendering it to civilians, and thus become subordinate to civilian authority." He added that continuous dialogue would be necessary to achieve a higher level of civilian control over the army.[25] Less than a month later, President Chamorro caught the military by surprise when she announced in an Army Day speech that she intended to replace General Ortega "sometime in 1994." The president also stated her intention to transfer the Defense Information Division (DID) from the EPS command to the executive branch under a civilian overseer and to change the name of the armed forces to "reflect more clearly its national character."[26] Although the latter move and several lesser initiatives had been negotiated with Ortega prior to the announcement, the decision to remove him and the transfer of the DID had not.[27] Ironically, just before her speech, Ortega presented Chamorro with the army's proposal for a new Military Code.

The EPS Military Council met in emergency session and issued a communiqué stating that President Chamorro could not dismiss the army chief, citing Article 30 of the 1991 Decree Law which gave the Military Council that authority. The communiqué underscored that making such changes would set "a dangerous precedent."[28] Ortega subsequently declared his willingness to resolve the tense situation, but he emphasized that the "president's intention" to discharge him should be strictly governed by the Constitution and the law and not be subject to "any internal or foreign political pressure which compromises the country's sovereignty and dignity."[29] The confrontation underscored once again how little headway Chamorro's government had made in asserting control over the EPS, and it placed a renewed sense of urgency on the negotiations between the army and the executive branch to agree on a draft of the former's proposed Military Code.

The 1994 Military Code

Negotiations over reforms to the military's organic law continued between the executive and the military high command during the early months of 1994. At a UN forum on the role of Nicaragua's armed forces, Luis Humberto Guzmán suggested that approval of a new Military Code would perhaps be "the best time . . . to announce replacements necessary to advance the institutionalization of the armed forces."[30] Ortega's analysis of the impasse was even more succinct. The general told a Latin American Studies Association delegation in June 1994 that "until the army has its Military Code, I can't retire. . . . Once we have such a law, the individual becomes less important to the institution."[31] Earlier, speaking at a Forum on Civil-Military Relations, he argued that Nicaragua's main problem was not the relationship between civilians and the military, but rather "the backwardness of a nation that has no democratic experience whatsoever and the conflict between those who want democracy and those who do not." He reminded the audience that the consolidation of democracy depends as much on civilians as it does on the military.[32]

On May 18, 1994, President Chamorro sent a draft of the proposed Military Code to the National Assembly. In her view, the new law, once promulgated, would provide Nicaragua for the first time in its history with an army clearly subordinated to civilian power. Most important, the draft provided for the president to appoint a new commander in chief on December 21, to take office on February 21, 1995. After four contentious years, Chamorro's government and the various interests represented by General Ortega had negotiated what the latter had insisted upon since the FSLN's electoral defeat, a "dignified withdrawal" that would preserve the institutional integrity of the military.

After three months of intense negotiation, the National Assembly approved the Military Code on August 23, 1994.[33] President Chamorro formally ratified it on September 2, which, appropriately, was Army Day. The new code established guidelines regarding the functions of the armed forces, their professionalism, and nonpartisan nature. It provided the basis for increased accountability to civilian authority by subordinating both the army's strategic orientations and its chief to the executive branch. Significantly, the new code did not empower the president to appoint directly the chief of the armed forces. Instead, it limited the executive's authority to reject the nominee proposed by the Military Council. The code did, however, specify for the first time the causes for which the army chief might be removed and limited him to a single five-year term. Other significant provisions banned members of the armed forces from having party affiliations and explicitly prohibited the use of military intelligence for political purposes. Legal reforms included a provision for the Supreme Court to name military judges and a restriction of military jurisdiction to military crimes, essentially eliminating the Hispanic tradition of military *fuero*.[34]

One of the most controversial aspects of the new code was the decision to allow the army to operate a special pension fund and to sanction military-owned businesses to sustain it. Although the National Assembly insisted that the military pay taxes and limit itself to operating nonprofit enterprises, organizations such as the Higher Council on Private Enterprise (COSEP) complained that the army should not be in economic competition with the private sector.[35] The new code specified that earnings from the army's investments be used exclusively for its new Military Pension Institute (IPSM), and that the minister of finance and the head of the National Social Security and Social Welfare Institute (INSSBI) serve on its governing board. Notwithstanding such provisions, as of late 1995, civilian authorities had yet to determine any legitimate limits to the army's business interests.

Professionalization

In addition to the issues mentioned above, the Military Code incorporated the basic revisions governing organization, structure and composition, command levels, and internal norms that the EPS had formulated in 1990. Together with the provisions on jurisdiction and retirement, they represented an indispensable element in consolidating the army's professionalization process. The army's dramatic reduction in size during the early years of the Chamorro government made it possible to establish a new command structure, increase efficiency, and strengthen cohesion of troops at all levels through improved professional training. Virtually all of the officers who remained on active duty after 1992 had undergone considerable practical military training in the 1980s, but most had limited general and professional military education backgrounds. In June 1993 the army took a fundamental step toward guaranteeing a professional corps of qualified officers when the Military Academy enrolled two hundred cadets in its first class since the overthrow of Anastasio Somoza.[36] The "Andrés Castro" School for Sergeants opened in March 1994, and specialized officer training courses were established for lieutenants and captains. Higher-ranking officers continued to train abroad, principally in Mexico, Spain, France, China, Russia, and Cuba.[37]

Despite the advances in recruitment and training and the development of a hierarchical system of rank and promotions after 1990, institutional concerns remained that were likely to work against the unity of the officer corps in the short term. For example, by 1995 competition was already keen among officers in the bloated middle ranks who were seeking promotion to the highly restricted grades. Additional competition simmered between noncoms and graduates; and among the latter, between those who either had or hoped to receive advanced training abroad. Finally, a problem remained for those senior officers who lacked the requisite skills and training now required for promotion to the highest command levels.[38]

After 1990 both the government and the "dissident" UNO sector understood professionalization of the army principally in terms of its complete divorce from the FSLN and its subordination to civilian authority. Although the military made the transition from the Sandinista period to the Chamorro government with its partisan designation intact, there is evidence that the military had lost some of its partisan character even before the FSLN's electoral defeat. General Ortega had stated on a number of occasions that he warned then President Daniel Ortega about the danger of using the EPS for partisan political purposes. Specifically, he feared that differences among FSLN leaders would be reflected within the officer corps and that the party-army-state alliance would not allow the EPS to develop its own professional and institutional identity.[39]

It was not easy for many Sandinistas, including Daniel Ortega, to accept uncritically Humberto Ortega's efforts to assert the military's nonpartisanship, especially since many of the EPS's pronouncements, attitudes, and policies after 1990 worked directly against the FSLN's interests. Disagreements between the Ortega brothers over the role of the army led the general to assert early in the transition period that the EPS would "never be the armed wing of the FSLN or any political party."[40] Not long afterward, he denounced Daniel for encouraging "civic insurrection" and said that political speeches directed at creating confrontations had no place in the Chamorro government's policy of reconciliation.[41] Ortega's order to counterattack rearmed former EPS soldiers who took over the city of Estelí in July 1993 is perhaps the clearest indication that the army had divorced itself from its partisan origins. It was a mere formality when the National Assembly voted in November 1994 to change the name of the EPS to the Nicaraguan National Army as part of the constitutional reform package. By that time, internal divisions among the Sandinistas had led Ortega to proclaim that "the FSLN can break up into as many pieces as it wants. . . . Our task in these difficult circumstances is to keep the army intact."[42]

Well before Ortega's departure, the EPS had effectively assumed a nonpartisan character. However, professionalization of the military has also traditionally been associated with the concept of an armed force that accepts civilian authority and ceases to make political statements on matters of professional or national concern.[43] If one accepts the premise that the military cannot exist without developing social and economic interests and is, therefore, by nature political, then the problem is not one of military participation in politics, but the nature of that participation. As Paul Zagorski reminds us, the armed forces "should not and cannot be excluded from the discussion of public policy in which they have a reasonable claim to expertise."[44]

Shortly after assuming command on February 21, 1995, General Joaquín Cuadra made it clear that no one, including Ortega, would influence the army's decisions from behind the scenes or from outside the military hierarchy. When asked about the military's political role, he stated that the army would not meddle in party politics or comment on political developments. However, he added that since the military shares "great responsibilities" with different sectors of the country, it would continue to express opinions "at the times they should be given and with the appropriate discretion and maturity."[45]

During the first year of his tenure as army chief, Cuadra reaffirmed on various occasions the military's subordination to civilian authority. At a ceremony on May 29, he stressed the army's impartiality in the controversy between the executive and legislative branches over constitutional reforms. However, in language highly reminiscent of his predecessor, he strongly criticized those people who, "blinded by partisan, group, or personal aspirations, intend to pursue personal interests at the expense of national interests."[46] Like Ortega before him, Cuadra sought to assure his civilian counterparts that the military would never seize power. In commenting on the 1996 elections, he stated that it would require a "major disruption" for the army to intervene, something he did not foresee under the political circumstances existing at the time.[47]

According to Cuadra, the military's principal political role in mid-1995 was to continue its professionalization. The Military Inspector General's Office, established in 1994, created the potential for closer internal control over personnel, command, and general discipline, making it less likely that military decisions would depend on individual perception and personal leadership. Under Cuadra's command, the army was expected to rely more on collegial decision making and to conduct its business more openly than was the case during Ortega's tenure.

Conclusion

The controversial relationship between the EPS and the Chamorro administration dated to the transition accord signed between the new government and the armed forces in March 1990. Although the EPS acceded to the transfer of power, it managed to retain significant prerogatives to control military affairs with only nominal direction from civilian elements within the executive and legislative branches.

An important element in the fabric of civil-military relations is civilian oversight of military activities to ensure that they conform to national policy and legal norms.[48] Civilian control over the military, as embodied in the 1994 Military Code, had broad support in principle in late 1995, but it appeared that it might be difficult to achieve in the short term. Nicaragua had few civilian experts in military affairs. The lack of civilian regulatory mechanisms had allowed the military to make decisions affecting its own socialization and organizational structure with only marginal input from civilian authorities. This state of affairs was especially evident during the period in which the juridical framework for the military's organization and behavior was being negotiated and promulgated.

The evidence suggests that after 1990 the EPS underwent substantial changes in its professionalization, most visibly a reduction in force levels unprecedented in Latin America and a redefinition of its mission. As of the mid-1990s it appeared that as Nicaragua's army became more professionalized, it might be expected to develop institutional interests, skills, concerns, and values shared by all developed military institutions, and to compete within the political arena for what it perceived to be its proper share of the society's limited resources. With the new Military Code, the legal framework was now largely in place to negotiate some of the more contentious institutional issues that are likely to affect civil-military relations in the near term, such as the demand for a "dignified" budget and the need to clarify the army's financial interests.

As elsewhere in Latin America, economic uncertainty was likely to contribute to an unstable pattern of civil-military relations in Nicaragua for some time. With little prospect for greater economic growth and equity, future governments, regardless of their political composition and orientation, were not likely to have the financial resources to assure either the military or the National Police of an adequate budget to fulfill their respective missions, much less pursue additional reforms. Although in the mid-1990s the army maintained a degree of autonomy in the disbursement of profits from the substantial number of commercial enterprises it owned and administered, it could not guarantee a method of funding the military budget completely independent of civilian oversight. As of late 1995 the civilian government had yet to lay the institutional foundations for greater civilian control, especially over the army's economic transactions.

As of the mid-1990s, Nicaragua's army no longer served the partisan interests of the FSLN—in fact, it seldom had, at least explicitly, during the transition period. Although the army's political role after 1990 was guided in part by its revolutionary origins, increasingly it had come to reflect the institution's growing corporate interests. The army's role in suppressing strikes and social protests had tarnished its image as an ally of popular movements, which has led to increasing contradictions between the officer corps' Sandinista roots and the institution's interest in promoting economic stability and growth, even at the expense of the country's popular sectors.

Debate within the Nicaraguan armed forces had converged by the mid-1990s with wider Latin American military trends in considering possible new roles ranging from antidrug-trafficking initiatives to environmental conservation. Perhaps more so than any other country in the region, Nicaragua had met the challenge of creating a model of civil-military relations that over time might yet delimit the army's role in the nation's political life. Apart from the small core of civilian abolitionists, there was surprisingly little dissent after 1990 within the officer corps or between it and civilian authorities over the proper function of the armed forces in society. Nor was there much uncertainty over the institution's primary missions. The fact that the military retained an internal mission centered on civic action programs was not on its own necessarily harmful to civilian control. In view of Nicaragua's extreme underdevelopment, some role expansion was probably desirable. The critical question was that such expansion be defined and ordered by elected political authorities, not by the military. Eventually, credible conventional missions would be needed to distance the military from civilian areas of responsibility, which was not likely to happen as long as the National Police remained poorly trained, understaffed, and underfunded.

On balance, the military's concerns and anxieties in the mid-1990s were not so different from other armed forces, including that of the United States, as they strove to accommodate their interests and redefine their institutional role to changing national, regional, and global conditions.

The transition period under consideration produced a paradox for the Nicaraguan military. The institution experienced an unprecedented reduction in its manpower, procurement, and general budget support from 1990 to 1995. Yet the constitutional system that evolved over the same period provided the basis for a permanent organizational structure, professionalization, and interest in the national economy that was certain to perpetuate, if not increase, the army's decision-making authority and ensure it a prominent role in Nicaragua's civilian society.

Although opportunities for dialogue and understanding between civilian and military authorities increased after 1990, several constitutional changes of government would be needed in Nicaragua before it would be possible to speak of any pattern of civil-military coexistence. And even then, it might not be until Nicaragua was less polarized politically and more economically developed that the military's role as a national institution could be fully understood or appreciated. Ultimately, the future role of the military and the boundaries between its professional and political conduct would be determined by the ability of the country's various political actors—including the military—to arrive at a viable consensus on national goals and the manner in which they were to be achieved. In this respect, the 1996 elections represented only a step, albeit a crucial one, in Nicaragua's efforts at democratic consolidation.

Notes

1. For an analysis of the origins and role of the EPS prior to the 1990 elections, see Thomas W. Walker, "The Armed Forces," in *Revolution and Counterrevolution in Nicaragua*, ed. Thomas W. Walker (Boulder, CO: Westview Press, 1991), 77–100.

2. *Barricada*, February 28, 1990. When asked later about his role in the transition, General Ortega stated that in his early conversations with President Chamorro he had insisted on "respect for the legitimacy of the armed institution, its chain of command, and its commanding officers." Gen. Humberto Ortega, interview with LASA delegation, Managua, June 22, 1994.

3. *La Tribuna*, April 5, 1994. The complete Transition Protocol and other documents relevant to the military's organic law are reproduced in Emilio Alvarez Montalván, *Las fuerzas armadas en Nicaragua: Sinopsis histórica, 1821–1994* (Managua: Jorge Eduardo Arrellano, 1994), appendix.

4. Quoted in *Debate acerca del Ejército Popular Sandinista de Nicaragua* (Managua: United Nations Development Program, July 1994), 25.

5. "Chamorro Turns Down Humberto Ortega for Cabinet" (text), Panama City ACAN in Spanish, 0209 GMT 7 Apr 90. Translation by the Foreign Broadcast

Information Service. Foreign Broadcast Information Service (hereafter cited as FBIS)
Daily Report: Latin America (April 9, 1990): 26.

6. Luis Humberto Guzmán, Christian Democratic leader and president of the
National Assembly from 1993 to 1996, contends that only Ortega could have main-
tained the unity of the armed forces during the crucial institutional changes ef-
fected during the early phase of the transition. See Guzmán, *Políticos en uniforme:
Un balance del poder del EPS* (Managua: Instituto Nicaragüense de Estudios Socio-
Políticos, 1992), 25.

7. These points are explored more fully in Margarita Castillo, "Las relaciones
cívico-militares en Nicaragua y la búsqueda de una nueva agenda de seguridad de
cara al siglo XXI" (Managua, unpublished manuscript, n.d.).

8. For an analysis of alternative strategies of civilian control, see Paul W.
Zagorski, *Democracy and National Security: Civil-Military Relations in Latin
America* (Boulder, CO: Lynne Rienner, 1992), esp. 77–83. This discussion makes
extensive use of his terminology and classification.

9. The Tocontín Accord and subsequent cease-fire agreements are found in
Oscar René Vargas, *¿Adónde va Nicaragua? Perspectivas de una revolución
latinoamericana* (Managua: Ediciones Nicarao, 1991), 87–90.

10. Angel Saldomando D., "El proceso de pacificación en Nicaragua, 1990–
1994" (Managua, draft manuscript, February 1995), 7–8.

11. "Reporting on Chamorro's Army Reduction Plan" (text), Managua Domestic Service in Spanish, 1757 GMT 15 Jun 90. FBIS *Daily Report: Latin America*
(June 18, 1990): 29. Further reductions dropped the level to 33,000 by November
1990.

12. Humberto Ortega, interview with LASA delegation, June 22, 1994.

13. "H. Ortega on Road Block, Armed Forces Reductions" (text), Managua
Domestic Service in Spanish, 1836 GMT 8 Nov 90. FBIS *Daily Report: Latin
America* (November 9, 1990): 42.

14. According to data provided by the Army's Office of Public Information, as
of December 6, 1994, the breakdown in personnel was 10,000 in ground units, 1,200
in the air force, 800 in the navy, and 3,200 officers. It is important to keep in mind
that Nicaragua's air force and navy function as integrated components of the army.
The operational capabilities of air and naval units are severely limited.

15. Although the details are sketchy, General Ortega's sudden dismissal of
Col. Javier Pichardo as chief of the air force on August 8, 1990, had overtones of
dissension within the officer corps reflecting the anxieties created by the reorganization in progress. According to one source, the conflict allegedly centered on the
emerging influence of *los cheles* (Nicaraguan slang for anyone of fair complexion),
headed by Joaquín Cuadra. Roberto Cajina, interview with author, Managua,
June 26, 1995.

16. *El Nuevo Diario*, December 16, 1990.

17. *La Prensa,* December 18, 1990.

18. Ibid., December 21, 1990. The military's budget for 1992 was reduced to
$42.9 million. From 1993 through 1995 it was in the range of $36 million, representing 8 to 9 percent of the national budget. Nicaragua's per capita expenditures
on the military had become the lowest in Latin America.

19. Ibid., February 7, 1991.

20. *El Nuevo Diario*, September 2, 1991.

21. *La Prensa,* November 28, 1991.

22. "Civic Movement Advocates Abolition of Militarism" (text), Managua Radio
Católica in Spanish 1100 GMT 4 Jun 92. FBIS *Daily Report: Latin America*
(June 9, 1992): 10–11.

23. "Humberto Ortega Statement on EPS Position Noted" (text), Managua Radio Sandino in Spanish, 1511 GMT 27 Oct 92. FBIS *Daily Report: Latin America* (October 28, 1992): 15–17.

24. *La Prensa,* November 5, 1992; *Miami Herald,* November 7, 1992. According to one source, Antonio Lacayo knew of and may even have approved Ortega's speech before it was delivered (*Envío* 6 [January–March 1993]). It was known at the time that Chamorro wanted still greater cutbacks, although not the complete elimination of the EPS being called for by the antimilitary movement.

25. "Lacayo on Subordinating the Armed Forces" (text), Managua Sistema Nacional de Televisión Network in Spanish, 0230 GMT 5 Aug 93. FBIS *Daily Report: Latin America* (August 9, 1993): 18.

26. Chamorro's address is reproduced in FBIS *Daily Report: Latin America* (September 3, 1993): 12–14.

27. According to General Cuadra, President Chamorro and General Ortega had met on several occasions during August to discuss his retirement and other military concerns, but only in general terms (General Joaquín Cuadra, interview with LASA delegation, Managua, June 26, 1995).

28. *Barricada,* September 3, 1993.

29. *La Nación* (San José), September 12, 1993; reported in FBIS *Daily Report: Latin America* (October 13, 1993): 22–23.

30. *El Nuevo Diario,* January 14, 1994. Actually, Carlos Chamorro had linked Ortega's retirement directly to the passage of the Military Code in a *Barricada* editorial as early as August 5, 1993.

31. Humberto Ortega, interview with LASA delegation, Managua, June 22, 1994. During the same interview, Ortega described the proposed Military Code as an attempt to provide better civil-military relations, although, he added, "there are some who would not accept it even if it were the Bible."

32. "H. Ortega: Warns against Disbanding Army" (text), Panama City ACAN in Spanish, 1934 GMT 25 Apr 94. FBIS *Daily Report: Latin America* (April 26, 1994): 37–38. A digest of Ortega's and other Nicaraguans' comments on the EPS have been compiled in *Debate acerca del Ejército Popular Sandinista.* For a more extensive collection of Ortega's views on civil-military relations and a selective chronology of events during the period from 1990 to 1992, see Humberto Ortega Saavedra, *Nicaragua: Revolución y democracia* (Mexico City: Organización Editorial Mexicana, 1992).

33. But without the support of the UNO coalition, whose leader, Luis Sánchez Sancho, complained that by granting the military legal and economic status the code essentially created "a state within a state." Ominously, former Assembly president Alfredo César suggested that the lack of a genuine consensus on the law could result in its repeal after the 1996 elections. See *Central America Report* (September 2, 1994): 3.

34. The final version of the code appeared in the September 2, 1994, edition of *La Gaceta,* the government's official organ, with the title of "Código de organización, jurisdicción y previsión social militar."

35. The military's involvement in business activity is thought to have increased dramatically during the early stages of the transition, although even civilian authorities such as Guzmán claim that there is little public information about the military's business interests. See his *Políticos en uniforme,* 32.

36. Copies of the academy's curriculum were not easily obtained in 1995, even for Nicaraguan scholars working on the military. According to one U.S. defense official familiar with the academy's operation, the faculty included a number of former Sandinista political officers. Interview with author, Managua, June 28, 1995.

37. Over one hundred senior officers received advanced training abroad in the period from 1992 to 1994. The information on professionalization is derived in large part from an EPS report presented to the OAS in April 1993, summarized in *El ejército en Nicaragua* (Managua: United Nations Development Program, January 1994).

38. Advancement after 1979 was based largely on combat experience. As a result, many officers rose through the ranks with a minimum of formal education and professional training. With the new Military Code, requirements for promotion dictate that advancement be based on seniority and merit. As of mid-1995 some dissatisfaction existed among the roughly 400 captains who faced rigid requirements for promotion to major. At the time, the officer hierarchy had been frozen at the upper ranks with 82 majors, 32 lieutenant colonels, 14 colonels, an unfilled brigadier general rank, one major general, and one general (Maj. Ernesto Medina, interview with author, Managua, June 29, 1995).

39. "Humberto Ortega Discusses Army, Government" (text), Managua Sistema Nacional de Televisión Network in Spanish, 0030 GMT 28 Jul 90. FBIS *Daily Report: Latin America* (August 2, 1990): 32–33. See also "Civic Movement," ibid. (June 9, 1992), cited in note 23.

40. *Barricada*, April 9, 1991.

41. *La Prensa*, June 5, 1991. Such statements led some Sandinista partisans ruefully to suggest that Ortega's effort to "departisanize" the EPS appeared, at times, to be more of an effort to obliterate the army's popular and Sandinista origins. See, for example, the editorial by Onofre Guevara in *Barricada*, June 18, 1992.

42. Humberto Ortega Saavedra, *El ejército va a permanecer unido: Tenemos el deber de conservarlo intacto* (Managua: Ediciones y Artes Gráficas Multiformas, June 1994), 25.

43. For a fuller treatment of this issue, see Elvira Cuadra, "El EPS y la transición" (Managua, unpublished manuscript, December 1993).

44. Zagorski, *Democracy and National Security*, 53.

45. *La Tribuna*, February 22, 1995. According to Major Medina, Cuadra made it clear in his early meetings with the officer corps that he did not want the army drawn into political controversies that did not concern it.

46. "Army's 'Impartiality' in Government Dispute Stressed" (text), Havana *Prensa Latina* in Spanish 1916 GMT 29 May 95. FBIS *Daily Report: Latin America* (May 30, 1995): 34.

47. General Joaquín Cuadra, interview with LASA delegation, Managua, June 26, 1995. However, Cuadra also acknowledged in the same interview that, as the "last guarantor of stability," the army would never allow anarchy to develop.

48. Zagorski, *Democracy and National Security*, 56.

5

General Economic Policy

Mario Arana

It would be unfair and inaccurate to attribute the poor performance of the economy during the first four years of the Chamorro administration to any one cause. It was the result of at least three factors: a neoliberal adjustment and stabilization program, a radical economic and political transition, and the economic legacy and constraints inherited from the Sandinista period.

For most of the first half of the 1990s, Nicaragua experienced severe economic difficulties. In some ways, what was happening was typical of a country in a poststabilization phase, moving from a period of hyperinflation and undergoing a structural adjustment program. Low levels of private investment, high interest rates and financial margins, an artificially overvalued currency, high dollarization (indexing to the dollar) levels, and economic stagnation were some of the characteristics shared by Nicaragua with other countries that had undergone a similar process in the 1980s. Nicaragua, however, arrived at this stage relatively late compared to other Latin American countries.[1] Thus, it was not until 1994, after more than a decade of repeated failed attempts at stabilization, that significant economic growth started to take place.[2]

However, the case of Nicaragua was also unique, not just in its lateness but also in that the country was simultaneously experiencing a triple transition.[3] It was moving from war to peace and the demobilization and resettlement of previous combatants; from a restriction of civil and political rights in the face of foreign aggression and domestic discontent to a more democratic and open society that enjoyed renewed press freedom; and from a highly regulated economy and state-centered accumulation model to a market-based system undergoing a neoliberal adjustment and stabilization program.

The Transition in Its Economic Context

Though often overlooked by critics and opponents of the Chamorro government, the new policymakers in 1990 confronted a deep economic crisis that constrained available economic options. The economy they inherited that year was afflicted by well-entrenched hyperinflation dating from 1988,[4] protracted economic stagnation that had begun in 1984, large distortions of relative prices, poorly defined property rights, the largest per capita foreign debt in the world, and severe gaps in the current account and in domestic spending.[5]

During the 1980s, Nicaragua had endured the frustrations of repeated unsuccessful attempts at stabilization. Until 1984, price control mechanisms had kept inflationary pressures under control. However, a timid attempt to adjust the economy in 1985, which included some price liberalization along with the continuation of significant deficit spending, brought a sharp increase in prices that eventually led to hyperinflation. Rates of inflation rose from 300, to 700, to 1,300 percent in 1985, 1986, and 1987, respectively.

Since the timid approach to dealing with inflation had clearly failed, a heterodox shock, including a change in currency, was introduced in 1988. A few months later, these adjustment policies were modified again in a more orthodox direction to include price and wage liberalization. Inflation reached 33,000 percent in 1988, in part the result of the inconsistency inherent in combining aggressive devaluations to align prices with increased deficit spending. In addition, Nicaragua by this time was almost totally without foreign exchange for stabilization purposes. It was clear by the end of 1988 that a new approach was very much in order.

A more consistent and strict program undertaken in 1989 succeeded in bringing inflation down to 1,700 percent that year. In the wake of the election campaign and the change in government in 1990, inflation rose again to 13,500 percent. Economic instability and price distortions that the economy had suffered in the second half of the 1980s were also reflected in losses in output and increased unemployment as different attempts at adjustment strove to reduce the government deficit by contracting credit and public investment.

Unemployment was five times higher in 1990 than it had been in 1984, when it had hit its lowest level of the decade. Indeed, the expansionary policies of the Sandinista government had brought unemployment and underemployment to the lowest level known in modern economic history. But these policies had been based on economic strategies that, financially, were clearly unsustainable. In 1990, Gross Domestic Product (GDP) per capita was about U.S. $400, about one-half that of 1980 (see table). Exports had dropped from a peak of U.S. $680 million in 1978 to an average of U.S. $436 million for the period 1980–1984, and to an average of U.S. $284 million for the period 1985–1990.

Expansionary economic policies, which included increased social spending, expansionary credit policies, subsidies for production and basic consumption, an aggressive public investment strategy, and increased defense spending all accounted for the country's worsening domestic and external

Basic Nicaraguan Economic Indicators

	1990	1991	1992	1993	1994	1995
GDP (U.S.$						
1980 millions)	1,815	1,812	1,820	1,813	1,874	1,949
GDP per capita	469	453	440	425	425	429
Inflation	13,490	865	3.5	19.5	12.4	11.1
Unemployment	11.1	14.2	17.8	21.8	20.7	18.2
Underemployment	33.2	38.0	32.5	28.3	32.9	35.0
Exports	330.6	272.4	223.1	267.0	351.2	491.3
Imports	636.4	751.4	855.1	744.0	874.7	956.7
Current account	(303)	(7.9)	(716)	(483)	(533)	–
Foreign debt						
(U.S. $ millions)	10,616	10,312	10,792	10,987	11,695	8,700
Foreign cooperation	484.3	1,158.6	633.1	459.4	632.4	517.6
Donations	254.4	622.5	322.4	318.9	223.4	192.1
Loans	229.9	536.1	310.7	140.5	409.0	325.5

Sources: The Nicaraguan Central Bank and the Ministry of Foreign Cooperation.

economic situation. The average fiscal deficit from 1983 to 1988 was about 23 percent of GDP, while the global deficit, which also included foreign exchange losses and nonrecoverable loans from the financial banking sector, reached over 30 percent of GDP. In addition, the Nicaraguan foreign debt, which made up for the lack of exports and helped finance the expansionary economic policies that characterized the Sandinista administration, had increased from U.S. $1.5 billion in 1980 (three-fourths of GDP) to U.S. $10 billion in 1990 (more than five times its GDP).

The new government, then, was saddled with a large foreign debt, an extreme dependence on foreign aid, and a deteriorated human and physical capital base that was technologically obsolete. In the short term, this situation meant that the government was in a weak bargaining position vis-à-vis multilateral organizations at precisely the moment when it was facing a desperate need of fresh liquid foreign resources for 1990. More important, Nicaragua had little room to maneuver at the macroeconomic level. Fiscal and monetary discipline, though very liberally managed during the first few months of the new government, could only be relaxed in the long run to the extent that the country found sources of foreign exchange.

This vehicle for flexibility was hard to come by. Many of the new funds from international sources were conditioned on the adoption of an adjustment and stabilization package under the supervision of the International Monetary Fund (IMF).[6] Negotiations with the IMF, which was inclined to recommend strict fiscal and monetary discipline, would take awhile. At the same time, access to new funds would require the servicing of old debts to multilateral financial institutions. As a result, much of new liquid foreign exchange funds obtained during the first few years ended up being used for direct support to the balance of payments[7] and the servicing of inherited foreign debt, and economic policy was contractionary in general. The direct support to the balance of payments brought a consumption bias in imports, to the detriment of savings and productive investment.[8]

In the short term, this environment inhibited a reactivation of the economy. Even so, a process of economic restructuring commenced to take place during the 1990s, as some sectors started expanding while others began or continued to contract.[9] Instances of expansion were the product of the new set of economic rules of the game as well as political stabilization and further institutionalization of democracy, which together generated a growing confidence on the part of a segment of the business sector.

In 1994, Nicaragua finally began to experience renewed overall economic growth, albeit under very fragile macro- and microeconomic circumstances. After a decade of stagnation or decline, the economy grew 3.2 percent in 1994 and 4 percent in 1995. However, competitiveness was limited by the high cost of basic services and the low productivity of labor. In addition, the country's international reserves remained low. Moreover, the social cost of adjustment, as reflected in high levels of unemployment and underemployment, was significant. Unemployment reached 20.2 percent by early 1995 while underemployment stood at 53.9 percent. Thus, by early 1995 the unemployment rate was twice that of 1990 and ten times that of 1984.

While it is true that macroeconomic options at the beginning of the 1990s were limited, it is also clear that, as time passed and the new administration and its own agenda became consolidated, there were many missed opportunities to reorient government actions to respond to the predominant socioeconomic structure of the country—consisting of small- and medium-size producers—and to the demands of the "reformed sector" created by the revolution.[10] The failure to do so was a major shortcoming. Indeed, by the mid-1990s, the country seemed to be heading toward a reconcentration of income while the reformed sector languished in economic and political disarray.[11] At the structural level, the Chamorro administration's uncritical and naive faith in market forces and its general disregard for market imperfections injected a bias which—by default, if not by design—favored large businesses and strengthened the positions of monopolies, oligopolies, and the business elite close to the government.[12] The administration was effective in co-opting the labor movement (especially Sandinista labor unions) by giving workers 25 percent of formerly state-owned enterprises. However, by the mid-1990s many of the by-now worker-owned entities found themselves heavily in debt, starved for working capital, and underutilized or close to collapse.

Like most other Latin American countries, Nicaragua in the first half of the 1990s also displayed a lack of institutionalization. Business relations were still based more on personal contacts than on the norms and the laws of institutions, which resulted in the lags in governability and economic and social inefficiency and, in turn, added uncertainty and risk to investment decisions. Rather than being oriented toward long-term investment, the economy remained driven by short-term profit motives, thus adding to a prevailing sense that only the elites were benefiting from economic growth. It is likely that this perception of elitism explained the rising popularity of the traditional Liberal Party.[13] On the one hand, that party embodied the interests of the middle class and important segments of the popular sectors. On the other, it was, for many, a way to settle accounts with a perceived implicit alliance between the Chamorro government and the Sandinistas.[14]

Although the government was slow to recognize the reality of market imperfections or to invest resources in supporting the emergence of competition and programs that might favor small- and medium-size producers, it did begin to change in the mid-1990s. In tune with the new demands and reorientation of funds from multilateral institutions such as the Inter-American Development Bank and the World Bank, new programs favoring these sectors began to be developed.[15] But these programs faced structural institutional shortcomings and, at the time of this writing, their impact was still limited.

The country's institutional inadequacies were evident in the fact that the National Development Bank (BANADES), the major state bank in charge of agricultural credit, tended to neglect medium and, especially, small producers. The relative lack of political or socioeconomic criteria in the decision making of the government and its many institutions, their concentration on the macroeconomics of the country, and the relatively strict predominance of the profit motive and efficiency considerations for the logic of governance favored large producers up to mid-1995, when individual credit ceilings were implemented and a major rural credit program got under way. The early policies had eventually led to serious financial consequences resulting from risk concentration and the hardships generated by adjustment policies for the state banking sector.[16] By the mid-1990s it was clear that the country had an institutionality that tended more to favor large and established businesses than informal sector activities or small- and medium-size operations where most of the employment was generated.[17] While the possibilities of democratizing credit and the economy were neglected, it took a major crisis in the state financial sector and the influence of multilateral institutions for these early trends to be reversed.

There was hardly any integration between economic and social policy. Not only did economic policy inflict social costs on the population as the country was undergoing a period of adjustment, but macroeconomic policy also was not thought out with a logic that would broaden access and income opportunities to the large poor majority of Nicaraguans. Most social programs had a universal character that failed to discriminate between the poor —especially the very poor—and the nonpoor. According to a survey conducted in 1993, 53 percent of the population were considered poor while

20 percent lived in extreme poverty.[18] Nevertheless, the adjustment compensation packages implemented during the period emphasized the temporary generation of employment, without the development of new skills or programs that could guarantee a permanent integration of these sectors into the productive side of the economy.

Often, the short-term focus of multilateral financial institutions or bilateral cooperation projects affected project sustainability. The government frequently lacked adequate counterparts to development projects, showed weaknesses in negotiating with international entities, or had problems in coordinating foreign assistance efforts.

In addition, levels of investment did not rise until 1994, and much of this rise is accounted for by the dynamics of public investment. There seemed to be a gap between national public investment priorities, as defined by the central government, and local needs. While the government officially stood committed to the decentralization of resources and decision making, municipalities remained weak. Although it is true that local governments eventually came to enjoy greater authority, resources became more centralized. As of the mid-1990s there were no clear mechanisms in place to rectify this situation. Finally, as was also true under the Sandinistas, the existence of a feudal institutional order in different government ministries and official institutions impeded the possibility of better coordination and articulation of policies and the improvement of government efficacy.

Stabilization and Adjustment Policies

The Chamorro administration brought a major shift in economic policy. The country moved from a state-centered model of accumulation and a significantly regulated economy to a market-oriented economy. This process brought a rapid privatization of state enterprises (which had accounted for about 30 percent of GDP in 1990), liberalization, and the opening up of the economy. By 1994 the National Corporation of State Enterprises (CORNAP) had privatized, returned to previous owners, or liquidated 343 businesses out of a total of 352 state enterprises. Transportation and the fishing sector, for instance, were completely privatized in 1992 and 1993, respectively.[19] The strategy of the new government relied heavily on the business sector to become the axis and engine of accumulation under new rules of the game. According to this rationale, the government would stabilize the economy, reestablish relations with multilateral institutions, and reactivate economic growth based initially on the availability of new external sources of foreign exchange.

Three misconceptions were present during the early phase of the new government: 1) the assumption that Sandinista mismanagement was the main source of Nicaragua's economic problems; 2) the illusion that there would be plenty of external aid, mainly from the United States, and that the country had an unlimited capacity to absorb that aid; and 3) the belief that agriculture would recuperate rapidly as peace and new rules of the game were established.[20] Nicaragua, however, had long passed the threshold where a quick rebound would be possible, given the deterioration of the infrastructure, lags in technology, decapitalization, and loss of healthy business practices in general.[21] Uncertainty, sociopolitical unrest, poorly defined property rights, weak institutional capacities, and high production costs, among other conditions, hardly provided the right mix for a quick economic recovery. Moreover, the pacification of the country and large-scale military demobilization of both sides of the conflict were top priorities in the agenda of the new government. These issues and the problem of political instability[22] received most of the government's attention and considerable amounts of its resources during the early years.

The Mayorga Plan

The economic policy of the Chamorro government fell under the responsibility of Francisco Mayorga, the president of the Central Bank. In many respects, the new economic plan was a continuation of the stabilization and adjustment package that the Sandinistas had been implementing in the late 1980s. However, there were some fundamental differences. While it, like that of the Sandinistas, called for a restrictive fiscal policy, Mayorga's plan was based on drastic cuts in military spending and tax reform.

A second important instrument of Mayorga's plan was monetary reform. A new currency, the gold *córdoba*, was introduced at parity with the U.S. dollar. The old and the new currencies coexisted while prices were expected to stabilize. At the same time, interest rates were raised to become less negative. More important, financial assets (loans and deposits) were indexed to the gold *córdoba*, laying the groundwork for the disappearance of the old currency. The exchange rate policy for the old currency continued the same pattern of frequent minidevaluations adopted by the Sandinistas, except at a faster pace after an initial drastic devaluation to catch up with inflation. Eventually, devaluations began to slow down as the pressure on the dollar diminished. The exchange rate for the gold *córdoba* remained at a 1-to-1 parity with the dollar until March 1991.

These two elements contributed to price stabilization in 1991, and the little price stability that was accomplished during 1990. Economic stabilization, however, took longer than expected. According to Mayorga, this delay was the result of sociopolitical unrest generated by Sandinista organizations which, he claimed, wanted to discredit the stabilization package of the new government and make it falter.[23] Also, to the extent that the new government honored salary increases for federal employees decreed by the Sandinistas before leaving office, significant fiscal pressure was exerted, which undermined the package. At the same time, major expenditures were

undertaken in order to replace the pillaging of state property that had occurred under the Sandinistas during the transition of power (the so-called
piñata). In fact, deficit spending was twice as high as in 1989, a year of
Sandinista austerity. Thus, in spite of Mayorga's intentions, fiscal and monetary behavior during the first year of the Chamorro administration was, in
fact, expansionary.[24]

The new policy included full normalization of international financial
relations. The government's strategy sought to bring its arrears with multilateral institutions quickly up to date in order to gain access to new funds.
However, this goal took longer than expected, and it was not until 1991 that
the government managed to put together a large-enough amount of aid to
pay its arrears. The confrontations between the Chamorro administration
and the Sandinista mass movement during Mayorga's initial days in office,
new wage increases, and two national strikes that brought significant economic losses to the country all contributed to the continuation of price instability and economic stagnation during the first year. Mayorga left the
government in December 1990 with the country's economic policy in disarray and after yet another year of economic decline.

The Lacayo Plan

The locus of economic policymaking after the departure of Mayorga moved
from the Central Bank to the Economic Cabinet coordinated by Minister of
the Presidency Antonio Lacayo. After an initial period of apparent indeci-
sion in economic policy in early 1991, the government addressed a number
of important issues.[25] The process of confrontation gave way to a new period of negotiations with labor and business organizations promoted by the
government in order to reach broad consensus over economic policy. This
process culminated in February 1991 with a social agreement that prepared
the way for the stabilization effort undertaken in March 1991.

In the previous October, initial progress had been made in achieving
peace when a social consensus pact was reached between employers, workers, and the Chamorro administration. The need for structural reform, trade
liberalization, removal of state monopolies, and the return of properties to
expropriated owners had been stressed.[26] Workers would eventually argue
that many of the commitments made—specifically, the implementation of a
gradual adjustment process with special attention to social costs—had not
been fulfilled by the government as promised. Similarly, it later proved difficult for it to fulfill business expectations that it be flexible in supporting
economic reactivation with generous credit.

The stabilization and adjustment package that was introduced in March
1991 was of a rather heterodox nature. On the one hand, it included a currency devaluation of 600 percent, with a 200 percent adjustment for public-
sector salaries; the anchoring of the exchange rate to stabilize prices; and a

commitment to cut government expenditures and to bring them in line with available foreign assistance. Credit and military expenditures, in particular, were to be drastically reduced. On the other hand, an income policy based on price controls of basic goods was also part of the package. On the monetary side, interest rates became positive in real terms, and the high rates for deposits contributed to a rapid decrease in liquidity during the period immediately after the announcement of the program. This component was consistent with new financial theories that associated high interest rates with high deposit levels and investment rates.[27]

The program was technically well developed and skillfully presented to the public. The targets for fiscal policy were rapidly met as gains in efficacy were quickly accomplished. Also, greater efficiency in tax collection was achieved. The deficit of the consolidated public sector fell from 17 percent of GDP (before grants) in 1990 to 6.4 percent in 1991.[28] However, the deficit remained high even after discounting for the arrears on service of the outstanding public external debt. Interest payments on public external debt increased from zero to 3.8 percent of GDP between 1990 and 1993, but arrears remained high (9.2 percent of GDP in 1992).

In 1990 and 1991 the Chamorro government was also able to reestablish relations with multilateral organizations and to pay pending arrears with the World Bank and the Inter-American Development Bank in order to regain access to their loans with support from bilateral donors. In addition, the Stand-by Agreement was negotiated with the IMF, and overdue bilateral foreign debt was renegotiated with the Paris Club, a forum of industrialized countries created for the purpose of dealing in a multilateral fashion with bilateral debts. On the structural side, the government began to completely finance its deficit with foreign resources; international reserves grew; the state apparatus began to shrink; and fiscal reform was undertaken. The privatization of state enterprises entered into full swing. The structural measures also included trade liberalization, agrarian reform, redistributing state-owned lands to individual farmers, and mechanisms to enforce property rights. The financial sector was reformed so as to allow private banks to operate in the country. Internal commerce and the prices of basic goods were eventually deregulated.

Hyperinflation was brought under control in 1991. Registering 13,500 percent in 1990, it came down to 866 percent in 1991. In fact, if we consider only the year from April 1991 to April 1992, the accumulated inflation rate amounted to only 8 percent. Yet, while hyperinflation was eliminated, the stagnation of the economy continued in spite of significant monetary aid. A large part of incoming foreign resources was used to pay foreign debt. Indeed, in 1991 the multilateral lending agencies (the World Bank and the Inter-American Development Bank) were paid about $0.5 billion.

While fiscal targets were achieved in 1992, a rise in current expenditures toward the end of the year (related to a wage increase) led to a disagreement with the IMF and the suspension of the Stand-by Agreement signed in 1991, which was supposed to have expired in April 1993. At the same time, the redress of the trade regime—accomplished through the elimination of the state trade monopoly, the abolition of quantitative restrictions on imports and exports, and tariff reductions[29]—brought a surge in private consumption. Since exports did not recover, foreign aid created a widening of the trade deficit (from 18 to 32 percent of GDP between 1990 and 1992) and facilitated the increase in private consumption from 57 to 74 percent of GDP.[30] In this context, even with fiscal austerity, foreign aid, together with liberalization, seemed to have stimulated private consumption at the expense of private savings and investment.[31]

The Foreign Exchange Crisis of 1993 and the ESAF Package of 1994

Foreign cooperation reached an extraordinary peak, amounting to close to 70 percent of GDP in 1991 as arrears of multilateral institutions were brought up to date. But the level of aid in 1992 was back to a more normal level of about 34 percent of GDP (the average for the 1990–1995 period was about 35 percent) amounting to U.S. $650 million. In other respects, however, 1992 was not a good year. The value of goods exported reached its lowest level for the first half of the decade, at U.S. $223 million. At the same time, there was also great political instability and serious conflict between the executive and the legislative branches. To make matters even worse, there was an eventual suspension of aid disbursements from the U.S. government while structural adjustment continued.

In January 1993, in order to respond to a number of adverse trends in economic balances, and in spite of the suspension of the Stand-by Agreement with the IMF, the government devalued the *córdoba* by 20 percent, thus inaugurating a new period of a more active exchange-rate policy along with other stabilization and adjustment measures. A crawling peg system with weekly adjustments to preserve the real value of the currency was adopted. However, Nicaragua's 1990 and 1993 devaluations proved that, while accomplishing an initial real depreciation in the short term, any long-term effect was undercut by the domestic inflationary process triggered by the same devaluation.

As it was, this devaluation took place within the framework of a larger set of economic policy measures aimed at stopping the persistent deterioration of the balance of payments and the lack of growth of the Nicaraguan economy.[32] However, economic stagnation persisted, and the devaluation (without adequate, complementary, and consistent fiscal and monetary policies) had to bear the burden of adjustment almost exclusively. In all, devaluation seemed more successful in undercutting imports than encouraging exports. Imports fell significantly, and an actual improvement in the balance of payments took place. These results strengthened the general hypothesis that export behavior was determined more by the constraints derived from structural bottlenecks than by a possibly overvalued domestic currency.

In general, however, the policies of 1993 failed to address major macroeconomic problems. Fiscal and monetary policy were inconsistent with the devaluation strategy and the desired objective of improving export performance. Public expenditures were not reduced as expected. The financial system was basically unchanged as unpaid loans and a technically broken state banking system remained in place. Monetary policy was contradictory to the goal of achieving price stability: in January the Central Bank reduced the discount rate, thereby reducing interest rates and easing monetary policy just as the devaluation was stimulating an inflationary surge.

During 1993 the negotiation of an Enhanced Structural Adjustment Facility (ESAF) loan was initiated with the International Monetary Fund. However, as the government did not reach an agreement until April 1994, international cooperation dropped significantly to U.S. $460 million compared to an average of about U.S. $650 million for the period 1990–1995. International reserves were reduced by U.S. $100 million, and inflation went to 19.5 percent. In general, the end result was a sense of disarray and a belief that the government had lost track of its economic objectives.

Economic Growth in 1994 and 1995

During 1994 the ESAF was signed with the IMF. With this agreement the government bought stability for the balance of payments for the following three years, with the stipulation that broad policy conditionality would be met. The first year of the IMF adjustment package saw the best performance that the economy had registered in a decade. With a growth rate of 3.2 percent, the economy seemed to be responding to the sustained framework of relative stability of the previous three years and the fact that balance-of-payments viability seemed secure for the medium term. Exports of goods increased from U.S. $267 million in 1983 to U.S. $350 million in 1994.

Economic growth continued at a pace of 4 percent in 1995, surpassing population growth, which was estimated to be 2.9 percent according to the new 1995 census. Exports of goods for 1995 reached U.S. $490 million, the result not only of unusually favorable coffee prices but also of the dynamism of a number of other sectors such as fishing, nontraditional exports in general, and the free-trade zone. A new, more focused, and aggressive foreign debt renegotiation strategy reduced Nicaragua's old foreign debt with the Paris Club and commercial debt by about U.S. $1.8 billion in 1995. This strategy called for a reduction of the foreign debt from U.S. $11 billion in 1994 to U.S. $3.5 billion for 1996, which, although it was an optimistic figure, would still leave Nicaragua a highly indebted country.

In spite of these positive developments, new problems emerged by mid-1995 as the government found that it was unable to meet the targets set in the IMF adjustment package. A new program (the Bridge Plan) was signed as a transitory measure in order to return to the objectives of the initial agreement. IMF approval of the performance of the government was critical in order for it to continue receiving important levels of foreign assistance. By the end of 1995 it appeared that, while performance was still not close enough to the standards set by the Bridge Plan, the government had generated enough goodwill for the IMF to continue supporting it. The final results remained to be seen as the country approached the elections of 1996.

Among the important issues of contention were the inability of the government to meet the targets on fiscal current savings, the viability of the state banking sector, the delays in the privatization of the telecommunications company, and the level of adjusted international reserves. All these by the mid-1990s had led to further contractions in the liquidity of the economy with the potential of harming the dynamism of economic growth. Nevertheless, by the end of 1995 a number of independent economists were predicting that growth would continue in 1996 at an even faster pace. The government was projecting in its development plan a 4.5 percent growth for the period 1996–97 and 6 to 7 percent per year for the period 1997–2000.[33] Thus, the balance by the mid-1990s seemed to promise more positive developments for Nicaragua in the years to come.

This economic growth, however, would need to have a broad base and to bring greater income equality if the country was to consolidate sociopolitical stability. The unemployment rate, which seemed to be lagging behind the economy by one year, began reacting positively in the second half of 1995 as it dropped from 20.7 percent in 1994 to 18 percent in 1995. However, since underemployment remained above 50 percent, poverty did not appear to be diminishing in any significant way, and the outlook for the country as a whole was still mixed. Major challenges remained ahead.

The structural adjustment process had caused such dislocations and underutilization of productive resources, including labor, that the social cost had become a political issue. This issue, in turn, was large enough to threaten not only the political continuity of the Chamorro current in the upcoming elections but also the sustainability of the adjustment package itself. By early 1995 opinion surveys indicated that the pro-government formula of Antonio Lacayo and his National Project (*proyecto nacional*) were in trouble.

Conclusion

The most readily visible achievements of the Chamorro administration had been relative peace and economic stability. The latter, however, had been bought at a high social cost as poverty, unemployment, and underemployment worsened throughout the first half of the 1990s. Since it is true that the costs would have been even greater had there been no adjustment, the question is not whether there should have been adjustment but rather what type could have served the country better.

Social indicators began to improve in 1994 when, after a decade of decline or stagnation, the economy started to grow. The structural adjustment process at the same time had been relatively effective in modifying the terms of trade in favor of savings and exports. This was not the case, however, with respect to agriculture, a key sector for the generation of employment in the economy. In addition, in spite of positive economic growth and important structural changes, income reconcentration was a worrisome trend; and social deterioration, after a decade of decline or stagnation, remained as a major challenge to be overcome.

By the mid-1990s it was evident that the government needed to concentrate its efforts on developing microeconomic and sectoral policies that would respond to the predominant socioeconomic structure of the country, made up of small- and medium-size producers in the countryside and of the informal sector in the cities (see Chapters 6 and 16, respectively, this volume). Similarly, a more systematic and integral socioeconomic approach needed to be developed to deal with the situation of poverty and extreme poverty that was affecting a large part of the population. The levels of poverty that existed were incompatible with sustainable economic development in the long term and were not helping the country prepare for global competition and the need to attract foreign investment. It would be imperative to restructure government spending in order to invest more in human capital—in particular, to make the country's education model (see Chapter 7, this volume) more compatible with its developmental model.

If the country were ever to gain more independence from the heavy policy conditioning of multilateral financial institutions, its reliance on foreign cooperation needed to give way to greater self-sufficiency. This change would not happen in the short term, given that even though aid was declining, Nicaragua would still need important levels of foreign resources. The dependence on foreign assistance was especially problematic in that it seemed to have given the state an autonomy from the society it represented. External actors had attained an increased predominance, often against the perceived interests of national players.

As of 1995, Nicaragua lacked an official development strategy. Consequently, the economic policies implemented were not the result of a national consensus. The relationship of the business sector with the government was more one of antagonists than of partners in the building of the nation. By early 1996 the government did begin debating its strategy with various sectors, but it was not clear whether this effort, at such a late stage of the Chamorro period, would make a difference in terms of national policy or contribute to building a national consensus. The proposal that the government presented was a reiteration of many of the policies implemented throughout the Chamorro administration. As of 1996, the country needed an overarching governmental body that would harmonize sectoral policies, alert the government about critical long-term development issues, coordinate public investment, and buttress the country's weakened institutional negotiating capacities vis-à-vis multilateral financial institutions, foreign cooperation, and national actors. Whether satisfaction of that need would be part of the agenda of the new administration remained to be seen, but even the international multilateral institutions were in agreement that it was required.

Notes

1. For a study on recent stabilization experiences, see Michael Bruno, Stanley Fischer, Elhanan Helpman, and Nissan Liviatan, eds., *Lessons of Economic Stabilization and Its Aftermath* (Cambridge, MA: MIT Press, 1992).
2. For new theories on growth after adjustment, see Luis Servén and Andrés Solimano, eds., *Striving for Growth after Adjustment: The Role of Capital Formation* (Washington DC: World Bank, 1993).
3. Unlike the most recent well-known transitions, the Nicaraguan transition did not have an empirical or theoretical reference point. The country did not have the features of a centrally planned economy, such as in the East European nations, and its political system was far from the typical authoritarian or dictatorial political regimes of the Southern Cone of South America.
4. For an analysis of Nicaraguan hyperinflation, see José Antonio Ocampo, "Collapse and (Incomplete) Stabilization of the Nicaraguan Economy," in *The Macroeconomics of Populism in Latin America*, ed. Rudiger Dornbusch and Sebastian Edwards (Chicago: University of Chicago Press, 1991), 331–68.
5. For an economic study for the first half of the 1980s, see Mario Arana, Richard Stahler-Sholk, Gerardo Timossi, and Carmen López, *Deuda, estabilización y ajuste: La transformación de Nicaragua, 1979–1986* (Managua: CRIES, 1987). For the second half of the 1980s, see Mario Arana, Richard Stahler-Sholk, and Carlos Vilas, "Políticas de ajuste en Nicaragua: Reflexiones sobre sus implicaciones estratégicas," in *Cuadernos de Pensamiento Propio*, Essay Series #18 (Managua: CRIES, 1990), 9–42. Also, for different perspectives, see various authors in Rose Spalding, ed., *The Political Economy of Revolutionary Nicaragua* (Boston: Allen and Unwin, 1987).
6. The USAID package for U.S. \$300 million, granted to the new government in 1990, made clear that the United States expected Nicaragua to submit to an IMF agreement. See United States Agency for International Development, "Nicaragua: A Commitment to Democracy, Reconciliation, and Reconstruction," *Fact Sheet* (Managua: USAID, 1990).
7. The direct support to the balance of payments helped sustain an artificially fixed foreign exchange rate, which was used as an anchor to hold down price increases.
8. For an analysis of the consumption-investment tradeoff, see Rob Vos, *The Macroeconomics of Aid in Nicaragua*, document prepared for the Swedish Agency for International Development, mimeo (The Hague, Netherlands: Institute of Social Studies, 1994).

9. For an official analysis of these trends, see Gobierno de Nicaragua, *La economía nicaragüense, 1995* (Managua: Ministerio de Economía y Desarrollo, 1995). Previous annual reports from the same source can be studied.

10. The "reformed sector" refers to the economic sector that emerged as a result of the agrarian reform, the privatization of state enterprises to the workers, and in general the popular sectors that were favored by the revolution during the 1980s and in the period between the elections and the transferring of power to the new government in 1990. This last period also witnessed a large transfer of properties into Sandinista hands, many of which were made through legally and ethically questionable means, which favored a new Sandinista business elite. This process was popularly and derisively known as *la piñata*.

11. The genuine interests and concerns of the members of the reformed sector, by their own inability, were mixed with the narrower interests and concerns of the new Sandinista business elite, to which many in the party leadership ended up belonging. The popular sectors in this respect were more or less left to their own devices, without necessarily having the same possibilities of defining and influencing the national agenda.

12. For an in-depth analysis of the business elite during the Chamorro government, see Chapter 15, this volume.

13. Beginning in 1992, different polls begin showing a rise in popularity of the Liberal Constitutionalist Party (PLC) under the leadership of Arnoldo Alemán, which surpassed in popularity the Sandinista National Liberation Front (FSLN) in 1994. CID-Gallup, *Opinion Pública #15*, Nicaragua, August 1995.

14. For the opposition, the alliance of the Chamorro government and the FSLN, which began with the transition protocol signed by three members of UNO and the FSLN, was responsible for the lack of economic reactivation since too much economic and political power remained in Sandinista hands.

15. See Chapter 15, this volume, in which Rose Spalding analyzes changes in the financial policies of the National Development Bank.

16. By 1995 the National Development Bank (BANADES) was technically broke in spite of having gone through a restructuring process with government support two years earlier.

17. There were new programs developed by the mid-1990s that attempted to fill this gap. These included nonconventional financial intermediation of credit and programs for the support of small- and medium-size enterprises and rural development. However, these efforts were still relatively new, and their efficacy remains to be seen.

18. For data and analysis on the poor, see World Bank, *Nicaragua: Poverty Assessment Report* (Washington, DC: World Bank, 1995).

19. See CORNAP, *Avance del proceso de privatización al 31 de diciembre de 1994* (Managua: República de Nicaragua, 1995).

20. See Renato Aguilar, *Nicaragua 1990: A New Leadership Takes Over*, Department of Economics, Macroeconomic Studies No. 24 (Gothenburg, Sweden: Gothenburg University, 1992), 13–14.

21. The practice of saving disappeared as high levels of inflation and later hyperinflation motivated people, instead, to convert money into foreign exchange or actual goods. Loans from the financial system were either not paid back or their real value was undermined by hyperinflation, so that a culture of subsidized loans became the norm and later affected the banking system to recover credits.

22. The country suffered two paralyzing national strikes during the first year of the new government.

23. Interview with Francisco Mayorga, Managua, September 1995.

24. While the fiscal deficit with respect to GDP was 8.1 percent in 1989 (the lowest for the decade, which averaged over 18 percent for the second half of the 1980s), in 1990 it was 17.2 percent. See Vos, *The Macroeconomics of Aid*, Table 5.1.

25. For a good summary of this period, see Renato Aguilar and Asa Stenman, *Transition in Nicaragua: Patterns of Growth and Stagnation*, Department of Economics (Gothenburg, Sweden: Gothenburg University, 1995), delivered at the 1995 meeting of the Latin American Studies Association, Washington, DC, September 1995.

26. See Vittorio Corbo, Michael Bruno, Stanley Fischer, Raul Laban, and Patricio Rojas, "An Economic Assessment of Nicaragua," mimeo, Swedish International Development Agency, March 1993.

27. The literature on financial repression has argued that the problem for underdeveloped economies is the lack of capital and not its cost. Therefore, high interest rates, to the extent that they attract deposits, help capital formation and growth. For a study testing this argument, see Maxwell J. Fry, *Money, Interest, and Banking in Economic Development* (Baltimore: Johns Hopkins University Press, 1991). The reactivation of private investment in the case of Nicaragua proved to be more difficult.

28. See Vos, *The Macroeconomics of Aid*, 5.

29. Tariffs and duties on imports were cut back from an average of 50 percent to 15 percent.

30. See Vos, *The Macroeconomics of Aid*.

31. Ibid., 46.

32. See Aguilar and Stenman, *Transition in Nicaragua*, 27.

33. See Gobierno de Nicaragua, "Plan nacional de desarrollo sostenible, 1996–2000" (rough draft for discussion), mimeo, Managua, May 1995.

6

Agrarian Policy

Jon Jonakin

The electoral defeat of the FSLN in 1990 presented Nicaragua, particularly its peasantry, with the prospect of a regime transition as significant as that ushered in following the Popular Sandinista Revolution of 1979. During the 1980s the Sandinista Agrarian Reform (SAR) had substantially altered the Somoza-era structure of land tenure as thousands of peasants and rural wage workers acquired rights to former latifundio estates. Land redistribution, along with policies that expanded access to education, agricultural technology, producer credit, and political participation, created what some argued were the "structural preconditions" for a democracy that aspired to more than an open electoral process.[1]

With the assumption of power by Violeta Chamorro in April 1990, the peasants again braced themselves for far-reaching change. The new president was quickly embroiled in political and legal battles over land-tenure issues with rural workers and peasants unwilling to surrender the greater access to work and land gained during the 1980s. These battles were also engaged with members of her diverse political coalition, notably large estate owners whose properties were confiscated in the SAR and who were unwilling to accommodate to the status quo. Economic policy, meanwhile, addressed the need to reactivate the rural economy through a series of market reforms that reflected the conditionality of structural adjustment and economic stabilization policies designed by the International Monetary Fund (IMF). With access to foreign exchange and debt renegotiation extended as the carrot, the stick fell as conditions that required massive elimination and/or privatization of the Sandinista state apparatus in the countryside, the elimination of many consumer and producer subsidies, and the tightening of farm credit.

Government policy under the Sandinistas was marked by considerable ambiguity: a pluralist party system under the aegis of a party that aspired to vanguard status, a carefully cultivated capitalist sector amid widespread confiscation of private property, populist economic policy eventually wedded to structural adjustment measures—all in an economy and society on a war footing. Under Chamorro, the transition to a neoliberal market-driven model directed by a president who headed a political coalition, but not a political party, proved difficult. Attempts to ease this passage were made through a series of pacts between the FSLN and the Chamorro administration that delimited areas wherein fundamental change could or could not be attempted. But the pacts angered as many as they pleased. By 1995 the continued failure to resolve ownership conflicts over many agricultural lands and the cumulative impact of restrictive fiscal and monetary policies had contributed to a profound recession. In this unstable political and economic setting, a flourishing land market emerged that threatened to reverse the redistributive gains attained under the SAR.

Sandinista Agrarian Reform and Policy

After World War II, the dynamic impulse to Nicaragua's economy came from the diversification and extension of its already prominent agricultural export sector.[2] While Gross Domestic Product (GDP) grew at impressive levels over the thirty years before 1979, the concentration of land, wealth, and income among agro-export elites denied the benefits of economic expansion to many people. Landless rural wage workers and poor peasant farmers, representing as much as 70 percent of the farm work force, served as temporary laborers in the coffee, cotton, sugarcane, and banana harvests.[3] Nicaragua's agro-export driven economy typified the theoretical constructs of "disarticulated" growth and "functional dualism."[4]

After 1979, Sandinista agrarian policy was designed less to alter the structure of production, or the crop mix, than it was to transform the rural social class structure by extending access of the landless and near-landless to land and work. The early confiscation by decree of the properties of the Somoza family and their affiliates was followed in 1981 by the promulgation of the Law of Agrarian Reform. Together, these actions greatly diminished the presence and power of the agro-export bourgeoisie. In their place appeared state farm and cooperative sectors. As reported in Table 1, the portion of agricultural land controlled by large-scale estates dropped from over 50 percent to around 20 percent by 1988. The greater part of this redistributed area was organized as either state farms in the Area of People's Property (Area de Propiedad del Pueblo, or APP) or as the collectively run Sandinista Agricultural Cooperatives (Cooperativas Agrícolas Sandinistas, or CAS). By one estimate, about 31,000 families, or 37 percent of the population of poor peasants and seasonal workers eligible for land grants, gained access to land under the SAR by the mid-1980s.[5] Thousands more acquired access to permanent work on state farms.

Table 1. Changes in Land Tenure Structure between 1978 and 1988 (in percentages)

Estate Size/Property Form	1978	1988
Small- and Medium-Scale Farms	*47.6*	*47.1*
Less than 50 mz[1]	17.5	18.7
50 to 200 mz	30.1	28.4
Large-Scale Estates	*52.4*	*21.0*
200 to 500 mz	16.2	13.5
Greater than 500 mz	36.2	7.5
SAR Sector	*00.0*	*31.8*
Cooperatives		
CAS	00.0	8.7
CCS[2]	00.0	11.4
State farms	00.0	11.7
Total	**100**	**99.9**

Source: Jaime Wheelock, *La reforma agraria sandinista: 10 años de revolución en el campo* (Managua: Editorial Vanguardia, 1990), 115.
[1]Abbreviation for *manzana*, or 1.7 acres.
[2]Credit and Service Cooperatives (Cooperativas de Crédito y Servicios).

Along with the material endowments of land and work that came with the SAR were Sandinista-affiliated political groups. The Rural Workers' Association (Asociación de los Trabajadores del Campo, or ATC) and the National Union of Farmers and Cattlemen (Unión Nacional de Agricultores y Ganaderos, or UNAG) attempted the often difficult task of reconciling the interests of rural wage workers and peasants with Sandinista government policy. As part of modernization efforts, the implementation of the SAR also incorporated an army of technical advisers charged with agricultural extension and credit dispensation.

The transformation of property relations realized by the SAR inevitably engendered problems apart from those that they were intended to resolve. Frictions developed among many SAR beneficiaries who were denied the option of fee-simple titles to land and instead were offered membership in the collective CAS or work on state farms. These frictions were only exacerbated in the case of the CAS, where state directives often restricted enterprise autonomy and cooperative property titles were typically "provisional."[6] Elsewhere, those affected by SAR confiscations were emboldened to, and abetted in, armed resistance by the Reagan administration's Central American policy. The Contra war came at tremendous human and material expense, a cost that fell with special vehemence over SAR cooperators.[7] While the elections of 1990 would end the fighting, the transitional period that they ushered in opened the door to a new level of social conflict over agrarian issues. Now the battle lines would be drawn in the courts and the legislature, among the picket lines of rural workers, in land seizures carried out by peasants and former soldiers, and in the boardrooms of the international lending agencies.

Post-Sandinista Property Rights and Agrarian Reform

Reflecting the varied composition and conflicting interests of the members of its domestic political coalition and its international advocates, the Chamorro government's agrarian policy incorporated both orthodox market-style adjustments and heterodox redistributive measures. The latter were evidenced by the implementation of a newly styled agrarian reform and the transfer of lands, primarily to former combatants in the war. Linked with agrarian reform was the generally recognized need to clarify property rights and the application of orthodox fiscal and monetary policies that were urged on President Chamorro by the IMF. Both directly through the assault on SAR lands and indirectly via market reforms, the new regime opened a process that threatened the rural status quo as it had developed under the Sandinistas.

During the period in 1990 between the February elections and the change of government in April, representatives of the Sandinista and Chamorro governments agreed to a Transition Protocol to orchestrate the segue between regimes. Among a range of topics, this social pact specifically addressed the need to assure "legal security" to those who had been the beneficiaries of lands granted under the SAR.[8] At the same time, lame-duck Sandinista legislators passed a series of decrees that attempted to rectify their earlier negligence in failing to assign definitive property rights to SAR beneficiaries. While these decrees were generally deemed tenable in their intent to formalize ownership of extant property allocations, important exceptions emerged as high officials in the departing government suddenly became recipients of rural and urban properties.[9]

Far from easing tensions, the Protocol and transitional legislation served both to deepen resistance to the status quo, as represented by the SAR, and to create serious fissures within the UNO coalition. Somoza-era landowners and UNO supporters who sought return of their lands resented any accommodation with the existing state of affairs. In an apparent attempt to placate internal dissension, Chamorro issued Decree No. 11-90 in May 1990, known as the Review of Confiscations. The decree presented a challenge both to the Protocol and transitional legislation with the establishment of a review commission whose mandate called for a reevaluation of contested confiscations in order to determine their final disposition. Turmoil prevailed, however, when a year later the Supreme Court declared unconstitutional important articles of Decree No. 11-90, but not before the review commission had heard nearly four thousand cases involving agricultural lands and issued over two thousand decisions calling for the return of properties taken under the SAR.[10] In the chaos that followed, properties were often left with two owners inscribed in the public register.

The immediate and enduring effect of attempts to clarify property issues was to generate a series of protracted legal and legislative conflicts that contributed to the paralysis of agriculture. Reports of SAR cooperatives faced with disputes over their property appeared regularly in the newspapers.[11] Even for those SAR properties, primarily cooperatives, that faced no challenge to their tenure rights, the mere possibility of such claims undermined morale, altered production and investment decisions, and contributed to the resolve by some people to sell SAR lands.[12] Moreover, the ambiguous position of the government regarding the terms of the Transition Protocol brought it into direct conflict with the FSLN and an ever more independent movement of rural workers and farmers.

Parallel with the legal and legislative maneuvers over property was the Chamorro government's promulgation of its own agrarian reform, now under a renamed and reorganized ministry: the Nicaraguan Institute of Agrarian Reform (Instituto Nicaragüense de Reforma Agraría, or INRA). The two central goals of INRA not only reasserted the basic terms of the Transition Protocol ("the economic and social consolidation of the existing reformed sector") but also promised "the broadening and deepening of agrarian reform to satisfy the peasantry's demand for lands."[13] The latter goal was expressed in several concrete objectives, the most notable proposing the delivery of almost 1 million *manzanas* of land to 86 percent of the estimated seventy thousand eligible peasant claimants.[14] By March 1992 the Chamorro government was reported to have transferred 701,500 *manzanas* to over twenty-four thousand families—an effort that, according to INRA, was almost equivalent to that realized by the SAR.[15]

Problems with the new agrarian reform appeared on various fronts. Since private property was now untouchable, the source of reform lands was often that of SAR cooperatives or the former APP.[16] In these circumstances, the fulfillment of one peasant claimant's demand served only to displace another peasant or rural worker or to reduce the per capita land area for each beneficiary. Also, the perceived slow pace of change and the failure of many claimants to acquire lands led to the seizure of cooperative and private estate acreage. In the province of Jinotega, demobilized members of the Contra army reportedly occupied sixty-three properties by 1992, mostly belonging to large- and medium-scale producers and covering almost 33,000 *manzanas*.[17] In an effort to forestall these occupations, many demoralized private owners offered their lands to the government for sale and subsequent redistribution.

Ironically, INRA's titling policies replicated many of the perceived weaknesses of the SAR. The delivery of INRA lands was often as a cooperative rather than to an individual. Instead of definitive fee-simple titles, lands were deeded with a provisional title not dissimilar to those initially granted under the SAR, which had provoked so much uncertainty.[18] At a minimum, these deeds permitted the holder to be eligible for agricultural credit. The viability of these new small-scale enterprises, however, was soon called into question as a market developed in the lands deeded by the provisional titles. A chagrined INRA responded by declaring the sales illegal, an action that deepened skepticism over the titles' value.[19]

Structural Adjustment and Fiscal Reform

While the Chamorro government's agrarian reform intended, in principle, to expand peasant access to land, its structural reforms and economic stabilization policies worked to restratify land tenure. The structural adjustment component was most dramatically felt by workers on state farms through the process of privatization of APP lands and the generalized withdrawal of the state from agriculture. Immediately following the installation of the new administration, 351 state industrial and agricultural enterprises were placed under the purview of the National Corporation of State Enterprises (CORNAP), where they began a process of dismemberment and sale.[20] By February 1992, five months after the first IMF accord was reached, 34 percent of these entities had been privatized. The pace then accelerated; and by the end of 1993, 80 percent had been sold.[21]

Since land was the asset in the most immediate demand, state agricultural enterprises were among the first to be liquidated. Their disposition became an explosive issue as former owners of confiscated cotton, coffee, and sugarcane acreage vied with workers and demobilized soldiers of both armies for the spoils. Accords negotiated in August 1991 agreed to the concept of an area of workers' property by setting aside a minimum of 25 percent of state lands for their ownership. By October 1993 a partial list of privatized state agricultural enterprises revealed that 35 percent of lands had been returned to former owners, 31 percent was divided among former state workers, while the remaining 34 percent was proportioned among former combatants.[22]

For workers, privatization meant a traumatic process involving massive layoffs and the need to determine new work forms and representational structures. The full-time salaried agricultural work force was reported to have decreased by about 72 percent, from 135,000 in 1990 to between 35,000 to 40,000 in 1992.[23] Notable disputes arose between the leadership in the Sandinista rural workers' syndicate, the ATC, and those members of the newly formed Area of Workers' Property (APT), which comprised a portion of state lands. Workers were often dissatisfied with the less confrontational attitude of the ATC in the negotiations over land partition, nor were they pleased with its suggestion of a centralized, corporate structure for the APT.[24] Instead, workers proposed and established so-called Anonymous Enterprise Societies wherein negotiations for prices paid for land, the terms of ownership, and work norms were determined in a more decentralized manner.[25]

The difficulties under the new circumstances were seen, for example, in the case of one privatized enterprise, AGROEXCO, that had historically been dedicated to cotton production. Within the APT as well as the area granted to demobilized soldiers, only a small portion of the associated workers were employed full-time on the enterprise. Due to the absence of credit, technical assistance, and crop changes, the required labor complement had fallen and many former APT members had been forced to seek work elsewhere.[26]

At a more global level, adherence to IMF conditionality meant the dramatic contraction of public expenditures and state services. Over a period in which the growth rates of real GDP were stagnant or falling, government spending fell steadily from 41.3 percent of GDP in 1988 to only 17.5 percent in 1992 and remained at that level for 1993.[27] Aside from removing tens of thousands of state agricultural workers from the public payroll, over 5,500 workers in the state-run financial system—63 percent of the total—were retired between 1990 and 1993 as the banking system was privatized and downsized.[28] These cuts hit agriculture especially hard since many of those laid off were located in rural branches of the National Development Bank (BANADES). Indeed, 64 percent of these branches were subsequently closed, a move that complicated farmers' physical access to credit.[29] In late 1994, and in keeping with the latest IMF package signed in June of that year, additional branch closings and layoffs were effected, again largely in rural areas.[30]

Along with the reduction in scope of the rural financial system was the disappearance of the country-wide agricultural extension services that the state had provided before 1990. This loss proved especially problematic for many former soldiers who now had access to land but had limited farming experience.[31] Elsewhere, the state enterprise that purchased and provisioned subsidized grain, known as ENABAS, was largely privatized. Although the withdrawal of the state from grain markets had begun before 1990, this exit accelerated after 1990, a move which caught the "free market" unprepared to fill the gap. Insufficient numbers of private traders and storage space contributed to increased marketing margins indicated by higher consumer prices and weaker farm gate prices of staple foods.[32]

Economic Stabilization and Monetary Reform

In the 1980s the central elements of Sandinista monetary and credit policy affecting agriculture were seen in real interest rates that frequently turned negative and in lavish long- and short-term producer loans targeted at the beneficiaries of the SAR. Incentives for responsible management of borrowed funds were often lacking, since collateral requirements were minimal and accumulated debts were at times forgiven. Imported inputs to agriculture were heavily subsidized. All these factors fueled the demand for credit, encouraged loan recuperation problems, and contributed to the hyperinflation.

For the new government, reining in inflation and the internal and external deficits that plagued the Sandinista regime dictated tight restrictions on the expansion of the money supply. Thus, along with privatization and the eschewal of deficit financing required by structural adjustment came tight monetary policies that responded to the rubric of "economic stabilization." In practice, these policies required a banking system prepared to tighten the screws on internal credit.[33] To implement this policy, new institutions were envisioned. With IMF assistance, the Chamorro government drafted banking legislation which laid out new rules for the operation of the Nicaraguan Central Bank (BCN) and BANADES while it also opened the door to the expansion of private commercial banks. As the role and size of BANADES diminished, it began to operate much as a commercial bank, concerned with cutting its losses and turning a profit.

A key BANADES policy became that of linking farm loan disbursement to the retrieval of prior loans, wherein the pool of net credit would increase only if loan recovery improved.[34] Also, interest rates were set at higher and generally positive real levels in order to attract private savings, so that by 1993 bank officials reported thousands of new accounts.[35] At the enterprise level, BANADES initiated rigorous technical assessments to determine loan eligibility and began to assess collateral requirements that could exceed the actual loan amount by 150 percent.

In practice, the new policies affecting credit failed to conform to an efficient and unbiased management of money. Three years of drought prior to 1993, growing cost-price pressures affecting agriculture, and the indexing of outstanding debt with currency devaluations had multiplied farm debt and elevated the number of loan defaults. With new loans refused to producers who fell behind in their payments, upwards of forty thousand producers—many of them SAR beneficiaries—faced possible foreclosure.[36] In this climate, BANADES's interest rate policy served to price many people out of the credit market. Ranging between 18 percent and 22 percent in 1993, the nominal loan rates set by BANADES were the highest in Central America and would climb to 30 percent by late 1994. Indeed, the level of interest rates demonstrated a disturbing nonmarket proclivity to remain unacceptably high even as inflation was brought under control.[37]

Ironically, as BANADES's private savings grew, the policy that tied available credit with loan repayment precluded their use as credit—especially, it seemed, in agriculture. Data from the BCN reveal that the cropped area financed and total money financing dropped precipitously after 1991. In the case of beans and corn, both the total areas funded and producer credits dropped in a range from 75 percent to over 80 percent between 1991 and 1993.[38] Similar or even greater cuts affected cotton, sesame, coffee, and bananas. By 1994 there was a strong recovery of over 30 percent in producer credit directed at coffee, but monies for beans and corn showed no recovery while loans for rice, sorghum, and sugarcane fell off sharply. Elsewhere, the repercussions of the farm credit squeeze were seen in a decline of imports of intermediate agricultural goods by 77 percent over the years from 1989 to 1992, while in the same period imports of commercial consumer goods rose by almost 200 percent.[39] Imports of Toyotas had replaced fertilizers. Interestingly, the deterioration of imports of farm inputs occurred over a period when most analysts agreed that the Nicaraguan currency, in spite of devaluations in 1991 and 1993, remained massively overvalued, a fact which underscored doubts about the priorities of credit policy.[40]

More than tight monetary policy alone served to provoke this drop in agricultural loans. Another explanation was the low execution rate for programmed credits, which was itself largely a reflection of low eligibility rates among loan applicants. In July 1993, at a time close to the end of the sowing period for the first planting season, official agricultural credit loaned out had reached only 55 percent of programmed amounts.[41] A similar disparity between programmed and dispensed credit had existed a year earlier as well.[42] The restrictive loan conditions that guided BANADES's technical assessment of borrowers typically disqualified most producers as "subjects of credit." In 1993 the portion of SAR cooperatives and other smallholders that attained subject-of-credit status varied between only 8 percent and 12 percent.[43] Thus, even though credit was ostensibly available and thousands of producers desired it, few were deemed creditworthy.

Coincident with the declining quantity of, and access to, agricultural credit was its concentration in the hands of large estate owners. Over the years 1990, 1991, and 1992 the portion of credit secured by large-scale farms grew steadily from 31 percent, to 56 percent, and finally to 71 percent, respectively. These gains came at the expense of medium- and small-scale producers who cultivated the vast bulk of Nicaragua's farmland. In the same period, these sectors saw their portion of producer credit drop from 56 percent to 29 percent, while it dried up altogether for workers on the state farms.[44] Not surprisingly, as credit was increasingly skewed toward large-scale farms between 1990 and 1992, the number of rural clients that received loans declined by 80 percent.[45]

The official explanation offered for this loan pattern argued, often at variance with the evidence, that elevated default rates and high administrative costs accompanied loans made to small- and medium-scale borrowers.[46] Citing the Nicaraguan Central Bank's own data, one study noted that small-scale producers realized higher loan repayment rates than large-scale producers.[47] A fuller explanation for the skewed loan pattern suggested a quite different reality. The issue of financing became politically charged when the president of BANADES and prominent members of the Chamorro government were reported to be recipients of exceedingly large noncollateralized loans and subsequently to have defaulted on their payments. Indeed, only twenty-two debtors accounted for one-half of BANADES's outstanding debt in 1994. The apparent extent of the corruption prompted one study to conclude: "[BANADES] is not a development bank; it is not even a bank. It lends huge amounts to large-scale producers based on friendship mixed with political criteria."[48]

In late 1993 policy changes were vowed as bank authorities promised to reduce the size of loans made to individuals in order to spread the remaining monies among more clients.[49] Contradictory directives from the IMF and the World Bank, however, appeared to undermine the resolve to reform credit policy. While suggesting that BANADES target small- and medium-scale farmers, these institutions simultaneously called for dramatic cuts in bank personnel and facilities. By mid-1995 more restrictive credit was assured as the BCN bowed to IMF pressure to raise the reserve ratio for *córdoba* deposits from already high levels that ranged between 10 percent and 15 percent.[50]

The failure of BANADES to underwrite production for thousands of farmers spurred UNAG to expand the credit, marketing, and processing activities of its Agricultural Producers' Cooperative Enterprise (Empresa Cooperativa de Productores Agrícolas, or ECODEPA). UNAG also initiated efforts aimed at creating a nongovernmental financing institution that targeted peasant producers.[51] Organized around the principles of the Grameen Bank in Bangladesh, the Peasants' Bank was inaugurated in August 1994 but could count on only limited funding.

The broadest measures of the impact of the policies of structural adjustment and economic stabilization were revealed in a set of dismal economic and social indicators for the country and, especially, the rural sector. For three of the five years from 1990 to 1994, official estimates of real GDP growth rates were negative, and they remained basically stagnant in the remaining two years. At the national level, unemployment reached 60 percent in 1993, and in some rural areas it ranged upward to 80 percent.[52] Significantly, the breakdown in the delivery of producer credit followed the return of thousands of demobilized combatants to the countryside. Real wages continued a downward trend that had begun in the mid-1980s, and, by late 1993, the national poverty index stood at 70 percent. In October 1994 full-time workers on coffee estates in the Matagalpa region earned the equivalent of less than U.S. $25 per month, a sum that was sufficient to buy only 36 percent of the basic market basket.[53] As wages dropped and the public health budget fell, cholera, dengue, and malnutrition spread in the countryside. Most dismal of all, the infant mortality rate reached 81 per thousand and was the highest in Central America, having increased 14 percent between 1991 and 1993.[54]

The structural adjustment and economic stabilization policies of the Chamorro government had brought the hyperinflation of the late 1980s under control, but in the process they had produced a grave economic depression. In the countryside, SAR beneficiaries faced desperate times. Hard-pressed by the limited access to producer credit, uncertain over the status of their property titles, and often facing considerable enterprise debt, many peasants began to sell their properties.

Land Markets and Their Impact on SAR Beneficiaries

A major expression of the market reforms introduced by Chamorro was seen in the explosion of activity in land markets that often involved acreage distributed under the SAR. In the 1980s, SAR lands that comprised the co-operative sector, in particular, were prohibited from sale. Members might enter and leave their association with the cooperative, as many thousands did, but indemnity in such cases did not include their right to sell some portion of the land.

After 1990 the continuing uncertainty over property rights, the sharply restrictive economic measures, growing farm debt, and the neoliberal emphasis on free markets all contributed to the emergence of markets in land. Under the combined impact of systematic and/or random bias in capital markets, land sales might be expected to tend toward *interclass* exchanges as land passed from relatively capital-scarce peasant producers to capital-abundant estate owners.[55] Systematic bias in the market for capital that favored large-scale producers could be rationalized, as noted earlier, on the basis of expected lower administrative costs and higher rates of loan repayment. Likewise, the random shock of drought or recession on producers of different scale was apt to affect more strongly and adversely the capital position of peasant farmers. Unable to insure against crop loss during drought or to borrow on the basis of future income in a recession, peasant farmers might sell land simply to ensure their survival. In such a climate, land transfers could be marked by distress sales wherein capital-constrained peasants discounted land prices far below their fair market value. In the Nicaragua of 1990 where both systematic and random bias effects in capital markets appeared present, land markets threatened, finally, the more egalitarian structure of land tenure that developed under the SAR.

Comprehensive data on the extent and nature of land sales involving SAR beneficiaries evidenced considerable discrepancy. As of 1993 the estimates of the portion of SAR land sold ranged upward to 100,000 *manzanas*—about 10 percent of the reform sector lands—and downward to 50,000 *manzanas*.[56] A more detailed, if somewhat ambiguous, picture of these sales emerged from regional surveys and anecdotal evidence.

A June 1993 survey of fifty-three CAS cooperatives in the northwest regions of Chinandega and León found that 6.5 percent of their total lands had been sold by that date.[57] Interestingly, 95 percent of the area sold occurred on those CAS that had previously parceled land among the membership and that had relinquished the former scale and collateral advantages they had shared as a collective. While the reasons for parceling were related to factors both internal and external to the cooperative, once parceled, the now family farms experienced relatively greater capital flow problems; were more prone to sell their tractors and equipment; and, finally, were drawn in greater numbers into the land market. Elsewhere, a 1994 regional study in Rivas in the southwest found that 13 percent of the area controlled by the CAS sampled had been sold.[58] Unlike sales in Chinandega and León, where the parcels sold accounted for only a small part of any one cooperative's total parceled area, the large majority of marketed land in Rivas (62 percent) represented the total liquidation of cooperative lands.

Both the Chinandega and León survey and the Rivas study confirmed the expectation that land sales were realized at distress prices. A *manzana* of agricultural land in the former regions brought 1,531 *córdobas* on average, while the reported fair market value was 4,993, a 226 percent difference.[59] In Rivas, marketed CAS lands garnered 660 *córdobas* per *manzana* on average but held a market value of 1,500 *córdobas*.[60] Moreover, in Rivas, large estate buyers made their purchases at prices below those paid by other classes of buyers. The reasons given for land sales acknowledged the general economic and, especially, capital flow difficulties associated with farming.

The expectation that such sales would be monopolized by rich estate owners showed evidence of regional differences. In the Chinandega and León survey, the large majority of land transactions (85 percent) were *intraclass* sales between small producers. In many cases, the peasant buyers and sellers were members of the same cooperative, a situation which evidenced an informal policy that granted other cooperators the first option to buy. Yet, in spite of the active participation of small-scale buyers in land markets, the majority of acreage sold among the CAS sampled in Chinandega and León (56 percent) was purchased by large estate owners.[61] In Rivas, where powerful "political functionaries" and latifundistas reportedly acquired 90 percent of marketed cooperative lands, the domination of markets by such buyers clearly pointed toward a restratification of land ownership.[62]

As seen in Table 2, by 1994 the combination of Chamorro-era land reform, legal and legislative maneuverings, economic policy, and the operation of land markets had resulted in a shift in the tenure structure as larger estates increased their share of agricultural properties. If in 1988 estates larger than 200 *manzanas* had occupied around 21 percent of farmland, by 1993 that figure had expanded to 26 percent. While the greatest percentage gain between 1988 and 1993 occurred among properties of less than 50 *manzanas*—rising from 18.7 percent to 39 percent of area in farms—the bulk of this increase simply represented the transfer of lands from the SAR sector that were already controlled or accessed by peasants. Indeed, the largest part of the increase in the small-scale sector had its origin in the parceled lands of the collective CAS. Regardless of the nominal increase in peasant-controlled land or of the actual extent of the interclass transfers, the likelihood of continued restratification of land control appeared great under the current policy matrix.

Table 2. Changes in Land Tenure Structure between 1988 and 1993 (in percentages)

Estate Size/Property Form	1988[1]	1993[2]
Small- and Medium-Scale Farms	47.1	71
Less than 50 mz	18.7	39
Non-SAR: private	–	21
SAR lands: parceled co-ops and individual lands	–	10
Post-SAR lands: primarily former combatants	–	6
Post-SAR lands: APT members	–	2
50 to 200 mz	28.4	32
Large-Scale Estates	21.0	26
200 to 500 mz	13.5	16
Greater than 500 mz	7.5	10
SAR Sector (Untransformed)	31.8	2
Cooperatives[3]	20.1	2
State farms	11.7	0
Other	–	2
Total	**99.9**	**101[4]**

[1]Data for 1988 are drawn from Table 1.
[2]Data for 1993 were compiled from NITPLAN reported in "Campesinos y finqueros: Los marginados de siempre," *Barricada*, November 1, 1993.
[3]Figures for 1993 represent only the unparceled collective cooperatives or CAS.
[4]Percentage figures from source document totaled 101 percent.

Conclusion

Five years after the electoral defeat of the Sandinistas, the agrarian policy of the Chamorro government had created a kind of transitional stasis—an oxymoronic state of affairs that resulted in a political and social impasse that pleased almost no one. While President Chamorro was successful in framing both the broad outline of the debate and the general direction of the farm economy on neoliberal terms, the social consensus required to formulate the details of the transition was not easily secured. Moreover, that consensus became more elusive with the onset of recession and misery.

The equivocal nature of much policy and legislation affecting SAR property rights exemplified the difficulty in balancing the interests of rural workers and peasants who benefited under the SAR with those of confiscated landowners. The early Protocol that promised to respect the property rights acquired under the SAR was undercut by legislative and legal maneuvers initiated by members of Chamorro's political coalition—actions that were, ostensibly, against her will. The post-1990 agrarian reform and the later agreement to permit an area of workers' property on former state lands were nonneoliberal policies that had further alienated segments of her erstwhile coalition.

Such compromises of the structural adjustment in process were a concession to the new "correlation of forces" that had emerged over the decade of social revolution in the 1980s. The political and economic empowerment of peasants and rural workers in the Sandinista era made them significant players in the transitional period. More independent of the strategic strictures that they faced as Sandinista-affiliated unions, rural workers assumed a confrontational attitude that often put them at odds with FSLN tactics after 1990. The seizure of private lands by former combatants and the reconstitution of armed bands of *recontras*, *recompas*, or even combinations of both, was evidence that peasants were active agents on their own behalf, not content to stand idly by while politicians and market forces worked their magic.

The capitalist sector present in the Nicaragua of 1990 had undergone, and was undergoing, considerable change as well.[63] Commercial, financial, and producer capitalists divided along lines of unyielding resistance to, or conciliation with, aspects of the Sandinista-era status quo and the perceived accommodationist policies of President Chamorro. The different stance of distinct fractions of capital contributed to the political stalemate. Agro-export elites, in particular, faced difficult times after 1990. Never enamored of the possibility of confiscation through the SAR, many of these producers had nonetheless remained in Nicaragua in the 1980s where they benefited from the low interest rates and generous credit and input subsidies. Now, with state aid largely withdrawn and facing weak world prices for coffee and cotton and import competition in some areas, these producers looked longingly at the 1980s with their guaranteed prices and low costs. On the other hand, those estate owners whose lands were confiscated under the SAR remained implacable in their opposition to accommodation. Elsewhere, entrepreneurial-minded UNAG officers tried to fill the void left by the diminution of the state's role in rural credit markets and extension services.

If the conservative forces were frustrated in their political efforts to roll back the SAR at a quicker pace, they could still be content to let market forces operate in order to restratify land tenure and society along former lines. The official policies fashioned to govern the market for short-term rural credit typically denied outright small- and medium-scale producers or set loan rates at levels that discouraged borrowing. Also, the limited reach of financing provided by the nascent Peasants' Bank in the mid-1990s ensured that large numbers of peasant producers could expect little help. In conjunction with substantial debt and the uncertainty over property rights, the denial of producer financing was the nail in the coffin for many SAR beneficiaries who began to sell land at below-market prices. The utter desperation inherent in such distress sales was appreciated when one considered that those selling land entered a labor market characterized by extremely high rates of unemployment and abysmally low real wages.

The supposed efficiency gains associated with structural adjustment and economic stabilization proved elusive five years into the Chamorro government. Indeed, and in spite of the orthodox litany of "getting the prices right," the imperfect nature of capital and labor markets in the revanchist political climate was hardly an accident. Those who sought to reconfigure both the control of land and, subsequently, the social class structure seemed to design market rules and institutional practices precisely to effect those ends. At the same time, the voice and power gained by peasants and rural workers in the 1980s meant that the struggle to determine and to maintain those rules and practices would be prolonged.

Notes

1. Philip J. Williams, "Dual Transitions from Authoritarian Rule: Popular and Electoral Democracy in Nicaragua," *Comparative Politics* 26, no. 2 (January 1994): 170.

2. Victor Bulmer-Thomas, *The Political Economy of Central America since 1920* (Cambridge, Eng.: Cambridge University Press, 1987), 156–60.

3. Carmen D. Deere and Peter Marchetti, "The Worker-Peasant Alliance in the First Year of the Nicaraguan Agrarian Reform," *Latin American Perspectives* 8 (Spring 1981): 42.

4. Alain de Janvry, *The Agrarian Question and Reformism in Latin America* (Baltimore: Johns Hopkins University Press, 1982).

5. Nola Reinhardt, "Contrast and Congruence in the Agrarian Reforms of El Salvador and Nicaragua," in *Searching for Agrarian Reform in Latin America*, ed. William C. Thiesenheusen (Winchester, MA: Unwin Hyman, 1988), 467.

6. Jon Jonakin, "The Transition from External Constraint to Enterprise Autonomy on Nicaraguan Agricultural Production Cooperatives," *Canadian Journal of Latin American and Caribbean Studies* 19 (1994): 61–88.

7. Orlando Nuñez et al., *La guerra en Nicaragua* (Managua: CIPRES, 1991), 314–19.

8. Freddy Amador, Rosario Ambrogi, and Gerardo Ribbink, *La reforma agraria en Nicaragua: De Rojinegro a Violeta* (Managua: Escuela de Economía Agrícola de la UNAN, 1991), 7.

9. David Stanfield, *Insecurity of Land Tenure in Nicaragua*, Working Paper (Madison, WI: Land Tenure Center, 1992), 9, 13.

10. Ibid., 10.

11. "Desalojo ronda a Cooperativa Caraceña," *Barricada*, July 27, 1993; "Cooperatives Hard-pressed by the Banks and the Law," *Barricada International* 374 (June 1994): 7.

12. Jon Jonakin, "The Impact of Structural Adjustment and Property Rights Conflicts on Nicaraguan Agrarian Reform Beneficiaries," *World Development* 24 (July 1996): 1179–92.

13. Freddy Amador and Gerardo Ribbink, *Nicaragua: Reforma agraria, propiedad y mercado de tierra* (Managua: Escuela de Economía Agrícola de la UNAN, 1992), 3.

14. Ibid., 3–5. One *manzana* equals 1.7 acres.

15. Ibid., 4, 34.

16. Ibid., 5; Rosario Ambrogi, "La privatización en el sector agrícola: Caso AGROEXCO," *Revista de Economía Agrícola* 5 (1992): 6, 7.

17. Amador and Ribbink, *Nicaragua: Reforma agraria*, 24.

18. Ibid., 1; Stanfield, *Insecurity of Land Tenure*, 14.

19. Amador and Ribbink, *Nicaragua: Reforma agraria*, 25.

20. Ambrogi, "La privatización," 3.

21. Renato Aguilar and Asa Stenman, *Nicaragua 1994: Back into the Ranks* (Stockholm, Sweden: Swedish International Development Authority, 1994), 17.

22. Freddy Amador and Ricardo Guevara. "El mercado de tierra en Nicaragua," in *El mercado de tierras en Nicaragua* (Managua: Centro de Investigaciones Económicas y Sociales, 1994), n.p.

23. Richard Stahler-Sholk, "El ajuste neoliberal y sus opciones: La respuesta del movimiento sindical nicaragüense," *Revista Mexicana de Sociología* 56 (July–September 1994): 68.

24. Richard Stahler-Sholk, "The Dog That Didn't Bark: Labor Autonomy and Economic Adjustment in Nicaragua under the Sandinista and UNO Governments," *Comparative Politics* 28 (October 1996): 77–102.

25. Ambrogi, "La privatización," 7, 8.

26. Ibid., 7–9.

27. Stahler-Sholk, "El ajuste neoliberal," 68.

28. Aguilar and Stenman, *Nicaragua 1994*, 17.

29. Adolfo Acevedo Vogl, *Nicaragua y el FMI: El pozo sin fondo del ajuste* (Managua: Ediciones CRIES, 1993), 106.

30. "Feeding the Big Fish," *Barricada International* 381 (January 1995): 12.

31. Ambrogi, "La privatización," 7.

32. Max Spoor, "Liberalization of Grain Markets in Nicaragua: From Substitution to State Minimalism," *Food Policy* 20 (1995): 103–5.

33. Acevedo, *Nicaragua y el FMI*, 69–123.

34. Ibid., 95–97.

35. "Un banco 'eficiente,' " *Barricada*, May 17, 1993.

36. "El peso de la deuda," ibid.

37. Alejandro Martínez, "La tasa de interés no es un molino de viento," *Barricada*, date lost.

38. BCN, *Indicadores económicos* 1, no. 4 (April 1995).

39. Acevedo, *Nicaragua y el FMI*, 93.

40. Ibid., 125.

41. "Así va la siembra," *Barricada*, July 19, 1993.

42. Acevedo, *Nicaragua y el FMI*, 96.

43. "Doce mil familias con hambre y 80 mil manzanas ociosas," *Barricada*, July 22, 1993; "Ciclo agrícola en la hora de la verdad," ibid., May 17, 1993.

44. Acevedo, *Nicaragua y el FMI*, 112.

45. "Campesinos a la ruina," *Barricada*, May 17, 1993.

46. "Feeding the Big Fish," 12, 13.

47. Stahler-Sholk, "El ajuste neoliberal," 68.

48. "Feeding the Big Fish," 13.

49. "Banco financiarán a pequeños productores," *Barricada*, November 3, 1993.

50. "Possible Restrictions on Credit," *Barricada International* 385 (June 1995): 8.

51. "The Farmers' Bank: Sowing the Seeds of Economic Recovery," *Barricada International* 381 (January 1995): 13–14.

52. Stahler-Sholk, "El ajuste neoliberal," 68; "A Year of Surprises, Crises, and Tensions," *Barricada International* 369 (January 1994): 7.

53. "Farm Workers Ask for Higher Wages," *Barricada International* 378–79 (October–November 1994): 10.

54. Figures on poverty and infant mortality were reported in "Pobreza crece," *Barricada*, November 16, 1993.

55. Michael Carter and Dina Mesbah, "Can Land Market Reform Mitigate the Exclusionary Aspects of Rapid Agro-Export Growth?" *World Development* 21 (July 1993): 1089–95.

56. Amador and Guevara, "El mercado de tierra en Nicaragua," n.p.; "Campesinos y finqueros: Los marginados de siempre," *Barricada*, November 1, 1993.

57. Jonakin, "The Impact of Structural Adjustment," 1185.

58. Javier L. Matus, "Monitoreo al mercado de tierras: Síntesis, Departamento de Rivas," 14, 18, prepared for the Comisión de las Comunidades Europeas, April 1994.

59. Jonakin, "The Impact of Structural Adjustment," 1186.

60. Matus, "Monitoreo al mercado de tierras," 22.

61. Jonakin, "The Impact of Structural Adjustment," 1187.

62. Matus, "Monitoreo al mercado de tierras," 20.

63. Rose Spalding, *Capitalists and Revolution in Nicaragua: Opposition and Accommodation, 1979–1993* (Chapel Hill: University of North Carolina Press, 1994), 180–87.

7

Social Policy

Karen Kampwirth

Where does social policy fit into the ongoing process of transition in Nicaragua? Cuts in spending for social programs might appear to have been an inevitable response to a national-level process of regime transition and economic restructuring, but the transformation of social policy was not just a passive reaction to external pressures. Instead, it resulted from a complicated negotiation process among many different social groups, only some of which enjoyed direct access to the Chamorro administration.

The changes that occurred in the three areas of social policy addressed in this chapter (social welfare, education, and health care) differed dramatically. The most notable, in structural terms, took place in social welfare: the ministry that had been entrusted with the provision of welfare services ceased to exist in January 1995, and it was replaced by new agencies with significantly different agendas. The most dramatic ideological changes occurred in education, which also saw some more limited structural transformation during this period. Finally, in the area of health care, there were no structural or ideological changes of comparable significance, although health policy was also refashioned, to some extent, in response to the realities of new national political priorities and budget cuts.

The differences between these policy areas can be attributed to the personalities, values, and political skills of high-level National Opposition Union (UNO) appointees in the relevant ministries combined with the responses of civil society in general, and the unions in particular,[1] to attempts to transform state social policy. One legacy of the Sandinista period, the expansion of "the 'space' available for autonomous social organization and mobilization,"[2] meant that certain groups within civil society were sometimes able to influence government policymaking. But that legacy was hardly static. During the first half of the 1990s, the nature of civil society continued to evolve; and as it evolved, its ability to influence policymaking varied.

Social Welfare

Before 1979, an agency known as the National Social Security Institute (Instituto Nacional de Seguridad Social, or INSS) provided social security for some workers in the formal sector and for some members of their families. Shortly after the overthrow of Anastasio Somoza, INSS redefined its mission to insure a greater proportion of the population and to improve on the services provided to the insured population. At the same time, in one of the first acts of the new revolutionary government, the Ministry of Social Welfare (Ministerio de Bienestar) was founded in July 1979, absorbing the Somoza-era National Assistance and Social Provision Board (Junta Nacional de Asistencia y Previsión Social) and taking over the functions of the Social Assistance Department of INSS.

In addition to taking over old ministries, the new one greatly expanded on the missions of its predecessors. This expansion involved creating departments of "Family and Child Welfare (day-care centers, nutrition programs, protection and reeducation, care for the elderly, scholarships, training, and family protection); Community Development; Integral Rehabilitation; State Production Collectives; Committee of Staple Foods; and the administration of the Popular Lottery."[3]

In 1982, INSS and the Ministry of Social Welfare were united under a new name, Nicaraguan Social Security and Social Welfare Institute (Instituto Nicaragüense de Seguridad Social y Bienestar, or INSSBI). The years following the change in name were characterized by a steady expansion of the type of services covered by the ministry, and of the number of people served. By increasing the numbers of workers who were insured by the ministry (from 122,597 in July 1979 to 286,945 in December 1989) and, more important, by offering a wide range of new services to uninsured Nicaraguans, INSSBI went from covering 202,518 people in 1979 to 1,813,415 in 1989.[4]

The authors of a report on the progress in INSSBI during the Sandinista period concluded that in early 1990 it was "one of the biggest and most complex institutions at the national level and [it] enjoyed a harmonious and efficient structure."[5] Popular opinion would seem to support this self-evaluation; INSSBI enjoyed a great deal of legitimacy.[6] Given this legitimacy, it was somewhat surprising that the Chamorro administration chose to eliminate the social welfare half of the ministry. It was even more surprising that it was eliminated with no public protest. But that was only possible after several years of carefully preparing civil society.

In 1990 and 1991, INSSBI's official position held that its policies had not changed at all from those of the Sandinista period. Although there were cuts in services during this time,[7] it is likely that they were driven more by economics than by ideology. In other words, those cuts are probably most fairly viewed as a continuation of the structural adjustment policies of the late 1980s rather than a policy shift due to the change in administration in 1990.

While the case of INSSBI suggests that a change in administration does not lead to an immediate transformation of all state ministries, the process of regime transformation often does catch up to lagging ministries. The new political climate caught up to INSSBI in January 1992 when Dr. Simeón Rizo replaced Dr. Silviano Matamoros (1990–1992) as the national director of INSSBI. Unlike his predecessor, who insisted that INSSBI would carry out the same mission in the 1990s as it had in the 1980s, Dr. Rizo explicitly rejected the legacy of the 1980s. As he explained: "In the 1980s social security was designed for a totalitarian society, in which the economic contributions, differences, and characteristics of the individual were forgotten in place of a concept of man as functioning within a class. . . . Social security was designed for a paternalistic state that would cover everything."[8]

Between the time when Rizo took over the administration of INSSBI in January 1992, and the separation of "INSS" (social security) from "BI" (social welfare) in January 1995, services and personnel were steadily reduced.[9] It could no longer be argued that this move was a continuation of the policies of the late 1980s and early 1990s that sought to reduce the size of the ministry for economic reasons. First, the discourse justifying those policies changed dramatically, as illustrated by the above quotation. And second, relations among the administration of the ministry, its employees, and the unions were also undergoing change.

Complaints by former employees that there were serious morale problems within INSSBI between 1992 and the division of the ministry in 1995 are supported quantitatively by the drop in personnel over the course of the 1990s (see note 9). The official explanation is that over one-half of the employees resigned so as to reap the short-term benefits of one of the state-reducing economic plans. While it is likely that some fraction of the resignation rate was due to economic decisions that were made without reference to working conditions at INSSBI, those same economic plans were offered to workers in other state agencies that did not witness anything approaching INSSBI's attrition rate.[10] Why did so many employees desert INSSBI to take their chances in a disastrous economy? Why, when the agency ceased to exist as INSSBI, was there no public protest from employees, union activists, the press, or the general public? Both questions may be answered by looking at the internal politics of the ministry.

During the first two years of the Chamorro administration, there were few dramatic changes. However, change was nearly inevitable after the appointment of Dr. Rizo as national director, since he made no secret of his contempt for the legacy of the revolutionary period. This contempt might have served to unite the employees of the ministry against his plans. It did not, however, because of a "policy of breaking the unity of the employees

... of discrediting all the work that had been done. That was more effective than firing people would have been."[11] In many cases, workers were transferred from fields in which they had years of experience to fields in which they had none. As experts on children found themselves working in programs for the elderly and vice versa, many became demoralized and resigned without protest.

This internal divide-and-conquer strategy helps to explain both the mass resignations from INSSBI and why the union that represented its workers led no protest when INSS and BI were separated, even though BI's successor sought to provide a small fraction of the services that had been previously provided. The secretary-general of the union that represented INSSBI employees explained that "we in the union considered that the division was better than to continue to be united within INSSBI, because Dr. Rizo was more interested in social security [than in welfare]."[12] The decision of the union not to protest, combined with the complicity or incompetence of the press,[13] meant that, shortly after one of the most far-reaching and popular ministries was basically privatized, few members of the general public knew that anything had changed.

What did the new ministry do, and why use the word "basically" privatized? According to a booklet that described the Nicaraguan Fund for Children and the Family (Fondo Nicaragüense de la Niñez y la Familia, or FONIF), the goal of the direct successor of the BI of INSSBI was to be "an instrument to set standards, to facilitate, to advise, and to channel funds to those nongovernmental organizations and to the civil society . . . that develop programs and projects for children."[14] No reference was made to directly providing services. Instead, over the course of two to four years, FONIF was to hand over the provision of all services to the private sector.[15]

The mission of FONIF (to seek solutions for children and families at risk) shared a great deal with the mission of INSSBI, but the means to fulfilling that mission contrasted sharply. The directors of INSSBI (until 1992) believed that the state played a legitimate role in the direct provision of social welfare services. The directors of FONIF did not make this assumption. Instead, they thought that once the state removed itself from the social welfare field, the private sector would step in to fill all unmet needs. Needless to say, this new model was controversial, seen by some as "complete irresponsibility"[16] and by others as a way for "everyone to take responsibility for everyone else."[17]

FONIF listed eight goals to be carried out during its first year, including "parental education about family responsibility . . . [improving] the infrastructure of day-care centers . . . [developing] a scholarship program for working boys and girls . . . [and submitting] proposals for reforms in family law."[18] The list of goals did not mention work with the disabled or elderly, as INSSBI had done. It was not clear if those groups were targeted: they were referred to elsewhere in the booklet, and there was debate (among the FONIF employees interviewed by the author) as to whether or not they were targets of FONIF's programs. Finally, women were another group that had been directly served by INSSBI. They, too, were not mentioned in FONIF's booklet (nor in the interviews) and were either not to be served at all or were subsumed within "the family."

Ending the section on social welfare policies at this point (the elimination of the ministry and its replacement with the more restricted FONIF) would give the impression that, by 1995, the state had dramatically retreated from its involvement in the field. In my opinion, that would be a fairly accurate impression—but it would not be completely accurate. Another new agency, while not a direct descendant of the BI of INSSBI, was also involved in social welfare policy. So it is appropriate to complete this section with a discussion of the Ministry of Social Action (Ministerio de Acción Social, or MAS).

MAS, formed in January 1993, might have had more in common with INSSBI than did FONIF, which largely restricted its mission to serving children. In contrast, like the INSSBI of the 1980s and early 1990s, MAS purported to address social welfare issues in a holistic way. But unlike the old INSSBI and like FONIF, MAS was not to provide services directly. "We are standard setters, directors. . . . [MAS] manages projects but they are transitory because that is not the function of MAS."[19]

MAS's activities during 1994 were nearly all economically oriented, with an emphasis on community participation. They included a job program in areas such as street repair, well digging, reforestation, and repair of health clinics, schools, and churches; credit for small producers and small business owners; an animal-raising program for peasant women who headed households; and coordination of disaster relief efforts. All together, these programs generated 160,419 jobs.[20] In emphasizing community participation, MAS could easily have been guided by the same slogan as INSSBI in the 1980s: "To Social Problems, Communal Solutions." But, unlike INSSBI, MAS proposed solutions that were nearly exclusively economic. While there was no call for MAS to address children's needs since that role belonged to FONIF, certain sectors, such as the elderly and women, may have fallen through the cracks between FONIF and MAS.

Finally, it is important to consider the short-term nature of MAS's economic solutions. The number served by these programs is unclear: the jobs were described as "temporary or permanent," but the MAS literature does not address this question in any greater detail, so the 160,419 jobs generated may or may not have gone to 160,419 different people. A related issue is compensation: the standard salary was 56 *córdobas* per week, the equivalent of U.S. $7.46, which is quite a low wage in Nicaragua.[21] Some jobs paid only 56 *córdobas*, some paid 56 *córdobas* plus a food stipend, while some paid only a food stipend.

According to MAS's figures, the single biggest program created positions in exchange for food (60,053 "jobs" were generated).[22] Food-for-work programs such as this one, that were funded through U.S. Public Law No. 480,[23] have come under serious criticism over the last several decades for exacerbating economic inequality, forestalling reform, and sometimes even making future reform more difficult to carry out by damaging local agricultural markets.[24]

The temporary, poorly compensated nature of these jobs means that MAS needs to be seen as an emergency agency rather than as an agency for the enhancement of social welfare over the long term. Of course, given the nature of the economic crisis that engulfed the country in the 1990s, emergency social welfare was important. The open question was whether this emergency welfare was organized in a way that would allow for long-term improvements in the welfare of the poorest.

Education

Education was central to Sandinista efforts to transform Nicaraguan society. The most famous instance of these efforts was the 1980 literacy campaign which, in the space of five months, brought the national illiteracy rate down from 50 to 12 percent.[25] The literacy campaign (and all other education under the Sandinistas) remained controversial well into the 1990s. For many of the Sandinistas' critics, the literacy campaign epitomized the destruction of traditional authority that the revolution had represented. In a speech on the fifth anniversary of her taking office, President Violeta Chamorro made the surprising claim that the tens of thousands who had volunteered to teach others to read had only done so because the Sandinistas had mixed drugs in the soda pop that the volunteers drank.[26] It is not known why she made this unsupported accusation, but the underlying sentiment—that the campaign was a blow to traditional "family values"—is common.

After the literacy campaign and until the electoral loss in 1990, Sandinista educational policy would continue to attempt to create "the new man"—that is, to inculcate new, more egalitarian values. The Chamorro administration's educational policies, though lacking the drama of the literacy campaign, also need to be viewed in these terms. Education is never only about teaching basic skills but is inevitably about values as well.

Although the Chamorro government seemed to share the Sandinistas' belief that education should shape societal values, UNO appointees had a different view of what those values should be. To begin, they tended to disagree with the Sandinista interpretation of education in the 1980s. While Sandinista writings on education proclaimed the importance of inclusion, UNO appointees tended to remember education in the 1980s as having been exclusive. According to one administrator at the Ministry of Education (Ministerio de Educación, or MED): "Everything was politicized. . . . These books [the Somoza-era Morals and Civics series] disappeared to leave room for politicized material. History of *sandinismo*: Sandino goes, Sandino always."[27] Under the Chamorro administration, textbooks were produced that were much less partisan than those issued by the Sandinistas. But their textbooks, and education as a whole in the 1990s, made far fewer efforts to transform old inequalities based on class, gender, and generation.

Textbooks in a series called Morals and Civics were written, published, and in children's hands less than a year after UNO took office thanks to a grant of $12.5 million from the U.S. Agency for International Development (AID). Officials with the AID insisted that they merely funded the textbooks and were not directly involved in writing them.[28] Apparently, that was true; in fact, very few people were involved in writing them. According to a MED administrator, the books "were produced without the participation of the teachers, by a group of three or four closed up with the Minister"[29]—a notable contrast with the Sandinista decision to use the old Somoza-era readers for the first year or two so that textbooks could be developed after a process of popular consultation.

The process through which the textbooks were developed was controversial, as was their content.[30] While the new ones were not partisan, they were quite political. In order to inculcate a version of traditional family values, the texts in the Morals and Civics series presented numerous images, as well as direct discussions, of ideal gender and generational relations. Happy mothers were pictured cooking or cleaning in their middle-class kitchens; happy fathers were shown sitting in overstuffed chairs or engaged in paid employment. The texts emphasized the value of legal marriage, the only form of marriage recognized by the writers of the books (although the 1987 Constitution recognized both common-law and legal unions), as well as the evils of abortion, which was illegal. An adviser to Minister of Education Humberto Belli[31] explained the need for the Morals and Civics series: "Education [under the Sandinistas] was devoid of a lot of traditional family values that Nicaragua had known under the Somozas. . . . Christian values were lost."[32]

The sixth-grade text illustrated these Christian values through an eight-page-long discussion of the Ten Commandments,[33] in apparent violation of the laws of the secular Republic of Nicaragua. MED officials denied that such discussions could be seen as an attempt to substitute Catholic for lay education, acknowledging that such a substitution would be a violation of the Constitution. Instead, their goal was simply for the "educational system to be open to values of Christian inspiration."[34]

The most significant change in the first half of the 1990s was in the ideological content of teaching materials. But that was not the only way in which Nicaraguan education was transformed: there also were changes in the relationship of the Ministry of Education to civil society. While the language in favor of community participation used by the ministry in the 1990s was remarkably similar to that used in the 1980s, the practical meaning of that discourse changed greatly.

According to the Sandinista conception, civil society was comprised of organizations (controlled, ideally, from below) that were to represent their members' interests to the relevant state agencies. During the 1980s the National Association of Educators of Nicaragua (Asociación Nacional de Educadores de Nicaragua, or ANDEN) had tremendous influence over the course of education in the country. ANDEN was the only teachers' union, and 1 percent of all teachers' salaries were deducted automatically to pay dues.[35]

In the first few months of the Chamorro administration, the new minister of education rejected this relationship by excluding ANDEN representatives from the process of formulating new textbooks, signaling a redefinition of civil society. The new MED sought to relate to a civil society that was organized from above—that is, by the MED itself. Starting in 1993, a structure of representative bodies was created so as to involve what the MED called "civil society" in educational decisions. At the department level (the rough equivalent of a U.S. state) each educational council was comprised of: 1) a representative of each municipal council; 2) a representative of "the Church" (presumably the Catholic Church); 3) a representative of private enterprise; and 4) the departmental director from the MED. The structure of the educational councils at the municipal level was similar, with the addition of representatives of parents and teachers. No union was represented at all.[36]

The representatives of civil society that oversaw the ministry were either individually selected by the ministry itself or appointed according to some impersonal mechanism (seniority, in the case of teachers, or their children's grades, in the case of parents). These people were not elected or appointed by the members of the organization they represented. In fact, they did not come from any organized group, with the exception of the Church.

While the ideal of autonomous social organizations was not always met during the Sandinista period, there is an important difference between the Sandinista conception of civil society as comprised of *organizations*, albeit imperfectly autonomous organizations, and the Chamorro administration's conception of civil society as based on *individuals* who are appointed by the very state agency they are to oversee. It is true that the special privileges given to ANDEN during the Sandinista period greatly diminished the potential for civil society to mediate between the state and the citizenry, and there were important advances under UNO as rival teachers' unions were permitted to organize. However, the work of those unions was marginalized. This marginalization provoked considerable anger from many union members, and teachers' strikes were a regular part of life in Nicaragua in the first half of the 1990s. Minister of Education Belli himself became a frequent topic of graffiti. "Get out, Belli" decorated walls all over the city of Managua; no other minister received such attention.

Linked to the transformation of the relationship between the MED and civil society was the initiation, in April 1993, of a decentralization program comprised of autonomous high schools (with plans to eventually create autonomous grade schools) and municipalization. Many schools became autonomous in the first two years of the program,[37] while municipalization was much slower, perhaps because there were clearer incentives for a school to become autonomous than for a municipality to take over the responsibility of paying for education.

An autonomous school continued to receive part of its budget from the MED and part from parents, just as regular public schools did. The main difference was that autonomous schools charged parents a fee while public schools could only request one. The administration of the autonomous schools could then use what it earned through fees to raise the miserable salaries of its teachers (see note 21) or to otherwise improve working conditions. Teachers who received higher salaries and other benefits were to work harder and more effectively, according to the proponents of autonomous schools. An article in the MED's newsletter reported that in 1993 "the drop-out rate in autonomous institutes was 8 percent while in other state centers it was 16 percent."[38]

This article (and various other articles in the MED's newsletters) implied that drop-out rates were lower because of autonomy. It was not clear if that was the case since the rates before those schools became autonomous were not reported. Since only schools that served children with relatively affluent parents who could pay a fixed monthly fee could become autonomous, it is possible that those schools already had lower drop-out rates, prior to becoming autonomous, than the average school. In any case, whatever class differences there were from one public school to another were probably enhanced as children from affluent families concentrated in the newly autonomous schools.

Health Care

One of the legacies of the Somoza era was a health system that was fragmented, inefficient, and elitist, even by Central American standards. As a result, one of the priorities of the Sandinista administration was the reform of health care. The many agencies that had provided such care under Somoza were consolidated into the Ministry of Health (Ministerio de Salud, or MINSA). A greater emphasis was placed on national health planning, which was facilitated by the creation of various regional offices. In both planning and providing health care, community participation was encouraged. A number of mass organizations took part in decision making through Popular Health Councils and in the provision of services through immunization campaigns, constructing latrines, surveying at-risk children, building new clinics, and health education.[39]

In many ways, these campaigns were effective. The vaccination campaign nearly eradicated polio and greatly reduced levels of other infectious diseases. While there were only 43 clinics in 1978, there were 532 by 1983. In 1979 only 50 percent of the population of Managua had access to drinking water, but by 1988 some 80 percent had access.[40] And, perhaps most important, health services were free.

When the Sandinistas handed over MINSA to the Chamorro administration in 1990, that ministry enjoyed a great deal of popular legitimacy. The value that the population placed upon health services could be part of the reason why MINSA did not change its approach significantly during the first half of the 1990s, certainly not compared to INSSBI and the MED. Despite external pressures to reduce state services, health policies saw only relatively insignificant changes in the early 1990s. The Ministry of Health remained intact, the basic priorities (services for mothers, children, and the poorest) were untouched,[41] and, while the budget for public health was lower in the 1990s than it had been during much of the 1980s, the number of personnel employed by the ministry remained steady.[42]

Just as a relational view of social welfare and educational policies helped explain the types of changes that occurred in those areas, a consideration of the relations between Ministry of Health officials and the Confederation of Health Workers (Confederación de Trabajadores de la Salud, or FETSALUD) can help explain the minimal changes in policy. In sharp contrast to the relations between INSSBI and MED officials and their respective unions, the relations between top officials of MINSA and FETSALUD were civil, if not always friendly.

MINSA officials made various efforts to depoliticize health services. For instance, a special session of the National Health Council was held on August 27, 1993, in which speeches were given by Marta Palacio, the minister of health, as well as by Lea Guido and Dora María Téllez (both ministers of health during the Sandinista period), and by Fernando Valle (a minister of health from the Somoza period).[43] Such an event—implying that political opponents might all make valuable contributions to health care—would have been difficult to imagine in the other social ministries. The rhetoric used by the ministry under Dr. Palacio (who took office in early 1993) and, to a slightly lesser extent, by her predecessor, Dr. Ernesto Salmerón (1990–1993), also demonstrated efforts to depolarize society.

At the same time as the ministers of health seemed more willing to negotiate with civil society and less quick to reject all the policies of the previous decade, FETSALUD, the union that represented health workers, strategized effectively. It retained an ability and willingness to organize, protest, and strike (unlike the union that represented social welfare workers) yet also retained civil and productive relations with the ministry (un-

like the union that represented teachers). Among the benefits of this strategy were collective agreements that were signed by MINSA and FETSALUD
in May 1990, May 1992, January 1993, and December 1993, with the final
agreement covering the period 1993–1995.[44]

The relative civility of relations between the health ministry and health
workers did not mean, however, that there were no changes in health care
during the 1990s. One notable change, beginning in 1991, was the initiation
of fees for services, to be paid according to a sliding scale. Another change
was the effort to decentralize services. In 1991, Local Holistic Health Care
Systems (Sistemas Locales de Atención Integral de Salud, or SILAIS) and
governing boards in hospitals began to be formed. According to one
FETSALUD representative, while decentralization was a good idea in theory,
it brought about few practical changes: "The idea was to get a little closer
to the population; but without resources, there is little that one can do."[45]

Resources were the crux of the problem. Despite a certain level of social agreement over policy, the health of the average Nicaraguan deteriorated as health workers tried to serve a rapidly growing population with a
stable (and small) budget.[46] For instance, the infant mortality rate, which
had dropped during the 1980s, rose again in the 1990s.[47] Epidemics such as
dengue fever, malaria, and cholera regularly swept through Nicaragua during the first half of the 1990s. These high levels of sickness and mortality
may be attributed, in part, to drops in the government's per capita spending
on health care.[48] But in large part, the poor health of the population was
simply a function of its steadily increasing poverty.

Conclusion

At the inauguration of the Ministry of Social Action, President Violeta Barrios de Chamorro explained that, through its social policy, her government
would bring about "the peace that my husband Pedro Joaquín Chamorro
imagined, the peace in Nicaragua for which he was assassinated fifteen years
ago. . . . [In his words:] 'We want peace based on a regime that creates the
economic, social, and political conditions that satisfy the needs of the people
. . . a just and egalitarian society where there is no lack of bread, education,
health, and housing for anyone.' "[49] By at least one economic measure,
progress was made in fulfilling this vision in the years following his assassination. In 1978, the year of his death, the Somoza administration spent
20 percent of its budget on the "social sector." That percentage climbed in
subsequent years: to 24 percent in 1985, 31 percent in 1990, and 44 percent
in 1994.[50]

That rising percentage of the national budget did not necessarily translate into a larger budget for each ministry. Instead, the rising percentage for
the social sector illustrates the fact that other areas of the state took even
deeper cuts during the 1990s. While these budgetary constraints could have

been foreseen, the development of social policy over the course of the Chamorro administration was not obvious at the onset.

One change that could have been predicted as early as the 1990 electoral campaign was an ideological one, as Violeta Chamorro was a conservative Catholic who rejected the threat to traditional power relations that the Sandinista revolution had represented.[51] Ideology alone, however, does not explain the shape of social policy in the 1990s. While the Ministry of Education embraced traditional Catholic values, the Ministry of Health seemed to ignore the ideological instructions from the administration.[52] To explain why social policies varied so much within the same administration, social welfare, education, and health policies have been analyzed here in relational terms. This analysis confirms the value of Philip Williams's two-level approach to political transitions, in which they occur within civil society as well as within the national political arena.[53]

By 1995, Pedro Joaquín Chamorro's vision of a country "where there is no lack of bread, education, health, and housing for anyone" was far from fulfilled. President Violeta Chamorro was not solely responsible for this lack of progress, as she was under severe pressure to eliminate many of the services that might have furthered her late husband's vision. But she and her administration deserve blame for the types of cuts that were made. Budgetary cuts and programmatic changes were consistently made in ways that reduced the power and resources of the most vulnerable, especially the elderly, women, and the poor. These sorts of changes were not unique to Nicaragua, of course. But the heightened expectations and mobilization of the 1980s meant that this return to marginalization was resisted, if sometimes ineffectively.

Notes

1. The focus here will be on unions, although the author recognizes that civil society also encompasses other groups. Some of those groups attempted to influence social policy (though less consistently than the unions) throughout the 1990s. For example, the women's movement actively opposed the ideological changes in education, and there were heated debates in the press over cuts in social welfare and health services.

2. Philip J. Williams, "Dual Transitions from Authoritarian Rule: Popular and Electoral Democracy in Nicaragua," *Comparative Politics* 26, no. 2 (January 1994): 171.

3. Instituto Nicaragüense de Seguridad Social y Bienestar, *Informe evaluativo de diez años y nueve meses de revolución en el INSSBI* (Managua: INSSBI, April 1990), 15.

4. Ibid., 32, 43.

5. Ibid., 43.

6. In response to a survey, INSSBI was mentioned, more than any other institution, as a good source for help with family-related legal problems. Karen Kampwirth, "Cambios y continuidades en las relaciones familiares de poder:

Resultados de una encuesta del Barrio Altagracia, Managua" (Managua, unpublished manuscript, 1992), 25–26.

7. One target for cuts in the early 1990s was child care. Perhaps because organized resistance was more difficult in rural areas than in cities, the rural child-care centers suffered the most cuts. By mid-1991 no centers had been closed in Region III (most of which is the city of Managua), but all twenty-two centers in Region I had been eliminated (Livia Chévez, interview with author, Managua, June 27, 1991; Reyna Isabel Velázquez, interview with author, Managua, June 26, 1991). There were also reductions in INSSBI's services for battered women. Workshops against domestic violence were eliminated and INSSBI had ceased to mediate between couples in cases of domestic violence by mid-1991 (Vanexa Moralla, interview with author, Managua, June 17, 1991).

8. Simeón Rizo Castellón, "Exigencias y posibilidades de una reforma al sistema de seguridad social en Nicaragua" (Managua, unpublished manuscript, September 10, 1992).

9. In December 1990, INSSBI had 4,341 employees; see INSSBI, *Memoria 1990* (Managua: INSSBI, 1991), 37. By 1995, INSSBI's predecessors had fewer than half as many employees, a total of 1,700, of whom 800 worked for FONIF (Arlé Martínez, interview with author, Managua, May 5, 1995) and 900 for INSS (Mario Flores, interview with author, Managua, May 11, 1995).

10. There were no equally significant changes in the numbers of teachers employed by the Ministry of Education: 26,503 teachers were employed in 1990, 27,560 in 1991, 26,685 in 1992, 28,994 in 1993, 21,888 in 1994, and 21,606 in February 1995 (Ministerio de Educación, Managua, unpublished documents). Similarly, the number of people employed by the Ministry of Health was quite stable: 19,206 employed in 1991, 19,977 in 1992, 21,043 in 1993, and 21,935 in 1994 (Ministerio de Salud, Dirección General de Recursos Humanos, "Series históricas de algunos cargos substantivos, 1991 a marzo de 1994," Managua, unpublished document).

11. Reyna Isabel Velázquez, interview with author, Managua, May 8, 1995.

12. Ana Esquivel, interview with author, Managua, May 12, 1995.

13. Two of Nicaragua's four daily newspapers (*Barricada* and *La Prensa*) did not report the ministerial change. One paper mentioned the creation of FONIF but not the elimination of the BI of INSSBI (Claudia Chamorro G., "Chamorro amplia aparato burocrático del Estado," *La Tribuna*, January 11, 1995). Only *El Nuevo Diario* got right the details of the state restructuring, but without expressing the concern one would have expected given that newspaper's editorial line (Aura Lila Morena, "Incorporan cinco mujeres al gabinete presidencial: Crean dos nuevos entes autónomos, INSSBI dividido en tres entidades," *El Nuevo Diario*, January 11, 1995).

14. Gobierno de Nicaragua, *FONIF, Fondo nicaragüense de la niñez y la familia* (Managua: Lotería Nacional, 1995), 3.

15. Arlé Martínez, interview with author.

16. Reyna Isabel Velázquez, interview with author, May 8, 1995.

17. Danilo Barrios, interview with author, Managua, May 12, 1995.

18. Gobierno de Nicaragua, *FONIF*, 21–22.

19. Idalia García, interview with author, Managua, May 9, 1995.

20. Ministerio de Acción Social, *Memoria institucional, 1994* (Managua: MAS, 1995).

21. Average salary from Idalia García, interview with author. The dollar value was calculated on the exchange rate at the time of the interview of 7.5 *córdobas* to U.S. $1. While MAS's salaries of 56 *córdobas* per week (the equivalent of 224 per month) were especially miserable, MAS was not the only ministry to pay low wages. The basic salary for a public grade-school teacher without experience or

professional qualifications was 400 *córdobas* per month (Mario Quintana, interview with author, Managua, May 8, 1995). An administrator and teacher with twenty-five years' experience told me she earned 600-some *córdobas* (Guadalupe Jarquín, interview with author, Managua, May 3, 1995). Wages varied greatly from agency to agency; for instance, a secretary with four years' experience at INSS and no prior work experience was paid 1,070 *córdobas* per month (Fátima Zelaya, interview with author, Managua, May 3, 1995).

22. MAS, *Memoria institucional, 1994,* 78.

23. Ibid., 25, 80.

24. See, for example, Frances Moore Lappé and Joseph Collins, *World Hunger: Twelve Myths* (San Francisco: Food First, 1986), 106–7, 189.

25. Deborah Brandt, "Popular Education," in *Nicaragua: The First Five Years,* ed. Thomas W. Walker (New York: Praeger, 1985), 328.

26. "La señora Chamorro debe una disculpa," *Barricada,* April 26, 1995; William Roiz Murillo, "Alfabetizadores rechazan afirmaciones de Chamorro, Tünnerman: Doña Violeta sabe que no fue así," *Barricada,* April 27, 1995.

27. César Escobar, interview with author, Managua, March 17, 1991.

28. Liliana Ayalde, interview with author, Managua, October 13, 1992; Ken Schofield, public talk, Managua, July 22, 1991.

29. Juan José Montenegro, interview with author, Managua, June 4, 1991.

30. The "textbooks" refer only to the Morals and Civics series. On others produced during the 1990s, see Robert F. Arnove, *La educación como terreno de conflicto* (Managua: Editorial UCA, 1995), 99–119, published in English as *Education as Contested Terrain: Nicaragua, 1979–1993* (Boulder, CO: Westview Press, 1994).

31. Humberto Belli was vice minister of education from April 1990, when the Chamorro administration took office, until he replaced the first minister of education, Sofonias Cisneros, in January 1991.

32. Elida Zelaya de Solórzano, interview with author, Managua, January 31, 1991.

33. César Escobar Morales, *Aprendemos a convivir: Civica, moral, y urbanidad, sexto grado* (Lima, Peru: Editorial Labrusa, n.d.), 4–12.

34. MED, *Lineamientos del Ministerio de Educación en el Nuevo Gobierno de Salvación Nacional* (Managua: MED, 1990), 13.

35. Arnove, *La educación como terreno de conflicto,* 55.

36. MED, "Guia operativa: Para la organización y funcionamiento de las instancias que participan en el proceso de descentralización educativa" (Managua, unpublished manuscript, April 3, 1995), 3–15.

37. By May 1995, sixty-two high schools had become autonomous. See MED, "62 centros en la autonomía," *Revista Maestro* (May 1995): 10.

38. Francisco Arellano Oviedo, "Autonomía administrativa: Modelo original, realista, y eficaz," *Revista Maestro* (November 1994): 11.

39. Thomas Bossert, "Health Care," in Walker, ed., *Nicaragua,* 352–53.

40. Paola Pérez-Alemán, "Economic Crisis and Women in Nicaragua," in *Unequal Burden: Economic Crises, Persistent Poverty, and Women's Work,* ed. Lourdes Beneria and Shelley Feldman (Boulder, CO: Westview Press, 1992), 241.

41. MINSA, *Política nacional de salud* (Managua: Ediciones Internacionales, 1993); ibid., *Plan maestro de salud, 1991–1996* (Managua: MINSA, 1991).

42. Throughout the 1980s the Ministry of Health's budget rose steadily until it reached a high point in 1988 of the equivalent of U.S. $146,440,000. Health budgets from 1990 to 1993, respectively, were $76,640,000, $67,500,000, $79,360,000, and $79,070,000. In the 1990s the number of people employed by the ministry

climbed slowly. By 1993 the number of employees had returned to 1987 levels, although the budget was much smaller. In 1987, MINSA employed 21,310 people with a budget of $101,770,000; in 1993 it employed 21,043 with a budget of only $79,070,000. MINSA, "Series históricas"; ibid., "Evolución de la fuerza de trabajo, 1980–1987" (Managua, unpublished document); ibid., Dirección de Presupuesto, "Ejecución presupuestaria institucional, Período 1980–1992" (Managua, unpublished document).

43. MINSA, *Política nacional de salud: Sesión extraordinaria* (Managua: no publisher, August 27, 1993).

44. FETSALUD et al., *Las reformas en los servicios de salud a partir de 1990* (Managua: no publisher, May 1994), 25.

45. José Humberto Murillo, interview with author, Managua, May 15, 1995.

46. In 1993, Nicaragua had a 3.5 percent annual growth rate; each mother had an average of 5.6 children (MINSA, *Política nacional de salud*, 13).

47. The infant mortality rate was 61 per 1,000 in 1989, 56 per 1,000 in 1990, and 71 per 1,000 in 1992. See "Why Social Conflict?" *Envío* 12, no. 138 (January–March 1993): 15.

48. One source estimated that spending averaged $35 per capita in 1987–1989 and only $16 per capita in 1993 and 1994 (FETSALUD et al., *Las reformas en los servicios de salud*, 6).

49. MAS, *La agenda social* (Managua: IMPRIMATUR, 1993), 4.

50. MAS, *Memoria institucional, 1994*, 88.

51. Karen Kampwirth, "The Mother of the Nicaraguans: Doña Violeta and the UNO's Gender Agenda," *Latin American Perspectives* 23, no. 1 (January 1996): 67–86.

52. The issue of population growth illustrates this division within the state. MED administrators were not concerned by rapid population growth; instead, they thought that the real problem was promiscuity. Sex education, therefore, taught abstinence and natural family planning methods, while artificial contraception was only mentioned in a negative way. In contrast, MINSA administrators thought of rapid population growth as a real problem and so promoted the use of contraception.

53. Williams, "Dual Transitions from Authoritarian Rule."

8

The Environment

Desirée Elizondo

Nicaragua has the greatest natural resource endowment of any Central American state.[1] In the vision of national utopias, only the idea of building an interoceanic canal competes with the conviction that sustainable natural resource use is Nicaragua's main road to development. Of the country's 130,000 square kilometers, approximately one-half consists of forests. The greatest potential is found in the tropical rainforest, which runs from the northern to southern borders and is being considered as a corridor for biodiversity. Another third of the territory is composed of aquatic environments, including the largest lake in the isthmus; marine and freshwater resources include the most underharvested fisheries in the region and several endemic freshwater fish species. Nonrenewable resources include large precious metal deposits, marble, and calcite. The Autonomous Regions on the Caribbean coast hold nearly two-thirds of the country's natural resources. Ninety percent of the river basins drain through the Miskito lowlands—part of the largest coastal plains in Mesoamerica—and empty into the Caribbean. The continental shelf provides a habitat for one of the most extensive seagrass meadows in the world and large banks of coral reefs and is home to more than 80 percent of the endangered green sea turtles remaining in the Atlantic Ocean basin.[2]

Fortunately, the environmental issue remained relatively free of the politicized or ideologized discussion that usually taints public debate in Nicaragua. After a decade of revolution in which all strategies were ultimately subordinated to national defense, the transition in the environmental area was less traumatic than in other state sectors. The first half of the 1990s opened a space in the international arena for formulating sustainable development policies, and the Chamorro government used it effectively. The problem was its failure to implement its own policy guidelines and thus put their repercussions to the test in national life, particularly among peasant producers. However, the debate and conflicts between a pro-investment wing and a pro-environmental one within the government itself was the period's most important feature. The conclusion of that unresolved debate, not to mention the future of the region's three most important biological reserves (discussed later), would depend on the 1996 elections and the political leanings of the new government that took office on January 10, 1997.

Sandinista Environmental Policy

In the euphoria of the triumph of the Sandinista revolution in July 1979, the Government Junta of National Reconstruction inaugurated a new natural resource policy. Its first step was to decree a series of laws nationalizing the renewable and nonrenewable natural resources conceded to local elites and international companies by the Somoza dictatorship. Cancellation of the forestry concessions and, especially, nationalization of the gold mines were among the national demands against the Somoza dynasty. They were also a logical consequence of the anti-imperialist nature of the Sandinista National Liberation Front (FSLN). The resource extraction enclaves created by the foreign companies in a large part of Nicaraguan territory had tremendous social and environmental consequences. Extensive pine forests in the center and north of the country had been converted into pastureland, while important rivers in the northeastern mining triangle of Siuna-Bonanza-Rosita had been contaminated by the toxic waste dumped into them over the decades by the mining companies.

In the improvisational atmosphere that reigned in the first months of the revolutionary government, environmentalists linked to the guerrilla movement influenced the new leaders, who in turn used such environmental problems to make political pronouncements to promote a new philosophy of natural resource use. Hand in hand with nationalizing lumbering and mining activities, the Sandinista government created the Nicaraguan Institute of Natural Resources and the Environment (IRENA) as an autonomous superinstitution. Although IRENA was endowed with the legal faculties required to manage and protect renewable and nonrenewable natural resources, this status had little practical effect.[3] It did, however, reflect the political importance originally assigned to the sector linked to natural resources.

This environmental idealism lasted only as long as it took the new leaders to realize the economic relevance of the natural resources. Also in the first year, other state institutions such as the People's Forestry Corporation (CORFOP), the Nicaraguan Mining Institute (INMINE), and the Nicaraguan Fisheries Institute (INPESCA) were created to set policies for managing and using the primary natural resources. These institutions established a political and economic power axis that ultimately turned them into either large sectoral state corporations or oversight bodies for such corporations.[4] Their approach to natural resource use differed little from the foreign companies in that the focal point was extraction without considering the ecological potential or the activities needed to reestablish the ecosystems.

The initial attention to the environmental sector was quickly displaced by other priorities. An agrarian reform law dramatically altering the land-tenure structure was passed in mid-1981, and it became one of the main underpinnings of rural policy during the 1980s. Although the regulatory component of this law contained important elements regarding sustainable land use, such environmental aspects were not consistently integrated into the agrarian policies that accompanied it. The law obliged any agrarian reform beneficiary to comply with soil protection and erosion control. These formal environmental norms were never put into practice, however, partly because the political and administrative apparatus that headed up the agrarian reform had neither the knowledge nor the technical instruments needed to ensure compliance.

Even with the radical changes in land tenure and the technical deployment aimed at fostering peasant crop production, these policies resulted in neither increased agro-ecological knowledge nor productivity of the agricultural and forestry systems. Rural technification was carried out through agricultural technology packages designed according to type of crop, which implied a massive use of inputs without taking into account soil fertility, climate, or other natural, environmental, and social factors that would adjust technology to the conditions of the Nicaraguan peasantry. The tasks of meeting the planned production goals, fulfilling the food security strategy, and socially and administratively organizing the state production complexes and cooperatives were better understood than agro-ecology. In addition, the U.S. economic blockade induced the government to import a huge back-up stock of pesticides from third countries, while the macroeconomic policy of overvaluing the domestic currency led to exponential growth in the use of these toxins, with negative environmental consequences.[5]

The war of aggression conducted by the Contras was the other phenomenon that severely affected forestry and agricultural activity in the country's central and northern zones. It ripped apart the peasantry's social and economic fabric and triggered the resettlement of many communities. The Sandinista government's priorities centered on defense, leading it to focus on consolidating the organizational and military aspects in these zones. The war had unimaginable social and economic costs in the rural areas.[6] Yet, paradoxically, during the years of greatest military confrontation, the National Forestry Service statistics reveal a drastic drop in the expansion of the agricultural frontier and register a regeneration of forest in important areas in the center and Caribbean coast of the country.[7]

With a new political and economic system oriented toward the war, the environmental debate ceased being a government priority, and no counterpart in civil society forced it back on the agenda. IRENA's weak institutional role facilitated its political relegation, to the extreme of being absorbed as a separate Department of Natural Resource Management in the Ministry of Agricultural Development and Agrarian Reform (Ministerio de Desarrollo Agrícola y Reforma Agraria, or MIDINRA) in 1988, when the government collapsed a number of institutions to deal with its financial crisis. Ecological disasters, resulting from a failure to make environmental impact studies of the government's major development projects, were a consequence of the absence of a credible environmental interlocutor during the Sandinista government. One of the best-known cases was the coffee modernization project known as CONARCA in the Department of Carazo, where 20,000 hectares of forest and coffee plants were razed to eliminate a coffee bean plague, which resulted in permanent environmental damage.

Despite the lack of an environmental policy that could reconcile economic development plans with the environment, the Sandinista government chalked up important achievements in getting natural resource conservation and management projects under way. A new approach to forestry use was formulated with the support of the Swedish government, and the sector was considerably strengthened. According to IRENA, "this plan was focused on industrial forestry development, having identified concrete actions as well as the investments required to put the forestry sector in a state to significantly contribute to national socioeconomic development."[8] IRENA's low profile allowed a concentration of technicians in base-line studies and planning, which gave the institution a more technical character. It carried out soil studies and management plans for the country's main river basins. With a statist vision, it also prepared strategic plans for areas of major social and economic importance such as the western watershed area where the project known as Heroes and Martyrs of Veracruz was developed.[9]

The revolution attracted significant foreign assistance, which promoted projects of rural development, alternative technology generation, reforestation, and watershed conservation. Important experiences in the field of agroecology and organic agriculture had a major local impact, as in the Santa Lucia municipality, where the Campesino a Campesino (Peasant to Peasant) project was initiated.[10] At an experimental level, numerous applied agronomy research projects were documented at the level of individual farms. The most significant investment of the revolutionary decade, however, was in preparing a generation of technical professionals, who now constitute Nicaragua's most valuable human resource capital in the environmental field.

The Chamorro Administration and the Environment

Rupture and Transition

After an initial phase in which negotiating the conditions of the transition as well as ending the war and disarming the armed groups took priority, the new government embraced a stabilization and structural adjustment plan within a classic neoliberal framework. In the state spheres administering this new economic, agrarian, and social model, the change of government indicated a significant break with the Sandinista revolution (see Chapters 5, 6, and 7, this volume). In the environmental sector, in contrast, the transition kept the existing institutions and even restored greater rank in the new governmental hierarchy to IRENA by unshackling it from the agricultural ministry when MIDINRA's entire structure was dismantled.[11] The born-again institute was restructured under the leadership of Dr. Jaime Incer Barquero, a respected scientist.[12] The professional and "environmentalist" ties between IRENA's technical elite and its new minister gave the institution stability and strength during the government transition.

The international community continued to support IRENA's work. Expecting the new government to undertake an economic policy in tune with the population's needs and Nicaragua's natural potential, cooperating agencies engaged in a strategic planning process coordinated by Incer. The overall framework of this planning process was laid out in the "Conservation Strategy for Sustainable Development" and the "Scheme of Environmental Territorial Planning." Land use planning and utilization of biological diversity constituted two crucial paradigms of sustainability in Nicaragua.

The quatrain of strategic policies drawn up during the Chamorro government was complemented by two important efforts: the Forestry Action Plan and the Environmental Action Plan. The first, with a more sectoral approach, set forth a policy aimed at reactivating the forestry sector's contribution to the economy in a sustained fashion. It included five key programs at an implementation cost of U.S. $272 million (14.2 percent of GDP). The Environmental Action Plan had a more institutional approach that attempted to relate sectoral policies with the environment. Signed into law by President Violeta Chamorro in 1993, it served as the foundation for the creation of IRENA's successor, the Ministry of the Environment and Natural Resources (Ministerio del Ambiente y Recursos Naturales, or MARENA), in January 1994.

Without question, the strategic planning guidelines were important accomplishments of the Chamorro government. Prepared with a participatory methodology, they were amply recognized by Nicaragua's environmental and scientific community. Nonetheless, the government sector more linked to traditional economic agents viewed these policies as mere "good intentions" that lacked economic viability. Although the government succeeded in formulating a coherent vision of the environment and natural resources and put a priority on attracting foreign financing for important conservation and development programs, both its public discourse and its practice revealed ambiguity from the outset. It showed little interest in articulating its environmental strategies with its economic program.

On the one hand, the economic program and the initiatives of the Ministry of Economy and Development (MEDE) were geared to promoting foreign investment and making use of the country's forestry, energy, fishing, and mining resources. The vision of the government's pro-investment wing grew out of the commercial underexploitation of renewable natural resources, which was generating considerable economic losses for the country.[13] The goal was thus to attract investors willing to bring capital into a politically high-risk setting, without the legal framework that would protect their investments in the medium and long term, and to recover the 1970s export figures in wood, shellfish, and ore. In exchange, the government promised to deregulate the economy, open up trade, provide protection from fees, apply export incentives, and streamline fiscal and administrative requirements. In fact, seafood exports rose from U.S. $10 million in 1990 to U.S. $80 million in 1995, in a context of restricted business competition.[14]

As of the mid-1990s, the ecological effect of this increased fishing effort had not been evaluated. The same ministry promoting fishing investment was also charged with monitoring and investigating the fishery resources. MEDE repeatedly declared that marine resources in Nicaragua are underexploited and inexhaustible. Others argued that this level of fishing, using legally permitted practices, was unsustainable and was destroying ecologically important habitats.

To promote mining activity, the government first privatized the assets of the old mines—a process in which the miners' unions participated—and gave exploitation rights to the new companies. Following that, it began to speed up the provision of exploration rights. By October 1995 the government had turned over 17 percent of the national territory in concessions and set a target of finishing the paperwork before the October 1996 elections on the additional 24 percent that had been requested.[15] MEDE projected that production of gold would go from 44,700 troy ounces in 1995 to 205,000 by the year 2000. This pro-investment vision gives a hint of Nicaragua's high economic potential and of the possibility of beginning to exploit the new deposits that might be found through the prospecting studies and exploration that the new companies would be conducting. Although government discourse emphasized the great technological development that the world had experienced in geological exploration, traditional methods were still being used in Nicaragua at the time.

On the other hand, major conservation and development projects for strategic natural areas of the country were prepared, inspired by national strategies and backed by the international community and the influence of the world environmental discourse. Pushed by its pro-environment wing, the government decreed a number of legally protected conservation areas totaling 13 percent of the national territory, in which natural resource use would be restricted and limited. The lack of coordination in state policy generated strong conflicts between MEDE and MARENA, which prepared contradictory action plans for the same areas.

Three important natural reserves constituted the largest and most important biological areas of the Central American region. They were also the sites of the greatest conflict and challenges to Nicaragua's environmental future. The Indio Maiz Reserve (3,000 sq. km.) and the Bosawás Reserve (8,000 sq. km.) contain the densest rainforests anywhere on the American continent except for the Amazon. Despite the scientific, ecotourist, and alternative development potential of these ecosystems due to the huge biological diversity found within them, the expansion of cattle ranching and traditional agriculture pushed the peasant population toward the reserves' buffer zones, where it was calculated that some 70,000 hectares of forest were being lost annually.[16] Important ore deposits are located in those reserves, and the nongovernmental organizations concerned with the environment developed their denunciation and vigilance work to ensure that the government did not offer concessions within the reserves.

The third strategic area is the Miskito Cays biological reserve, located on the Caribbean Sea's marine platform. It includes the Miskito Cays archipelago and a large part of the coastal wetlands, including many coastal lagoons on the mainland. The coral reefs and other marine ecosystems there provide food and habitat for numerous marine species, including traditional, commercially important species. However, the nature of the Río Coco sedimentary basin also creates conditions for petroleum reserves, and the government's plans to open that river basin to petroleum exploration raised a great risk regarding the area's future sustainability. Beyond the major strategies, the government had no plan of action to promote sustainable development of the buffer zones and conservation of the natural reserves. In that field, the most important achievements were in the work of civil society. Local-level projects of nongovernmental organizations with a more developmental than conservational vision generated knowledge and promoted sustainable management practices in the buffer zones.

Very few studies had been carried out inside Nicaragua on the potential of its biodiversity and the ecology of its rainforests. Perhaps the greatest knowledge resided with the indigenous communities that had cohabited with the forest since ancestral times. The national universities had neither the financial resources nor the links with the indigenous communities to promote and study the natural ecosystems. Among the few initiatives, the most consistent one was promoted by the Center for Research and Documentation of the Atlantic Coast (Centro de Investigación y Documentación de la Costa Atlántica, or CIDCA) with U.S. academics who scientifically followed the evolution of the southern Caribbean region's rainforest, which was devastated by Hurricane Joan in 1988.[17]

The environmental issue most broadly debated by the population and avidly covered by the media during the Chamorro administration was its provision of concessions. After the government's frustrated attempt to concede vast forest lands in the northern Caribbean region to a Taiwanese corporation's megaproject in 1991, public concern for the destiny of Nicaragua's natural resources grew significantly. Although debate centered on questioning the handing over of concessions in legally protected conservation areas, the fear of environmental professionals and the university community was that huge areas of national territory were being offered in concessions without any legal and normative framework to protect the country's interests.

The presence of two environmental philosophies within the same government contributed to weakening MARENA and repeating its predecessor's history of political isolation and limited ability to influence state development plans during the 1980s. Despite MARENA's impeccable institutional and legal mandate, it did not escape the national tradition of palace intrigue. The executive branch awarded its vice ministerial posts to political allies, resulting in an inevitable clash between the scientific minister and the political vice ministers. Mutual charges of corruption seriously undermined the institution's credibility.

The International Context of the 1990s

The United Nations Conference on the Environment and Development (UNCED) in 1992 in Rio de Janeiro, also known as the Earth Summit, was the first such international event to occur during the Chamorro administration. Preparations for it provided an important guideline for environmental mobilization, since the government managed to present a national vision of the environmental problem in drawing up its strategies. Its report pulled together existing knowledge in sectoral studies made by specialists from both public and private institutions.

The leadership on environmental issues within the new government team also succeeded in projecting itself at the regional level. Nicaragua set itself up as the main promoter of a Central American environmental agenda and strategy within a framework of sustainable development. One of the first results of all these efforts was that the Central American countries went to the Earth Summit with a unified report on the environmental problems in the isthmus. The conference was the first international event to give the new government signals about the need to incorporate the environment into its national and international agenda.

Since copious financial resources were expected to become available to developing countries after the conference, and Nicaragua was the Latin American country with the most forests after Brazil, the government went to work. President Chamorro capitalized on the region's political efforts to attract world attention with its thesis of Sustainable Development for the region, even holding an ecological presidential summit in Managua in 1993, which was attended by renowned world leaders. The main political backing came from Washington with the presence of Vice President Al Gore. But the expected economic backing never came. The government lacked the ability to market the priorities and projects outlined in its strategic plans. Within a few weeks, the greatest ecological event in Nicaragua's history was passé.

The international context of the 1990s unquestionably had a positive political influence on the institutionalization of the state, and thus on its environmental policies. Greatly dependent on bilateral and multilateral foreign aid, the government was very sensitive to the oversight that donors and the international lending agencies exercise over that aid. Despite its limitations in concretizing projects and seeking new financial resources, international cooperation and the national budget for the environmental sector increased during the Chamorro government.[18] The presence of donors and interlocutors from the international lending agencies was one factor that cushioned the de facto isolation of environmental policies and catalyzed the main reforms in the environmental management framework.

In the last two years of its term, the government made significant strides in the institutional sphere, with a new MARENA minister who enjoyed greater political confidence from the executive branch.[19] It also made important advances in preparing major investment projects for the environmental and natural resource sector with international financial agencies. One of the results was that a reform was pushed through in MARENA itself, turning an institution oriented toward forestry and an operative role in implementing field projects into an environmental ministry with normative and regulatory functions. That challenge required the creation of a technical area specializing in the protection of environmental quality and the reconceptualization of the institution's overall vision.

In the context of state reform and the conditioning of credits from the World Bank and the Inter-American Development Bank, the greatest institutional and juridical changes occurred in the 1990s. Although the environmental commitments of these credits were seen as conditions placed on the government, they paradoxically allowed the development of a more integral view of environmental management, which was capitalized on by MARENA. One visible result was that in reordering the public sector and reforming the public utilities, the inclusion of environmental considerations became a requirement in all investment projects for generating and distributing energy, as well as in the regulatory laws for the provision of services and exploitation of natural resources. Together with the creation of regulatory bodies to oversee the new utility companies, environmental units were created within the new institutions and financial resources were earmarked to strengthen them. Another result was the promotion of a juridical reform of the environmental framework, which sought to organize and modernize natural resource and environmental legislation. Important bills were drafted with a more sustainable and integral vision of natural resource utilization and greater coherence with the international environmental agreements that Nicaragua had signed.

One very important event in environmental legislation was an initiative by nongovernmental organizations to submit a comprehensive environmental bill to the National Assembly in 1993. The government responded by quickly drafting its own bill. The resulting existence of two competing bills led to the creation of a mixed commission to reconcile them into a joint effort by the state and the nongovernmental organizations. The legislative package that originated with that global bill, the General Law on the Environment and Natural Resources, was completed with specific legislation for each natural resource (forests, fishing, and mines). Strong obstacles existed to approving that set of bills. During the 1995 legislative session, the Higher Council on Private Enterprise (COSEP) requested that the National Assembly suspend debate on it and succeeded in getting it temporarily shelved. However, according to declarations of the president of the Assembly's Environmental Commission, the first set of laws was expected to go into effect before the end of the Chamorro government's term.

The inclusion of prevention and control of environmental contamination as a priority for MARENA allowed the development of new strategies and regulations to reduce ecological damage caused by the economy.[20] The new model of environmental administration was not conceptualized according to a traditional strictly regulatory and centralized approach. Rather, it recognized the responsibility of society and the role of local institutions and governments to protect the environment. Although the Chamorro government promoted the decentralization of public administration in its discourse in general terms, it made no effort to regulate the 1988 Municipal Law and transferred neither clear responsibility nor the necessary financial resources to the municipal mayoralties.

One pending point on the environmental agenda was the relationship between the governments of the North and South Atlantic Autonomous Regions and the Managua government regarding management and usufruct of the natural resources in that vast and resource-rich area. The absence of a regulatory law to buttress the 1987 Autonomy Statute undermined the autonomous governments' negotiating capacity. Throughout the Chamorro administration's term it signed only partial agreements giving the autonomous authorities some participation in providing forestry concessions and collecting taxes, fees, and lease payments on them.

The development of the central government's environmental protection philosophy was influenced by the environmental model of Denmark, which became the leading donor for this sector—thus allowing a more dynamic environmental vision to be promoted to the private sector, with a flexible framework of norms for the industrial sector that would permit the companies to self-regulate their environmental management (clean technology, environmental auditing, etc.). Although Nicaraguan private enterprise at first appeared receptive to the environmental discussion, its conservative character led it eventually to dismiss the government's environmental norms as just another tax. This position devolved into the traditional discourse that disqualifies environmental protection as a brake on economic development. Very few companies proposed improving the atmosphere of their factories and reducing the load of contaminants that they were dumping into the environment. However, under pressure from public opinion and the fledgling environmental organizations, the government did occasionally interfere. For instance, it requested the petroleum sector to make an environmental study of the whole zone affected by the Esso oil refinery and related activity in the immediate environs of Lake Xolotlán and the Asososca Lagoon, which is an important drinking water reservoir for the city of Managua.

With Nicaragua's reinsertion into the international financial community, financing opportunities opened up in the multilateral organizations for the environmental sector. With little coordination on the part of the government institutions, technical units financed by the World Bank and the Inter-American Development Bank proliferated. These units began preparing investment projects that would have a considerable medium- and long-term impact on the quality of Nicaragua's environment and the state of its natural resources.

Three projects, with a short-term investment projection of U.S. $126 million, were scheduled to enter into the implementation phase in 1996: the cleanup and recovery of Lake Xolotlán; the Protierra project, related to natural resource management in the northwest; and the Socioenvironmental and Forestry Development Program, to be implemented in the north-central part of the country. After many years of discussion and the preparation of plans to begin cleaning up Lake Xolotlán, which receives the city's waste water and untreated residue from its factories, for the first time an action plan was prepared with financial backing. In its first phase, the project would develop the sanitary infrastructure needed to collect and treat sewage and clean up the lake's southwestern edge. In addition, it contemplated conservation works and management of the lake's watershed. Protierra contemplated tax incentives and municipal funds to develop investment projects in conservation and development works. Together with the forestry program to be implemented in the country's north-central zone, these projects were aimed at initiating a process in which the local government would appropriate the strategies.

This package of internationally financed projects would represent one of the principal environmental challenges for the government elected in 1996. The increased foreign debt demanded efficient and coherent administration as a counterpart so society could enjoy the long-term benefits. If that did not happen, the country would run the risk that its future would continue to be mortgaged. In short, at issue was the move from a theory of sustainable development to its practice.

Final Reflections

The greatest success of the transition process propelled by the government of President Chamorro in the environmental sphere was the correct interpretation of the opportunities that the international context of the 1990s offered. The governmental leadership was visionary in formulating sustainable development policies, articulating international cooperation, and going forward with an institutional reform process. Its main deficit, however, lay in the fact that these very strategies were conceived more for external than internal consumption. In other words, the new policies responded more to the dynamic and requirements of the international organizations and less to the raw domestic realities that urged immediate change. The challenge that remained, therefore, was to turn the environmental strategy around so that it faced inward, toward a country submerged in poverty that had not yet derived any benefit from these policies.

Going against the grain of the governmental discourse about sustainable development, an accelerated deterioration of the country's natural resource base was under way. The rural population's needs for firewood, the colonization of new land and the burning of forests, the inexorable advance of the agricultural frontier, together with the confusion about land tenure, were generating a social pressure that seriously threatened the forest reserves. Those reserves, it should not be forgotten, constitute the patrimony of all humanity, given their extension and biodiversity. Soils clearly appropriate for forests were being devoured year after year by producers, pushed by an agricultural model so deeply in crisis that peasants could not even resolve their own subsistence needs and were turned into net purchasers of basic grains. That potential danger for Nicaragua's reserves began to knock on the doors of the buffer zones, where financial policies offered credits for felling timber.

Thus, by the mid-1990s, a change in the relationship between economic policy, natural resources, and sustainable development appeared imperative. It would be necessary to comprehend the rural population's identity and its relation to the natural resources. Cultural and social diversity required that the government's sustainable development strategies be adapted so that they would have an impact on people's lives. The macropolicies would have to reach down to the local level and put into effect coherent action plans that incorporated the environmental component as an integral part of the economic policy, not as an accessory to it. During the Chamorro administration, long-term concessions were given to foreign investors to exploit resources in the fishing, mining, and forestry sectors without the government having the oversight capacity or normative development required to ensure that environmental protection would be included and respected.

Nicaragua is a country in which individuals, not laws, and individual leaders, not institutions, have prevailed. Despite the advances of the last two years of the Chamorro administration as a result of constitutional reforms, institutions remained weak. Although the adjustment and reform of the state would have long-term benefits, that very process weakened institutions in the short term, generating a kind of impasse in the decision-making process. Concerns about this institutional weakness and uncertainty about what the next government would do grew as the 1996 electoral campaign got under way.

The government does not have exclusive responsibility for everything, however. The diverse expressions of civil society also have a share of responsibility for the success or failure of environmental policies. The proliferation of nongovernmental organizations in the 1990s did not correspond to the goals and expectations that they put forward. The majority wasted their energies in political denunciations (necessary but insufficient), and only a few directed ongoing efforts to the educational work that, over time, would bear fruit in transforming the productive culture. For its part, the traditional private sector, with its myopic mentality, remained a prisoner of its backwardness and prejudices. It perceived investment in the environment as a cost and any governmental regulation as highly suspicious. The lack of business modernization was also a consequence of the lack of social responsibility so typical of the neoliberal age.

By the mid-1990s it was obvious that the government would have to adjust its sustainable development plans to the sectors and regions that would have to implement them, encouraging the local communities and governments to participate in and take ownership of them. But much more than good governance, subjected to the scrutiny of the citizenry, is required to execute an effective environmental strategy. Only a genuine investment in environmental education would permit farmers, peasants, business people, and other individuals to incorporate an environmental vision into their personal decisions.

Notes

1. World Resources Institute, *World Resources, 1992–93* (New York: Oxford University Press, 1992).

2. J. Ryan, "Seagrass Meadows and Marine Plants on the Nicaraguan Caribbean Coast," WANI pamphlet # 15 (Managua: Universidad Centroamericana, 1994).

3. Among others, the mandate given to IRENA included policy development and enforcement, research and monitoring, management of conservation parks, river basin planning, and pollution abatement. Also placed under the same institution were the economic use of natural resources. All the tutelage related to natural

resources was given to one institution. Besides the lack of viability, this law reflected the double role often found in state organizations: on the one hand, the role of regulator and rule setter; and on the other, the role of user or game player.

4. The corporation's main role was to promote the economic development of state companies and to implement policies for the use of the natural resource base. As an example, the forestry corporation (CORFOP) had the mandate to dictate policy; manage all the tree plantations; implement lumbering activities (such as cutting, transporting, industrialization, marketing, and export); manage all the sawmills; and enforce the forestry law.

5. The import and distribution of agricultural inputs was centralized in one state company, which also oversaw huge stocks of pesticides. In 1993, MARENA found 1,500 metric tons of expired, banned, or toxic substances in the company's warehouses stored in nonsecured conditions. During this investigation, MARENA learned that underground dumping to get rid of expired products had been a common practice. The degree of soil and water contamination is not known. Studies were under way to examine this problem.

6. For details, see *Costos materiales y humanos de la guerra* (Managua: Instituto Histórico Centroamericano, Universidad Centroamericana, 1984).

7. Gobierno de Nicaragua, Plan de Acción Forestal, 1992.

8. Instituto Nicaragüense de Recursos Naturales, *Plan de Desarrollo Forestal, 1985* (Managua: IRENA, 1985).

9. The increase in cotton production between 1960 and 1980 and the misuse of pesticides and machinery generated an ecological crisis that reached alarming levels in this area. To restore the ecology, a project known as Erosion Control of the West (PCEO) was launched in 1982, with a very positive impact in establishing forestry plantations and windbreaks. After this experience, the project called Héroes y Mártires de Veracruz was designed with the goal of rehabilitating a greater portion of the degraded river basin.

10. The Campesino a Campesino program was initiated in 1987 after an exchange of experiences between members of the National Union of Farmers and Cattlemen (Unión Nacional de Agricultores y Ganaderos, or UNAG) and the Mexican association known as Development and Peace Service (Servicio de Desarrollo y Pacificación, or SEDEPAC). It had the objective of disseminating technology and strengthening ties between peasants. The program began in Santa Lucia with sixteen farmers and developed local technology to achieve sustainable agriculture. Farmers affiliated with the program sought training in sustainable practices, and in 1995 the program had a presence in twenty-six municipalities with two hundred promoters.

11. During the transition of power between the Sandinista and the Chamorro governments, the status of IRENA was reestablished by law. With the argument of fulfilling regional agreements, President Daniel Ortega signed a bill in April 1990 giving back the status assigned in 1979 to IRENA. The Chamorro government ratified it, and the legal status of IRENA was affirmed.

12. Jaime Incer Barquero is considered the father of environmentalism in Nicaragua. He is the founder of the Ecology School at the Universidad Centroamericana, Managua, where most ecologists in the country have been his students. Dr. Incer joined IRENA in 1983 for a short period. Under his influence, the Sandinista government declared a series of protected areas. He took over IRENA in 1990.

13. Author's interview with Carlos Abaunza, general director of the Natural Resources Division, Ministry of Economy and Development, Managua, January 5, 1996.

14. Ministerio de Economía y Desarrollo, *Comportamiento de los sectores productivos en 1995*, December 1995.

15. Ibid.

16. Different values are registered in relation to the deforestation rate. The rate given is taken from the Plan de Acción Forestal, 1992.

17. John H. Vandermeer and Ivvette Perfecto of the University of Michigan and Douglas H. Boucher of the University of Maryland have coordinated research projects and expeditions to the Nicaraguan rainforest. See especially two final reports to CIDCA—K. Yih, D. H. Boucher, and J. H. Vandermeer, "Efectos ecológicos del huracán Joan en el bosque tropical húmedo del sudeste de Nicaragua a los cuatro meses: Posibilidades de regeneración del bosque y recomendaciones," May 27, 1989; and J. H. Vandermeer and I. Perfecto, "Los bosques de la costa caribeña de Nicaragua: Tres años después del huracán Juana," 1991.

18. Foreign aid increased from U.S. $1.8 million in 1990 to U.S. $9.5 million in 1995, and the national budget increased from 2 million *córdobas* in 1990 to 16 million *córdobas* in 1995.

19. After the crisis of MARENA and the conflicts between Dr. Incer and the two vice ministers in October 1994, the team was replaced completely and Milton Caldera was appointed minister in November.

20. Two important by-laws were approved and implemented in 1995. The first law requires environmental impact assessment studies for major infrastructure and development projects. Although the system that was developed considers public hearings and participation of local governments in the evaluation process, only a few studies had been completed with public participation. The second law, "Measures for the Control of Pollution Generated by Domestic Sewage Discharge, Industry, and Agro-industry Waste Discharge," dictates the first set of effluent discharge standards for industry, agro-industry, and water treatment plants.

III

Groups and Institutions

It would be difficult to understand Nicaragua in the 1990s without taking into consideration how various groups and institutions were impacting and being impacted by the process of change. The first three chapters in this section focus on some of the principal political actors on the scene: parties and grass-roots organizations. In the lead chapter on the FSLN, Gary Prevost shows how various tensions—some having their origins in the 1970s and 1980s and others peculiar to the 1990s—led ultimately to a major fracturing of the Sandinista movement in the mid-1990s. In their chapter, Kenneth Coleman and Douglas Stuart H. discuss the evolution of seven party "families" and the tremendous fractionalization that developed over decades and was accentuated in the 1990s. Erica Polakoff and Pierre La Ramée describe the "resilient" grass-roots organizations, which, though besieged from several sides, were nevertheless able to play a significant role in the ongoing process of change.

This section continues with an examination of other groups and institutions and their relationship with the national political system: the former Contras, the peoples of the Atlantic Coast, the Church, the economic elite, the urban informal economic sector, and the mass media. Ariel Armony notes how the former Contras, struggling to hold the Chamorro government to promises made in 1990, evolved into several organizations with different types of leadership and strategy. Judy Butler traces the history of the peoples of the Atlantic Coast—long marginalized, misunderstood, and abused—from conflicts with pre-Sandinista governments to tension and open warfare with the Sandinistas themselves, to the successful negotiation of a landmark Autonomy Law in 1987, to renewed misunderstanding and abuse after 1990. Andrew Stein shows the complex reasons why the Catholic Church, which had opposed the Somoza regime and the Sandinistas, was also frequently critical of the Chamorro administration. In their chapters on the economic elite and the informal sector, Rose Spalding and John Speer expose what may be, to some, a surprising lack of unity within both of those groups in regard to the neoliberal economic policies of the 1990s. Finally, Kent Norsworthy describes striking changes in the character of the mass media from the Somoza period to the Sandinista era and into the Chamorro period.

9

The FSLN

Gary Prevost

In 1990 the Sandinista National Liberation Front suffered a surprising and devastating electoral defeat. In an unprecedented development, the FSLN, a party that had achieved power through revolutionary means, accepted its defeat and passed on the reins of government to the conservative coalition led by President Violeta Chamorro. The election defeat was a stunning blow to the FSLN, which was not prepared for its new role as the democratic opposition. As a result, the ensuing five years saw significant changes in the party as it turned away from its revolutionary past and plotted for a return to power by electoral means in 1996. The election defeat brought to the surface divisions within the FSLN that had been suppressed during the years of state power. In 1995 the Sandinista movement underwent a serious split with the formation of the Sandinista Renovation Movement (Movimiento Renovadora Sandinista, or MRS). This split cannot be understood without a close review of the party's pre-1990 history.

The party also faced a populace that was deeply alienated from politics and seemed to view the Sandinistas as part of the country's traditional political elite that had failed to address their fundamental social and economic problems. The FSLN was probably Nicaragua's largest single political party, with thousands of dedicated followers, but it faced a difficult task if it was to avoid becoming a permanently marginalized force in national politics.

Early History

The FSLN was founded in 1961 at a meeting in Tegucigalpa, Honduras, as a relatively small political-military organization. Over the course of the next eighteen years the organization slowly grew in influence and eventually assumed the leadership of a broad multiclass alliance that confronted the Somoza dictatorship and overthrew it in July 1979. The Sandinista movement emerged during the era of the triumph of the Cuban revolution, drawing heavily on the Cuban experience and the writings of Che Guevara and

Fidel Castro. The young revolutionaries were also inspired by the struggle thirty years earlier by Augusto César Sandino against the occupation of Nicaragua by the U.S. Marines and the domination of the country's politics by the elitist Liberal and Conservative parties. By studying their own fight for national identity and liberation in light of similar struggles in Cuba, Vietnam, and elsewhere, the Sandinistas were able to build on Sandino's tactics and infuse their movement with a coherent ideology.[1]

Like other young Fidelistas throughout Latin America, they adopted a tactical strategy based primarily on rural guerrilla warfare. As in other countries, these efforts in the early 1960s were a failure, but the Sandinistas learned from their early mistakes and survived with a more diversified strategy. While more military defeats occurred in the countryside, the FSLN slowly built up its influence in factories, neighborhoods, and at the university during the late 1960s. However, on entering the 1970s, the hold of the Somoza dictatorship on Nicaragua remained very strong. The small Sandinista organization, numbering fewer than five hundred members, began to fragment into differences over the proper tactics to be pursued. For example, from 1970 to 1975 the National Directorate (Dirección Nacional) of the party did not hold a single meeting.

Separate groups carried out their political work in isolation from the others, and many cadres were in prison during that period. By the time the national leadership met in Cuba in 1975, the division of the organization into three factions was clear: Prolonged Popular War, Proletarian, and Insurrectionalist. The Prolonged Popular War (Guerra Popular Prolongada, or GPP), basically Maoist in orientation, included party founder Tomás Borge. Their strategy and concrete political work emphasized rural guerrilla warfare. They were probably the slowest to acknowledge the developing revolutionary situation of the late 1970s, isolated as they were in the more conservative areas of rural Nicaragua.

The Proletarian Tendency (Tendencia Proletaria, or TP), which included Luis Carrión and Jaime Wheelock, based itself in large measure on dependency theory and the traditional Marxist-Leninist emphasis on the industrial working class. Nicaragua's urban working class, small as it was, was seen as the main motor force of a coming revolution. Political work in the cities was emphasized, and this group also built a base among students. The Insurrectionalist Tendency (Tendencia Insurrectionalista, or TI), which included Daniel and Humberto Ortega, was the last one to emerge. It did not represent an entirely new approach; rather, it served primarily as a mediator between the two existing tendencies. The Terceristas (or Third Force) did not draw a sharp distinction between a rural and urban emphasis, seeing the need for action in both arenas. The Terceristas' provocative contribution was the promotion of a multiclass alliance strategy. This idea was not new. Carlos Fonseca, the party's leader until his death in 1976, had advocated it; and there was also ample historical precedent for it in the strategy of both

Sandino and the July 26th Movement in Cuba. However, the contribution of the Terceristas was placing it at the center of political work.

The depth of the divisions within the FSLN should not be underestimated. The Borge faction sought to expel the Proletarians from the party, and sharp differences still existed well after the revolutionary upsurge began to take form in 1977. It is important to note the depth of these divisions as one explores the split that occurred in the FSLN in 1995, although they eventually became secondary to the developing revolutionary situation. In hindsight, the turning point for the Somoza dictatorship was the December 1972 earthquake that destroyed Managua. The disaster reversed the relative economic prosperity of the middle sectors and served to underscore further the brutality and undemocratic character of the Somoza regime.

The FSLN was weak and divided, as was the rest of the political opposition in this period, so the transformation of political consciousness was slow. However, the FSLN reemerged with boldness, first at the end of 1974 when its partisans raided a social gathering at the home of the U.S. ambassador, and again in 1977 when they seized the National Assembly. The upsurge of mass struggle opened in late 1977, and the urban masses moved into action after Pedro Joaquín Chamorro was murdered in early 1978. The independent uprising of the Indian community of Monimbó in February 1978 pushed the FSLN in all of its factions to move toward general insurrection. Disagreement over the question of alliances had led the Insurrectionalists to participate in the Broad Opposition Front (Frente Amplio Opositor, or FAO) through their supporters in the Group of Twelve, while the GPP and the TP were concentrating on what was to become the United Peoples' Movement (Movimiento del Pueblo Unido, or MPU). Although the Terceristas are often credited with the alliance strategy that ultimately proved successful in overthrowing Somoza, their flirtation with the FAO ended in October 1978 when many of the key backers cooperated with a U.S.-sponsored mediation that was intended to keep the FSLN out of power. A new group, the National Patriotic Front, using the MPU as its axis, was formed and brought a variety of anti-Somoza organizations together under the hegemony of a new, united FSLN.

A vital addition to the ranks of the Sandinistas during the 1977–1979 period was the Group of Twelve, which emerged in October 1977 in a document printed on the front page of *La Prensa*. Its members were known opponents of Somoza but were not connected to any prior political activity. They boldly declared that no political solution could be found in Nicaragua without the full participation of the FSLN. Several of these men would later appear as members of the Sandinista party and officials in the revolutionary government: Fernando Cardenal (minister of education), Miguel D'Escoto (foreign minister), Sergio Ramírez (vice president), Carlos Tunnerman (ambassador to the United States), and Joaquín Cuadra (deputy army chief). Their inclusion in the Sandinista movement not only opened important links to the bourgeois opposition but also broadened the ideological spectrum of the FSLN itself. Prior to that time, the differences within the party were all differences among revolutionaries. With the triumph of the revolution and the inclusion of key figures from the Group of Twelve, a social democratic unit had been injected into the party for the first time.

In the short term the inclusion of these social democratic figures did not materially alter the course of the revolution. The complete military victory of the FSLN, with its three tendencies united in March 1979, allowed the party to make its choices within the nine-person National Directorate made up of three persons from each of the tendencies. The social democrats from the Group of Twelve had some influence from their important government posts, but they were not a part of the strategic decisions that would be made in the directorate throughout the years of state power. Only after the electoral defeat and in the wake of two departures from the directorate was Ramírez elevated to the top level of leadership. His time at the top would be limited, since he was removed at the May 1994 special congress. Not surprisingly, in January 1995, Ramírez led a split from the FSLN to form the MRS.

Most studies of the Sandinistas in power have tended to focus on a single strategic vision.[2] In reality, the FSLN evolved only in relationship to the various challenges that were faced during the 1980s. Such studies downplayed the divisions that predated July 1979 and focused only occasionally on small differences over tactics and personalities. Whatever differences that may have existed in the National Directorate were contained within it, so that it successfully put forward a united front of democratic centralism throughout its years in power.

The FSLN in Power

In July 1979 the FSLN, marked by a clear history of Marxist ideology significantly influenced by the struggle of Sandino, liberation theology, and the triumph of the July 26th Movement in Cuba, assumed power. It also assumed power as a small vanguard organization that had carried out armed struggle for nearly twenty years. The ten years of state power transformed both the character and ideology of the FSLN.[3] Some of the changes, especially in the structure and function of the organization, were brought on almost exclusively by its new role as a governing party. Other changes, especially in ideology and in the arena of turning ideological commitments into public policy, came about as the result of choices made by the FSLN leadership. In general, these transformations took the party away from its revolutionary principles and set the stage for an even more rapid move toward social democracy that occurred after the 1990 election defeat. By the middle of the 1980s the political rhetoric of the FSLN was considerably changed from its historic program of 1969. When the Sandinistas left office in 1990, this changed ideological commitment was mirrored in the political practice of the FSLN as the ruling party. The 1984 election platform of the FSLN had declared that the philosophy of the revolution was embodied in three principles: political pluralism, a mixed economy, and nonalignment.

Throughout the 1980s the Sandinista leaders downplayed the real role of Marxism in the formation of the FSLN and instead focused almost exclusively on the figure of Sandino and other Nicaraguan heroes such as Benjamín Zeledón, who had resisted U.S. domination. Even the historic figure of Carlos Fonseca was not emphasized and his writings were not widely published.[4] This deemphasis of the Marxist role can be explained in part by the FSLN's life-and-death struggle with the United States in a Cold War context. While the FSLN relied heavily on aid from Cuba and the Soviet Union throughout the 1980s, it strove mightily to throw off its label as a Soviet client state in a desperate bid to retain support from West European governments and liberals in the U.S. Congress. However, the decline of a Marxist viewpoint had actually become a reality in the practice of the Sandinistas by the middle of the decade.

The emphasis on political pluralism and the organization of a constitution and elections primarily along Western liberal democratic ideals represented a shift in the thinking of the FSLN leadership. The 1969 program did not specifically deny political pluralism by a commitment to one-party rule, but it called it into question by demanding "the replacement of the constitutional theory of elected representation with a revolutionary government that would promote direct popular participation." Freedom of expression was supported but hedged by the phrase "in the interest of the people."[5] A slight revision of the 1969 document, published in 1978, was more explicit in defending democratic liberties by saying that everyone would enjoy the right to free expression. However, the real shift in FSLN thinking on political structures came with the construction of the 1984 elections. From July 1979 until January 1985, Nicaragua was governed by an executive junta and a legislative council of state.

The Council of State, in some ways, reflected the commitment to direct popular participation. As it evolved, the council had fifty-one seats: thirteen went to political parties, including the FSLN, but most of the rest were awarded to grass-roots organizations that had emerged during the revolutionary struggle—Sandinista Defense Committees (Comités de Defensa Sandinista, or CDS), Sandinista Workers' Central (Central Sandinista de Trabajadores, or CST), Rural Workers' Association (Asociación de los Trabajadores del Campo, or ATC), Women's Association (Asociación de Mujeres Nicaragüenses Luisa Amanda Espinosa, or AMNLAE), and Sandinista Youth (Juventud Sandinista-19 de Julio, or JS-19J). The representatives, chosen by their respective organizations, were thus directly involved at the highest level of government decision making. The grass-roots organizations pressed for the continuation of some representation when the permanent political structures were adopted for the 1984 elections, but the FSLN leadership opted instead for a liberal, democratic, unicameral National Assembly elected on a proportional basis.

The 1984 elections were conducted in some measure to give the revolutionary government legitimacy in the eyes of Western nations, so the Sandinista leaders bent over backwards not to offend their liberal and social democratic allies with revolutionary structures. This parliamentary system also represented a concession to Nicaragua's traditional conservative parties, although many of them boycotted the elections anyway under pressure from the United States. By 1984 the FSLN leaders were convinced that such concessions were necessary in confronting Washington. However, in hindsight, it can be noted that the concessions also represented a shift away from revolutionary principles and provided an opening to the United States and its Nicaraguan allies that was successfully exploited in the 1990 elections.

The practice of the FSLN in the economic arena also drifted toward the right during the 1980s. The mixed economy constructed by the Sandinistas could have been gleaned from the 1969 program's commitment to the "protection of small- and medium-sized proprietors," but the general thrust of the program's economic pronouncements was more anticapitalist and prosocialist. It called for the nationalization of the property of the Somozas and associates of the ruling government, U.S.-based companies, natural resources, and foreign commerce. The rural sector was to be drastically affected with major land expropriations. Other socialist recommendations included national economic planning and worker participation in state enterprises. Once in power, the Sandinista perspective underwent a subtle shift, and a "strategic commitment" was made to a mixed economy, which meant the maintenance of a private sector far into the future. Bayardo Arce outlined the Sandinista perspective: "Looking at Nicaragua's experience, our economic and social configuration, and knowing the experience of other countries, we decided that a completely state-run economy wouldn't work for us. Given our circumstances—a developing country without technology or the economic resources to exploit our natural riches—we could not make the state the administrator of everything."[6]

In the early years of the revolution the FSLN did pursue a clear socialist orientation and did not see itself as representing the interests of the landlord class, which continued to exist and even prosper under Sandinista rule. Tomás Borge explained this seeming contradiction by declaring that "the FSLN defends the owners of this country's wealth and it represents them in terms of the nation. But in terms of the popular and class struggle, we cannot represent them because we have made the decision to base ourselves in the worker-campesino alliance."[7] The FSLN walked this tightrope between the bourgeoisie and the popular classes for several years, generally tilting toward the popular classes and socialism, but after 1985 it began to move away from a socialist orientation.

In the agrarian reform program the revolutionary government, feeling the pressure of successful recruitment of the peasantry to the Contras, began providing private ownership to individual peasants at the expense of cooperatives that initially had been favored. However, it was during the final two years of Sandinista rule (1988–1990) that the socialist orientation of the mixed economy was significantly gutted by Sandinista policies. Prior to June 1988 all economic measures had significantly cushioned Nicaragua's poorest people. The FSLN seemed to keep in mind Borge's creed of a "mixed economy in the service of the workers." However, the June 1988 measures and other reforms that followed in 1989 affected all elements of the society, lifting price controls on almost all goods and services and removing almost all of the remaining subsidies to consumers. As a result, transportation and food prices rose sharply. Nicaragua's poor people, some of the most dedicated supporters of the FSLN, were hit the hardest.

In contrast to the hard-hit poorer sectors, the Sandinista economic reforms gave significant benefits to the private agro-export sector. The government maintained this strategy despite no significant increase in productivity and growing evidence that the subsidies were largely being squandered or sent to bank accounts in the United States. This shift in economic policy was a significant step toward the right by the FSLN and represented the triumph of more conservative elements in the party leadership, as embodied in presidential adviser Alejandro Martínez Cuenca, a U.S.-trained economist.[8] While the elimination of many subsidies may have been necessitated by the near economic collapse brought on by the years of war, the FLSN leaders went well beyond short-term belt-tightening arguments to justify the changes. In a two-part interview in *Barricada* on March 15, 1989, Borge justified this policy course by arguing that market mechanisms are an expression of "objective relations and general economic laws" that transcend capitalism and socialism and can be used to serve "specific class interests."[9] He sought to maintain a Marxist framework for his argument by making a questionable comparison of the Sandinista reforms to the New Economic Policy undertaken by the Soviet Union in 1921.

The retreat from a socialist orientation might have only been temporary had the FSLN retained power in 1990, but that was not likely. A definite shift in FSLN thinking was apparently under way, representing the dominance of more social democratic rather than revolutionary socialist ways of thinking. Sandinista leaders increasingly pointed to countries such as Sweden, not Cuba, as representing their model. This shift would be played out in many complex ways as the party moved from state power to the opposition.

The FSLN in the 1990s

A process of reflection and debate over the electoral defeat began almost immediately within the ranks of the FSLN. The first phase of that discussion ended with a historic Sandinista meeting at El Crucero in June 1990, where several resolutions analyzing the defeat were passed.[10] The evaluation and reorientation of the FSLN continued at the party's first congress in July 1991. For one year before the congress, the debates over the party's future largely took place in the pages of the nation's newspapers and magazines, primarily *Barricada* and *El Nuevo Diario*. These debates previewed the issues that would eventually split the FSLN in 1995.

Not unexpectedly, the El Crucero document placed primary blame for the defeat on externally generated factors—the Contra war, the economic blockade, Third World economic crises, and the relative weakness of the revolutionary forces in the Western Hemisphere. The document also acknowledged the importance of such internal issues as the military draft, indiscriminate confiscations of land, forced purchase of basic grains, harsh attitudes toward the informal sector, and abuses by the police and army. However, most significant in the document was the public admission of many long-standing party errors that had never been publicly acknowledged. These errors, as stated in the document, included authoritarianism, lack of sensitivity to rank-and-file concerns, imposition of leaders and organizational structures without democratic discussion, excessive professionalism of party structures, a more demanding approach to granting membership at the grass-roots level than at the administrative level, and arrogant behavior and abuse of power on the part of Sandinistas with civilian and military responsibilities.

The El Crucero document was important to an understanding of the debates that were developing within the party, but it was far from adequate. A much better understanding was found in speeches and newspaper columns prepared by party activists from the National Directorate on down through the ranks. The debates centered around the type of party that the FSLN should be and around the political positions that it should take in the face of the country's economic and political crises.

On the question of the nature of the FSLN, several leading members of the National Directorate led by Arce and Daniel Ortega stressed that the FSLN must become a "modern" political party. Starting from the position that there was no viable revolutionary path to power, the FSLN leadership argued that the party had to shed its old political-military structure and become primarily a party built around winning back power through elections. Proponents of this perspective said that the FSLN should become a social democratic party and seek full integration into the Second International.[11]

However, this proposed turn to the right did not meet with universal approval. To many Sandinistas, social democracy was identified with antiworker governments such as those of Carlos Andrés Pérez in Venezuela. Arce acknowledged this opposition when he pleaded with opponents to Second International membership to acknowledge that the organization was heterogeneous and had included such "friends" of Nicaragua as West Germany's Willy Brandt and Sweden's Olof Palme.[12] Party leaders had initially expected the idea of membership in the Second International to be readily passed, but it was shelved at the June 1990 meeting at El Crucero when significant opposition developed.[13] The issue was placed on the back burner when Sandinista leaders realized that opposition to Second International membership could become the rallying point of a diverse left opposition. Opponents of the notion of a modernized social democratic party argued strongly that the FSLN should not become primarily a vote-getting machine. They argued that while the FSLN should greatly expand its ranks, it should remain in part a party of cadres involved chiefly in day-to-day struggles in the unions, the neighborhood, and the countryside.[14]

These two different visions of the FSLN began to take shape during the response to the Chamorro administration's draconian policies in the spring and summer of 1990. In a speech soon after the February election defeat, Daniel Ortega pledged to the FSLN supporters that their movement would "govern from below." For a time in 1990 that promise seemed to ring true as mass demonstrations and strikes led by FSLN militants paralyzed the country in response to plans by the Chamorro administration to reverse the gains of the revolution in education, health care, and land reform. A new Sandinista-led workers' movement, the National Workers' Front (Frente Nacional de Trabajadores, or FNT), emerged to lead and coordinate a variety of mobilizations. During the height of these protests in the summer of 1990, it was not even clear that the Chamorro government would survive, in part because deep divisions had developed within the UNO coalition. Political forces, led by Vice President Virgilio Godoy, attacked some of the agreements made between the outgoing Sandinista government and Violeta Chamorro and her advisers. Both Chamorro and Godoy wanted to marginalize the FSLN, but the latter wanted to do it with a quick frontal assault. Chamorro, with a more realistic assessment of the party's remaining strength, opted for a slower approach.

In the face of the two enemies, Chamorro and Godoy, sharp differences emerged within the FSLN. The central leadership, led by Daniel Ortega, developed an analysis of Nicaraguan society that became the basis of the party's political strategy. Party leaders argued that there were essentially four political factions at work in the country.[15] On the extremes there were two distinct groups. The far right, headed by Godoy, was seen as the main enemy desiring to roll back all of the revolutionary gains and beginning a process of physically liquidating the FSLN. This group was viewed as having the strong support of the U.S. embassy in Managua. On the far left were the sectarian left parties and some Sandinistas who were seen as unwilling to accept the electoral defeat and itching to return to power by revolutionary means. One forthright expression of the FSLN leadership's position was offered by National Assembly member Edmundo Jarquín, with his equation of the Godoy faction and the FNT trade union leaders who organized the July 1990 general strike.[16]

Top FSLN leaders avoided such a characterization of the FNT, but they did not distance themselves from Jarquín's point of view. In this analysis the political center was occupied by Chamorro and her closest advisers, including her son-in-law, Minister of the Presidency Antonio Lacayo, and the bulk of the FSLN. Using this characterization of the Nicaraguan political scene, the party leadership argued for a "pragmatist" position: that the defense of the revolution lay in a social pact between the two centrist forces (mainstream FSLN and the Chamorro government) that would serve to isolate both the Left and Right opposition.

The strategy was carried out with the signing of the *concertación* between the FSLN and the government in October 1990. This agreement, coming after a long series of strikes by the FNT, won some minor concessions from the government but largely ratified the wholesale privatization program of the Chamorro administration and its supporters in Washington. The FNT leaders were generally skeptical of the pact, and as a result it was not formally endorsed by them. The pragmatist alliance strategy was eventually carried out in the National Assembly, where in early 1993 the FSLN entered into a tactical bloc with many UNO delegates to force Alfredo César, an ally of Godoy, out of the Assembly leadership. This alliance and the continuing social pacts would eventually lead to the analysis by some that the FSLN was engaged in "co-governance" with Chamorro and Lacayo.

Not surprisingly, some Sandinistas challenged both the social pact and the basic framework of analysis from which it came. Critics of the framework argued that in strategic terms the Chamorro government, not the Godoy faction, was the principal enemy. U.S. policy against the revolution was seen as working primarily through the Chamorro administration rather than the marginalized factors around Godoy, who was never even allowed to assume his duties as vice president.[17] Critics of the party leadership pointed out that the unions were leading the way in defending the gains of the revolution and accused it of selling out the unions and tempering their forthright militancy. The unions, not the National Directorate of the FSLN, were credited with leading the major strikes. These critics were also vehemently against the social pacts, which were viewed as giving cover to attacks on the revolution and disarming the potential opposition. Many Sandinistas also questioned the characterization of the left as being "dangerous radicals." They willingly accepted the label as "principled" and argued that the future of the FSLN was in staking out a revolutionary position uncompromising to the Chamorro government. They directly defended the workers

and farmers who were most directly affected by the administration's policies. The "principled" forces particularly rejected the idea that revolutionary socialism was discredited by the events in Eastern Europe, leaving social
democracy as the only viable path. They argued that socialism, still based
on principles from Marx and Lenin, was fully relevant for the Third World
and Nicaragua.

During 1990 and 1991 these disagreements festered within the party,
but the National Directorate largely maintained its tight hold on the direction of the organization. In the summer of 1990, FSLN leaders were elected
for the first time at the departmental and regional levels. Former Ambassador to the United States Tunnerman raised the idea in a *Barricada* column
that the National Directorate should also stand for election.[18] This call was
rejected in the short term, but it built momentum for the view that such an
election was essential at the first party congress, scheduled for 1991. At the
El Crucero meeting the party leaders had owned up to the lack of democracy within the ranks, but in reality they were very slow to yield any real
control to the base.

The 1991 party congress was supposed to represent a break from the
FSLN's undemocratic past, but it did not advance very far. Preparations for
the July meeting were tightly controlled by commissions headed by the various members of the National Directorate. While elections were held to produce delegates from throughout the country, all members of the old
Sandinista assembly were guaranteed speaking and voting rights at the congress. In addition, the National Directorate did not issue a political report
for discussion beforehand. This failure to lay out the party's political strategy denied the opposition any real opportunity to question the leadership's
alliance policies and to elect delegates to reflect that challenge. The limitations on internal democracy were also highlighted when the National Directorate decreed that the new directorate would be elected by slate.
Delegates were presented with a slate of candidates chosen by the outgoing
directorate and were only given the opportunity to accept or reject the list.
This procedure was disputed by a vocal minority at the congress who were
also particularly upset over the exclusion of the outspoken Managua party
leader, Dora María Téllez, who would have been the first woman elected to
the directorate.

As a result, the only changes that occurred were the election of Ramírez and René Núñez to replace Carlos Núñez, who had died in 1990, and
of Humberto Ortega, who resigned in order to retain his position as the
head of the army. At that congress, Daniel Ortega's de facto leadership of
the party was codified by his election to the newly created position of
secretary-general. The congress also created a new party decision-making
structure whereby the congress was formally established as the organization's
highest decision-making body and the Sandinista assembly was made the

highest body between sessions of congresses. Prior to 1991 the assembly had only been an advisory body to the National Directorate. Previously appointed by the latter, the Sandinista assembly became a body elected by the congress in secret ballot. At the July 1991 congress a new assembly of ninety-eight representatives was chosen in a hotly contested election. There was a 60 percent turnover from the previous body, but the overwhelming majority was still loyal to the Ortega leadership.

For the two years after the 1991 party congress the FSLN pursued its alliance strategy with President Violeta Chamorro, and its leadership went largely unchallenged. The turning point came in July 1993 when many prominent Sandinistas outside of the National Directorate published an open letter harshly critical of the party's direction. Known as the Group of 29, they called on the party leaders to distance themselves definitively from the Chamorro government and resume close ties with the social base of the FSLN, the workers and the peasants. They argued that the tactical alliance with Chamorro had considerable political cost for the FSLN. They stated that the alliance gave the Sandinistas no real control over Chamorro administration politics (it was not co-governance), but it meant that the FSLN was seen as bearing some of the responsibility for the dire economic circumstances of the country. In practice, the FSLN's support for social and economic stability meant that the economic interests of the popular sectors had taken a back seat to the political priorities of the party.

The July 1993 document was signed by many prominent Sandinistas, especially those with strong links to the popular movements. The list included Victor Hugo Tinoco, political secretary of Managua; Doris Tijerino, former chief of police; Gustavo Porras, head of the Confederation of Health Workers (FETSALUD); Fanor Herrera, party head in León; Felipe Pérez, mayor of León; Henry Petrie, former head of the Sandinista Youth (JS-19J); and Lumberto Campbell, former presidential delegate to South Zelaya. The document spurred considerable discussion throughout the party and received especially strong support from Sandinista unionists and members of the Sandinista Youth.[19]

Following the publication of the letter of the Group of 29, Daniel Ortega made an important tactical shift. Fearing a challenge from the left, he began to reposition himself within the party debates. Beginning with his July 19, 1993, revolution commemoration speech that replied to the Group of 29, Ortega began to identify more closely with the popular sectors and to distance himself somewhat, at least in rhetoric, from Chamorro and Lacayo. Ortega's shift to the left made FSLN leaders with more clearly social democratic tendencies (Ramírez, Carrión, and Téllez) vulnerable. Two events in the fall of 1993 apparently widened the differences within the national leadership. At a meeting of the National Directorate, Ramírez declared an interest in running for the presidency in light of his positive standing in the polls in comparison to Ortega.[20] In hindsight, Ortega may have seen this declaration as the signaling of a power struggle for control of the party. In addition, sharp divisions of opinion within the National Directorate over a national strike that turned violent publicly boiled over. Ramírez and others criticized the tactics of the strikers, while Ortega clearly sided with those in the streets.

These differences were formalized with the emergence of two tendencies prior to the special May 1994 party congress. Ramírez formed the group For a Return to a Sandinista Majority, and Ortega led the Democratic Left tendency. The Ramírez group made it clear that it thought the FSLN needed to move toward the center if it was to regain political power in the 1996 elections. The Democratic Left also stressed the importance of winning the 1996 elections but questioned the more definitively centrist-leaning tactics of the Ramírez group. It stressed the importance of maintaining the historic principles of the FSLN and identifying with the popular sectors. The Democratic Left was clearly responding to the challenge from the Group of 29. In reality, the Ortega group had reestablished its revolutionary credentials without really critiquing or changing its controversial alliance strategy.

The May 1994 congress represented a solid victory for the Democratic Left tendency, which dominated the elections to the new Sandinista assembly and National Directorate.[21] The congress, however, also laid the groundwork for the split that occurred several months later. The overall spirit of the congress was deeply divisive and marked by harsh personal attacks. In a seemingly vindictive act, Ramírez was excluded from an expanded National Directorate in spite of his prominent position in the party and his leadership of an obviously important minority sector. Many rank-and-file Sandinistas were shocked by the harshness of the divisions and hoped that the differences would not lead to a split, but such a breakup may have been inevitable. Since the Sandinista movement incorporated the relatively conservative Group of Twelve in 1978, it had been a broadly heterogeneous political party. That heterogeneity had been suppressed during the years of state power, but the disorientation caused by the electoral defeat and the challenge of being a revolutionary party in the post-Cold War era were too great to overcome without a split.

The split was formalized in January 1995 with the departure from the FSLN of several key figures, including Ramírez and National Directorate members Téllez, Carrión, and Mirna Cunningham. Many prominent intellectuals, including Ernesto and Fernando Cardenal, also left the party. As noted earlier, several of those who left organized the MRS, which was formally launched as a political party at a congress in May 1995. The gulf between those who stayed in the FSLN and those in the newly formed MRS was quite wide. Reconciliation seemed improbable, and both parties appeared likely to field candidates in the 1996 elections. The MRS claimed a membership of 24,000, compared to that of 350,000 for the FSLN.[22] At any rate, the MRS dominated the Sandinista bench in the National Assembly. Of the thirty-eight Sandinistas in the Assembly, only seven were clearly affiliated with the FSLN. Not all the rest formally joined the MRS, but they tended to vote with them on important legislative matters, including the 1995 reform of the constitution.

The split and the controversial alliance strategy were not the only major challenges facing the FSLN. The party suffered from the widespread belief, both within it and outside it, that individual members unfairly benefited from the distribution of goods that occurred during the transition to the Chamorro government. Known as the *piñata*, this process apparently resulted in the transfer of considerable property to the leadership ranks of the FSLN throughout the country. Many of the transactions may well have been justified by years of low-paid services, but it was ultimately viewed as unjust by many rank-and-file Sandinistas who did not benefit materially during the transition as well as by the wider population.[23] The *piñata* appeared to have significantly undercut the moral authority of the Sandinista movement and also helped to magnify class divisions within the FSLN that made it difficult for the party to mount a sustained alternative to the neoliberal economic policies of the government.

Conclusion

The FSLN of 1996 was doubtless not the political party that had assumed power in 1979 with a clear revolutionary stance and the widespread support of the Nicaraguan people. It had been hurt by association with a decade-long war with the United States and by the accompanying decay and collapse of the economy in the late 1980s. And, in spite of its graceful acceptance of defeat in the elections of February 1990, its image had been tarnished even further by the behavior of some of its leaders during the *piñata* of the next two months.

What damaged the Sandinistas the most, however, was the party split, eventually formalized in 1995. A long time in the making, this division was a product of the gradual evolution of thinking and practice within the FSLN. It had its roots in the final months of the insurrectionary effort and evolved further over issues of policy and program during the period of Sandinista rule. In the 1990s divisions were finally strained to the breaking point over disagreements concerning the proper role of the FSLN as an opposition party and the ideal strategy for an eventual return to power. True, the FSLN had retained the strong support of an important segment of the people and had secured political space in the relatively democratic system that it had brought into being. However, for a majority of politics-weary Nicaraguans, it had become just another political party that had failed to address their basic needs.

Notes

1. For a fuller treatment, see Harry E. Vanden and Gary Prevost, *Democracy and Socialism in Sandinista Nicaragua* (Boulder, CO: Lynne Rienner, 1993), chap. 2; and Donald Hodges, *Intellectual Foundations of the Nicaraguan Revolution* (Austin: University of Texas Press, 1986).

2. For example, John Booth, *The End and the Beginning: The Nicaraguan Revolution*, 2d ed. (Boulder, CO: Westview Press, 1985).

3. For more details, see Vanden and Prevost, *Democracy and Socialism*.

4. His best-known work in Nicaragua in the 1980s was his book on Sandino. Carlos Fonseca, *Long Live Sandino* (Managua: Department of Propaganda and Political Education of the FSLN, 1984).

5. "Programa histórico del FSLN" (Managua: Departamento de Propaganda y Educación Política del FSLN, 1981).

6. Interview with Bayardo Arce in *Excelsior* (Mexico City), June 25, 1986, excerpted in *Barricada International* (July 16, 1987).

7. Tomás Borge, quoted in Gabriele Invernizzi, *Sandinistas* (Managua: Editorial Vanguardia, 1986).

8. For a full exposition of his views, see Alejandro Martínez Cuenca, *Sandinista Economics in Practice* (Boston: South End Press, 1992).

9. Interview with Tomás Borge, *Barricada*, March 15, 1989.

10. For a complete text in English of the El Crucero document, see *Barricada International* (July 14, 1990).

11. Interviews reflecting this "modernizing" perspective include Bayardo Arce, "El Frente pasa a la oposición," *Barricada*, April 25, 1990; Luis Carrión, "Revisión a fondo en FSLN," ibid., June 20, 1990; and Victor Tirado, "Seremos partido de cuadros y partido de masas," ibid., July 5, 1990.

12. Erick Aguirre and Luis Hernández, "No tenemos por que golpearnos el pecho" (interview with Bayardo Arce), ibid., July 5, 1990.

13. *Barricada International* (July 14, 1990).

14. Representative of this position is Daniel Abud Vivas, "El congreso del FSLN: Entre definiciones y coyuntura," *Crítica* (September–October 1990): 21–22.

15. The most articulate statement of this theoretical perspective was provided in "Polarization and Depolarization," *Envío* (October 1990): 3–11. A similar theoretical framework was expressed by several key Sandinistas interviewed in November 1990, particularly former presidential adviser and economist Alejandro Martínez Cuenca. See also Daniel Ortega, "The Country Needs Dialogue and Consensus," *Barricada International* (July 28, 1990): 13–17.

16. Edmundo Jarquín, opinion page article, *Barricada*, November 15, 1990.

17. Carlos Fonseca Terán, "Concertación solo si está al servicio de la Patria, la democracia, y el proletariado," *El Nuevo Diario*, August 7, 1990.

18. Carlos Tunnerman, "The Democratization of the FSLN," *Barricada International* (August 25, 1990): 17.

19. Support for the Group of 29 was evidenced in many interviews in January 1994, especially with Lily Soto of the ATC and Leonidas Pulidas of the CST, and in discussions with Sandinista Youth leaders. However, many of these people questioned the motives of the signers who were not closely associated with the popular sectors.

20. Interview by author with Luis Carrión, former member of the National Directorate, Managua, July 3, 1995.

21. For an overview of the May 1994 congress, see Gary Prevost, "Political Infighting at Sandinista Special Congress," *NACLA Report on the Americas* (July–August 1994): 1–2.

22. The membership figure for MRS was announced at the party's founding congress and reported in *El Nuevo Diario*, May 22, 1995. The FSLN figure was reported in *Barricada International* (February 1995).

23. This view was confirmed in many interviews by the author, especially with Ramón Meneses, Sandinista journalist and former FSLN Department of International Relations official, and with Francisco Campbell, secretary-general of the Autonomous University of the Caribbean Coast, Bluefields, Nicaragua.

10

The Other Parties

Kenneth M. Coleman and Douglas Stuart H. *

The 1995 separation from the Sandinista National Liberation Front (FSLN) of the Sandinista Renovation Movement (Movimiento Renovadora Sandinista, or MRS) was only the most dramatic symbol of the fractionalization of Nicaragua's postrevolutionary party system.[1] Media coverage of the breakup of the FSLN emphasized personalities and ambitions, so the split was portrayed as one between Sergio Ramírez and Daniel Ortega prior to the 1996 national elections. As Gary Prevost indicates in Chapter 9 (this volume), the issues underlying the breakup of the FSLN were far more complex.

Similarly, the reasons why Nicaragua had over twenty additional non-Sandinista political parties encompassed more than mere conflicts between personalities. We see the major cleavages generating the contemporary party structure as responding to political issues: 1) how best to deal with the Somoza governments prior to 1979, specifically a) whether to work for change within the Somozas' Liberal Nationalist Party (Partido Liberal Nacionalista, or PLN) or seek change outside of the PLN, and b) whether to take an intransigent stance toward the Somoza regime or seek to bargain with the Somozas over the opening of the prerevolutionary polity; and 2) how best to deal with the Sandinista government of 1979 to 1990, specifically a) whether to work to affect the policy orientation and political pluralism of the revolutionary experience from within the revolutionary coalition or via open opposition to the FSLN-dominated government, and b) whether to adopt a position of intransigent opposition or to seek to bargain with the FSLN. Imposed on top of each of these parallel cleavage

*Kenneth Coleman expresses gratitude to the Council for International Exchange of Scholars for a Fulbright award at the National Autonomous University of Nicaragua and to Jessica Bartholow at the University of New Mexico for research assistance. Thanks are also extended to Ms. Bartholow, Thomas W. Walker, Steven K. Smith, and William A. Barnes for comments on earlier drafts.

structures were issues that became deeply personal, such as whether the leaders of those parties that came into being to oppose the Somozas or the FSLN were ever imprisoned, killed, or otherwise repressed by the governments they opposed. Those experiences often help to explain the particular choice of party tactics.

By the mid-1990s there were five major and two minor party "families" in Nicaragua: 1) the Liberals; 2) the Conservatives;[2] 3) the Christian Democrats; 4) the revolutionary family of parties;[3] 5) the Social Democrats; and the lesser 6) regional integrationist party family as well as 7) two counterrevolutionary parties. Historically, like the rest of Central and Latin America, the first political organizations to emerge in Nicaragua were the Liberal and Conservative parties. With only two exceptions to be noted below, the partisan structure did not change until the 1950s with the emergence of the Christian Democratic Party, which would later fractionalize into a family.[4] Thereafter, revolutionary organizations came forward in the 1970s to be transformed into political parties with a stroke of the revolutionary pen in 1979, from which most of the social democratic parties emerged as dissidents in the 1980s.[5]

Political issues stimulated the formation of the parties of the 1990s, often through splits from preexisting organizations in response to two quite different but strong governments—those of the Somozas and the Sandinistas. However, legal processes involving changing standards of revolutionary legality affected the timing, pace, and difficulty of gaining formal registration.

Prior to 1979 only two political party families were permanently recognized in Nicaragua, the Liberals and Conservatives. The revolution made a lasting change in this artificial constriction of the partisan landscape. After 1979 there were five periods during which new political parties gained legal registration: 1) a 1980 legitimation of eight parties participating in the anti-Somoza struggle (the FSLN as well as two liberal, one conservative, two Christian democratic, and two social democratic parties); 2) three parties were registered in time to compete in the November 1984 national elections (two revolutionary family parties and one social democratic party); 3) two parties were registered in 1984 but not in time to compete in the 1984 elections; 4) parties were registered under the terms of the 1987 Constitution, stimulated by the Central American Peace Accords, in time for the 1990 elections (two liberal, three conservative, and two Christian democratic parties as well as one revolutionary family); and 5) parties were registered under a new and tougher set of requirements in the post-1990 era (one conservative, one integrationist, one Evangelical (Protestant), and two counterrevolutionary parties). Fractionalization persisted because, as of mid-1995, there was no provision in Nicaraguan electoral law requiring that parties draw a certain percentage of the vote to retain their registration— that is, once established, the law permitted parties to persist forever. The table below identifies these five periods in the attainment of legal registration. However, some interpretation is necessary.

Granting of Legal Registration to Nicaragua's Current Political Parties

First Period: 1980, via participation in the Council of State
Liberal Independent Party (Partido Liberal Independiente, or PLI), 1944*
Nicaraguan Socialist Party (Partido Socialista Nicaragüense, or PSN), 1944
Social Christian Party (Partido Social Cristiano, or PSC), 1959
Sandinista National Liberation Front (Frente Sandinista de Liberación Nacional, or FSLN), 1961
Liberal Constitutionalist Party (Partido Liberal Constitucionalista, or PLC), 1968
Popular Social Christian Party (Partido Popular Social Cristiano, or PPSC), 1976
Nicaraguan Democratic Movement (Movimiento Democrático Nicaragüense, or MDN), 1976
Democratic Conservative Party of Nicaragua (Partido Conservador Demócrata de Nicaragua, or PCDN), 1979

Second Period: 1984 registration, in time for election
Communist Party of Nicaragua (Partido Comunista de Nicaragua, or PCdeN), 1970
Marxist-Leninist Popular Action Movement (Movimiento de Acción Popular Marxista-Leninista, or MAP-ML), 1972
Social Democratic Party (Partido Social Demócrata, or PSD), 1979

Third Period: 1984 registration, too late for election
Revolutionary Workers' Party [Trotskyite] (Partido Revolucionario de Trabajadores, or PRT), 1984; previously Marxist Revolutionary League (Liga Marxista Revolucionaria, or LMR), 1975
Central American Unionist Party (Partido Unionista Centroamericana, or PUCA), 1984

Fourth Period: 1989 registration, in time for 1990 election
Liberal Party of National Unity (Partido Liberal de Unidad Nacional, or PLIUN), 1989
Social Conservatism Party (Partido Social Conservatismo, or PSOC), 1989
Popular Conservative Alliance (Alianza Popular Conservatismo, or APC), 1989
Movement of Revolutionary Unity (Movimiento de Unidad Revolucionaria, or MUR), 1989
Democratic Party of National Confidence (Partido Democrático de Confianza Nacional, or PDCN), 1989
National Action Party (Partido Acción Nacional, or PAN), 1989
National Conservative Party (Partido Nacional Conservador, or PNC), 1989
Neo-Liberal Party (Partido Neo-Liberal, or PALI), 1989

Fifth Period: 1990 postelection registrations
Central American Integrationist Party (Partido Integracionista de América Central, or PIAC), 1992
Conservative National Action (Acción Nacional Conservadora, or ANC), 1992
Democratic Alliance Party of Nicaragua (Partido Alianza Democrática Nicaragüense, or PADENIC), 1992
Nicaraguan Resistance Party (Partido Resistencia Nicaragüense, or PRN), 1993
National Justice Party (Partido Justicia Nacional, or PJN), 1994

Parties Seeking Registration in 1994–95: '96 Force (Fuerza '96); Liberal Nationalist Party; Sandinista Renovation Movement; Democratic National Party (Partido Demócrata Nacional, or PDN).

Fusions: Conservative Party of Nicaragua (Partido Conservador de Nicaragua, or PCN),
    1992, from PSOC and PCDN; Christian Democratic Union (Unión Demócrata Cristiana,
    or UDC), 1994, from PPSC and PDCN

Source: Hugo Mejía (see note 6).
*Year following name is the date of the formation of the political organization as interpreted
by Mejía.

The first group of parties to receive legal registration did so by virtue
of accepting invitations to participate in the Council of State of the revolutionary government, as authorized by Chapter III of the Fundamental Statute of the Governing Junta of the Government of National Reconstruction
of 1979.[6] These parties had been created at various times between 1944 and
1979, yet all had been denied legal recognition by the Somoza regime. Their
participation in the revolutionary struggle through civic or armed opposition and their acceptance of a role in the Council of State were sufficient
to warrant legal registration in the eyes of a revolutionary government.
With only one exception (the Democratic Conservative Party), all of these
parties did have a prior trajectory in Nicaraguan politics and could probably have met the more rigorous demands of the post-1990 registration
requirements.

It should be noted that Somoza's PLN was proscribed by the Government of National Reconstruction in 1979 and did not seek to reemerge as a
political force until 1994. The party that inherited by default a leadership
role within the Liberal family was the Independent Liberal Party (PLI), which
had the longest history of open opposition to the Somozas. The Conservative parties were fractionalized in 1979 at the time of the triumph of the
revolution because of earlier disagreements over how to confront the
Somozas.

The parties that were registered in 1984 did so under the terms of the
Law of Political Parties established by the Council of State on September 17, 1983, which created the Council of Political Parties that existed
until May 4, 1995.[7] The law established the right of ideologically like-minded
citizens to organize themselves into political parties but assigned to the
Council of Parties the obligation to extend registration only when certain
requisites had been met, including the filing of a set of party statutes and a
program of government. Once again, the obligations were minimal, although
now slightly more rigorous—requiring statutes, a program, and a list of
officials. Under duress from the U.S.-sponsored Contra war, special "expedited" procedures were made available to permit registration in time for the
1984 elections, but only three new parties were granted recognition in order to participate in that election (the Communist Party of Nicaragua, the
Marxist-Leninist Popular Action Movement, and the Social Democratic
Party). Two others were recognized in the late fall of 1984: the Trotskyite
Revolutionary Workers' Party and the Central American Unionist Party.[8]
Collectively, these 1984 registrations represent the second and third peri-

ods in the configuration of Nicaragua's party system as it existed in the mid-1990s.

In the fourth period, that of 1989, entirely new parties emerged, though always within one of the preexisting political families. These parties came into being largely as a result of differences over just how confrontational to be vis-à-vis the Sandinista regime. A good example on one end of the spectrum is the Liberal Party of National Unity (PLIUN), which objected to the growing drift to the right of the PLI and would have bargained with the FSLN. The PLIUN initially took part in discussions about the formation of the National Opposition Union (UNO) coalition in 1989, but it decided to run its own presidential candidate, Rodolfo Robelo, because of the excessively harsh line that the PLI and other participants in UNO were taking on the FSLN.[9]

At the other end of this spectrum of parties registered in 1989 we might place the National Conservative Party (PNC), an organization whose leaders participated initially in the anti-Somoza Broad Opposition Front (FAO) in 1977 but who opposed the FSLN emerging as the dominant force in the revolutionary government. Not recognized in 1980, one leader of the PNC (Roger Mendieta) alleged that he had been offered and had rejected positions in the Sandinista government, while another such leader, Adolfo Calero Portacarrero, went into exile and became a spokesman for the Contras. The PNC represented one of the few legally registered vehicles for leading Contra figures to reenter the political process in time to compete in the 1990 elections.[10]

Once again, all eight parties receiving registration did so under expedited procedures, generated under external pressure,[11] so as to permit participation in the 1990 elections. As Hugo Mejía, the president of the Council of Political Parties, put it: "In February of 1989 the Nicaraguan executive branch introduced a reform to the Electoral Law that was approved by the National Assembly, by which various political groups, in their majority descended from preexisting political parties, who claimed for themselves the right to participate immediately in the 1990 elections, could obtain legal registration via the briefest of (three-week) application processes and with minimal requisites similar to those used in the prior (1983) Law of Political Parties."[12] Again, there were no extensive procedures for circulating petitions, for organizing local chapters, or the like. The process of gaining registration was essentially political.

It is important to understand that the first twenty-one parties to receive legal registration in Nicaragua's fractionalized post-1979 polity did so for political reasons—the first eight because they supported the revolution (and had been proscribed by the Somozas), the next thirteen because they solicited their registration under expedited procedures so as to permit the holding of competitive elections in 1984 and 1990. Those expedited procedures were defined by external parties (the United States or the signatories to the

Esquipulas Accords) as necessary evidence of good faith by a revolutionary government presumed to be unenthusiastic about democratization.

Among Nicaraguan party activists in the mid-1990s there was a mythology of conscious Sandinista manipulation of the party registration process so as "to divide and weaken opposition to the FSLN." Such an interpretation, however, misreads the history of the post-1979 era. Although Mejía was a Sandinista, the Council of Political Parties over which he presided appeared to take seriously the operating rules that it had been handed. Those rules were influenced by two macropolitical processes: the revolution itself; and external forces in the counterrevolution and peacemaking efforts. If there was manipulation, it was by external forces who pressed for registering political parties with no evidence that they had any popular appeal.

In the post-1990 period of registering parties, a more demanding set of regulations was in place. Political considerations still prevailed in the registration of the Nicaraguan Resistance Party (PRN), which was exempted from certain requirements on political grounds.[13] But other parties faced a bracing set of requirements, the most important of which was the need to organize leadership councils in each of the 143 municipalities and to present in each local statutes and minutes of organizational meetings as well as lists of local party leaders and their addresses. As of mid-1994, three additional parties—a splinter integrationist party; a splinter conservative party; and the Democratic Alliance Party of Nicaragua (PADENIC), a personalistic vehicle led by an exile of the 1980s—had met these new criteria, and other requests for registration were in process. Among the groups awaiting formal registration was the Christian Democratic Union (UDC), a fusion of preexisting organizations that was playing an increasingly important role through the service of Luis Humberto Guzmán, its leader, as president of the National Assembly in 1994 and 1995. And by 1995 that list now included the MRS and Antonio Lacayo's National Project.[14] It was possible that a spurt of party registrations would occur in 1995–96 in anticipation of the 1996 national elections. If so, this spurt would happen via the newer, more demanding registration process.

What was the overall structure of the array of parties found in Nicaragua in the mid-1990s? It is best to begin with the two traditional families, the Liberals and the Conservatives.

The Liberal Family

The PLI was organizationally the strongest party within this family by virtue of: 1) having been founded in 1944 precisely so as to oppose the continuation of the Somozas in power as a personalistic regime; 2) having participated in the revolutionary struggle and in the first revolutionary governments; and 3) having its senior leader, Virgilio Godoy, elected vice president under Violeta Barrios de Chamorro.[15] The PLI took an intransigent position of open opposition to the Somozas. It originally participated within the revolutionary coalition but moved into open opposition by 1984; but it never took an intransigent position against the FSLN, favoring instead the "civic struggle." After 1990, however, the PLI hardened its position, refusing to bargain on most issues in the National Assembly with the Chamorro-FSLN-Christian Democratic-Social Democratic "co-government."[16]

While Godoy and Chamorro became political antagonists immediately upon the inauguration of the Chamorro presidency,[17] the PLI still has a political organization intact. By late 1995, Godoy and his party had not joined the coalition of four Liberal parties that nominated a joint candidate in midyear. Rather, they offered Godoy as the "independent" Liberal candidate, which he was both nominally and figuratively. It was by no means clear that the PLI's organizational base would translate automatically into votes. In the 1994 elections in the two Autonomous Regions of the Atlantic Coast, the PLI did not offer an independent slate of candidates; rather, it supported a slate representing UNO. That slate did poorly, finishing a distant third in the Southern Autonomous Region and in a dismal, totally noncompetitive eighth place in the Northern Autonomus Region. Hence, the drawing power of the PLI in 1996 remained unclear.

In 1995 the electorally strongest member of the Liberal family appeared to be the Liberal Constitutionalist Party (PLC). Born in 1968 as a faction within the PLN which argued for rotation of leadership and the selection of civilian leaders as PLN presidential nominees, the PLC was registered in 1980 as one of the parties which opposed the Somozas during the final denouement and which accepted a position on the Council of State.[18] While the Constitutionalist Liberal Movement (as it was known before 1979) took the position of seeking to negotiate from within the PLN nearly until the triumph of the revolution, once the Sandinistas emerged as the strongest force within the new revolutionary government the PLC moved into open opposition, but again not of an intransigent nature. The leadership chose to remain in Nicaragua and take part in the "civic struggle." For that reason it was somewhat unexpected that the PLC would emerge as one of the most effectively hard-line elements within the UNO coalition.

Arnoldo Alemán, the mayor of Managua under the Chamorro government and post-1990 president of the PLC, led his party into a belligerently anti-FSLN, anti-"co-government" posture. His gift for trenchant verbal simplifications of complex political realities brought him considerable mass appeal, as did his capacity as mayor to improve the visible infrastructure. Alemán paved roads, invested in plazas, and made sure that all such high-profile improvements advertised his administration. International relief funds flowed into post-1990 Nicaragua and were put to good political use by Mayor Alemán, creating jobs, producing collective goods, and reminding the public of the source of these benefits. Aleman's PLC remained nominally within the UNO coalition but ran its own candidates in the Atlantic Coast regional elections. In those 1994 contests the PLC was the major winner, demonstrating surprising electoral strength. In both Autonomous Regions it won a plurality of the valid vote (35.2 percent in the North and 35.5 percent in the South). The performance on the Atlantic Coast, plus the high visibility of Alemán, made the PLC mayor the eventual nominee of a four-party liberal coalition in the 1996 presidential elections.[19]

The others joining this coalition were the Neo-Liberal Party (PALI), the PLN, and the PLIUN. As previously indicated, the PLIUN saw the FSLN as a reality in 1989 and found the posture of UNO to be excessively nonreconciliatory. While the PLIUN maintained such a posture into the 1990s, it knew it could not compete effectively on its own and joined the four-party coalition. By contrast, the PALI alleged that it had emerged from the ranks of "Somocistas without tails"—that is, Somocistas from the PLN not involved in the corruption of the Somoza government.[20] PALI leaders accused the FSLN of being a "totalitarian government" in the 1980s and continued to criticize institutional infrastructures inherited from the FSLN years. Yet these leaders stayed in Nicaragua and seemed to have no visible ties to the armed opposition; PALI's president did admit to having received money from the U.S. government "to host seminars and conduct educational campaigns." Having failed to establish an independent political voice,[21] the PALI appeared likely to slowly disappear in the future. Somewhat amazingly, the name of the Somocistas' PLN was reclaimed in late 1994 by a few Nicaraguans who sought registration as a party and joined the Liberal alliance in time for the 1996 elections.

The Conservative Family

Carlos Vilas argues that Conservatives had better relations with the FSLN government than did Liberals, in part because Conservatives had long held material grievances against the Somozas and in part because many of their sons and daughters became leaders of the FSLN and other revolutionary organizations.[22] Indeed, it was the murder of Conservative publisher Pedro Joaquín Chamorro that provoked the popular mobilization that led to the fall of the Somozas.[23] What is clear is that the experience of the Sandinista years clearly did not unify the Conservative family; rather, it added a process of fractionalization on top of preexisting defections to Christian democracy. In 1990 the Conservative Party family was deeply divided, and unity was not attained subsequently in the Chamorro presidency.

Central to that conflict were not only the fault lines mentioned earlier but also the question of which leaders elected to stay in Nicaragua during the Sandinista years and which elected to leave. An example was the dispute between Dr. Fernando Agüero Rocha, a charismatic Conservative leader of the 1950s and 1960s, who left the country when apprised of threats to his life in the early post-triumph days, and his one-time disciple, Miriam Argüello, who remained in Nicaragua and participated in political life throughout the entire Sandinista era. Argüello deeply resented the expectation of Dr. Agüero that he could immediately return to the leadership of the Conservative Party.

In the mid-1990s, Agüero was head of an organization known as the Conservative Party of Nicaragua (PCN), upon which the Council of Political Parties bestowed this preferred "historic" name in 1992 when the Democratic Conservative Party (registered in 1980) and the Social Conservatism Party (registered in 1989) decided to fuse.[24] Argüello was secretary-general of the Popular Conservative Alliance (APC), which gained legal registration in 1989. Both leaders were "progressive conservatives"[25] and one was the political protégé of the other. Yet Argüello believed that she had "earned her spurs" and had no reason to defer to Agüero, who chose to leave the country rather than fight difficult battles at home with the Sandinistas.

Both the PCN and the APC should be characterized as consistently reconciliatory in their orientations. Although Agüero failed in an attempt to bargain with the Somozas in the triumvirate, one of the most despised events in Nicaraguan political history,[26] he remained in the mid-1990s an engaging individual and a powerful orator. Argüello led her APC out of UNO in December 1993, and the seven deputies of this party comprised an important element of the "center group" that was playing a crucial role in the governance of Nicaragua in 1994. In June 1995 she was nominated as a presidential candidate by the APC.

Two other Conservative parties played minor roles in the mid-1990s in Nicaragua. The National Conservative Party (PNC), discussed earlier, a party which took a role of open intransigent opposition in the Sandinista years and retained its anti-FSLN stance in the 1990s, stayed within the UNO coalition. By contrast, Conservative National Action (ANC) was the direct descendant of the political forces led by Pedro Joaquín Chamorro and had impeccably anti-Somoza credentials.[27] The ANC initially supported the Sandinista government, since five of the first seven Supreme Court justices appointed by the FSLN were members of the ANC. One of those justices resigned in protest against a government decision in 1987.[28] The ANC attempted to be a critic "within the revolution" and generally succeeded in doing so. In the early 1990s it had three deputies as a result of participating in the UNO slate, one cabinet ministry, the Supreme Court seat of Santiago Rivas Haslam, and several ambassadorships. Clearly, the ANC was supportive of the Chamorro government's calculus of reconciliation, in contrast to the PNC. On balance, three of the four Conservative parties of Nicaragua exhibited a propensity toward reconciliation in the Chamorro years, while only one of the four Liberal parties exhibited such an orientation. Indeed, the three Conservative parties were the most consequential ones, whereas the one Liberal party favoring conciliation was a minor one.

The Revolutionary Family

As mentioned earlier, the revolutionary family was dysfunctional. The various parties that existed in this group were either: 1) disappointed contenders for power in the Government of National Reconstruction of 1979; 2) left-wing organizations that underestimated the probability of armed insurrection succeeding; or 3) groups that supported some, but not all, aspects of the revolution in power and sought to build bridges between the FSLN government and a wider array of social forces as they saw the revolution's support shrinking. Whatever the subcategory, these were all left-wing groups critical of the FSLN. The degree of disaffection was exacerbated because the FSLN had imprisoned leaders of many of these parties.

In the first subcategory, disappointed contenders for power in the government of 1979 included the Marxist-Leninist Popular Action Movement (MAP-ML). This group had its origins in 1971–72, when it left the FSLN in a disagreement over tactics, taking more or less the position of the Proletarian Tendency that urban organization was necessary.[29] The MAP-ML subsequently organized construction workers (in the Workers' Front) and students, published small newspapers, and participated in the armed insurrection of 1977–1979 by starting the Anti-Somoza Popular Militias (MILPAS). Upon the triumph, conflict immediately broke out with the FSLN, which wanted to disarm the popular militias. The MAP-ML resisted "because the bourgeoisie form part of the new government," and it criticized the government program as being "too social democratic."[30] The FSLN came down hard on the MAP-ML, imprisoning several of its leaders. The MAP-ML was registered as a party in 1984, ran its own candidates, and received 10,000 votes and two assembly seats. But in 1990 it again ran alone against stronger competition and won nothing.

By the mid-1990s its leader was confessing "that the party is in very difficult shape; what with the collapse of most Nicaraguan industries, we have few workers to organize." The party leader was thinking about 1996 in terms of an alliance or abstention. In either case, the MAP-ML had probably passed its moment in Nicaraguan politics. Similarly, the Trotskyite Revolutionary Workers' Party (PRT) had its origins in the prerevolutionary struggle, was also repressed in the immediate revolutionary era by the FSLN, and by the mid-1990s was limited to participating in published debates on how to reconfigure the left. The party leadership had come to see an electoral role for the PRT in 1996 only "if the FSLN moved totally toward the center," thus opening up a space on the left for a coalition of parties—the MAP-ML, the PRT, and the MUR.[31]

The prime example of a party that underestimated the possibilities of insurrection in the late 1970s was the Communist Party of Nicaragua (PCdeN), led by Eli Altimirano. Proscribed for many years, the PCdeN emerged from antecedent organizations, the Nicaraguan Workers' Party

(PTN, 1937) and the Nicaraguan Socialist Party (PSN, 1944). Disputes over how to proceed in the 1967 election campaign (that of Dr. Agüero) led those who were to form the Communist Party to separate from the PSN, warning that the Somozas would use force to prevent an electoral defeat. According to Altimirano, Anastasio Somoza, fearing the end in the 1970s, once offered legal status for the PCdeN in exchange for support for a controlled devolution of power to others (presumably non-Somocistas, but acceptable to the Somozas). Altimirano rejected the offer, and the PCdeN remained proscribed until it gained recognition in 1984 under the FSLN government. Early in the Sandinista years, Altimirano was imprisoned by the FSLN regime for having criticized the "excessive speed" with which some Frente leaders were arguing for a transition to socialism[32] and their "authoritarian tendencies." These experiences of mutual distrust led to the remarkable fact that the PCdeN participated in the UNO coalition for the 1990 elections, remaining with UNO as late as 1994. Indeed, Altimirano served in 1994 as the chairman of the UNO council. The Communist Party in the post-1990 era continued to exhibit an anti-FSLN orientation.

Finally, within the revolutionary family, there were two additional organizations. The Movement of Revolutionary Unity (MUR) was led in the mid-1990s by Francisco Samper (initially of the MAP-ML) but had once been led by Moisés Hassán. The latter served on the original Governing Junta of 1979, stayed with the FSLN regime throughout most of the 1980s as vice minister of government (under Tomás Borge) at the cost of growing personal doubts, and finally resigned after the Peace Accords to form the MUR and to offer himself as a presidential candidate in 1990. As a defeated presidential candidate, Hassán won enough votes to warrant a seat in the National Assembly in the Chamorro years. He used that post to criticize the FSLN for "corruption" and for "continued commitment to strikes, disruption, and violence," which upset other leaders of the MUR. He left to form the Renovating Action Movement (MAR), which, as of mid-1994, had yet to decide if it would seek registration as a political party. Having sought to change the FSLN from within for a decade, Hassán gave up and took an increasingly anti-FSLN stance in the 1990s, as did the MAR, while the MUR still sought to keep the doors open to an all-embracing coalition of the left looking toward the 1996 elections.[33]

The biggest addition to the revolutionary family in the mid-1990s was the Sandinista Renovation Movement (MRS), through which numerous senior officials of the FSLN exited in January 1995. The birth and nature of this party are discussed in Chapter 9.

The Christian Democratic Family

The first political party other than the Liberals or Conservatives to enjoy representation in the National Assembly was the Social Christian Party of

Nicaragua (PSCN) through its participation in a 1967 coalition.[34] By the 1990s the Christian Democratic Union[35] had emerged as a major force for compromise in the bargaining that produced a working "co-government" for Violeta Chamorro based on the defection of a "center group" from the UNO coalition. The UDC held the presidency of the National Assembly for two years under Luis Humberto Guzmán, who published an independent weekly newspaper, *The Chronicle*, during the late Sandinista era. The UDC held six deputy slots in the Chamorro years[36] and, with other members of the "center group," provided much needed leadership on negotiating difficult issues, such as the 1995 constitutional reform package.

As of 1994, the UDC had not chosen an electoral strategy for 1996, indicating that it was focusing on major issues in the National Assembly. Other parties were approaching it as possible allies. Two UDC leaders indicated that "we have to avoid the election of Arnoldo Alemán or the FSLN. We need to stabilize the country—for this reason we are not seeking to lead any coalition. First come the needs of the country. But, yes, we want to see the country in good condition and stabilized by the year 2002, at which point you could see a Christian Democratic government in this country."[37]

In fact, it appeared that the UDC strategy might prove productive, with the package of constitutional reforms finally published in mid-1995. Yet the UDC had not captured the imagination of the Nicaraguan public. Three long-time Christian Democrats serving as ambassadors for the Chamorro government expressed concern in a joint press conference in early August 1995 that the UDC and other Christian Democratic parties were showing very poorly in public opinion polls, and they urged the unification of the three parties that remained.[38]

The authors' interviews with Agustín Jarquín, leader of the PDCN, which collapsed itself into the new UDC, revealed a leader similarly bent on reconciliation. Indeed, Jarquín served as vice minister and executive director of INIFOM (Institute of Municipal Development), in which he organized courses on negotiation processes for municipal councilors throughout the country, noting that "in this country we have always practiced the politics of opposition—opposition to Somoza, then opposition to the Sandinistas. Now we need to govern and to learn how to negotiate so as to do so . . . we need the politics of proposition instead of those of opposition."[39]

By contrast, those Christian Democrats who stayed within the National Action Party (PAN) appeared in the summer of 1994 to be heavily invested in an anti-Sandinista posture.[40] But mid-1995 news reports include the PAN among parties supporting the constitutional reform package and speculate about it as a potential electoral ally of the Nicaraguan Democratic Movement (MDN), the UDC, the MRS, and the APC.[41] It is interesting that the PAN leadership made negative comments about a new Protestant political organization, not for being Protestant but because (allegedly) "these were the same people who worked with the FSLN in the past."[42] An interview with the young physician president of that party, the National Justice Party (PJN), revealed a posture that seemed to be progressive and reconciliation-oriented, much like that of the UDC leadership, but distinguishable by the emphasis that it placed on family planning.[43] The PJN was looking to an independent campaign in 1996, expecting that its ties to the growing Evangelical community would win it 20,000 to 50,000 votes and a seat in the National Assembly.[44] The last party in the tendency was the original Social Christian Party (PSC), which dated to the 1960s. By mid-1994 the PSC no longer was recognized by the international Christian Democratic movement and no offices could be located in Managua.[45]

On balance, then, political parties inspired by Christian social thought had reemerged as an important political force in the Nicaragua of Violeta Chamorro's government. But as it looked to 1996, the Christian Democratic movement had yet to prove its electoral appeal. The most dynamic religious force in the country was probably Evangelical Protestantism,[46] so it remained unclear whether Christian Democracy could overcome partisan factionalism to become a powerful electoral contender.

The Social Democratic Family

Three major political organizations constitute this family: the Nicaraguan Socialist Party (PSN), the Nicaraguan Democratic Movement (MDN), and the Social Democratic Party (PSD). As of mid-1994, each of these organizations was playing a role on the center left of the political spectrum, with the MDN perhaps the most conservative of the three.[47] The PSN had been born in 1944 during the Popular Front era of World War II, when the West and the USSR were war-time allies. It brought the organized working class and left-wing intellectuals into the Nicaraguan political process. Forced underground shortly after the war, the PSN had some success in labor organizing in the 1960s during the Central American Common Market boom. Those who stayed in the party after fissures in 1967 and 1977 always favored participation in broad alliances and the "civic struggle." But early in the revolutionary government, the FSLN wanted the PSN to disappear and made offers to that end.[48] These overtures produced resentment, and the PSN went into overt opposition, which led to some brief jailings of its leaders. The party has played a centrist role in the 1990s, with Gustavo Tablada serving as president of the National Assembly for one year, after having served as minister of agrarian reform early in the Chamorro government. The PSN was looking to alliances with other center-left parties in 1996, including those of the social democratic and christian democratic families.[49]

The MDN was a vehicle created after the assassination of Pedro Joaquín Chamorro to mobilize business, labor, and professionals against Anastasio Somoza. Alfonso Robelo, a major figure in the MDN, accepted a position in the Governing Junta along with Violeta Chamorro. Both resigned in 1981, and Robelo eventually played a figurehead role in the armed opposition. But MDN leaders returned from exile and joined the UNO coalition. In the mid-1990s, Robelo remained a senior adviser in the party, while Doña Violeta's foreign minister, Ernesto Leal, was a member of the MDN. The MDN entered into an alliance with the PSD looking to the 1996 elections.

The PSD, from its registry in 1984 until early 1994, was very much a vehicle for Alfredo César, a one-time official in the FSLN government who became the leading public spokesman for the Contras. A participant in UNO in the 1990 elections, the party rebelled in early 1994 and booted the right-wing César and Guillermo Potoy from leadership positions, after which it offered an ideology similar to European social democrats and looked toward participation in a coalition of the center or center-left in 1996.[50]

With the departure of the most virulently anti-Sandinista leaders from the PSD, as of mid-1994 the prospects for cooperative behavior within the social democratic family in the 1996 elections appeared plausible, perhaps more than such prospects within the Christian democratic family.

The Central American Integrationist Family

The Central American Unionist Party (PUCA) was the only "player" among this small family, and it was not represented in the National Assembly. Granted registration too late to compete in the 1984 elections, the PUCA in 1990 subsequently ran an independent female presidential candidate, Blanca Rojas, who won an insufficient number of votes to warrant a seat in the National Assembly. Rojas and her husband, Giovanni D'Ciofalo, were the dominant figures in this party. But the PUCA had a history of anti-Somocista activity that stood it in good stead in Nicaraguan politics. It competed in the 1994 Atlantic Coast elections and did poorly. While not a powerful voice for Central American integration, the PUCA was a voice for moderation and compromise. By contrast, the Central American Integrationist Party (PIAC) seems to have started as a personalistic vehicle for a disappointed politician, Alejandro Pérez Arévalo, who was closely allied with UNO and subsequently replaced by others. No coherent ideological message emanated from an interview in 1994, although a propensity to stay allied with UNO was clear.[51] There was little reason to believe that the integrationist family was primarily concerned about regional integration or an electoral force of consequence. But the PUCA could provide occasional officials in centrist governments.

The Counterrevolutionary Family

The PRN was registered in 1993, following the logic that it made more sense to have the Contras represented in the political process than excluded from it. While some people hoped for a while that the PRN might prove to be a powerful electoral ally, the party leadership itself seemed more interested in using its formal status to press the Chamorro government to honor land claims to those who had laid down their arms.[52] Indeed, the PRN competed in the 1994 Atlantic Coast elections and finished fourth in the northern Autonomous Region (6.9 percent of the valid vote) and seventh in the South with 2.6 percent of the vote. If substantial violence could be averted in Nicaraguan politics, the PRN seemed most likely to degenerate into an interest group operating under the name of a political party. Another small group, the Democratic Alliance Party of Nicaragua (PADENIC), was created by an Afro-Nicaraguan non-Contra leader, Pedro Mayorga, who spent the Sandinista years in exile in Costa Rica. Along with Laura Patterson, he succeeded in obtaining nationwide registration under the difficult post-1990 standards, although Mayorga himself was from the Atlantic Coast. But PADENIC's vision of "sustainable development"[53] failed to generate support in the 1994 Atlantic Coast elections, and the novelty of Mayorga's candidacy as an Afro-Nicaraguan was unlikely to make PADENIC a more powerful player in 1996. The PRN remained anti-Sandinista, while PADENIC was less so.

Conclusion

The apparent fractionalization of the Nicaraguan party system by 1995 was severe. Party leaders were aware, of course, that alliance building would be crucial to political success in such an environment. In 1994 a number of leaders of minor parties were inclined to attribute the proliferation of parties to the Machiavellian tendencies of the FSLN in establishing the Council of Political Parties in the 1980s and conceding registration easily so as to divide and conquer the opposition. From the perspective of late 1995, that interpretation seemed implausible. The FSLN had now itself fractured. And, with historical distance, it was easy to see that thirteen parties were registered in 1984 and 1989–90 because the world demanded that Nicaragua have "democratic" elections—democracy being provable by the presence of opposition (and ultimately only by a Sandinista defeat). Registration requirements were stiffened for the first time in the 1990s, but parties continued to seek and to gain registration.

Existing parties seemed unwilling in mid-1994 to propose electoral legislation requiring a performance criterion for continuing to exist. That issue was critical. The Nicaraguan party system would remain fractionalized until such time as parties disappeared when they could not compete effectively in the electoral arena. Coalitions would emerge on a short-term basis in electoral contests, such as in 1996, but would be disbanded thereafter under the pressures of governance or as a result of personal or institutional interest.

The fractionalization of the party system in the mid-1990s was neither a result of clever Machiavellian design by the FSLN nor of ineptitude or malevolence by the Chamorro administration. Rather, it resulted from a lack of planning in a polity buffeted by external forces and in which freedom of political organization had been long denied. It was understandable if Nicaraguans tended to believe in the early 1990s that the freedom to organize was fundamental. But if democracy was to be consolidated, perhaps their views might need to change. Electorates have finite cognitive capacities; and too many political parties can generate confusion, the image of contentious politicians, and a consequent distrust of the polity. By the mid-1990s, Nicaragua appeared to need a smaller and more coherent array of electoral choices. To have adopted a standard of abolishing political parties that fail to attract 2 or 2.5 percent of the vote in national elections might have been wise.

Notes

1. Various methods exist to estimate the degree to which party systems are fractionalized. Applying NP, an index designed to avoid "overcounting of large parties and excessive sensitivity to small ones," we calculate the values for 1994 Nicaraguan elections in the two Autonomous Regions of the Atlantic Coast to be extremely high: 7.24 in the North and 6.71 in the South. These NP values are nearly twice as high as those which would be found in France and more than two and one-half times those found in Italy, two European polities noted for their multiparty systems. See Juan Molinar, "Counting the Number of Parties: An Alternate Index," *American Political Science Review* 85, no. 4 (December 1991): 1383–91.

2. In the nineteenth century, Liberal and Conservative parties were the first to be formed in Latin America, distinguished by the Conservatives' propensity to support the secular powers of the Catholic Church (over the registry of marriages, which had practical consequences for property inheritance, and over education) versus the propensity of Liberals to favor the coexistence of civil institutions (of marriage and education). In Central America, Liberal governments of the nineteenth century were often associated with efforts to redistribute lands from indigenous communities to those who sought to grow coffee for export.

3. The revolutionary family of parties was less than friendly among its members. This state of affairs illustrates a wider point—each family had come to exist because of disagreements among its members. Consequently, the building of alliances within the family was not automatic. Indeed, it may have been easier to build alliances across party families than within them.

4. See Thomas W. Walker, *The Christian Democratic Movement in Nicaragua* (Tucson: Institute of Government Research Publication Series, University of Arizona Press, 1970).

5. One exception to these generalizations is that the Nicaraguan Socialist Party (PSN) was born in 1944. The PSN initially supported the revolution but eventually moved in a social democratic direction. A second exception is that an attempt was made by Salvador Mendieta to create a reform-oriented Central American integrationist party in 1899, but it was proscribed for generations until the revolutionary government granted legal registration to a body bearing a similar name in 1984—

just prior, but too late, to compete in the 1984 elections. The timing of registrations conceded by the Council of Political Parties in 1984 became a topic of debate and resentment.

6. See Hugo Mejía, "Resúmen de la Conferencia del Lic. Hugo Mejía B. en la Facultad de Ciencias de Comunicación de la Universidad Centroamericana," April 15, 1993, reprinted in Consejo de Partidos Políticos, *Boletín Informativo* 10 (May 1993): 4–5.

7. On the abolition of the Council, see "Nicaragua: Reformas electorales serán aprobadas en setiembre," *La Nación* (San José, Costa Rica), August 4, 1995, electronic version.

8. Leaders of both parties alleged in 1994 that their applications had been purposefully delayed by the then newly created Council of Political Parties in order to prevent their participation in the 1984 elections.

9. Robelo, then a justice of the Supreme Court of Nicaragua and vice president of the PLIUN, said: "We didn't have any problems with the FSLN in 1989–1990. Our posture has always been that the FSLN is a reality. You have to take it into account because it represents a strong political force in the country. We need national solutions and we cannot attain them without including the FSLN. . . . When we attain a government of true national unity, as the name of our party indicates, we will need to have a national program of governance, including elements that all parties can accept, and everyone should agree to implement that program. You cannot do this without the FSLN." Interview by the authors, Managua, July 20, 1994. Unless otherwise noted, all of the interviews cited below were also conducted jointly by the authors in Managua.

10. The Social Democratic Party (PSD), from 1989 to 1994, was also such a vehicle and the party of Alfredo César, another spokesman for the Contras.

11. This time, coming from Nicaragua's commitments under the 1987 Esquipulas II Peace Accords and subsequent implementing agreements.

12. Mejía, "Resúmen": 8.

13. As a pretext for exempting the PRN from the post-1990 requirement of organizing branches of the party in all 143 municipalities of Nicaragua, the argument was made and accepted that "an effective state of war" still prohibited entry of certain exiled leaders into their home communities, for which reason it was impossible to have party leaders in all the municipalities.

14. The MRS was shooting for presentation of its organizational documents for all 143 municipalities as of September 1995. Antonio Lacayo, son-in-law of Violeta Chamorro, resigned after five years as minister of the presidency to seek the presidency itself in the fall of 1995.

15. Virgilio Godoy served early in the Sandinista government as minister of labor.

16. By 1994, UNO, the coalition that nominated Violeta Barrios de Chamorro, was no longer supporting her. Doña Violeta's government dealt with a "center group" in the National Assembly (consisting of Christian democrats, social democrats, and various defectors from other party families) and the "renovating wing" of the FSLN, which dominated the Frente's legislative delegation. When approval of legislation was needed, the Chamorro administration looked to this group, not to the seven parties that remained in UNO. The PLI stayed in UNO and took a belligerent stance toward the Chamorro government, of which its leader was nominally a member. The parties remaining in UNO spoke disparagingly of "co-government" between the administration and the FSLN as if it were a betrayal of the anti-Sandinista cause. In fact, the "co-government" included about half of the prior UNO coalition.

17. Godoy showed up for work on his first day as vice president only to be told that there was no office for him in the Presidential Palace in Managua. For years he operated from his personal office not far from the Mercado Oriental.

18. Interview of June 28, 1994, with Eliseo Nuñez H., vice president of the PLC. On the opposition of the PLC to Somozas during 1978–79, see Ramiro Sacasa G., "Nuestra causa es la del pueblo," speech given to the National Assembly of the Liberal Constitutionalist Movement, La Cuesta Country Club, Managua, July 30, 1978, and reprinted subsequently in a pamphlet.

19. See *Notisur* 5, no. 28, July 28, 1995 (electronic newsletter).

20. In Nicaraguan slang, to "have a tail" implies to have left traces of illegal activity. Interview with Dr. Ricardo Vega, PALI president, on July 28, 1994.

21. The PALI initially had three deputies in the National Assembly, elected in 1990 as part of the UNO coalition, but two defected to join the "center group." Vega accused these two of taking bribes to do so. Thus, the PALI was down to one deputy, who was not highly visible in the National Assembly.

22. See Carlos Vilas, "Asuntos de familia: Clases, linaje y política en Nicaragua," *Polémica* 18 (September–December 1992): 16–30, a publication of the Latin American Social Science Faculty (FLACSO) in San José, Costa Rica.

23. To describe Pedro Joaquín as a Conservative is to oversimplify his complex relationship to the Christian democratic forces of modernization, of which he was an important part. Some of the Christian democrats left to form a new party; others, like Chamorro, stayed nominally within the Conservative Party.

24. Argüello's party objected in the Council of Political Parties, to no avail, to the concession of this "historic" party name to Agüero's new organization. For a discussion of the two parties that joined to reconstitute the PCN, see Oscar René Vargas, *Partidos políticos y la búsqueda de un nuevo modelo* (Managua: Centro de Investigación y Ecodesarrollo ECOTEXTURA y Comunicaciones Nicaragüenses, 1990): 66–69, 73–75.

25. There has long been a tendency within the conservative parties of Latin America to reflect on European Catholic social thought, which argues for social responsibility. For an exposition of the content of such thought, see Alfred Stepan, *State and Society: Peru in Comparative Perspective* (Princeton: Princeton University Press, 1979), chap. 2. Elsewhere, many who were attracted to such views left conservative parties to establish Christian democratic ones. Some also did so in Nicaragua, but Agüero did not—yet he distressed other Conservative Party leaders by his calls for land reforms and the formation of cooperatives in the 1950s. Similarly, Argüello was instrumental in negotiating constitutional reforms in the 1993–94 period; as chair of the Constitutional Reforms Commission of the National Assembly, she brokered a deal with the FSLN and the "center group." Indeed, her skill as a centrist negotiator was such that one interviewee suggested that "the most probable alliance for the 1996 elections would be between the FSLN and Miriam Argüello's APC."

26. See Walker, *Christian Democratic Movement*, 29–30, for other bases of resentment toward Agüero.

27. Interestingly, Violeta Barrios de Chamorro professes affiliation to no political party.

28. The justice was Santiago Rivas Haslam, who was subsequently reappointed by Doña Violeta in the 1990s and confirmed with the unanimous support of the FSLN legislative delegation. Interview with Rivas Haslam, July 26, 1994.

29. Interview with Isidro Téllez, president of MAP-ML, July 4, 1994.

30. Ibid.

31. Interview of authors with three leaders of the PRT, including Bonifacio Miranda, secretary-general of the party, on June 6, 1994.

32. In interviews of May 20 and June 3, 23, and 28, 1994, with Altimirano, he gave his version of Marxist theory by which the productive forces of capitalism must come to full maturity, transforming both the productive system and the polity toward "bourgeois democracy" (which he argued is not to be dismissed as inconsequential) before a transition to socialism should be attempted.

33. Interviews with Samper, July 8, 1994, and Hassán, June 6, 1994.

34. Walker, *Christian Democratic Movement*, 41.

35. A result of the 1993 fusion of the Popular Social Christian Party (PPSC), the Democratic Party of National Confidence (PDCN), and a segment of the National Action Party (PAN).

36. Originally, their portion of the UNO slate yielded seven representatives, but the UDC lost one to the Nicaraguan Resistance Party (PRN). In the fluid political environment of the 1990s defections were common, as were expulsions for "failure to exhibit party discipline."

37. Interview of July 8, 1994, with Alfredo Rodríguez and Fanor Avedaño, Jr.

38. "Intentarán unir a tres partidos demócratacristianos," in "Centro América: A portada Nicaragua," *La Nación* (San José, Costa Rica), August 5, 1995, electronic version.

39. Interview of July 28, 1994, with Jarquín.

40. Interviews with Humberto Doña, first vice president of PAN, July 22 and 23, 1994.

41. "Disidentes sandinistas formarán partido político," *La Nación*, 23 July 1995 (San José, Costa Rica), electronic version.

42. Ibid.

43. Interview with Dr. Jorge A. Díaz Cruz, June 30, 1994.

44. Ibid., assuming a continuation of the rule that losing presidential candidates passing a minimum threshold gain a legislative seat.

45. The authors repeatedly left notes requesting interviews at the office of one PSC leader to no avail. The party headquarters listed as the official address with the Council on Political Parties had been closed.

46. In 1994 the Evangelicals, protesting against proposed constitutional reforms that would have reinstituted (Catholic) religious education in public schools, claimed to represent 25 percent of the Nicaraguan population. Robert Zub, dean of a Protestant seminary in Managua, estimates the figure much more modestly, at probably not exceeding 15 to 18 percent. Various interviews of Coleman with Zub, Managua, May–July 1994.

47. For those familiar with Nicaraguan political history, the very idea of a social democratic family may seem questionable. The Socialist Party might be seen as best placed in the revolutionary family, while the "center-left" credentials of the MDN and the PSD might be questioned. Yet the fact that right-wing leaders were expelled from the PSD in early 1994 and that the MDN and PSD had agreed upon an electoral alliance while discussions about expanding that alliance were under way with the Socialists led to what seemed (in 1994) a very real possibility that a coherent center-left bloc was on the verge of emerging. The break-off of the MRS from the FSLN heightened the prospects that a center-left social democratic family would emerge, one that would eschew violent struggle in favor of parliamentary routes to public policymaking inspired by a social, and not merely a political, vision of democracy.

48. According to PSN President Gustavo Tablada, in an interview of June 29, 1994. Indeed, that effort persisted for five years. Tablada indicated that the FSLN

proposed to include seven slots for the PSN in its legislative slate of 1984 if the party would agree to disband. The PSN rejected that offer.

49. As of this writing, the authors had no evidence of the PSN's posture toward the MRS, but it seemed a possible alliance partner.

50. Interviews with Adolfo Jarquín, Gonzalo Rodríguez, and Jorge Balladares, May 16 and 18, 1994. These leaders argued that the press of May 18, 1994, was in error in alleging that the PSD had already agreed to support Antonio Lacayo.

51. Interview with Narciso Lacayo Barreto, July 29, 1994.

52. Interview with Edgardo Molinares Blandón ("Comandante Richard"), June 27, 1994. Molinares was director of agrarian affairs for the PRN and negotiated with the Chamorro government over land claims. Interestingly, he expressed some sympathy for the Chamorro administration's challenge in allocating finite lands between the desperate needs of former Contras and demobilized Sandinista soldiers.

53. Interview with Laura Patterson of July 26, 1994; press release of November 6, 1995.

11

Grass-Roots Organizations*

Erica Polakoff and Pierre La Ramée

Before the 1979 Sandinista triumph over the Somoza dictatorship, the organized popular sectors—peasants, labor, women, and youth—served as the FSLN's mass base of support in both rural and urban areas. Because of widespread mobilization of the popular sectors in the revolutionary struggle, the Sandinistas could lay claim to the support of the majority of the population in the aftermath of the triumph. Indeed, during the first five years (1979–1984), the Sandinista mass organizations experienced rapid growth and carried out essential tasks (the consolidation of the revolutionary state and the development of popular democracy) in the transition from the old system to the new. The six major organizations—the Sandinista Defense Committees (CDS), the Luisa Amanda Espinosa Women's Association (AMNLAE), the Sandinista Youth (JS), the Sandinista Workers' Central (CST), the Rural Workers' Association (ATC) and its 1981 spin-off, the National Union of Farmers and Cattlemen (UNAG)—were involved in the process of socioeconomic development, overall defense, and the building of a democratic political system.[1]

By the mid-1980s, however, the mass organizations had become chiefly mechanisms through which party policy was implemented; they were plagued by problems of sectarianism, verticalism, and abuses of authority, all consequences of the Frente's democratic centralism and the government's increasing bureaucratization. As the economic crisis and the demands of the counterrevolutionary war intensified, and as resources became increasingly scarce, Nicaraguans grew disenchanted with the mass organizations for their apparent inability to help them meet their most pressing and immediate

*Both the research for and writing of this chapter were collaborative efforts. Parts of this chapter have been adapted from Pierre La Ramée and Erica Polakoff, "The Evolution of the Popular Organizations in Nicaragua," in *The Undermining of the Sandinista Revolution*, ed. Gary Prevost and Harry Vanden (London: MacMillan, 1997), 141–206.

needs, and participation in all of these organizations declined (with the exception of UNAG) throughout the second half of the 1980s. The Chamorro government's neoliberal policies between 1990 and 1996 had an even more devastating impact on the material conditions of life for the majority. With official unemployment and underemployment at over 70 percent[2] and the virtual privatization of health care services and education, the standard of living deteriorated substantially.

The popular organizations thus confronted the daunting challenges of surviving a difficult political transition, rebuilding their structures and memberships, and opposing the socially retrograde policies of the new regime. In this chapter the impact of the political and economic crisis on these organizations will be discussed. We focus on five—the Community Movement (Movimiento Comunal, or MC, formerly the CDS), AMNLAE and the Women's Movement, the CST, the ATC, and UNAG—and analyze their relationship to the Frente and their transformation after the 1990 elections. We also attempt to assess the ways in which the grass-roots organizations created in the 1980s changed the nature of politics in the 1990s.

The Community Movement

The main challenge facing the Community Movement was how to recover from the electoral defeat and reactivate what had once been a mass movement. In the words of MC national coordinator Enrique Picado, "The electoral defeat hit us all like an earthquake. The Frente didn't prepare us for the possibility of defeat. Imagine . . . if I was unprepared, how unprepared were the leaders of the communities, most of whom did not have much education or political awareness. The local leaders were completely demoralized."[3] The MC's transformation from a mass organization that had been created by, and was primarily responsible to, the FSLN into an independent organization embodying a social movement began well before the 1990 elections.[4] It was therefore better able to cope with the political crisis, compared with the other mass organizations. As the MC vice coordinator noted, "As an organization, we succeeded in confronting the election. We didn't need to know who voted for whom, but rather how to undertake the tasks of the community without seeing it connected to a political party."[5]

To gain acceptance from those who either had become disillusioned with the Frente or had been opposed to it, the Community Movement had to change its focus. Picado explained that during the decade of the 1980s, the CDS emphasized ideology and abstract ideas: "There wasn't much correspondence between 'a free country or death' (*patria libre o morir*) and resolving community problems. We focused on the masses and forgot about the person. Now we have substituted the individual for the masses."[6] Changing its focus from "the masses" as the unit of development to the individual and her (or his) community meant concentrating on local problems. This change helped the MC to gain people's support and participation in that "it is not reasonable [for the government] to demand that people make sacrifice after sacrifice. And although the economic situation has limited all of us, the MC has proven itself to be an alternative for them to find solutions to their social problems. It has been possible to gain acceptance in this way. The MC is a collective, serving the community. We talk about concrete problems that people have, and not about politics. Before, it was reversed."[7]

Furthermore, to legitimate the MC as a truly *democratic* organization, all leadership positions had to be elected rather than appointed.[8] Its national assembly of over six hundred directly elected municipal leaders convened to elect the national coordinator, vice coordinator, and treasurer; to evaluate policy; and to determine priorities. Building democracy at the base through local elections and the training of elected leaders was considered to be one of the MC's most important tasks.

Given the political and economic climate under the Chamorro presidency, building democracy at the base was even more difficult for the MC to achieve than it had been in the previous decade for the CDS. Since extreme political polarization created neighborhood conflicts that made community organizing difficult, becoming a nongovernmental autonomous organization independent of party politics was crucial to the Community Movement's survival and recovery. Breaking away from the party, however, created a great deal of tension among FSLN members and sympathizers who resented the MC's independence and exclusive preoccupation with the community. As explained by the vice coordinator:

> We focus on the problems of the community. We don't belong to any political party, nor to any government. We make our own decisions. We are an organization that corresponds directly to the needs of the community. It seems to us that this is where the power of the organization lies—precisely because we don't respond to anyone's politics. . . . This change was difficult to implement. Many people in the Frente questioned our style and our concept of community-based struggle. Our autonomy has cost us a great deal. . . . We are a threat to the political parties, including the Frente, because of our nonpartisan, nonsectarian style.[9]

In spite of attempts to disassociate its development policy from party politics, the Community Movement nevertheless continued to be identified with the Frente, especially by its detractors. Indeed, many of its leaders at all levels—its national coordinators, department coordinators, and community leaders—considered themselves to be "revolutionaries."

Virtually all of them were either FSLN militants or community activists in the struggle leading up to the Sandinista triumph and during the eleven years of Sandinista rule—that is, the overwhelming majority of MC leaders had a history of personal involvement in various aspects of the economic and social development of their communities.[10] Many of them maintained their membership in and allegiance to the Frente, although this loyalty became complicated after February 1995 when the FSLN split into two parties, the Sandinista Renovation Movement (MRS) and the existing Frente Sandinista (FSLN). While both parties were represented among the leadership of the Community Movement, some of these people were reluctant to discuss their own affiliation, emphasizing that it was a personal decision and had little to do with their actual work in the community. Moreover, adherents of both parties were critical of the public announcements by MC leaders Enrique Picado and Máxima Bermúdez in which they identified themselves as members of the MRS.[11]

The fact that MC leaders and activists not only were demonized by members of UNO for being "Sandinistas" but also were criticized by the leadership of the Frente for supporting a civic method of struggle as opposed to a more aggressive one, and for "betraying the revolution," can be viewed as a testament to the MC's nonpartisanship.[12] In one region, FSLN leaders threatened to start their own "community movement" to compete with the MC because the latter was "too independent of the party," while in another an MC coordinator found herself unwelcome in both the FSLN and the MRS.[13]

What stood out in sharp contrast to the criticisms that MC leaders received from the Frente is the fact that they maintained their allegiance to the revolutionary project. In the words of one community leader and activist, "To be a revolutionary means to be able to change as the context and conditions change. The revolution isn't this thing out there. The revolution is us. We are the revolution. It's not this political party thing—it's working for progress, for the children, for the community."[14] The political nature of the MC's work was clarified by its national coordinator: "Our work is not sectarian, but it *is* political. To work to transform reality, that's political. It's a revolutionary project that has its own ideology."[15]

Essential to the revolutionary project both ideologically and in practice was the Sandinistas' commitment to social justice and their "preferential option for the poor"—relieving hunger, malnutrition, and misery, and improving housing, health, sanitation, and ultimately the material conditions of life. While in power, the FSLN successfully carried out more than thirty popular health campaigns, reduced the infant mortality rate, increased accessibility to medical attention, drastically reduced the illiteracy rate, increased school enrollments and retention rates at all levels, improved housing standards, and established a national social security system.[16] What characterized MC leaders and activists was their continued commitment to social justice, especially in the areas of health and education.

The largest and most widespread project coordinated by the MC targeted children in very poor neighborhoods. The Community Movement operated over two hundred children's community centers (*casas comunales del niño*, or CCN), which offered a variety of services including day care or preschool, first- and second-grade classes, rehabilitation, and occupational training for young teens. The day-care centers and preschools had their origins in the children's community canteens (*comedores infantiles comunales*, or CICs) of the previous decade, which were established to respond to high mortality rates among infants and children. During the 1980s the centers received support from the Sandinista ministries of Social Welfare (INSSBI), Health (MINSA), Education (MED), and numerous nongovernmental international organizations and solidarity committees. Because hunger and malnutrition were viewed as community problems with community solutions, it was considered crucial to organize parents to participate in building and maintaining the centers.

By the late 1980s, Frente and community leaders involved in the CICs found that many of the centers suffered from instability caused by inconsistency in the delivery of food, difficulties in getting parents to provide supplementary food, insufficient follow-up on the nutritional status of children, and a high rate of staff turnover.[17] After 1990 these problems were exacerbated as a result of cuts in education and welfare and the virtual privatization of the health-care system. The children's centers had to depend on assistance from external sources—the Evangelical Committee for Development Assistance (CEPAD), the World Food Program, and international solidarity committees and organizations (although these, too, reduced their support after the 1990 elections). In addition, because the Chamorro government's neoliberal policies disproportionately burdened and most severely affected poor families, many centers experienced a decline in parents' ability to contribute their time and support. Such participation, conceptualized as the foundation of the children's centers, and essential to the success of all social-sector programs, became increasingly difficult to realize and sustain. Also, rising costs in services such as water and electricity left centers with these "luxuries" unable to afford them.

A few centers solved these problems by becoming virtually self-sufficient. In the municipality of Matagalpa, for example, there were five day-care centers, each of them affiliated with a micro-enterprise collective that earned just enough to ensure that the center always had electricity and that well-rounded meals were provided on a daily basis for 80 to 120 children. Each member of the collective—the workers in the business, the teachers, the cook, and the administrator of the school—was paid approximately 200 *córdobas* per month (or just under $30 in U.S. currency).[18]

Community Movement projects also included popular education, health, and sanitation, all of which were based on earlier Sandinista social programs. The popular educators were young people in their teens who volunteered to teach reading and writing to adults in their community. The MC also organized and trained over 20,000 health volunteers to educate the residents in their community on disease prevention, to provide basic health services, and to organize committees for potable water, vaccination campaigns, and latrine construction.[19]

The children's centers and the health projects highlighted both the extent to which the MC was decentralized and the disadvantages of decentralization. There appeared to be little communication among communities regarding their successes and failures in implementing projects, raising money, obtaining supplies, or organizing cooperation and participation. Ironically, decentralization, taken to this extreme, may have contributed to low levels of participation by detaching local concerns from the wider social context. According to one community leader, organizing was difficult because "people have changed a lot since the '80s. Now, people don't have as much motivation to participate. They'll say, 'What for? What's the point?' And the economic situation is so horrifying that one doesn't see a way out of it. They become disillusioned and lose all hope."[20]

In addition to these obstacles, the Community Movement had to overcome political polarization, which created conflicts in communities throughout the country. Managua, in particular, was a deeply divided city. In 1990, after Arnoldo Alemán became mayor, he created a city-wide organization called the Community Juntas of Time and Progress (Juntas Comunitarias de Hora y Progreso, or JCOHP). According to the District Three delegate to the mayor's office, community committees of the JCOHP existed in all of Managua's neighborhoods as early as 1991.[21] Picado criticized the JCOHP and the mayor for trying to convert community activists into JCOHP supporters and for their antidemocratic tendencies: "The municipal districts are returning to a Somocista structure. The mayor's representatives were always the ears of the authorities of Somoza's National Guard. They have a mentality of revenge. They certainly don't go around thinking about democracy."[22]

Political polarization was most evident in the struggle over property. Many property owners who had fled Nicaragua in 1979 returned after 1990 to reclaim their former lands, houses, and factories. In September 1994 the government created the Office of Territorial Organization (OOT) to settle property disputes and review all of the land, home, and property titles granted by the Sandinistas (especially in Laws Nos. 85, 86, and 88). The Community Movement was involved in legal proceedings on behalf of individual families and community organizations that occupied contested properties, regardless of their political affiliation. In addition, the MC assisted in organizing brigades against evictions and lobbied political parties, the Church, the government, and members of the National Assembly to influence legislation regarding property rights.[23]

Deterioration of the quality of life for the majority, which began with the counterrevolutionary war and the U.S. economic embargo of Nicaragua in the 1980s, accelerated rapidly during Violeta Barrios de Chamorro's term in office. What the MC was able to salvage was minute in comparison to what was lost. The UNO government's structural adjustment program and its neoliberal policies privileged the wealthy and assaulted the poor. Many people who had been managing to survive fell into abject poverty. Still, the MC carried on. In the words of one of its leaders, "we can't just stand by and watch everyone die of hunger. We have to do *something*."[24] As of 1996, the central question was, Could the Community Movement really make a difference in an environment hostile to social justice? Could it reach enough people, provide them with the desire to take control of their lives again, organize them to defend their rights, and convince them that they could make a difference—that it would be worth fighting back, worth the sacrifices necessary to attain a truly equitable and democratic society?

AMNLAE and the Women's Movement

The Frente's relationship to the women's movement was typical of its relations with the mass organizations in general in that AMNLAE had relatively little autonomy to determine its own agenda. Despite the Sandinistas' formal commitment to the emancipation of women, demonstrated as early as 1969 in the Historic Program of the FSLN, the outcome was mixed in terms of the top leadership's response to women's needs and their willingness to develop policy in a timely fashion to improve the status of women.

The women's movement, as embodied in a mass organization, suffered on two counts. First, it labored under the expectation that a single organization could adequately represent all women and address the diversity in their material conditions of life, social class, ethnicity, and aspirations. In other words, treating "women" as an undifferentiated or homogeneous "category" was problematic since they have distinct and conflicting interests, experiences, needs, identities, and allegiances.[25] In particular, AMNLAE was criticized as having had primarily a middle-class orientation[26] and thereby being unable to attend to the needs of rural women, the urban poor, and indigenous women.

Second, AMNLAE always had an ambiguous and contradictory role vis-à-vis the revolutionary state. Even though the state and the party both had a formal commitment to women's emancipation and participatory democracy, AMNLAE was still an organization created by and for the party, and not by and for women. As it became clear that it would defer its own agenda in preference to the Frente's, membership and participation declined. The feminist and Labor Party adviser to the National Workers' Front (FNT), Ruth Herrera, explained: "The Frente always had the AMNLAE leadership more committed to its membership in the party than to its leadership role for women. . . . The tasks carried out by AMNLAE placed a higher priority on the party than on women. . . . The FSLN listened to us, but they never took our demands seriously."[27] In other words, "women's issues and the needs of the revolution were too often placed in opposition to one another."[28]

The Sandinistas' defeat at the polls was a tremendous blow to AMNLAE. Community leader and activist Rosa Ceballo stated, "Of all the mass organizations, AMNLAE was the most dependent upon the party, so that when the FSLN lost the elections in 1990, AMNLAE was devastated the most."[29] In response to past criticisms, and in line with the plan for its reorganization as outlined in the Sandinistas' 1987 Proclamation on Women, AMNLAE underwent a major restructuring. Dora Zeledón, the new national coordinator, emphasized the organization's independence from the party: "AMNLAE is an autonomous movement that defines its own policies and actions, without being subordinated to any political party or government body. Without losing sight that it is a revolutionary project, its character is broad-based and has wide appeal."[30] However, it is still perceived to be primarily responsible to the Frente. According to the vice coordinator of the Community Movement, "AMNLAE is not yet an autonomous organization. . . . It was the organization hardest hit by the elections, and it is diminishing in its strength and influence. It can't offer women what we need."[31] Ceballo noted that "AMNLAE still has close ties to the party. It has stayed above everyone. Women can accomplish more and are better represented by the Community Movement, which doesn't distinguish between women— whether we are feminists or nonfeminists."[32] Benigna Mendiola, the leader of the women's section of UNAG and member of the National Assembly, criticized AMNLAE's tendency to centralize and its insensitivity to peasant women's realities:

> There's no need to centralize the movement. Each woman's way of thinking must be respected, but we must meet when there are problems which impede our collective development. . . . I respect the work of the women organizing this meeting. On the other hand, we haven't always had their support. It's not the same to be in the reality of the countryside as it is to contemplate philosophical questions. . . . In the past we've had problems with certain AMNLAE activists. They want to transform the mentality of the peasant overnight.[33]

Both Ceballo and Mendiola articulated the position that women's interests would be better served and women would be better represented by local organizations. Decentralization together with an emphasis on local solutions to local problems did, in fact, ensue.

Beginning in the late 1980s, and especially after the election of 1990, the "women's movement" resurged as an obvious challenge to "the FSLN's reluctance to move feminist issues off the back burner."[34] It manifested itself in the proliferation of women's organizations from small, local groups with very specific goals to larger organizations with a broader presence that surfaced throughout the country. Though fragmented, locally specific, and generally lacking national coordination, these nongovernmental organizations were independent of party politics and responded to women's specific experiences and needs through such activities as consciousness-raising workshops; theater groups that dealt with domestic violence, gender relations, and sexually transmitted diseases; special radio programs for youth and adolescents; agricultural and craft production collectives; retraining institutes; reproductive rights; and family planning and health services.

The most significant impact of the revolution on women was their mobilization and participation, leading to a transformation of their consciousness from passive victims or objects to active subjects capable of promoting policy and effecting social change. The legacy of the revolution was the continued mobilization of Nicaraguan women:

> The impact of the Revolution on women has been very positive. It has awakened our consciousness so that we are more sensitized to the problems in the community. It has taught us to collaborate with each other. It has given us an awareness of ourselves as active subjects in the process of social change. The revolution depended on women's participation in public life. It was a radical change from before and provided a foundation for further action. Once your consciousness is raised, you can't go backwards; once your eyes are opened, you can't close them again.[35]

The CST, the ATC, and UNAG

By 1989 an estimated half-million adult Nicaraguans were members of the popular organizations, and over one-half of them belonged to those groups representing working-class and peasant economic interests: UNAG, with 125,000 members; the ATC, with 50,000 members; and the CST, with 120,000 members.[36] These organizations played a key role in developing the country's productive forces and transforming the relations of production in agriculture and industry. But because of their pivotal role in economic reactivation and development, their relations with the Frente were difficult and contradictory, especially in the areas of institutional autonomy and the independent representation of their members' interests. Thus, while the ATC and the CST played important roles in the struggle against decapitalization, and the ATC influenced the timing and content of the first agrarian reform law passed in 1981, only UNAG (founded as an offshoot of the ATC in 1981), among all the mass organizations, developed and retained a significant degree of autonomy from the Frente.[37]

The CST and the ATC were instrumental in building, almost from scratch, a broad-based Nicaraguan labor movement. They were also instrumental in mobilizing support for Sandinista development policy as well as for the revolutionary project more generally. Both the CST and the ATC, however, became subordinate to party and state, acting to incorporate all labor activism under the FSLN[38] and to ensure general labor discipline. External aggression and economic scarcity, coupled with the newness and inexperience of the labor movement, contributed to a centralized and authoritarian approach to labor relations which polarized the movement into pro- and anti-Sandinista factions.[39]

Under the Sandinistas, unions were seen as exercising more of a political role than an economic one in the sense that the interests of the working class were ostensibly already enshrined in the ruling party and the revolutionary state. Without the existence of objective class contradictions between workers and the state, the role of the unions was to be one of consciousness-raising and mobilization. They were also to act as intermediaries between workers and the state in promoting a program of economic reactivation and growth that required the sacrifice of short-term economic gains for long-term socialist development. In practice, workers' economic needs and priorities were subordinated to the political imperatives of ensuring production, restraining inflation, and winning or retaining the cooperation of the capitalist class within the mixed economy. While this conception of trade unionism constrained labor militancy through the prohibition of strikes and other restrictions, such as those on wage increases, it did give workers important gains in their working conditions (the eighthour day), labor relations (the right to associate), and standard of living (the social wage). It also planted the seeds of labor self-management via formal mechanisms of participation in enterprise management (Councils of Production and Enterprise Committees).[40]

By 1988 the CST and the ATC (as was the case with the CDS and AMNLAE) began to challenge Sandinista hegemony, move toward a more autonomous stance, and take more aggressive action in defense of their members' interests. The sharp decline in real wages and the rapid growth in unemployment beginning with the February 1988 austerity program affected the working class more severely than any other sector of Nicaraguan society. When the 1989 *concertación* negotiations between the government and broad social sectors offered massive subsidies to large-scale cotton producers but no wage concessions to rank-and-file workers, the push to make the union movement more independent of political parties began in earnest, including internal reforms to promote union democracy and demands for a new labor code. Strikes in defense of jobs and wages also increased in number and intensity after the watershed June 1989 teachers' strike, when the Sandinista teachers' union (ANDEN) went on a wildcat strike and succeeded in negotiating an agreement with the government.[41]

The CST, already at a low ebb, was hit particularly hard by the Sandinistas' electoral defeat. Dependent on party and state, it lost at least one patron and was forced to confront a hostile neoliberal regime bent on rolling back whatever remained of the revolutionary legacy. The new regime was heralded by cutbacks in social services, plant closings, massive layoffs, salary freezes, and further retrenchment in government departments. The first preelection gropings toward union autonomy and worker remobilization were greatly accelerated by the formation of the National Workers' Front (FNT) during the strikes and uprisings of May and July 1990, in which a rejuvenated union movement played a leading role. Furthermore, the FSLN's attempt to impose its will on striking workers and to singlehandedly direct the course of these chaotic events provided greater impetus to grass-roots desires for independence from party dictates. Under the new FNT umbrella, the CST became one of twenty-two labor federations with a total of 240,000 members. At the same time, the apparent ineffectiveness of company unions grouped under anti-Sandinista labor federations, such as the General Confederation of Labor (CGT), swelled the ranks of an increasingly militant and independent labor movement. In fact, 70 percent of unions in the CST experienced steady growth in the first two years after the electoral defeat. CST leader Damaso Vargas pointed out that while most of the union leaders were FSLN militants or sympathizers, there was no longer a formal relationship between the unions and the party: "It's a friendly relationship . . . we listen to their advice and they listen to ours. Their advice carried more weight before than it does today. Nonetheless, the FSLN continues to represent the people's interests which the FNT defends."[42]

The FSLN displayed complex and contradictory positions on the labor movement and its new-found militancy, positions that reflected the party's own contradictory position vis-à-vis the government (the so-called co-government) and the growing split within the party between "orthodox leftists" (the Democratic Left current) and "social democrats" (the Renovation Movement), which culminated in the latter's departure from the Frente in February 1995.[43] One of the major bones of contention between the two currents was an alleged disagreement concerning the permissible degree of militancy leading up to and during strike action, the "social democrats" criticizing the tendency for the labor movement to engage in violent protest using aggressive tactics such as erecting barricades and burning tires. Ironically, many of the self-styled hard-liners (Daniel Ortega, Tomás Borge, and Victor Hugo Tinoco) who later upheld the centrality of militant civic action were among those most critical of striking CST workers during the first three years of the Chamorro administration, counseling caution and moderation during negotiations with the government on impending privatizations but later encouraging strikes and occupations to enforce agreements.[44] Not surprisingly, the Sandinista current within the labor movement also began to experience divisions, partly sectoral and partly ideological, around issues of strategy and tactics.

For one thing, the CST soon discovered that the guidelines for peaceful union struggles embedded in the *concertación* agreements between the government and the Frente did not provide unions with much leverage to enforce their demands and hold the government to its promises.[45] The unions learned that only turning up the heat had any impact on a neoliberal state which systematically violated both the letter and the spirit of its contracts by decapitalizing state enterprises before turning over previously agreed-upon shares to the workers. Only militant protest and strike action by sugar workers in the state's CONAZUCAR enterprise—in alliance with the anti-Sandinista CGT labor federation—forced the government and plant managers to comply with agreements to privatize shares of the sugar refineries to the workers. By backing up negotiations with a show of strength, and by forcing the government to negotiate privatization on an industry-wide basis, unions obtained total or majority control over important production units rather than the weaker 25 percent across-the-board negotiated by the Frente in the *concertación* agreement. The union movement thus learned to form broad alliances across ideological divisions and to strike by sector or industry rather than on a plant-by-plant basis; and, with the sugar, transport, and hospital strikes, they also learned that timing was of the essence by exploiting windows of opportunity opened by the international financial community's occasional scrutiny of the Nicaraguan situation. By one assessment, the success of the CST in devising its own guidelines for struggle independently of and in opposition to the party clearly demonstrated a substantial degree of autonomy from the FSLN.[46]

By the end of 1992, some 234 of 351 state companies had been privatized—that is, workers obtained shares in 131 agricultural companies and 99 industry and transport concerns, with full control in 122 and 43 of these, respectively. While some of the worker-owned businesses were successful, others struggled to survive in an inhospitable political and economic climate exacerbated by onerous repayment terms for workers' shares (ten years at 6 percent interest). While the ownership of enterprises provided the labor movement with opportunities unique to Nicaragua—a share of the economic pie, the possibility of maintaining social services and a reasonable standard of living for at least some workers, and the potential to influence economic policy in the future—the creation of an Area of Workers' Property also generated significant conflicts and contradictions within the labor movement.

The ATC, for instance, was criticized for its lukewarm attitude toward land occupations by its members, with some observers alleging that this was due to the potential threat that labor unrest might later pose to its own entrepreneurial ambitions. Others noted that once state farms were privatized, they tended to be run by professional union managers rather than by the workers themselves.[47] The Concrete Products Industry (PROCON) was a model of internecine labor strife and recrimination. The divisions within the PROCON union were reflections of a growing split within the CST between its "moderate" general secretary, Lucio Jiménez, and "hard-liner" Roberto González, head of the CST splinter Broad Front for Struggle (FAL). The takeover of this highly profitable concern by the radical FAL faction and its dismissal of sixty-five non-FAL workers did not bode well for the future of the new trade unionism in Nicaragua.[48]

In the agricultural sector, one of the first moves by the incoming Chamorro administration was to put members of the old Somocista agro-export bourgeoisie in charge of the rural public sector. They set out to reprivatize state farms, deliberately underfinancing operations and renting out much of the land to former owners. Only strikes and demonstrations on the part of the state farm workers obtained a partial reversal of this process.[49] The co-operative movement also found itself under attack as former landlords and demobilized combatants from both the Sandinista People's Army (EPS) and the former Contras or Nicaraguan Resistance (ex-RN) began to demand or invade cooperative landholdings. Cooperatives also encountered difficulties in obtaining credit if their lands were in conflict, if they were not properly registered as cooperatives, or if they did not have properly registered titles. These problems were widespread given the many competing claims over property and challenges to the Sandinista agrarian reform laws and subsequent executive decrees governing titles to landed property.

The leaders of UNAG responded by initiating negotiations with the new government, which led to preliminary agreements on land titling, credit, and other issues affecting the cooperatives. UNAG also organized marketing cooperatives and expanded its network of peasant stores to allow cooperatives and small producers to compete more effectively with the large export-crop producers. UNAG's own ECODEPA distribution network made farm inputs available at lower prices and offered credit in the form of crop loans. According to Daniel Núñez, UNAG's national coordinator, a revolving loan fund made more than 30 million *córdobas* available to producers. Without UNAG, there would have been virtually no food production.[50]

Perhaps UNAG's greatest success was in the area of political reconciliation through its work with the demobilized ex-RN and ex-EPS. UNAG took on the claims of both of these former adversaries when they were denied the land promised to them by the Chamorro government in return for, respectively, laying down their weapons and accepting massive reductions in the armed forces. In April 1992, largely through the efforts of Nuñez, ex-RN, ex-EPS, and UNAG representatives established the National Peasant Coordination (CNC), an alliance including more than 200,000 peasants and 60 percent of the agricultural land in the country. Nuñez described this organization as multiparty and independent, with economic rather than political goals: "Without us there is no agricultural production. Commerce, the ports, and the banks would come to a standstill. . . . Those who think the peasants were born just to plant corn and beans can think again. . . . We want to be the big counterpart to COSEP."[51]

For all of UNAG's efforts, however, conditions for small-to-medium agricultural producers grew increasingly precarious, and a slow but inexorable reversal of the agrarian reform was under way as growing numbers of Nicaraguan peasants sold their land. Much of the turnover of land resulted from changes in the agrarian reform statutes that now permitted the sale of reformed land, but insecurity of tenure and lack of credit drove the process. Indeed, one of the most serious problems in the agricultural sector was the rapid individualization of formerly collective lands and the ensuing uncertainty as to title and responsibility for debts.[52] Ariel Bucardo, a member of UNAG's executive council, pointed out that before 1990 more than 80,000 producers had access to bank credit, whereas in 1995 only 16,000, mostly large-scale producers, were considered eligible.[53] In June 1995, thousands of peasants participated in a march coordinated by UNAG, calling for the government to resolve the property problem in three months, failing which a massive civic protest campaign would be launched. Settling the issue required, according to Bucardo, the awarding of titles to 20,000 beneficiaries of the agrarian reform involving 300,000 *manzanas* of land. The march also called for the capitalization of the state bank to provide credit to medium and small producers.[54]

Conclusion

While the obstacles to achieving popular democracy during the decade of the 1980s were the counterrevolutionary war and the economic embargo (which exacerbated the Frente's sectarianism and verticalism), the principal obstacle in the 1990s became the state itself and its promotion of elite interests via neoliberal economic policies. On the one hand, it could be argued that decentralizing the "movements," while solving some of the problems and correcting some of the mistakes previously made by the Sandinistas, diluted the potential power and influence of the masses and thereby weakened their ability to effect social change under the Chamorro government. On the other hand, however, it is difficult to imagine any other strategy that could have overcome the crisis confronting popular democracy in Nicaragua.

In his analysis of the "regime transformation" literature, Philip Williams argues that Nicaragua might be seen as a unique case in having created a more inclusive model of democracy by incorporating both representative and participatory components. Although constraints, both inherited and acquired, thwarted the full development of grass-roots democracy, the legacy of ten years of popular mobilization made the consolidation of a limited elite-dominated democracy problematic.[55] Certainly, it is remarkable that the popular organizations proved to be as resilient, and the commitment to social justice as ineradicable, as they were.

This legacy also made it impossible for the FSLN, as a self-styled, reborn "orthodox" left party, to reassert its dominion over the popular organizations which it had created and once effectively controlled. Confronted by the neoliberal state and the inexorable rollback of the modest gains in social justice and development experienced during the 1980s, "the same strata that were once mobilized for insurrection began to reorganize to demand what they had come to see as their rights. Evidently, whether the FSLN remains at the forefront of those struggles or not, the Sandinista revolution made social subjects out of those who were once the mere objects of policy."[56] The leaders of the popular organizations were, however, unmistakably at the forefront of those struggles. They were the true "Sandinistas"—the living legacy of the revolution, regardless of their party affiliation. They demonstrated an unshakable dedication to their communities, a profound commitment to the revolutionary project, and an unwavering hope for a better future.

Notes

1. Luis Hector Serra, "The Grass-roots Organizations," in *Revolution and Counterrevolution in Nicaragua*, ed. Thomas W. Walker (Boulder, CO: Westview Press, 1991).

2. *Envío* 14, no. 166 (May 1995): 5.

3. Authors' interview with Enrique Picado, Managua, January 1991. After the 1990 elections, Picado continued as vice coordinator. He was later elected national coordinator, and Máxima Bermúdez was elected vice coordinator.

4. The transformation of the CDS began in 1988 under the leadership of Omar Cabezas. The CDS was renamed Committee for Community Development (CDC) and was drastically decentralized. Essentially, communities were left to organize themselves and develop their own initiatives. See Pierre La Ramée and Erica Polakoff, "Transformation of the CDS and Breakdown of Grass-Roots Democracy in Revolutionary Nicaragua," *New Political Science* 18/19 (Fall/Winter 1990): 103–23.

5. Authors' interview with Máxima Bermúdez, Managua, December 1994.

6. Authors' interview with Picado.

7. Authors' interview with Sergio Obando, MC department coordinator, Granada, June 1995.

8. Before 1990 only local-level representatives were elected by the membership at large; others were generally designated by the FSLN.

9. Authors' interview with Máxima Bermúdez, Managua, June 1995.

10. Authors' interviews with MC department and municipal coordinators in Managua, Masaya, Granada, Diriamba, León, Matagalpa, and Estelí, June 1995.

11. Authors' interviews with MC coordinators and Máxima Bermúdez, June 1995.

12. Authors' interview with Bermúdez, June 1995. The Frente launched a campaign against the MC in *Barricada*, with headlines such as "Dangerous passivity of leaders: They don't act nor permit you to act in the Community Movement."

13. Authors' interviews with MC department and municipal coordinators in Managua, etc.

14. Authors' interview with María Auxiliadora Romero Cruz, MC coordinator of the day-care centers in Matagalpa, June 1995.

15. Authors' interview with Picado.

16. For an analysis of the FSLN's achievements in the areas of health, education, housing, and social welfare, see Harvey Williams, "The Social Programs," in *Revolution and Counterrevolution in Nicaragua*, ed. Thomas W. Walker (Boulder, CO: Westview Press, 1991), 187–212.

17. Braulio Urcuyo, *Casas Comunales del Niño* (Managua: Valdez & Valdez, 1994).

18. Authors' interview and site visits with Romero Cruz.

19. Author's interview with Bermúdez, December 1994.

20. Authors' interview with Romero Cruz.

21. Authors' interview with District Three delegate to the mayor's office, Managua, January 1991.

22. Authors' interview with Picado.

23. Authors' interview with Bermúdez, June 1995.

24. Authors' interview with Jeanette Castillo, MC municipal coordinator, Matagalpa, June 1995.

25. Maxine Molyneux, "Mobilization without Emancipation: Women's Interests, State, and Revolution," in *Transition and Development: Problems of Third World Socialism*, ed. Richard Fagen et al. (New York: Monthly Review Press, 1986), 280–302; Helen Collinson, *Women and Revolution in Nicaragua* (London: Zed, 1990).

26. See Jane Deighton et al., *Sweet Ramparts* (London: Spider Web Offset, 1983); and Collinson, *Women and Revolution in Nicaragua*.

27. Quoted in "Seeking Unity in Diversity," *Barricada Internacional* 12, no. 347 (March 1992): 22–31.

28. Margaret Randall, *Sandino's Daughters Revisited* (New Brunswick, NJ: Rutgers University Press), 28.

29. Authors' interview with Rosa Ceballo, MC district coordinator, Condega, Estelí, June 1995.

30. Dora Zeledón, "Mujer y Poder," *Barricada*, 1993.

31. Authors' interview with Bermúdez, June 1995.

32. Authors' interview with Ceballo.

33. Quoted in "Seeking Unity in Diversity," 25–26. The meeting referred to here was a women's conference convened by a group of non-AMNLAE allied feminists, Managua, January 1992.

34. Richard Stahler-Sholk, "Sandinista Economic and Social Policy: The Mixed Blessings of Hindsight," *Latin American Research Review* 30, no. 2 (1995): 238.

35. Authors' interview with María Auxiliadora Chiong, assistant director, Institute "Women and Community," Estelí, June 1995.

36. Serra, "The Grass-roots Organizations," 49.

37. Ibid., 62.

38. Serra (ibid., 56) describes the tactics used by "the party, government, or FSLN-oriented unions . . . to prevent delegates from other unions from running for leadership positions."

39. Scarlet Cuadra and Gabriela Selser, "The Labor Movement in Nicaragua: Change and Challenges," *Barricada Internacional* 11, no. 337 (May 1991): 21.

40. See Serra, "The Grass-roots Organizations," 50; and Carlos Vilas, "The Workers' Movement in the Sandinista Revolution," in *Nicaragua: A Revolution under Siege*, ed. Richard Harris and Carlos Vilas (London: Zed, 1985), 124.

41. Serra, "The Grass-roots Organizations," 69–71.

42. Interview with Damaso Vargas in *Barricada Internacional* 11, no. 337 (May 1991): 23–24. See also "The Urban Movement: Out from Under the FSLN's Wing," *Envío* (July 1992): 26–30.

43. See Pierre La Ramée, "Differences of Opinion: Interviews with Sandinistas," *NACLA Report on the Americas* 28, no. 5 (March/April 1995): 11–14.

44. Midge Quandt, "Unbinding the Ties: Popular Movements and the FSLN," *NACLA Report on the Americas* 26, no. 4 (February 1993): 11–14.

45. The *concertación* agreements of September 1991 gave workers in 350 state enterprises the right to at least a 25 percent share of those companies. Scarlet Cuadra, "Workers' Property in Nicaragua: New Dilemmas Every Day," *Barricada*

Internacional 12, no. 349 (May 1992): 19–25; idem, "Workers in the Privatization of State Companies: Challenged to Succeed," *Barricada Internacional* 13, no. 361 (May 1993): 11–18.

46. *Envío* (July 1992): 26–30.

47. Quandt, "Unbinding the Ties," 12.

48. See "Worker-owned Businesses: No Gift Horse," *Barricada Internacional* 15, no. 384 (May 1995): 18–24.

49. Eduardo Baumeister, "Agrarian Reform," in *Revolution and Counterrevolution in Nicaragua*, ed. Thomas W. Walker (Boulder, CO: Westview Press, 1991), 243.

50. Ibid.

51. "Hoisting Just One Flag," *Barricada Internacional* 12, no. 349 (May 1992): 23–24. COSEP is the Higher Council on Private Enterprise.

52. "Decollectivization: Agrarian Reform 'From Below,' " *Envío* 13, no. 161 (December 1994): 21–25.

53. Scarlet Cuadra, "Fighting to Democratize the Economy and Property," *Barricada Internacional* 15, no. 386 (July 1995): 26–27.

54. Moisés Castillo Zeas, "3 meses para resolver problema de propiedad," *El Nuevo Diario* (Managua), June 17, 1995.

55. Philip J. Williams, "Dual Transitions from Authoritarian Rule: Popular and Electoral Democracy in Nicaragua," *Comparative Politics* 26, no. 2 (January 1994): 169–85.

56. Stahler-Sholk, "Sandinista Economic and Social Policy," 250.

12

The Former Contras

Ariel C. Armony

In the early 1990s, Nicaragua underwent a transition toward liberal democracy characterized by the concurrence of a peace process and a political transition largely determined by external pressures, particularly from the United States. The nature and pace of the Nicaraguan transition were dictated by elite pacts or agreements, which incorporated the interests of the domestic political elites while restricting the participation of the popular sector in the decision-making process. As the literature has argued for other cases in Latin America, these agreements functioned as mechanisms that sought to minimize open conflict by assigning "winners" and "losers" in the competition for scarce political and economic resources. While facilitating the political transition, these types of negotiations impinged upon future democratization because they functioned as "elite manipulations" that restricted the prospects for popular participation. Not only did relevant political choices made during the "founding moments" of the new liberal democratic system seriously threaten the democratization process by undermining the notion of majority rule and compromising the policy agenda, but also the negotiated transition in Nicaragua failed to establish well-defined rules of the game because of the lack of commitment on the part of elites to comply with the agreements that they themselves had crafted.[1]

The decision of Nicaragua's prime political actors to enter a process of consensus building for achieving peace and political stability resulted from a convergence of several factors—among them, the country's serious economic crisis and the erosion of mass support for the war against the Contras, the realization on the part of the Sandinista government that the Contra forces could not be eliminated so long as the United States was willing to sustain them, the simultaneous recognition by the opposition that the counterrevolutionary military effort could not succeed in overthrowing the Sandinista regime, the intense pressure of regional actors on the Sandinistas and opposition to enter into peace negotiations, and the decline in U.S. congressional support for the Contra war following the Iran-Contra scandal.

Esquipulas I (1986) and Esquipulas II (1987) provided a framework for negotiations between the Sandinistas and the opposition that culminated in the Sapoá Accord of 1988 and the decision of the ruling FSLN to move the 1990 elections ahead from November to February.[2]

Following the 1990 electoral triumph of the UNO coalition, the process of consensus building focused on three areas: 1) the March 1990 transition protocol between the Sandinistas and the government-elect, which sought to establish ground rules for political stability and viable conditions for governance; 2) the disarmament and demobilization accords between the Nicaraguan Resistance (Resistencia Nicaragüense, or RN, formerly Nicaraguan Democratic Force, or FDN) and the administration of Violeta Chamorro; and 3) the efforts to reach a social consensus in order to guarantee social stability in the context of structural economic reforms.[3]

The impact of elite agreements and the marginalization of mass actors in the transition and posttransition processes helped to shape the role played by the social grouping known as the "former Contras" in the 1990s. Even though the Chamorro administration succeeded in disarming the Resistance forces and discharging thousands of Sandinista People's Army (Ejército Popular Sandinista, or EPS) and Ministry of Government (Ministerio de Gobierno, or MINGOB, formerly Ministry of the Interior) personnel in the first two and one-half years, it failed to provide the necessary assistance to reinsert the former combatants into production (see Chapter 4, this volume). Reaching a formal end to the military confrontation was relatively easier than achieving consensus on the political and social conflicts inherited from the war. Since elites were committed only to the demobilization process— a key issue in the negotiated transition—the necessity of providing effective responses to the population uprooted by the war was never a priority at the bargaining table. The consequences of the Contra war were to be dealt with in the framework of neoliberal policies favored by the new government and with very scarce resources available for redistribution among societal actors, particularly among the former Contra peasants who were promised land and credit to facilitate their reintegration into civilian life.[4]

Determined to implement sweeping free-market economic reforms, the Chamorro administration could not face the costs of broadening its social agenda to include former combatants from both sides, internally displaced families, and repatriated refugees. Consequently, the system became overloaded with increasing demands from those sectors most affected by the dismantling of the state and the imposition of "the market" in Nicaragua. The low effectiveness and, sometimes, obliteration of state legality, a consequence of the drastic structural adjustment of the early 1990s, also posed important obstacles to the effective implementation of the peace accords and the social reinsertion of marginalized groups. As a result, violence escalated when bands of demobilized Resistance combatants (known as *recontras*), demobilized Sandinista armed forces personnel (known as *recompas*), and, later, mixed groups of former Contras and Sandinista peasants (known as *revueltos*) took up arms to press the government to respond to their demands.[5]

The situation of tension and polarization in the countryside led to an upsurge of violent action, including assassinations of former Contras and Sandinistas, politically inspired kidnappings, takeovers of towns, public buildings, and roads, armed attacks against security forces, and land invasions.[6] By mid-1992 there were some 22,000 rearmed former combatants from both sides operating throughout Nicaragua, mainly in the northern region. At the peak of the political crisis the Chamorro administration entered into a succession of short-term agreements with the rebels in order to control the chaotic situation and prevent the country from moving toward rampant social violence and renewed civil war. Rearmed groups of former Contras and Sandinistas continued their actions in northern Nicaragua and the Atlantic Coast through the mid-1990s.[7]

On July 21, 1993, a band of rearmed peasants, largely former EPS soldiers organized in the self-proclaimed Revolutionary Front of Workers and Peasants (FROC), took over Estelí to demand credit, property titles, access to education, improvements in health care, and the fulfillment of the agreements between the government and demobilized combatants. The EPS responded with a strong military offensive that led to a bloody confrontation resulting in forty-five dead and ninety-eight injured, about 90 percent of whom were FROC rebels and civilians. The army's response showed the determination of the government to act "with a strong hand" to impede the rise of the insurrectionary phenomenon in the countryside to the levels reached in 1992. The fragility of Nicaragua's political stability was exposed again in August 1993 in a double hostage crisis. A group of *recontras* (the 3-80 Northern Front) took hostage a peace delegation of Sandinista parliamentary deputies, government officials, and Special Disarmament Brigade (BED) officers in Quilalí. The rebels were demanding the dismissal of Gen. Humberto Ortega, Col. Lenín Cerna, and Antonio Lacayo. In response, a group of former Sandinista soldiers organized in the Dignity and Sovereignty Commando took over the UNO headquarters in Managua, where the coalition's political council was in session, and demanded the release of the *recontras'* hostages in Quilalí. The ensuing political crisis forced the government, the UNO's stand-in political council, and the national directorate of the FSLN to join efforts in order to reach a peaceful solution.[8]

The recourse to violence by marginalized groups in the post-Sandinista period cannot be seen as a mere legacy of the Contra war. It should be construed as a new phenomenon determined by an extremely polarized national context, the rapid failure of the RN's development strategy for the reinsertion of former Contra combatants and their families, the decomposition of the Resistance movement, the state's growing inability to successfully claim the monopoly of the legitimate use of physical force and to disarm the civilian population, and the drastic retrenchment of the state as guarantor of the rule of law and provider of welfare assistance and support to those groups most affected by economic structural reform. The absence of a political space of representation, the increasing obstacles to civil society activity, and the lack of solutions to long-standing agrarian conflicts invited marginalized actors to take up arms, seeking to pressure the government into finding solutions to their demands.[9] "We decided to opt for armed struggle because we are tired of waiting," said a member of an armed group formed by demobilized Contras and Sandinistas in early 1995. "It's been more than five years since the government promised to give us property titles and bank credits."[10] General frustration and skepticism among the disenfranchised population, reinforced by worsening economic and institutional crises, translated into a spiral of grass-roots violence that contributed to weaken Nicaragua's already fragile democratic structure.[11]

Background

Although the Sandinistas embarked on an ambitious agrarian reform program shortly after coming to power in 1979, their relations with at least a segment of the peasantry soon proved to be disappointing to both sides.[12] The welfare of many peasants was undermined by economic policies that resulted in a stark decline in terms of trade for the countryside, thus frustrating income-redistribution policies in the rural sector, and by the unintended effects of centralizing in urban areas the distribution of credit and consumer goods. Some peasants were also antagonized by the state-promoted policy of agricultural collectivization that focused attention on large state-managed rural units of production (considered vital for the reactivation of the economy), overlooking the demands of private peasant producers. The attempt to impose an administrative model that did not correspond to historical patterns of rural organization of production resulted in the disaffection of a large sector of the peasantry. The pressure on peasants to enter into forms of collective farming in order to gain access to land, and the state's goal of destroying the traditional individualistic peasant economy of production and replacing it with cooperative production, were also major causes of alienation.[13]

Other important reasons for the increasing appeal of the counterrevolution among rural inhabitants were ideological and religious dissent and ethnic conflict. U.S.-promoted anti-Communist propaganda and fear of a one-party Marxist state by Nicaragua's Roman Catholic Church hierarchy, which also opposed the identification of Sandinismo with Christianity, permeated the core of the peasantry. Furthermore, the mistakes committed by Sandinista officials in their relations with the ethnic minorities of the Atlantic region (Miskitos, Sumus, and Ramas) accentuated a historical legacy of conflict between the coastal peoples and western Nicaraguans. Early

Miskito-Sandinista tensions resulted in spiraling Contra activity on the Atlantic Coast.[14]

The rich and middle peasantry,[15] who were among the first to organize anti-Sandinista armed bands following the triumph of the revolution, played a major role in the recruitment of rank-and-file troops for the Contra forces. As a strategic link between the agrarian bourgeoisie and the poor peasantry, rich and middle peasants articulated interests that crosscut class alignments.[16] Outside mobilizers provided the resources for peasant insurrection against the Sandinista regime, but they shaped the struggle in terms of their elite interests—namely, the goal to regain their prerevolutionary socioeconomic and political privileges. Counterrevolutionary domestic and foreign actors with independent but complementary agendas were able to gather strength when large peasant groups became highly dissatisfied with state policies. Their discontent was thus channeled through armed resistance under a movement that consistently ignored the rank and file's demands and identity. This pattern continued under the "elite-dominated" negotiation process that accompanied the transition from FSLN to UNO rule in 1990: contrary to their expectation of immediate benefits from the UNO electoral victory, poor Contra peasants were marginalized in the process of consensus building. The RN leadership's inability to craft a strategy of negotiation aimed at securing mechanisms to guarantee government support for the reinsertion of former foot soldiers—as the Farabundo Martí National Liberation Front (Frente Farabundo Martí de Liberación Nacional, or FMLN) did in El Salvador, linking the demobilization process to government compliance with the peace accords—contributed to the mounting crisis that led to postwar rural violence.[17]

More than 600,000 people (about 15 percent of the total population) had been uprooted by the Contra war during the 1980s and an estimated 30,000 civilians and combatants died during that confrontation.[18] About 83 percent of the Contra foot soldiers were poor peasants and wage laborers from Nicaragua's northern and central regions, the area known as the agricultural frontier—vast vacant lowlands between the central and Atlantic regions.[19] Only 25 percent of the Contra combatants owned any form of property, 60 percent were under twenty-five years old, and 90 percent were illiterate or semiliterate. At the end of the war, the Nicaraguan Resistance organization claimed to represent more than 170,000 people in rural areas, including over 22,000 officially demobilized Contras and their families plus some 70,000 repatriates and 3,000 refugees. More than 50 percent of the Contra combatants' returning relatives were minors.[20]

The 1990 government-RN accords included an attempt to provide a comprehensive solution to the problem of the veterans' reinsertion by establishing areas designated for "development poles." The Disarmament Protocol of May 30, 1990, defined a "development pole" as "a production unit designed to benefit members of the community and the country, acting as a center for services and development for the surrounding region." It was agreed that each pole had to include housing and private plots of land for subsistence farming and ranching, potable water and electricity, schools, roads, and hospitals. Even though 80 percent of the Contra veterans who received land were concentrated around the development poles in El Almendro (Chontales), Río Blanco (Matagalpa), and Bocay-Ayapal (Jinotega), serious funding limitations and property conflicts frustrated the implementation of the project.[21]

In the postwar period the negotiations between the Chamorro administration and the irregular armed bands of *recontras* were bounded by the official decision to respond only to demands that did not pose obstacles to the ongoing program of structural reform. This decision led to an atomistic and disorganized bargaining process focused on transient, partial solutions to critical socioeconomic problems. The government's policy of conceding tangible benefits to the earliest rebel groups, in an attempt to control the growing turmoil in the countryside, unwittingly encouraged the use of violence and civic disruption by former Contras and former Sandinistas. As the socioeconomic situation in rural areas worsened, many uprooted teenagers joined those rearmed groups. In 1994 only 30 percent of the members of irregular bands detained for rural banditry were war veterans. This figure indicates that a nucleus of experienced former combatants was leading an increasing number of rural youth who viewed armed action as the only option for remuneration.[22]

By 1992 there were almost 23,000 rearmed insurgents operating in rural Nicaragua (see table). Following emergency negotiations and new agreements between the government and dissident groups throughout 1992, the number of rebels decreased significantly by the end of that year. The effectiveness of the disarmament process was primarily a function of the government's program to buy weapons from civilians and rearmed groups, the presence of the BEDs in the most conflictive areas, and the army's offensive in the northern region of the country. By the end of 1992, eighty-two *recontra* and *recompa* groups had been disarmed (the BED claimed to have recovered over forty-three thousand weapons). However, growing discontent among demobilized combatants soon led to an increase in the number of armed actions.

Having realized that the weapons purchase program had turned rearming into a profitable activity for rural dwellers, the government declared a State of Emergency, suspended all negotiations with rearmed groups, declared them outlaws, and urged them to move into security zones to avoid a definitive military strike. The limited response to the government's ultimatum forced the Chamorro administration to offer amnesty and renewed assistance to the rebel groups in return for their disarmament. Late in 1994 the government decided to make good on previous commitments to former combatants from both sides via cash payments, distribution of land and

Postwar Rural Violence (*recontras, recompas, revueltos*)

Year	Armed Actions	Participants
1991	238	n.a.
1992	378	22,893*
1993	554	1,300
1994	390	1,200

Source: Angel Saldomando, "El proceso de pacificación en Nicaragua, 1990–1994," draft manuscript, Managua, February 1995, p. 95.
*From 1991 to late 1992
n.a.: not available

housing, and employment as police or BED personnel. The former Contra forces were the principal beneficiaries of the government's compensation: the RN received 72 percent of the total disbursement (estimated at $97 million), and some 11,600 former RN troops received about 80 percent of the land distributed in this last phase. At the end of 1994 the government estimated that most of the rebel groups had been disbanded, but by mid-1995 the number of insurgents escalated again to some 1,000 men.[23]

Unfulfilled Promises

The 1990 peace accords had resulted in the demobilization of thousands of Contra combatants under the supervision of the Organization of American States' International Support and Verification Commission (Comisión Internacional de Apoyo y Verificación, or CIAV-OEA) and the United Nations' Organization for Central America (Organización de las Naciones Unidas para Centroamérica, or ONUCA). The Chamorro administration had promised a series of welfare policies designed to facilitate the reinsertion of demobilized Contras into civilian life in return for the assurance that the RN would recognize the legitimacy of the new government and would support the process of national reconciliation. This agreement with the Resistance was vital to promote the peace and stability needed for the success of the administration's economic reform package. In turn, the RN leadership faced the pressure to reach a compromise with the government-elect in light of the new scenario opened up by the political transition. The FSLN's electoral defeat and its peaceful extrication from power meant that the primary Contra military objective had been achieved, demanding the Resistance to evolve into a democratic political organization in order to maintain its cohesion and the continuing support of its rank and file.[24]

The demands of the former Contra troops were used by the Chamorro administration's executive branch and the UNO's extreme right-wing bloc as a clientalistic device to win over political allies. The government's negotiation strategy with rearmed groups was aimed at the co-optation of leaders and foot soldiers, proffering bribes according to rank.[25] Increasingly, former Contras, and demobilized Sandinistas as well, perceived that their chances to obtain state support depended upon their capacity to stage "spectacular" military actions and to develop local "areas of influence" that would give them some legitimacy to sustain their claims before local authorities. The competition for scarce resources led to growing tensions among irregular groups of former Contras and former Sandinistas.[26]

The demand for land was a critical issue for the Contra peasants, who had been promised individual plots in return for their disarming. This issue turned out to be a main source of discontent and tension among former combatants when it became clear that the Chamorro administration could not comply with the commitment to distribute land to all demobilized Contras. While the government's Nicaraguan Institute of Agrarian Reform (Instituto Nicaragüense de Reforma Agraria, or INRA) asserted that it had distributed land to 11,580 demobilized Contras (a total of 409,916 *manzanas*, with one *manzana* equaling 1.7 acres) by 1992 (when postwar rural violence reached its peak), the RN argued that government-allocated land constituted only 27 percent (277,672 *manzanas*) of the total promised, benefiting merely 6,573 demobilized combatants. As the figure below shows, the conflict over the distribution of land affected particularly the central region (Boaco and Chontales, which correspond to Region V) and the northern region (Matagalpa and Jinotega, which correspond to Region VI), where 61 percent of the demobilized Contra troops were concentrated. The difference between the INRA and RN's estimations apparently corresponded to land given to *colonos* (peasants without land titles) and *precaristas* (squatters), plots illegally occupied by demobilized Contras and land privatized or returned to its original holders. Numerous conflicts erupted between demobilized Contra soldiers and poor peasants because the latter were already settled on plots assigned to the former Contras, thus creating a tense situation in which two marginalized poor groups were compelled to compete with each other for subsistence land.[27]

The demobilization accords also stipulated that the government was to guarantee the privatization of land held by state-owned rural enterprises (HATONIC, CAFENIC, and AGROEXCO) for distribution, in equal parts, among their workers, former owners, demobilized EPS and MINGOB personnel, and demobilized RN troops. However, by 1992 the government had allocated only 6.2 of the 25 percent assigned to the Resistance. In sum, only 8 percent of the total land distributed by the government to the former Contras came from the privatization of state-owned rural corporations.[28]

Another critical problem decried by the RN was the INRA's failure to issue legal titles for the land distributed to demobilized Contra troops. When rural violence by rearmed groups skyrocketed in 1992, only 3 percent of recipients had been granted legal entitlement by the INRA. Those who received land but no titles could not have access to credit. In addition to this problem, the lack of technical support and other government services trans-

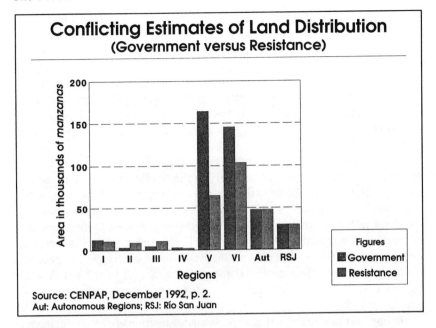

Conflicting Estimates of Land Distribution
(Government versus Resistance)

Source: CENPAP, December 1992, p. 2.
Aut: Autonomous Regions; RSJ: Río San Juan

lated into a growing informal land market that led to a reconcentration of property in few hands, threatening to alter the structure of land tenure in favor of large landowners (see Chapter 6, this volume). The INRA estimated that 30 percent of former combatants who received land sold it at low prices. It is important to note that most of the plots allocated to veterans were not suitable for traditional agriculture but rather for cattle ranching and forestation. Furthermore, since a large portion of the Contra rank and file had joined as adolescents and spent most of their adult life as guerrilla foot soldiers, they had had little or no farming experience.[29]

The severe national crisis triggered by the demobilization of over 94,000 RN and EPS/MINGOB troops and personnel was deepened by the deteriorating socioeconomic rural conditions in the late 1980s and early 1990s. Particularly serious was the situation in Jinotega, Matagalpa, Estelí, Madriz, and Nueva Segovia, where 40 percent of the demobilized Contras were concentrated. About 46 percent of the country's extremely poor lived in those departments, which shared only 22.9 percent of Nicaragua's total population.[30]

Civil Society or Parochialization?

Based on the assumption that the transition to liberal democracy leads to the "resurrection of civil society," various authors argue that civil society can be a solid base for new democracies if it provides individuals real opportunities to participate in shaping the political agenda.[31] Scholars also argue that democratic stability and consolidation must rest on a moderate civil society that holds back decisive claims until democratic institutions are capable of absorbing these demands without threatening the entire system. Civil society, according to this perspective, is locked into a conflicting situation. It is called to provide legitimacy to the democratic system; but, at the same time, it is advised to refrain from advancing "democratic" substantive demands that may conflict with political prudence, moderation, and accommodation—conditions that are deemed critical in a process of democratization.[32]

Civil society is defined here as the realm of voluntary, autonomous citizen action that operates collectively in the public sphere. Civil society defies assimilation to the privatism of the marketplace and challenges the established logic of the party system.[33] The development of civil society is closely related to the concurrent strengthening of state institutions and the market. Public policies have a key role in shaping social action because they nourish particular interests at the expense of others. These policies can have a strong effect on social inequalities, access to the policymaking process, and the institution of rules of conduct relevant to all civil associations.[34]

In contrast to countries that experienced transitions from exclusionary authoritarian regimes, Nicaragua already had—before undergoing a transition to a liberal form of democracy—an array of highly mobilized and largely democratic grass-roots organizations whose rank and file came largely from traditionally marginalized groups (see Chapter 11, this volume). If civil society is conceived as autonomous from the state, then civil society was relatively weak during the Sandinista period. However, several organizations created in the 1980s gradually gained autonomy from the state, thus laying down a basis for a potential civil society in Nicaragua. In addition to the post-Sandinista grass-roots movement, the former Contra rank and file began acting collectively in the public sphere following the demobilization process. These actors initially accepted the idea of making demands on the state under the rules of "democratic" bargaining—that is, desisting from violence and respecting the new institutional order. However, as the government consistently blocked their access to the policymaking structure, it became increasingly arduous for them to advance their claims while remaining committed to the established rules of the game.

During most of the first half of the 1990s the former Contras made demands on the state by employing largely "undemocratic" means that involved outright violence. These rebellious groups remained centered on the key, unresolved issue of the peasantry's welfare. While making essentially "democratic" demands and using violence as a means of strategic action, the former Contras tended to hinder the development of a viable civil society in Nicaragua. These actions exacerbated conflicts and overloaded the decision-making process, eventually making the system almost ungovernable.[35]

Preoccupation with the role of the former Contras in the construction of civil society in Nicaragua requires attention to the problem of incorporation of undemocratic actors in a liberal democratic system. It has been suggested that new democracies have to accommodate authoritarian groups, providing adequate channels for their participation within the democratic game. According to its proponents, this strategy reduces the risks of extrainstitutional attacks on the democratic system and strengthens the chances for democratic coexistence.[36] Even though in Nicaragua the Contras were not in power prior to the transition to liberal democracy, one needs to ask to what extent their record of widespread violations of human rights during their low-intensity war against the Sandinista regime could prevent them from becoming potential builders of civil society.[37] In addition, the provision of institutional and civic channels to participate in democratic politics for this kind of voluntary association—largely characterized by intolerance and endorsement of violence—could help to erode the support for democracy by those groups that could provide the seeds for the coalescence of civil society.[38]

Organizations of former Contras that continued to employ violence as a means of resistance could not be considered elements of civil society. Increasing mobilization of anticivil groups posed a threat to Nicaragua's incipient civil society and hence to the prospects for deepening democracy. A weak civil society coupled with seriously eroded state capacities to administer and enforce the rule of law accentuated the dominant trend of parochialization in Nicaragua. As an alternative to civil society, which "provides an adhesive that brings together disparate groups and interests within a common framework," parochialization is characterized by the prevalence of particularistic forms of organization centered on "attempts to colonize all or some parts of the state apparatus or, alternatively, to place one's own group beyond the reach of the law and of state power generally."[39] Parochialization was common in Nicaragua under the Chamorro administration. Furthermore, economic decay, weakness of institutional power, and paralysis of collective action (dominant features in many Latin American polities) helped to consolidate a "democracy by default" in Nicaragua— that is, "a political regime that survives because no other alternatives are available."[40]

Conclusion

In the 1990s the Contra movement unfolded into several organizations with different kinds of leadership, strategies, and goals. The Nicaraguan Resistance Civic Association (Asociación Cívica Resistencia Nicaragüense, or

ACRN) was the most effective in terms of its capacity of negotiation with government authorities and cooperation with national and international institutions and nongovernmental organizations. Set up by former RN field commanders as an intermediate voluntary association aimed at facilitating the reinsertion of demobilized Contras into civilian life, the ACRN focused attention on working with the Chamorro administration to establish viable mechanisms of cooperation and on strengthening support networks among Nicaragua's peasantry. In turn, another former Contra group, the Nicaraguan Resistance Party (Partido Resistencia Nicaragüense, or PRN), sought to channel the organizational resources of the Contra movement into a national political party. One of the PRN's key objectives was to position its members in important government posts—for example, as INRA representatives in areas with large demobilized Contra populations. As of 1994 the PRN was unable to integrate the personal agenda of its leadership (former Contra commanders) with the demands of the rank and file.[41]

The array of rearmed bands of Contras represented a complex phenomenon of postwar violence that included criminal activities, personal and political feuds, self-defense motivations, and socioeconomic claims. Some groups worked as armed thugs for large landowners or adopted banditry as a way of life, while others espoused demands for land, housing, and basic government services. The stream of grass-roots collective action generated by the latter groups led to the emergence of new leaders, usually with strong popular support at the local level, who first promoted armed action to advance peasants' demands but soon rejected the government's strategy of co-optation and advocated the need for reconciliation and collective action by formerly mutually hostile disenfranchised groups. This emerging leadership helped to form alliances between units of the demobilized Contra and Sandinista rank and file. Among the new organizations formed by Contra and Sandinista veterans were the Foundation of Ex-Combatants of War and the Alliance for Peace. In addition, the National Union of Farmers and Cattlemen (Unión Nacional de Agricultores y Ganaderos, or UNAG) integrated demobilized Contras and Sandinistas to promote a unified agenda of negotiation with the Chamorro government.[42]

These developments indicate that some groups associated with the wave of violence of the early 1990s began using their organizational resources and growing sense of identity to enter the democratic arena as civil society actors aimed at increasing, through self-organization, their means of resistance against exploitation and marginalization. The transformative potential of the groups that incorporated peasants who fought on the side of the Contras or the Sandinistas would be directly linked to their ability to overcome the limitations of both Sandinista and anti-Sandinista dominant political discourses, and to move from violent and parochial resistance to democratic participation. In addition, the prospects for a viable civil society would be tied to the decision of economic and political elites to commit to opening the political system to all organized social actors and to strengthening pluralist institutional channels for participation. As of the mid-1990s it remained an open question whether a stronger and more inclusive civil society in Nicaragua would be able to redress long-standing structures of economic inequality, extreme poverty, and domination.[43]

Notes

1. See Terry Lynn Karl, "Dilemmas of Democratization in Latin America," *Comparative Politics* 23 (October 1990): 1–21; idem, "Petroleum and Political Pacts: The Transition to Democracy in Venezuela," in *Transitions from Authoritarian Rule: Latin America*, ed. Guillermo O'Donnell, Philippe C. Schmitter, and Lawrence Whitehead (Baltimore: Johns Hopkins University Press, 1986); Frances Hagopian, " 'Democracy by Undemocratic Means'? Elites, Political Pacts, and Regime Transition in Brazil," *Comparative Political Studies* 23 (July 1990): 147–70; Guillermo O'Donnell and Philippe C. Schmitter, *Transitions from Authoritarian Rule: Tentative Conclusions about Uncertain Democracies* (Baltimore: Johns Hopkins University Press, 1986); and John Higley and Richard Gunther, eds., *Elites and Democratic Consolidation in Latin America and Southern Europe* (Cambridge, Eng.: Cambridge University Press, 1992).

2. Angel Saldomando and Elvira Cuadra, "Los problemas de la pacificación en Nicaragua: Recomposición de grupos armados y conflictos sociales," working paper, Coordinadora Regional de Investigaciones Económicas y Sociales (CRIES), Managua, February 1994, 4.

3. Ibid., 5.

4. See *Envío* 14 (May 1995): 4.

5. The groups of *recompas* were organized by demobilized EPS and MINGOB personnel. The *revueltos* incorporated former combatants from both sides in a unique blend that overcame ideological and political discrepancies and converged on collective peasant demands. The Democratic Front for National Salvation (Frente Democrático de Salvación Nacional, or FDSN) coordinated the rearmed Contra groups while the National Self-Defense Movement (Movimiento de Autodefensa Nacional, or MADNA) coordinated the *recompa* groups. Saldomando and Cuadra, "Los problemas de la pacificación," 16–17; Angel Saldomando, "El proceso de pacificación en Nicaragua, 1990–1994," draft manuscript, Managua, February 1995, 18–21; Guillermo Fernández Ampié, "Rumors of War," *Barricada Internacional* (March 1993): 4–6.

6. See Human Rights Watch/Americas, "Separating Facts from Fiction: The Work of the Tripartite Commission in Nicaragua," New York, October 1994.

7. Saldomando, "El proceso de pacificación," 13–17, 95.

8. *Barricada Internacional* (August 1993): 4–6; Saldomando, "El proceso de pacificación," 31; Guillermo Fernández Ampié, "The Country Held Hostage," *Barricada Internacional* (September 1993): 4–6.

9. See Saldomando and Cuadra, "Los problemas de la pacificación," 20–23.

10. As quoted in *Barricada Internacional* (March 1995): 5.

11. See Terry Lynn Karl, "The Hybrid Regimes of Central America," *Journal of Democracy* 6 (July 1995): 72–86.

12. This section is largely based on Ariel Armony and Robert Chisholm, "Is Social Revolution Possible in a Liberal Era? Revolution and Compromise in Nicaragua, 1979–1990," paper delivered at the Annual Meeting of the American Political Science Association, New York, September 1994.

13. Forrest D. Colburn, *Post-Revolutionary Nicaragua: State, Class, and the Dilemmas of Agrarian Policy* (Berkeley: University of California Press, 1986), 114 (table); Vera Gianotten, Ton de Wit, and Rodrigo Montoya, *Nicaragua: Cuestión agraria y participación campesina* (Lima, Peru: DESCO, 1987), 43–46. See Alejandro Bendaña, ed., *Una tragedia campesina: Testimonios de la resistencia* (Managua: CEI, 1991). As the Contra war escalated, the agrarian reform program changed in 1985 from an emphasis on the creation of a state-owned agricultural sector and the promotion of production cooperatives to the distribution of individual land titles in the hope of winning back peasant support.

14. Orlando Núñez, ed., *La guerra en Nicaragua* (Managua: CIPRES, 1991), 30–39; Thomas W. Walker, *Nicaragua: The Land of Sandino* (Boulder, CO: Westview Press, 1991), 98–99.

15. The rich and middle peasantry is defined here as a landed group (10 to 50 *manzanas*) whose main activity was the production of crops for the domestic market. See Laura Enríquez, *Harvesting Change: Labor and Agrarian Reform in Nicaragua, 1979–1990* (Chapel Hill: University of North Carolina Press, 1991), 7–8.

16. See Eric Wolf, *Peasant Wars of the Twentieth Century* (New York: Harper and Row, 1969), 289–90.

17. Colburn, *Post-Revolutionary Nicaragua*, 22; Philip J. Williams, "Dual Transitions from Authoritarian Rule: Popular and Electoral Democracy in Nicaragua," *Comparative Politics* 5 (January 1994): 180–82; Oscar Sobalvarro García ("Comandante Rubén"), interview with author, Managua, July 7, 1993; Saldomando and Cuadra, "Los problemas de la pacificación," 11; Judy Butler, "Nicaragua's Lessons in the Four Rs: Reconciliation, Reconstruction, Reinsertion, and Rehabilitation," paper delivered at the XIX International Congress of the Latin American Studies Association, Washington, DC, September 1995, 4; *Barricada Internacional* (March 1992): 6–7; *Envío* (May 1995): 5–6.

18. Butler, "Nicaragua's Lessons," 4; *Envío* (May 1995): 4; Michael Clodfelter, *Warfare and Armed Conflicts: A Statistical Reference to Casualty and Other Figures, 1618–1991* (Jefferson, NC: McFarland and Co., 1987), 1169.

19. Centro Nacional de Planificación y Administración de los Polos (CENPAP), Asociación Cívica Resistencia Nicaragüense (ACRN), "Balance del proceso de reinserción," 1990, 4; Centro de Investigaciones y Estudios de la Reforma Agraria (CIERA), *La reforma agraria en Nicaragua, 1979–1989* (Managua: CIERA, 1989), 6: 35; Eduardo Baumeister, "Farmers' Organizations and Agrarian Transformation in Nicaragua," in *The New Politics of Survival: Grass-roots Movements in Central America*, ed. Minor Sinclair (New York: Monthly Review Press, 1995), 245–46.

20. CENPAP, "Balance del proceso," 4; Butler, "Nicaragua's Lessons," 5; CENPAP, "Aportes para la estrategia de desarrollo agropecuario en Nicaragua," mimeo, December 1992, 1. As of June 1990 the exact figure of demobilized Contras was 22,413. During the following months some 5,000 Contras laid down their arms under the supervision of CIAV-OEA and ONUCA.

21. Butler, "Nicaragua's Lessons," 3; CENPAP, "La reforma agraria y los polos de desarrollo," January 1992, 17.

22. CENPAP, "Aportes para la estrategia," 21–24; Saldomando and Cuadra, "Los problemas de la pacificación," 18–24, 32–33; Butler, "Nicaragua's Lessons," 21, citing United Nations Development Program (UNDP), "Contribuciones al análisis de la transición nicaragüense," June 1995.

23. Saldomando, "El proceso de pacificación," 55–74; Saldomando and Cuadra, "Los problemas de la pacificación," 31; Butler, "Nicaragua's Lessons," 16–18.

24. Saldomando and Cuadra, "Los problemas de la pacificación," 9.

25. It is important to note that the military structure of the Contra forces paralleled Nicaragua's rural social stratification. When the government paid *recontra* groups to disarm, resources were distributed according to that very structure. Baumeister, "Farmers' Organizations," 251; Saldomando and Cuadra, "Los problemas de la pacificación," 33.

26. Saldomando and Cuadra, "Los problemas de la pacificación," 11, 23–24; *Barricada Internacional* (March 1992): 6–8; *Envío* (May 1995): 5–6.

27. CENPAP, "La reforma agraria," 19–21; idem, "Aportes para la estrategia," 2–3, 29, 33. It is important to point out that 8 percent of the land allocated by the government to the RN was assigned to families headed by women—widows or single mothers associated with the Contra movement.

28. CENPAP, "Aportes para la estrategia," 3–4.

29. Butler, "Nicaragua's Lessons," 5, 22; CENPAP, "Balance del proceso," 4; idem, "La reforma agraria," 30–31, 33; idem, "Aportes para la estrategia," 4–8.

30. About 78 percent of the extremely poor lived in Nicaragua's rural areas. Renato Aguilar and Asa Stenman, "Nicaragua 1994: Back into the Ranks," Department of Economics, University of Gothenburg, September 1994, 29–30, citing World Bank, Living Standards Measurement Survey (LSMS), 1993; Saldomando, "El proceso de pacificación," 94.

31. See, for instance, O'Donnell and Schmitter, *Transitions from Authoritarian Rule*, chap. 5.

32. Larry Diamond and Juan J. Linz, "Introduction: Politics, Society, and Democracy in Latin America," in *Democracy in Developing Countries: Latin America*, ed. Larry Diamond, Juan J. Linz, and Seymour Martin Lipset (Boulder, CO: Lynne Rienner, 1989), 12.

33. See M. Steven Fish, "Russia's Fourth Transition," *Journal of Democracy* 5 (July 1994): 31, 41; Larry Diamond, "Toward Democratic Consolidation," ibid, 4–17; and Philippe C. Schmitter and Terry Lynn Karl, "What Democracy Is . . . and Is Not," *Journal of Democracy* 2 (Summer 1991): 79–80. See also Jean L. Cohen and Andrew Arato, *Civil Society and Political Theory* (Cambridge, MA: MIT Press, 1992), 1–26.

34. Naomi Chazan, "Africa's Democratic Challenge," *World Policy Journal* 9 (Spring 1992): 279–307.

35. See Schmitter and Karl, "What Democracy Is," 80, 88n.9.

36. O'Donnell and Schmitter, *Transitions from Authoritarian Rule*, 69–72.

37. On Contra human rights violations see reports by Washington Office on Latin America and Human Rights Watch/Americas (formerly Americas Watch). See also Catholic Institute for International Relations, *Right to Survive: Human Rights in Nicaragua* (London: CIIR, 1987); and Sam Dillon, *Comandos: The CIA and Nicaragua's Contra Rebels* (New York: Henry Holt and Co., 1991).

38. See Leigh A. Payne, "Authoritarian Movements in the New Latin American Democracies: A Case Study of the Argentine Carapintada," paper delivered at the Annual Meeting of the American Political Science Association, Chicago, August–September 1995; and Chazan, "Africa's Democratic Challenge," 283.

39. Chazan, "Africa's Democratic Challenge," 282; Fish, "Russia's Fourth Transition," 39.

40. Giorgio Alberti, "Democracy by Default: Economic Crisis, Movimientismo, and Social Anomie in Latin America," paper delivered at the University of Bologna, May 1991, 6, cited in Luigi Manzetti, "Institutional Decay and Distributional Coalitions in Developing Countries: The Argentine Riddle Reconsidered," *Studies in Comparative International Development* 29 (Summer 1994): 82–114.

41. CENPAP, "Aportes para la estrategia," 10–12; Saldomando and Cuadra, "Los problemas de la pacificación," 10–13.

42. Camilo Dormóz ("Comandante Búfalo"), interview with author, Bluefields, June 29, 1993; Saldomando and Cuadra, "Los problemas de la pacificación," 37; Butler, "Nicaragua's Lessons," 20; Baumeister, "Farmers' Organizations," 257–63.

43. See Saldomando, "El proceso de pacificación," 100, 103; Jeffrey L. Gould, *To Lead as Equals: Rural Protest and Political Consciousness in Chinandega, Nicaragua, 1912–1990* (Chapel Hill: University of North Carolina Press, 1990), 292–305; Iris Young, "Civil Society and Social Change," *Theoria* 83/84 (October 1994): 73–94; and Manuel Garretón, *Dictaduras y democratización* (Santiago, Chile: FLACSO, 1984).

13

The Peoples of the Atlantic Coast

Judy Butler

The part of Nicaragua commonly called the Atlantic Coast was undergoing the same transitions as the rest of the country in the early 1990s, although its distinct historic evolution, economic base, and ethnic makeup, as well as its geographic isolation from the center of state power, gave them a different character. At the same time, it was grappling with a far older transition that was uniquely its own: from what many coast people term internal colonialism to incorporation into the nation on acceptable terms. The origins of this transition date back a century, but it only began making headway in 1984, when the Sandinista government broke with Nicaragua's concept of unitary government to accept the validity of autonomous government in the region.

Background

The term "Atlantic Coast" is misleading, since the region covers nearly half of the national territory, and erroneous, since its coastline is in fact Caribbean. The coast is home to three aboriginal peoples (Miskitos, Sumus, and Ramas) and two African-based groups (Garífunas and Creoles). Due to internal migration over the past century, the majority population now is mestizo (mixed Spanish and indigenous), the politically and culturally dominant group in the Pacific.

In 1894, President José Santos Zelaya ordered the military occupation of the port city of Bluefields. At the time, Bluefields was the seat of a Miskito-governed "district," demarcated in an 1860 treaty between the Managua government and the British, who had indirectly controlled the coast for over two hundred years. Although that treaty had finally recognized Nicaraguan sovereignty over the coast, a British flag rather than a Nicaraguan one still flew alongside the Miskito royal banner above Bluefields's Court of Justice. The court itself administered British common law, which blended better with Miskito legal concepts than the Roman law practiced in the Pacific later would.

Zelaya's goal was to bring the coast under national rule so as to gain control of its economic boom, begun a decade earlier with the arrival of U.S.-run banana companies. His move put an end to the Miskito monarchy that the British had fostered, as well as to the Miskitos' long military alliance with the British against Spanish encroachment, which had also allowed them to subordinate other indigenous groups from Costa Rica to Guatemala.

The agreement that headmen of the Miskito communities were forced to sign with the Managua government in 1894 was known in the Pacific as the *reincorporación* and in the coast as an overthrow. Politicians from the Pacific assumed local administrative posts; Spanish was decreed the official language, and teaching in any other language was forbidden. By 1905, Zelaya's natural resource concessions to U.S. companies had violated indigenous lands so extensively that the British stepped in one last time to assist its erstwhile "protectorate." The resulting Harrison-Altamirano Treaty—negotiated, as always, without coast participation—committed the Managua government, among other actions, to ratify indigenous land titles acquired before 1894 or, when impossible, to deed to each family a tiny plot of land.

The coast's banana boom collapsed in the 1930s, but the North American companies revived the extractive economy again and again until 1979, providing low-wage jobs to indigenous laborers in mines, lumber camps, and fishing operations. The companies invested nothing in the domestic social or productive infrastructure, but the locals focused their resentment for the underdevelopment on the central government, on those they even today call "Spaniards."

While the various movements to overthrow the government in the first half of this century found some echo on the coast, life there was otherwise generally uneventful until the 1970s. By then, the Somoza government's postwar development schemes, reminiscent of Zelaya's own nation-building moves, had reached the coast. Spanish-speaking teachers replaced Miskito ones on the Río Coco; peasant colonization of the agricultural frontier, including Sumu lands, was encouraged; state forest reserves were declared on Miskito lands, and villagers were forbidden to cut trees. Miskitos and Sumus began to organize and make contact with the growing international indigenous movement.

From Guarded Hope to a War of Rage to Autonomy

Even though the FSLN was rooted exclusively in the Pacific, the coast greeted its toppling of the Somoza regime in 1979 with cautious enthusiasm. In particular, local intellectual elites and coast youth studying in the Pacific knew that the FSLN's revolutionary program included a section devoted specifically to the region. They expected the age-old grievances with Managua finally to be redressed. In the first year and one-half, the new government invested more per capita on the coast than in the rest of Nicaragua and tried to deal with Miskitos, Sumus, Ramas, Sandinistas Working Together (MISURASATA), the burgeoning and ever more militant new indigenous organization, even after its better judgment counseled otherwise. The uneasy honeymoon between MISURASATA and the Sandinistas ended in a violent divorce by February 1981.

The underlying conflicts were not well understood then, but the specific trigger was clear.[1] On the eve of negotiations with MISURASATA over Miskito land rights and a month after President Ronald Reagan took office vowing to roll back the revolution, the Sandinista government arrested some two dozen MISURASATA leaders with the argument that they were promoting separatism. Within days, several thousand Miskito youth fled to Honduras, ready to make war on the Sandinistas. Top MISURASATA leader Stedman Fagoth soon contacted the CIA, which underwrote the effort of his incipient armed organization, Miskitos, Sumus, Ramas (MISURA).

Over the previous year, MISURASATA had continually raised its demands but had never presented a coherent alternative vision for the coast, and there is no evidence that the war itself had a strategic goal or was even planned. Donald Horowitz suggests that this "episodic character" of ethnic conflict helps explain shortcomings in understanding ethnicity: "It comes and goes, suddenly shattering periods of apparent tranquility."[2] Perhaps the most succinct explanation of Miskito motives was later given by MISURASATA activist Uriel Vanegas, who, at age sixteen, went to Honduras with the first wave, received intelligence training from the CIA, and ended up commanding four hundred warriors: "My objective was to get revenge."[3] If it was a war of rage more than of defined objectives, the road to lasting peace, based on a just resolution of the essence of that rage, was yet to be discovered.

Between December 1981, when MISURA attacked communities and military bases all along the Rió Coco, and mid-1984, when the Sandinista government began to rectify its policies on the coast, the war there expanded such that no village or city was left untouched. MISURA infiltrated down from Honduras, while MISURASATA, now turned into a military organization based in Costa Rica, worked its way up. Both attracted or coerced new fighters to join their ranks as they went.

Given Sandinista ignorance of the coast and the ethnic question in general, as well as the dearth of constructive clues coming from the coast, the government's announcement in October 1984 that autonomy was a legitimate aspiration was a conceptual shock. It was also a political shock, coming in the midst of a war in which the revolution's adversaries, even in that region, were financed and trained by the U.S. government. The Sandinista regime set in motion an intimately linked triple process: pacify the coast, encourage the return of the thousands of indigenous refugees in Honduras, and weave the various ideas of autonomy into a consensual legal framework for some measure of self-government. It had already demonstrated its new perspective by granting amnesty for Miskito prisoners of war, facilitating the return of undocumented Miskito refugees, and naming qualified locals to top administrative and political posts in the coast. In mid-1985, in response to a cease-fire accord with several hundred dissidents from MISURA, it demilitarized the border with Honduras, allowing thousands of forcibly displaced Miskitos to return home.

By 1988 some twenty such accords with about a thousand other MISURA dissidents combined with an on-again, off-again truce with Brooklyn Rivera, who headed MISURASATA in its incarnation as an armed organization, to reduce military activity on the coast to infrequent skirmishes. The accords grew mainly out of pressure on the fighters from civilian relatives anguished by the war's destructive effects and encouraged by the changes in government attitudes and policies. Those in the communities—mainly, women, children, and the elderly—wanted their men back to participate in the autonomy discussions. The government agreed, drawing the line only at those who refused a cease-fire.

The return of Miskito refugees gathered speed as news of the changes made its way to the refugee settlements in Honduras. Just over 17,000 returned with help from the United Nations High Commissioner for Refugees (UNHCR) between 1985 and 1989, and a similar number came back on their own. The most fearful waited for the 1990 elections; 10,486 returned under UNHCR auspices that year.[4]

Unite the Nation in Diversity

The autonomy project developed in fits and starts. Each setback raised the fear of skeptics that it was only a tactic to pacify the region, but Sandinista leaders working on the coast—if not the party as a whole—were convinced that peace would not last without effective autonomy, and that autonomy would not be effective without lasting peace. The setbacks were a result of the war, the economic crisis, and even a devastating hurricane, as well as the fact that no one had a clear vision of what autonomy should be. There was not even a word for it in the Miskito or Sumu language.[5]

Rivera had found an answer, but not on the coast. A segment of the international indigenous movement was arguing that native peoples, as the original inhabitants of an entire conquered hemisphere, have the right to a sovereign territory within the nation-state. Rivera took up that claim in a draft treaty he presented in 1987, in which he gave the central government virtually no role other than to financially subsidize indigenous autonomy in the coast.

Rivera's argument nurtured Miskito aspirations to again rule the coast, but consultations in the region showed that his scheme had no appeal to the other ethnic groups. Although MISURASATA had purported to speak for Sumus, Ramas, and even Creoles, it was never more than a Miskito organization. Its activists even warned Creole-Miskitos that they would have to identify as Miskitos or live elsewhere. Rivera's plan gave no specific indication of how Sumu and Rama voices would be heeded, or what to do with nonindigenous or mixed populations who had long lived in the territory. Such issues must be dealt with in the coast, since the six different groups are bonded by many elements of a common history but have distinct identities and aspirations. Complicating matters further, the region holds much of the nation's resource wealth but only one-twelfth of its population—many of whom are illiterate and over half of whom belong to the country's dominant group. Rivera's proposed system most likely would not have been governable.

The FSLN came to the idea of autonomy through another door. In addition to looking to other autonomy experiences for lessons starting as early as 1981,[6] Sandinista analysts studied ethnic-state relations in the Americas, thus coming face to face with the negative aspects of their own early assumptions. They found that governments had long been applying assimilation policies much like Anastasio Somoza's, a capitalist variant on the Sandinista thesis that the problem was native peoples' own "backwardness" and consequent lack of "development."[7] The analysts saw that loss of identity through assimilation was "rewarded" with low-level participation in the nation's economic life, while those who did not integrate were marginalized and, if they protested, repressed. Both marginalization and assimilation, these analysts recognized, meant second-class citizenship.

Indigenous populations were increasingly demanding recognition as "peoples" and thus the right to "freely determine their political status and freely pursue their economic, social, and cultural development," as expressed in the first article of the 1966 International Covenant on Civil and Political Rights. But that article was only being applied to decolonization. As one anthropologist explained in a symposium on autonomy in Managua, "The United Nations has stated in various resolutions that this sacred principle does not apply to groups or parts of nations within recognized independent states that respect human rights and are democratic."[8]

Even such governments see self-determination as a threat to territorial sovereignty, national unity, and, of course, the rights of the dominant group. Perhaps projecting subconscious guilt, they tend to equate it with secession, even though many other options exist. Given a history of separatist sentiments on the coast, and a war that was threatening the revolution itself, Sandinistas were not exempt from such fears. They skirted the term "peoples" to avoid creating a legal precedent should a definition of it be ratified internationally, but otherwise they tried to think through their fears more constructively.

They concluded that the demand for self-determination was, in essence, a demand for full expression of the group's social, political, economic, and cultural identity—in other words, for first-class citizenship without sacrificing that identity. Since second-class status inhibits a group's identification with the nation-state, the Sandinistas reasoned, the threat is not the demand, but the state's refusal to recognize it. Approached from that perspective, first-class citizenship is a right of all subordinated groups, not just aboriginal peoples. This thesis reflects elements of the "consociational democracy" theory developed by Arend Lijphart to explain the existence of stable polyethnic countries such as Switzerland within the ethnocratic system of nation-states.[9]

The challenge to the FSLN was not to shift the revolution's hierarchy of potentially competing principles, but to harmonize this new one with the others, including defense of the revolution itself. Modifying the FSLN's tenets on the primacy of class struggle, Comandante Tomás Borge, president of the National Autonomy Commission formed at the end of 1994, proclaimed two years later: "It has been demonstrated in practice that it is not scientifically correct to reduce social reality exclusively to class distinctions. Though class struggle determines social change and is always present, explicitly or implicitly, sociocultural formations still exist in contemporary societies that are the basis of specific ethnic identities. We thus recognize that social and ethnic diversity are among the moving forces of the revolution."[10]

His five-member multiethnic commission was charged with developing the theoretical framework for autonomy. Two regional commissions, which intellectuals in both Puerto Cabezas and Bluefields had spontaneously formed to discuss the implications of this new turn of events, were ratified and expanded to represent different ethnic and political perspectives and a rural-urban mix. They would delve into the specifics of the ideas on the coast itself and organize a grass-roots consultation there. Out of a week-long deliberation in June 1985 by the eighty members of all three commissions came a document entitled "Principles and Policies for the Exercise of Autonomy," the departure point for the consultation. At that point, the commissions also merged into one, with most responsibility transferred to the coast; the three members from the Pacific lowered their profile to advisory status.

Over six hundred local volunteers carried out the consultations, which were most productive in the south, where the war was winding down faster. By June 1986 the autonomy commission there had a first draft of a law reflecting the majority opinions and ideas from the various rounds of consultations. The draft was debated in Managua in the next month by over one hundred international indigenous leaders, Indian rights lawyers, and anthropologists invited by the government to a symposium with coast leaders on "The State, Autonomy, and Indigenous Rights."[11]

The north was to have had its draft by the same time, but life was still in turmoil in that Miskito-dominant region. Families were geographically scattered and politically divided, planting lands were inaccessible, roads were unsafe, and the fear of being caught in cross fire was a constant. Villagers also had trouble dealing with the legal abstractions. For them, autonomy was not a philosophical debate about forms of government but the word for their most immediate prayers. In 1985 it meant returning to the river; in 1986 it was synonymous with peace; in 1987, with family reunification; in 1988, with rebuilding their communities; and in 1989, with resuming economic activity. As in the south, it also had different meanings to different ethnic groups: economic control to the Creoles, protection of their environment to the Sumus, cultural identity and political control to the Miskitos, and so forth. Only educated urban elites and autonomy commission members fought over phraseology and concerned themselves with such issues as the structure and prerogatives of local government or where to draw the line between regional and central powers.

By April 1987 a joint draft had been hammered out and was debated in a multiethnic assembly in Puerto Cabezas with 220 elected delegates from the north and south, 2,000 coast observers, and scores of foreign visitors and press. Participants were asked to offer concrete alternatives to articles they opposed, but there was not always that level of clarity. The basic premise was not disputed: autonomy would be exercised within the coast as a distinct political territory in which each ethnic group would enjoy equal rights. The most substantive debate centered on the issue of earnings from the state's resource exploitation. Most delegates were dissatisfied with the relevant article, which simply stated that use of natural resources would benefit the coast population in "just proportions." They wanted a percentage fixed in the law. National Autonomy Commission director Ray Hooker, a Creole legislator, explained that the country's economic crisis and the destruction of the coast's productive apparatus by the war made it a bad moment to nail down this issue. Managua was still subsidizing the coast, as it had since the first year of the revolution. His argument that it would be better to negotiate percentages each year was accepted, albeit reluctantly.

There were also heated debates about whether to permanently divide the region and what to call it. Largely due to a lack of communication infrastructure, it remained divided. Miskitos wanted the name Yapti Tasba—Mother Earth in their language—but non-Miskitos were opposed. In the end, the unromantic names North and South Atlantic Autonomous Regions (RAAN and RAAS, respectively) were adopted.

The approved draft pleased everyone somewhat and no one completely. Each group recognized issues that it alone had pushed. The Sumus, for example, had been the only ones to propose environmental protection, and women had fought virtually alone to promote their participation in all aspects of regional life. At the same time, it was a common denominator of ideas that avoided conflictive interethnic and interregional issues. RAAS Regional Autonomy Commission director Johnny Hodgson consoled Creoles from the south who had seen "some of their brightest ideas fall out of the joint version" with the promise that these would be referred to their new government for future debate, since each region would have some latitude in implementing the law.

A review of early drafts, however, shows that some excluded ideas were not specific to one region or one group—for example, a proposal for an autonomy tribunal to decide cases of disputed authority between the central and autonomous governments, and another for a judicial structure to interpret the correct adaptation of national legal norms to local culture. A member of the National Assembly's judicial review commission explained that some such ideas would have required a constitutional reform, while others were not thought out well enough to be included.[12] "This law is just the port of entry," Borge assured the Assembly. "When time has passed and we have discovered the possible, inevitable defects, we will enter into a new phase of ratification and rectification, seizing the opportunity as it occurs."

The National Assembly passed the bill almost unanimously and without major changes in September 1987. Given the hue and cry in the Pacific at the original announcement of the autonomy process, virulent opposition might have been expected, but the opposition parties that had "defended" the coast against the Sandinistas were in no position to oppose what it ratified. One right-wing Assemblyman was heard to say privately that he opposed "giving control of half the country and its resources to a bunch of backward Indians"; but, though the issue of economic control haunted the debate, it never came out in the open.

By that time, Nicaragua's new Constitution had been approved as well. It contained thirteen articles directly or indirectly related to the coast, including one acknowledging its right to autonomous government. Another political-philosophical landmark was its new definition of the state. Article 8 declared, for the first time, that "the Nicaraguan people are multiethnic." It was the legal end of the ethnocratic nation-state concept.

Both documents guaranteed coast inhabitants the same rights and duties of citizenship as the rest of the population, although some of those rights, such as official use of their own languages and bilingual education, were limited to the Autonomous Regions. They are not inherently "special" rights, but those the dominant culture had historically taken for granted for itself and denied to all others.

The Autonomy Statute did not spell out the central government's areas of exclusive control, but they could be deduced from what was not given over to the regional governments. Beyond obvious ones such as the monetary system, citizenship, and the like, its prerogatives included four general areas found in most autonomy agreements: national defense, international relations, juridical norms, and overall economic planning. The latter two, however, acquired a different meaning in a revolutionary state. For example, the Sandinista government's first legal act had been to abolish the death penalty; it was not prepared to see such a progressive juridical norm overturned by a Miskito culture that still adhered to the concept of an eye for an eye. Instead, certain norms would be adapted to local cultural traditions. The communities consulted also proposed that they deal with petty crimes according to custom and that courts in the region deal with the major ones.

As to economic planning, the nation's resources were viewed in revolutionary terms as the patrimony of all citizens. The revolution was fought to more evenly distribute the nation's wealth, among both social classes and regions. The FSLN did not want one region to remain economically strapped while another grew fat on resources that happened to be within its boundaries, as often happens in a federated system. In addition, control over strategic resources is a different issue when the government backs powerful transnational corporations wanting to appropriate them privately than when resources are nationalized and the government protects them against such corporations. The possibility that the regime could revert to the former was not considered, however, and much of the statute's language was left too imprecise to protect the fledgling autonomous governments from the neoliberal central government voted into office in 1990.

The First Experience in Self-Government

It took another year to rewrite the electoral law and design special electoral districts for the coast. Each autonomous government would consist of a Regional Council of forty-five directly elected members from fifteen districts, plus the National Assembly representatives from that region. The Council would then elect a regional coordinator from among its members. The concept is not a legislative-executive division of powers but a modern version of a traditional indigenous assembly; the coordinator—or governor, as the post is known on the coast—also sits on the Council.

All six groups—Miskitos, Sumus, Creoles, mestizos, Ramas, and Garífunas—are found in the RAAS, while only the first four live in the RAAN, all in very uneven numbers. To ensure both ethnic equality and ethnic proportionality, the districts were drawn so that all members of each smaller group were in their own district. The revised Electoral Law then specified that the first candidate on any slate in that district must belong to the respective group. To avoid mere tokenism, the statute also determined that the seven-member Regional Council executive boards must include at least one member of each group. The board's functions make it a liaison between the Council, the coordinator, and central ministry officials in the region. In practice, however, it quickly came to serve the coordinator in the RAAS and the Council in the RAAN.

In a September 1988 speech celebrating the first anniversary of the Autonomy Statute, Borge announced that elections would be held the following April, but Hurricane Joan dashed that plan a month later by devastating the South Atlantic region. The elections were postponed to February 1990, to coincide with the national ones. The new governments were to be the first test of whether the historic tensions between Managua and the coast, between Miskitos and Sandinistas, and among the ethnic groups themselves, as well as between competing concepts of autonomy, could be successfully dealt with in a political forum. However, they took office with several circumstantial handicaps that put them at a major disadvantage in dealing with these fundamental problems.

Simultaneous elections. Had the autonomy elections occurred when planned, the autonomous governments would have overlapped a year with the central government that had sponsored the process and intended to assist the transition; for example, it had drawn up plans to progressively turn over the local administration of social ministries to the new authorities. As it was, the Chamorro administration, ignorant of and opposed to autonomy, refused to accept the regional governments' lists of names to head ministry offices in the two regions, and the new education minister soon gutted the Sandinista government's bilingual-multicultural education program. In addition, key elements that had been set aside so the regional governments could participate—demarcating new municipalities and drafting detailed regulatory legislation to buttress the Autonomy Statute—also fell victim to the new central government, which shelved them

Unqualified Council members. UNO won 22 seats to the FSLN's 18 in the RAAS, and YATAMA won 22 to the FSLN's 21 in the RAAN, but neither winner had chosen qualified candidates (see table). In the RAAS, most intellectuals and experienced politicians were either identified with the FSLN or did not want to run as candidates for an unknown coalition of Managua-based parties. In the RAAN, YATAMA leaders gave independent Miskito professionals a wide berth, suspicious that they were secret FSLN sympathizers; it used its candidacies instead to reward loyal former combatants. (YATAMA was the name adopted by the various Miskito armed groups when they unified in 1987 and kept when YATAMA reverted to a social-political organization in 1989.) Even the FSLN sacrificed some qualified party members to accept community-selected ethnic candidates on its slate.

Unaccountable coordinators. Even though neither winning party gained a clear majority, the Councils in both regions were so politically polarized that the two coordinators were free to give vent to self-serving and corrupt interests. The coordinator in the RAAS, a Creole, belonged to a UNO party and enjoyed good relations with business interests in Managua and the United States, but he had little base in the population. Ignoring the Sandinista bench and even his own, he waffled between the Chamorro government's central-ist actions and coast people's regionalist demands. His counterpart in the RAAN was initially a conciliatory Miskito who had joined the YATAMA slate only after Rivera smashed an attempt to forge an independent one. But YATAMA was increasingly embroiled in a leadership fight between Rivera and Fagoth, so for the first two years it did not concern itself with the coordinator's increasing corruption.

Conflicts among former combatants. The violent response of former combatants to the central government's unfulfilled promises, which reached worrisome heights in the Pacific in 1991–92, was minimal in the RAAS but flared early in the RAAN. It also had a unique twist there: those who had signed early peace agreements with the Sandinista government lost their subsidies, while those who signed with the new one began receiving assistance from an OAS commission set up to handle demobilization. Armed and feeling betrayed, the former posed major security problems for two years. These problems made it even harder to address the real obstacle to autonomy, which was in Managua.

The Chamorro government, which feared losing control over coast resources far more than any rupture of national unity, used every mechanism within its reach to subtly asphyxiate autonomy. To do so, it had three important factors in its favor:

• ECONOMIC PROSTRATION. Autonomy without a material base is a contradiction in terms. With local production destroyed by war and the hurricane, and even subsistence cropping paralyzed for years by massive population displacements, the Autonomous Regions were almost wholly dependent on central government financing. By 1991 an estimated 70 percent of the economically active population in the RAAS was un- or underemployed; in the RAAN the figure was an astounding 90 percent.[13] Control of the region's resource base was thus a prime expression of the conflict between the two government levels. Central government authorities separately negotiated resource concessions with foreign companies (and, in one case, their own relatives), forcing the regional governments into constant battles to gain some of the licensing and tax revenues. They tried numerous times, separately and jointly, to negotiate an agreement with the central government on resource control and other issues but were rudely turned away.

• AUTONOMY LAW AMBIGUITIES. The FSLN's residual fears of coast hostility as well as a desire to help the new governments develop their skills gradually had led it to keep the Autonomy Statute's language imprecise regarding the assigning of authority to either government level. With a law so open to interpretation, the autonomous governments had no legal defense against a new central regime that wanted to keep them powerless. The single major achievement of the first governments was to jointly draft a regulatory bill in their last year of office, but Managua simply shelved it rather than pass it on to the National Assembly for approval.

• LACK OF POPULAR SUPPORT. The Chamorro government quickly showed that it only responded to popular demands when they were backed by strong mobilization, but the coast population did not mount a defense of autonomy. It is hard to plumb the depths of multiethnic sentiments, but the problem appeared to be rejection not of autonomy but of the powerless, inept, and corrupt regional governments, which did not meet people's basic needs even as well as the FSLN had during the war.

As a regional Miskito expression, YATAMA could have mobilized community sentiment in the RAAN, but the acrimonious power struggle between Rivera and Fagoth alienated its base. That decade-old rivalry had acquired new organizational battlefields when President Violeta Chamorro appointed Rivera minister of a new central government agency called the Institute for Development of the Autonomous Regions (INDERA). In response, Fagoth, who like Rivera had not run for office in 1990, opted to defend the regional government as a key adviser to the coordinator. In a complete role reversal, he cast himself as a moderate, ready to reconcile with the Sandinistas, thus defining Rivera as an anti-Sandinista sellout to the central government.

INDERA was the central government's most blatant insult to both the letter and spirit of the Autonomy Statute, which states that the regional governments will "participate effectively in the preparation of national development plans and programs."[14] President Chamorro failed even to advise them prior to announcing INDERA's creation. Its budget was greater than that of the two regional governments combined, and Rivera ran it with no input from them. Their strongest joint demand throughout their four-year term was to dissolve INDERA, which finally happened on the eve of the new coast elections in 1994. Rivera was renamed vice minister of the new Social Action Ministry, still responsible for the coast.

Local FSLN strategy differed in the two regions. In the north, where YATAMA was one seat short of a majority, the FSLN gained seats on the executive board and worked constructively with those in YATAMA who were willing to put the war behind them. But all the problems combined to prevent any concrete gains, even after the first coordinator was unseated for corruption a year before his term ended. His replacement, a former YATAMA military leader allied with Rivera, was no better; he was the prime suspect in a fire that destroyed the government building and all of its financial and other records on the night after YATAMA lost the 1994 elections.

In the south, the FSLN was unable to forge an alliance with YATAMA in the first years to offset UNO's similar lack of a majority. The FSLN refused the two low-level seats that the UNO coordinator offered it on the executive board, preferring to limit itself to constructive opposition rather than legitimize UNO activities with its token presence. That government's main accomplishment, with FSLN help on the respective committee, was to win 50 percent of the payments to be made by the companies that had won bids to lease the state fishing companies. The payments, however, were made to a central government agency, which never turned over any of them to the region. In 1993 the FSLN pulled together enough votes (60 percent) from YATAMA and some dissident UNO councilors to unseat the largely repudiated coordinator, but he employed various maneuvers to finish out his full term.

Regional Elections (number of seats won on Regional Council + National Assembly representatives)

	RAAS				*RAAN*		
1990		*1994*		*1990*		*1994*	
YATAMA	5	YATAMA	5	YATAMA	22+1	YATAMA	7+1
FSLN	18+1	FSLN	14+1	FSLN	21+1	FSLN	19+1
UNO	22+1	UNO	5	UNO	2+1	UNO	0+1
		PLC	18			PLC	19
		ADECO*	1+1				
		MAAC*	2				
Total	**45+2**		**45+2**		**45+3**		**45+3**

Source: Supreme Electoral Council
*Coastal Democratic Alliance (Alianza Democrática Costeña, or ADECO) and Coastal Authentic Autonomous Movement (Movimiento Auténtico Autónomo Costeño, or MAAC) were local electoral associations, the former created by the incumbent regional coordinator after his own political party expelled him. Four such associations ran in the RAAN but won no seats.

1994—The Second Round

Given their poor showing, the incumbent parties in both regions lost heavily in the 1994 elections, while the FSLN dropped only a few seats. The losses were mainly picked up by the Liberal Constitutionalist Party (PLC) of Managua Mayor Arnoldo Alemán, at that time the front-runner for the 1996 national elections. The well-funded PLC had begun building its base the previous year, offering major party posts to well-known coast figures. It even attracted numerous YATAMA members as candidates in the RAAN, among them Fagoth. Interviews suggest that, in addition to the draw of Fagoth's charisma, the PLC's strong showing was due to dormant Liberal sentiments among mestizo migrants to the coast and a hazy memory that life had been better in Somoza's day, combined with a contradictory view that the PLC, as a "new" party, was worth a try. FSLN candidates suffered mainly from lack of financial support by the party, which was preoccupied with preparations for its upcoming special congress and with the divisions that would lead to a formal split at the end of that year.

In both regions, the quality of the newly elected Council members was slightly higher, and the Swedish government, interested in advancing democracy and the autonomy process, enhanced it further by financing seminars for them on administrative and legal issues. It also financed an institutional support program and a liaison office for the two governments in Managua, thus facilitating access between them and with the central government.[15]

In the RAAN, a stronger YATAMA-FSLN alliance and good working relations between the new coordinator (YATAMA) and board president (FSLN) augured well at the outset. The two even persuaded the health minister to decentralize health administration under the autonomous government. In the RAAS, the second term began as the first had ended, with the FSLN excluded from any seat on the board. In August 1995 the local PLC chief in the RAAS, without presenting any evidence of wrongdoing, even tried to unseat the regional coordinator, who had switched from the FSLN to the PLC. Since PLC councilor Fagoth led a campaign to do the same to the YATAMA coordinator in the RAAN, some observers surmised that the maneuvers aimed to give the PLC more control over the region before the national elections. In both cases, the conflict brought Council sessions to a temporary halt. By that same time, the FSLN split in Managua began affecting members on the coast, despite their earlier insistence that the issues had nothing to do with them and despite the decision-making autonomy that the coast chapters had won at the special FSLN congress a year earlier.

Another potentially serious problem was the language of the redrafted constitutional article referring to the Autonomy Statute, approved along with other reforms in mid-1995. While the intent was to put more teeth in it, the drafters did not update the first sentence to indicate that a law already existed, thus opening the possibility of an entirely new one and leaving unclear who would draft it.[16] Interviews with regional officials suggested that it was an inadvertent error, but some were optimistic that the National Assembly alliance that had pushed through the constitutional reforms favored approval of a stronger law than the original. That opinion was questionable, since that new alignment was already breaking up under pressure from the upcoming electoral campaign.

Given the excessive weight of national politics and parties on the coast, perhaps the best hope on the horizon in late 1995 was an initiative launched by Faran Dometz, a prestigious Creole pastor from the RAAS who had been elected Moravian Church superintendent earlier that year. Under church auspices, he began calling together coast leaders of all ethnicities and political persuasions to bring about common positions to present to any national party seeking the coast vote in the national elections.

Dometz admitted that it would be hard to surmount the multiple political and regional differences and personal and ethnic rivalries, but he was in an unprecedented position. Superintendent is a powerful post in Moravian structures; and, for the first time, the person holding it was also a politician. Dometz had created the electoral association called MAAC, was elected a regional councilor in 1994, and fell only one vote short of being elected regional coordinator of the RAAS by a voting bloc made up of the FSLN, MAAC, and YATAMA. If his own sincere diplomacy and the best instincts of others involved ultimately prevailed, the initiative stood to make some national parties take a stronger position on autonomy in their electoral platform. In the best-case scenario, it could later lead to a regional coalition or even party among those people—Sandinistas included—who believe that coast interests cannot be adequately represented by any national party.

The worst-case scenario, which always lurks in the wings on the coast but was being whispered about more ardently at that same point than it had been for some time, was a separatist movement. One of many issues rekindling that sentiment was the central government's abuse of communal land rights based on the old Harrison-Altamirano titles and a new wave of mestizo migration onto indigenous lands. The same issues had touched off indigenous organizing in the 1970s and were powerful mobilizing tools for MISURASATA in 1980–81.[17] There was no indication that the sentiment was any more rooted in realistic analysis and alternatives this time than at any other since 1894; the difference was the easy availability of weapons left over from the war and the still fresh military experience.

Notes

1. Useful readings on the underlying causes include: Center for Research and Documentation of the Atlantic Coast (CIDCA), ed., *Ethnic Groups and the Nation-State: The Case of the Atlantic Coast in Nicaragua* (Stockholm, Sweden: Development Study Unit, Department of Social Anthropology, University of Stockholm, 1987); Hector Díaz Polanco and Gilberto López y Rivas, eds., *Nicaragua: Autonomía y revolución* (Panama City, Panama: Centro de Capacitación Social, 1986); Charles R. Hale, *Resistance and Contradiction: Miskitu Indians and the Nicaraguan State, 1894–1987* (Stanford, CA: Stanford University Press, 1994); Klaudine Ohland and Robin Schneider, eds., *National Revolution and Indigenous Identity: The Conflict between Sandinists and Miskito Indians on Nicaragua's Atlantic Coast*, International Work Group for Indigenous Affairs (IWGIA), Document No. 47 (Copenhagen, Denmark, November 1983); Carlos M. Vilas, *State, Class, and Ethnicity in Nicaragua: Capitalist Modernization and Revolutionary Change on the Atlantic Coast* (Boulder, CO: Lynne Rienner, 1989).

2. Donald L. Horowitz, *Ethnic Groups in Conflict* (Berkeley: University of California Press, 1985), 13.

3. Douglas Carcache, "The Atlantic Coast—Two Leaders' Paths Join," *Envío* 7, no. 87 (September–October 1988), 12.

4. The official UNHCR figure for 1984–1990 is 27,510.

5. The Sumu organization SUKAWALA translated it as *alas yalahnin lani*: "to live our system of life." According to a SUKAWALA document prepared for its assembly to discuss autonomy, "It does not deny the right to development, but it should be in accord with our reality."

6. By 1985 they had looked at Spain, Canada, China, Denmark, Panama, and the Soviet Union. Interview by author with Autonomy Commission member Manuel Ortega Hegg, Managua, June 1986.

7. Modernization theory, which began to predominate after World War II, posited "the persistence of 'traditional' ethnic solidarities as an indicator of political underdevelopment" and argued that ethnic identities should give way to an emphasis on individual rights, abandoning group affiliation. Milton J. Esman and Itamar Rabinovich, eds., *Ethnicity, Pluralism, and the State in the Middle East* (Ithaca: Cornell University Press, 1988), as discussed in Billie Michele Mandel, *Conflict Resolution in Nicaragua: The Autonomy of the Ethnic Minorities of the Atlantic Coast*, senior honors thesis for Stanford University Department of International Relations, Center for Latin American Studies, 1994.

8. Rodolfo Stavenhagen, symposium on "The State, Autonomy, and Indigenous Rights," Managua, July 11–12, 1986.

9. Ibid. The model recognizes polyethnicity and the value of group identities, and it replaces power competition with power sharing as the overriding principle of political organization.

10. Speech to the Multiethnic Assembly, Puerto Cabezas, April 22, 1987.

11. The international experts considered that the draft integrated the most important aspirations of both the revolution and the coastal peoples. See "Considerations on the Autonomy Process," signed by seventy international participants in the autonomy symposium, July 1986.

12. Interview by author with Sandinista legislator Dorotea Wilson, a Creole from the mining district of the RAAN, Managua, March 1988.

13. Official central government figures.

14. Article 8, point 1, of Law No. 27—the Autonomy Statute.

15. I would like to thank Henningston Hodgson, coordinator of that program at the time of this study, for the useful documentation he provided for this chapter and for his valuable insights as a *costeño* to the first draft.

16. The original sentence of Art. 181 read: "The state shall implement, through a law, autonomous governments in the regions inhabited by the Communities of the Atlantic Coast for the exercise of their rights." An unofficial translation of the new first sentence is: "The state, through a Law, shall organize the autonomy system for the indigenous peoples and ethnic communities of the Atlantic Coast, which should contain among other norms: the attributions of its government bodies, its relation to the Executive and Legislative Branch and to the municipalities, and the exercise of its rights."

17. See Hazel Law, "Propuesta preliminar para la demarcación y legalización de las tierras comunales de la Costa Atlántica de Nicaragua," May 1995, for background and details of this issue. A copy of this proposal is available at the Center for Research and Documentation of the Atlantic Coast (CIDCA), Managua.

14

The Church

Andrew J. Stein*

The political positions of the leadership of the Nicaraguan Catholic Church from the mid-1970s through the mid-1990s varied considerably. Beginning in about 1974, no Nicaraguan government—left, right, or center—was spared the bishops' criticism of economic policy and human rights. In the 1970s the bishops ended more than three decades of cooperative church-state relations and support for the Somoza family dictatorship, deeming the revolutionary uprising against the Somozas to be legitimate. Soon, however, they opposed and challenged the revolutionary government of the Sandinista National Liberation Front (FSLN). Later, in the 1990s, they were even somewhat at odds with the democratically elected, center-rightist Chamorro government that replaced the Sandinistas in 1990. The almost unwavering political support that the Catholic Church had given Nicaraguan governments during the period of Anastasio Somoza García (1936–1956) appeared by the 1990s to have been permanently lost. At the same time that the Church exercised influence in public policy areas that traditionally had been among its pastoral concerns—conditions of its personnel and parishes, education, family law and public morality, the government's stance on religious competitors, and poverty and basic human needs—it also played an unprecedented role in the negotiated settlement to the civil war of the 1980s, the demobilization and reintegration of former combatants from the Sandinista army and the Contras, the monitoring of human rights violations, and the electoral transition of 1990.

*The author is grateful to Margaret Crahan, Brian Smith, Mitchell Seligson, Laura N. O'Shaughnessy, Thomas Walker, and John Booth for comments on earlier drafts of this paper. Funding for 1991 and 1993–94 field work was provided by the Center for Latin American Studies at the University of Pittsburgh, the Tinker Foundation, and a Fulbright-IIE fellowship. The author is grateful for this support without which the study would have been impossible. An earlier version of this chapter was presented at the 1995 meeting of the Latin American Studies Association in Washington, DC.

A key to understanding what might develop in religion and politics in Nicaragua after the mid-1990s lay in the difference of visions or models of the Church's proper role in society, and how that institution should relate to the political powers that be. Such "models" include assumptions about what is rightful authority within the Church as an institution, which interests are vital to the mission of salvation (the Catholic Church's proclaimed reason for being), and, by extension, what kind of activities the Church might legitimately promote in society and politics.[1] The assumptions that its leaders have about their institution and which matters are central concerns for its mission are varied and complex.

It is a gross simplification to say that a priest, a bishop, or a member of the religious hierarchy is "conservative" or "progressive" based on one dimension. Their motives and orientations are the product of a complex web of beliefs and perceptions. The different emphases of Church leaders have substantial implications for how the vital interests of the Church are defined, what are seen as its legitimate roles in social and political affairs, and how authority is exercised within the Church itself. No one image is held exclusively by the clergy at any given time, but there exists a series of competing models. For instance, bishops and priests may agree that the mission of the Church is the salvation of mankind, but they will not agree on how to legitimately achieve it. Related to this discussion is the renewed emphasis given to social change, democracy, and social justice by Catholicism after Vatican II (1962–1965) and the Medellín, Colombia, meeting of the Latin American Bishops' Council (Consejo Episcopal Latinoamericano, or CELAM) in 1968. While Church people of widely divergent political ideologies and theological and ecclesiological viewpoints tended to agree on the need for change, there was no agreement on how to achieve these changes, or which measures were most appropriate in the pursuit of the "preferential option for the poor."

Church-State Ties under the Somozas and the FSLN

From its inception in the 1930s to the beginning of the 1960s the Somoza dictatorship benefited greatly from the support of most bishops (with important exceptions such as Msgr. Calderón y Padilla in Matagalpa) and from a shared view of the Somoza family and much of the Church leadership that the latter would have close, cooperative relations with the state, be a central source of values for the nation and legitimacy for the government, and, in return, would confine its message to the spiritual realm. This close church-state cooperation characterized the period of the founder of the dynasty, Somoza García. The pattern of church-state interaction began to change under heirs Luis (1957–1963) and Anastasio Somoza Debayle (1967–1979), in part related to the impact of Vatican II and Medellín, as increasing differences emerged (particularly after 1968) between what the regime considered the appropriate mission and socio-political role for the Church and what Church leaders thought on the same issues. Although there were a few priests who were also active duty members of the National Guard, by the 1970s the Catholic Church became a principal critic of the human rights abuses and killings carried out by Somoza's army against rising opposition. There was anything but unanimity among the clergy over the proper stance of the Church toward the dictatorship, the desirability of social and political change, or the morality of the revolutionary insurrection (although the Episcopal Conference came out in favor of it in June 1979).

Once the Sandinistas took power, the polarization of the revolution badly split the Church. As Margaret Crahan observed in the 1980s, "attitudes within the Church toward the Sandinistas and the Contras cover the full spectrum from strong support to strong opposition, with many Church people being uncomfortable with both options."[2] Within the Sandinista government there was also a range of views about religion and the nature and interests of the Church in the country. Some leaders within the new political system that took shape after 1979 may indeed have wanted to view the Catholic Church as nothing more than one among many mass organizations that represented the majority, but one that should be loyal to the revolution's goals and policies. Another tendency within the FSLN government was the Christian tendency exemplified by the clergy and former lay Catholic organization leaders who conceived of the Church as the "People of God" and saw a close identification between the struggle for social justice and the welfare of the poor majority, on the one hand, and the program of the revolutionary government, on the other. Within the framework of a new revolutionary culture, political institutions, and society, the historical view of the Catholic Church as the sole moral authority within society would face a severe challenge. Its right to question the legitimacy of governments was also debated.[3]

Church-state relations shifted in 1980–1985 from apparent coexistence to open confrontation between the Catholic Church and the FSLN, mutual accusations of betrayal of the Nicaraguan people, and the bishops' effort to delegitimize the Sandinistas as usurpers of national sovereignty and totalitarian Marxists. Many of the issues and incidents of that decade are well known—the conflict over the creation of an FSLN-controlled revolutionary army, the debate over educational content and standards, the expulsion of priests in 1984 and of Monsignor Vega in 1986 for "counterrevolutionary" activities—and have been detailed in the ample literature on the FSLN period.[4] The course of events (and, it might be added, radically different models of the Church and preferred political systems) had led to confrontation as the de facto position. Although the mediation of the Vatican and the negotiated settlement to the Nicaraguan conflict reduced church-state tensions at the end of the 1980s, the legacy of the revolution continued to have an impact on the Church's role in the transition and how it influenced national politics.

The Church under Chamorro

When discussing the influence of the Catholic hierarchy and clergy in general during the transition process, one has to distinguish between the activities of the institution and its personnel in the sphere of politics related to the peace settlement, on the one hand, and traditional concerns related to public policy, on the other. The Church was an important mediator between the two sides in the negotiations of the Esquipulas Accords and the 1988 Sapoá agreement, with Cardinal Miguel Obando y Bravo serving on the National Reconciliation Commission. In the period after the FSLN defeat, the hierarchy pressed for investigations of unsolved political murders and decried the rise of kidnapping. As a continuation of work begun under the peace process in coordination with the OAS's International Support and Verification Commission, Cardinal Obando, several dioceses, and government representatives guaranteed the implementation of the accords, and they conducted investigations of revenge killings of demobilized former Contras and government soldiers.[5]

The Church later took an active role in the demobilization of the Contras and the reduction of the Sandinista army, and it subsequently worked to bring about a negotiated end to the problem of the rearmed groups of former combatants on both sides (see Chapter 12, this volume). It is not surprising that the bishops tried to mediate and act as peacemakers, since this was a role that they had increasingly assumed since the 1970s. However, denunciations of "renewed military oppression" surfaced during the controversy over the delayed retirement of Gen. Humberto Ortega as head of the army (see Chapter 4, this volume), and the passage of new military legislation in the National Assembly. Part of the Church's concern in this area stemmed from a genuine interest in avoiding the ill effects of rampant militarism on Nicaraguan society and politics. One bishop spoke of the Church's fear of authoritarianism in this way: "[It is] a mentality of strongmen on horseback (*caudillos*) that we have in Latin America, [where] the people are misled very easily to accept tyranny in their desperation, and do not commit themselves to the transformation of their own history. The Church would never accept this."[6]

While the political elites in the National Assembly negotiated reforms that were passed in September 1994 and early 1995, the Church continued to support a constitutional referendum. Even though only one in five Nicaraguans showed support for the idea of a referendum on a new Constituent Assembly, the majority of the priests in the parishes (69 percent), like the Episcopal Conference (Conferencia Episcopal de Nicaragua, or CEN), supported this option.[7] The Sandinista-created document was seen as an obstacle to the oft-cited "Rule of Law" that the bishops demanded.[8] They were of the opinion that the legal system did not work impartially during the 1980s and that a similar pattern of unequal application of the laws among

Nicaraguan citizens continued, depending on the accused person's social and political connections and influence.

The Church and the Electoral Process

Procedurally fair, inclusive, and democratic elections were never a hallmark of Nicaraguan politics.[9] With the exception of Archbishop Obando's public declarations against the fraudulent nature of Somoza's 1974 reelection, there was little documented concern by Catholic bishops for the integrity and competitiveness of the electoral process during the ten elections under the Somozas.[10] However, in a path-breaking pastoral letter issued in 1974, the CEN reminded Somoza and the citizenry that "a Christian cannot vote in good conscience against the principles of liberty that their faith demands."[11] The document also stressed the importance of ideological pluralism; and, in an indirect reference to the traditional parties that dealt with Somoza in return for personal gain, it noted that "political parties exist for the people and not only for themselves, nor to dominate the rest of the citizenry."

During the 1990 election campaign the Church was accused of openly taking the side of the Chamorro-UNO candidacy. Bishops and priests denied this allegation but granted that they gave general guidelines for voting according to the teachings of Catholicism. It is worth asking whether the guidelines were based primarily on the "teachings of the faith," or rather on the well-being of the institutional authority of the Church leaders. After repeating the same points as in 1974 regarding procedural guarantees and freedom of conscience, the first document on the 1990 elections pleaded for "maturity and respect" in the conduct of the party leaders and candidates and encouraged all citizens to register to vote (which they had not done in either 1974 or 1984).[12] Five weeks prior to the February 25, 1990, election, the bishops issued another letter in which they said, also for the first time, that whatever the outcome, the result should be respected.[13] Was the Church's call for a heavy voter turnout and respect for duly elected representatives based solely on democratic principles? Given the subsequent, more cooperative church-state relations under Violeta Barrios de Chamorro, consideration of the Church's institutional fortunes within Nicaraguan society and politics was also a likely motive for its stand.

The CEN publicly reminded the new administration of unsolved national problems such as the economic crisis and moral and social decay, and they urged "that power be exercised by those who were elected." It also noted "a growing frustration in large sectors of the population [over] the implementation of measures and programs different from those for which they voted."[14] When determining whether the Church was officially in favor of the UNO coalition, a distinction has to be made between the personal partisan and ideological preferences suggested by the statements and actions of key ecclesiastical leaders and the official position of the Church itself. While particular bishops and priests may have openly supported the UNO candidates, other priests supported the FSLN. What is clear, as the efforts of then-Monsignor Obando in Caracas to avert a Sandinista take-over in 1979 indicate, and as Crahan has pointed out, is that the Church had a clear preference in terms of political systems and a strongly negative response to Marxist revolutionaries and their vision of change and political organization:

> The Church cannot be characterized as consistently supporting any particular stances even though traditionally it has been identified with conservatives. Such an identification has flowed, in part, from its criticism of class warfare to achieve change. In general, however, the Church has tended to support reforms of existing Western liberal political institutions and capitalism.[15]

The Church and Public Policy

Church officials have seen a legitimate role for themselves to guide and shape public debate; and even though the Chamorro period was one of relatively less conflict than the 1980s, bishops were very assertive on a number of issues. Educational policy and the transmission of religious values had long been a central concern. Once the Sandinistas were defeated, both the Chamorro-UNO coalition and the Church hierarchy pointed to educational reform as a priority. Cardinal Obando mentioned this policy area during the inauguration of Doña Violeta in April 1990.[16]

The new administration's Ministry of Education praised the Sandinista government's efforts to extend coverage to marginalized sectors of the population and to develop agricultural and vocational education programs. However, the new regime's view of the educational legacy of the 1980s was mostly negative, both in terms of the quality of education and its "materialistic and pseudo-scientific" goals: "The ideological distortion of the educational system occurred when it was subordinated to the interests of a party elite . . . that was more interested in indoctrinating and in ensuring support for their political project than in educating."[17] This general assessment of the FSLN educational legacy was shared by the Church hierarchy.[18] In a pastoral letter, the top clergy attributed hatred, cruelty, ambition, injustice, and criminality to "years of atheistic education and a systematic and persistent campaign against Catholic morality."[19]

Other Church concerns taken up by the Ministries of Education and Health included public morality issues, religious values, and sex education. Unlike Sandinista policy, which favored greater preventative measures and contraception, the 1994 sex education program—as seen in a draft policy paper—stressed abstinence and morality rather than merely informing students.[20] This approach was very much a reflection of Church thinking.

The Sandinistas had made secular education an important goal, but once the Chamorro administration came to power, there was an effort to modify this position. Article 124 of the 1987 Constitution stipulated that education is secular but that religion may be taught in private schools as an additional subject. By mid-1994 the CEN was organizing a public campaign to allow voluntary religious instruction in public schools as well.[21]

Family law, religious marriage, and opposition to abortion constituted other areas where the Church influenced public policy. Article 74 of the 1987 Constitution stated that "the state grants special protection to the human reproductive process," yet in the 1990s the Church took an increasingly activist stance against abortion. Immediately before the 1994 United Nations Population Conference in Cairo, the bishops voiced alarm over the "dangerous and systematic attacks, including those by economically powerful governments and institutions, against life and the family."[22] The controversy intensified in June 1994 when members of the National Assembly proposed abortion-related reforms to the Penal Code and Article 74. In response, the bishops handed the president of the legislature a pro-life petition with more than seventy thousand signatures. In the same period, President Chamorro condemned abortion as "murder."[23]

Church-State Relations at the Parish and National Levels

Two major changes in the characteristics of priests in Nicaragua in the 1990s appeared to be the result of an increase in vocations (young men entering the priesthood) since 1980. First, prior to the revolution a substantial segment of the clergy had been of foreign origin, but by the mid-1990s the segment of the clergy which was of Nicaraguan nationality constituted two-thirds of all priests in the parishes. And second, most active priests at the parish level had been ordained after the revolution began.

In a survey undertaken by the author, the results showed that almost all priests thought that relations with the Sandinistas had been confrontational; only one person out of 170 said that there was no conflict. In addition, although many stressed that the degree of conflict and the nature of issues involved was in no way comparable, the majority of priests also noted conflict in the Chamorro period. These responses echoed the bishops' complaints about the political leadership of President Chamorro and the UNO government. Concerning the period after the Sandinistas left power, bishops and priests agreed that the causes of the conflict were threefold: 1) the government did not respond favorably to the Church's criticisms of its shortcomings (nearly one-third of priests cited this as the primary reason for conflict); 2) excessive decision-making power was being exercised by Sandinistas and nonelected officials, especially by Gen. Humberto Ortega and Doña Violeta's son-in-law, Minister of the Presidency Antonio Lacayo

(15 percent of priests stated this view); and 3) the government had failed to keep its promises made during the 1990 campaign.[24]

Regarding concrete policy initiatives by the Chamorro government, the clergy generally viewed the administration's educational policy in positive terms (nearly two-thirds rated it as "excellent" or "good" both at the primary and secondary levels), while opinion was much more mixed on policy toward the armed forces and demobilization of both sides in the war, or on broader social economic policies. It is worth noting that support for policies of central interest to the Church, such as education, was much higher than on economic or social policy, by as much as twenty percentage points. This pattern may reflect qualified support for measures that furthered the institutional interests of the Church but by no means guaranteed support across issue areas. In fact, the majority assessment of other Chamorro policy initiatives was negative by a large margin—perhaps due in part to a possible concurrence between bishops and priests in their assessment of the impact on the poor of neoliberal stabilization programs and the privatization of state industries.[25]

Priests' Evaluations of Chamorro Government Policies (in percentages)

	Health Care	Primary Education	Secondary Education	Privatize Industries	Demobili- zation	Stabilization
Excellent	0.0	13.6	13.6	6.0	15.8	2.0
Good	10.0	47.4	44.1	28.0	26.3	20.4
Fair	45.0	23.7	25.3	44.0	24.6	34.7
Poor	33.3	10.2	10.2	10.0	24.5	28.6
Very poor	11.7	5.1	6.8	12.0	8.8	14.3
Totals	**100.0**	**100.0**	**100.0**	**100.0**	**100.0**	**100.0**

Source: Author's survey of priests, N=170, 1993–94. The fifth policy area, Demobilization, refers to the disarmament and dissolution of both the government armed forces and the Contras after the 1987 Esquipulas and 1988 Sapoá peace accords were signed.

The Church and Social and Economic Policy

Another matter worth consideration is the degree to which church-state conflict was caused or heightened by differing positions on social policy, and on the eventual institutional arrangements and agreements among the political elite for the rules of political competition in the wake of the February 1990 elections. For more than twenty years Church leaders had spoken out against an ever-worsening situation of economic inequality and poverty. The critique of poverty was, in part, a result of the shift toward an emphasis on regarding poverty as due to unjust and sinful structures (a position that became common with Medellín) rather than individual moral failings. In their view as spiritual guides of Nicaragua, the bishops believed that they had a right to offer general guidelines and moral critiques, but not concrete policies.

A common theme in pastoral letters during the Chamorro administration was the scandalous degree of social and economic inequality. The U.S.-imposed embargo, and the destruction of crops, infrastructure, and human life during the insurrection (1978–79) and the Contra war (1981–1988) made the situation worse, and complaints by the clergy regarding the suffering of the poor did not cease.[26] Unemployment rose from an average of 26.8 percent in the period from 1985 to 1989 to 55–65 percent in 1992–1994, and the standard of living and threat to survival for the vast majority of the population worsened dramatically.[27]

Much of the critique of economic injustice was rooted in the ideas of the social function of property and the dignity of each human being (found in the encyclical letters of Popes Leo XIII, Pius XI, John XXIII, Paul VI, and John Paul II, and in the documents of CELAM). When Cardinal Obando was asked about the Church's critique of neoliberal economic policies (CELAM, 1992) and the ability of the market to solve Nicaragua's problems, he replied: "If it is a market economy that is not well controlled by the government, I consider it problematical. There is an enormous gap (between rich and poor), and many do not have anything to eat. And we have 60 percent unemployment. . . . I think that one has to regulate a market economy. If it is not controlled, [the market] creates even greater inequality."[28]

The bishops' concerns were not confined to abstract laments over the suffering of the poor. At the national level the bishops suggested to the Chamorro government that it fight official corruption and change its economic team in the cabinet, given the failure of existing policy and in the face of $3 billion in foreign aid and loans during the first three years in power.[29] On the diocesan level, one prelate pointed to practical programs to level the differences in society. Such measures extended beyond help with health care, housing, and education. The cleric spoke with conviction about the invisibility and abuse of the poor by the rest of society, referring to the judicial system: "Generally, lawyers defend institutionalized injustice, financial interests. . . . When it comes to matters of money, political differences disappear."[30]

Conclusion

The principal causes of church-state conflict in Nicaragua from the late 1960s through the mid-1990s flowed from a redefinition of the Church's political obligations and right to involve itself in political matters, and the protection of the Church in constitutional provisions and policy areas that affected its core institutional interests (education, social morality, the need to control access to foreign personnel and supplies necessary for its pastoral mission, and its ability to maintain unity among Nicaraguan lay

Catholics irrespective of social class or political allegiance). In the Chamorro period, the conflict was much less intense than under the Sandinistas. Now it was primarily rooted in three matters: 1) the traditional Church defense of its privileged areas of influence by gaining greater access over the direction of public policy, as in the period before the revolution; 2) the effort to rid the Chamorro administration of Sandinista influence; and 3) the Church leadership's repudiation of the government's record on reducing poverty, human rights abuses, and corruption among cabinet members or their subordinates in a time of unparalleled economic hardship for the poor majority of Nicaraguans.[31]

If we speak in terms of models, it could be argued that a majority within the hierarchy and a plurality among the younger priests who constituted nearly one-half of the clerics in charge of parishes in the early 1990s held a view of the Church as "institution"—that is, the Church's institutional health and interests were seen as paramount for the implementation of its mission in Nicaraguan society and politics. The model of the Church as "servant," or as the community of believers—the "People of God" in the language of Vatican II—was still an important one held by a substantial segment of the clergy and the laity. For many priests and bishops the commitment to promoting social justice had not waned. However, the relative emphasis among the competing models was on the "institution."

In 1972 the CEN had made the distinction between "politics in a broad sense" rooted in the rights of the community and in pursuit of the common good, and politics in a "concrete, individual, and partisan sense."[32] Cardinal Obando raised the same argument when he was asked whether the Church had become a political actor in its own right, taking a particular political line. Obando denied the accusation, saying that the Church mediated between the FSLN and Somoza and that it had denounced injustices under Somoza, the Sandinistas, and Chamorro equally, showing preference for none. At the same time he noted, "I think that we as hierarchy, bishops and priests, should not participate in partisan politics, but rather in politics in a broad sense."[33] The ideal for the Church hierarchy and lower level clergy from Vatican II onward had been to have a religious institution that was nonpartisan and independent from the constraints and favors of the state. There were many sincere efforts by the Nicaraguan Church to pursue this goal under Somoza, the FSLN, and Chamorro, but in practice the degree to which clerical involvement in public affairs avoided partisan commitments was uneven depending on bishop, diocese, and socio-political context.

Notes

1. For a discussion of the notion of models of authority and the Church, see Daniel H. Levine, *Religion and Politics in Latin America: The Catholic Church in Venezuela and Colombia* (Princeton: Princeton University Press, 1981), 144–54;

and Michael Fleet and Brian H. Smith, *The Catholic Church and Democracy in Chile and Peru* (Notre Dame: University of Notre Dame Press, 1997). Levine speaks of beliefs on dimensions of ecclesiology (how the Church as institution should be structured and administered) and socio-political views. Fleet and Smith add to this discussion a focus on a third dimension, theological differences (that is, religious beliefs about the nature of God, sin, and, by implication, the mission of the Church that have an impact on politics). For further discussion of models, see Margaret E. Crahan, "Church and State in Latin America: Assassinating Some Old and New Stereotypes," *Daedalus* (Summer 1991): 134–40; idem, "Religion, Church, Change" (unpublished manuscript, 1991); and Avery Dulles, *Models of the Church*, rev. ed. (New York: Image Books, 1987).

2. Crahan, "Church and State in Latin America," 146–47.

3. For more on the notion of the Church as a moral authority in society, see Joseph Mulligan, *The Nicaraguan Church and the Revolution* (Kansas City: Sheed and Ward, 1991).

4. See Philip Berryman, *The Religious Roots of Rebellion: Christians in Central American Revolutions* (Maryknoll, NY: Orbis Books, 1984); Philip Williams, *The Catholic Church and Politics in Nicaragua and Costa Rica* (Pittsburgh: University of Pittsburgh Press, 1989); and Michael Dodson and Laura N. O'Shaughnessy, *Nicaragua's Other Revolution: Religious Faith and Political Struggle* (Chapel Hill: University of North Carolina Press, 1990).

5. Comisión Tripartita, *Memoria de trabajo, 1992–1993* (Managua: Comisión de Verificación Cardenal Obando–Gobierno de la República de Nicaragua–OEA-CIAV, 1993). In their report, the three entities that made up the Commission stressed the need for a reform of military codes of justice as they pertained to crimes against civilians, and they pointed to lawlessness and the weak court system as obstacles to full peace in the country: "Impunity is considered by the Commission to be one of the negative factors most relevant for the true application of justice in Nicaragua. The recommendations should be a clear signal to Nicaraguan society, highly polarized, that it is not acceptable to take the law into one's own hands, and that it is possible [to achieve it] by means of the procedures established by law, enforcing justice and strengthening reconciliation and peace," 51.

6. Author's interview, Managua, July 1994.

7. Author's survey of Nicaraguan priests, 1993–94. During 1993–94 fieldwork, I interviewed 170 parish priests in all eight dioceses of Nicaragua. The parameters from which to draw a representative sample were not known, so I interviewed all of the parish priests whom I could find in the 197 parishes (some with more than one priest)—more than 60 percent nationally. In the dioceses that contain a majority of the country's population—the Archdiocese of Managua and the dioceses of León and Granada—I interviewed 70 to 83 percent of all priests active in pastoral work in the parishes. In each case I met beforehand with each respective bishop and diocesan vicar for a letter of introduction and permission to conduct the study, and I was given access to church directories of clergy in each diocese.

Topics covered in the survey included priests' background and training, pastoral activities, church-state relations, and political attitudes of the clergy. For a fuller discussion of the other issues covered in the priest survey and the distribution of interviews by region, see Andrew J. Stein, "The Prophetic Mission, the Catholic Church, and Politics: Nicaragua in the Context of Central America" (Ph.D. diss., University of Pittsburgh, 1995), apps. 2–4.

8. When reforms were eventually passed by the legislative branch in early 1995 and an open conflict with the executive branch ensued, Cardinal Obando negotiated a successful settlement to the constitutional crisis (in June 1995).

9. John A. Booth, *The End and the Beginning: The Nicaraguan Revolution* (Boulder, CO: Westview Press, 1982); Knut Walter, *The Regime of Anastasio Somoza, 1936–1956* (Chapel Hill: University of North Carolina Press, 1993).

10. See also Richard Millett, *The Guardians of the Dynasty* (Maryknoll, NY: Orbis Books, 1977).

11. Conferencia Episcopal de Nicaragua, "El hombre, la Iglesia, y la sociedad" (Granada: CEN, August 6, 1974), 7.

12. Conferencia Episcopal de Nicaragua, "Orientaciones con el motivo del período electoral y de las elecciones de febrero de 1990" (Managua: CEN, September 24, 1989), 3.

13. Conferencia Episcopal de Nicaragua, "Comunicado sobre la emboscada el día primero de enero, 1990" (Managua: CEN, January 3, 1990). For analyses of the role of the Church in the campaign, see Guillermo Cortés Domínguez, *La lucha por el poder: Revés electoral sandinista* (Managua: Editorial Vanguardia, 1990); Oscar René Vargas, *¿Adónde va Nicaragua?* (Managua: Ediciones Nicarao, 1991).

14. Conferencia Episcopal de Nicaragua, "Orientaciones con el motivo de las elecciones del 25 de febrero" (Managua: CEN, February 15, 1990b), 2. Part of this concern was over the Chamorro administration's "co-government" with the Sandinista opposition in the National Assembly and retention of Sandinistas in control of the police and armed forces. Further discontent was in response to the deep splits in the fourteen-party UNO coalition that won the elections.

15. Margaret E. Crahan, "Religion and Democratization in Central America," in *Political Parties and Democracy in Central America*, ed. Louis W. Goodman, William LeoGrande, and Johanna Mendelson Forman (Boulder, CO: Westview Press, 1992), 349.

16. Philip Berryman has discussed the purge of Sandinista influence in the teaching materials and personnel of the Education Ministry in his *Stubborn Hope: Religion, Politics, and Revolution in Central America* (Maryknoll, NY: Orbis Books-The New Press, 1994), 61–62. See also Robert F. Arnove, *Education as Contested Terrain: Nicaragua, 1979–1993* (Boulder, CO: Westview Press, 1994).

17. Ministerio de Educación, "Lineamientos del Ministerio de Educación en el nuevo Gobierno de Salvación Nacional" (Managua: MED, 1990), 4.

18. It is worth noting that Education Ministers Cisneros and Belli were fervent critics of FSLN rule and were active lay members of Catholic organizations such as the City of God during the 1980s.

19. Conferencia Episcopal de Nicaragua, "Para avivar la esperanza del Pueblo de Dios" (Managua: CEN, 1994), 4.

20. Ministerio de Educación, "Política de educación sexual del Ministerio de Educación" (Managua: MED, n.d.); *La Prensa*, July 8, 1994.

21. In a sense, such instruction would be a return to policy under the Somozas, with the important difference being that religion would be an extracurricular subject, taught after school hours, and instructors would not be paid by the state, as was done before the revolution.

22. Conferencia Episcopal de Nicaragua, "Para avivar la esperanza del Pueblo de Dios," 1.

23. *La Tribuna*, June 24, 1994.

24. Among the chief complaints are the lack of progress in reintegration into society of former Contras (or, as the clergy and the press now call them, the ex-Resistance), the failure to foster economic growth, and reducing and reforming the military and the police (including the delayed retirement of Gen. Humberto Ortega from his position at the head of the armed forces).

25. In the first three years of the Chamorro government, 237 of 351 state enterprises were privatized, according to Rose J. Spalding, *Capitalists and Revolution in Nicaragua: Opposition and Accommodation, 1979–1993* (Chapel Hill: University of North Carolina Press, 1994), 168.

26. Conferencia Episcopal de Nicaragua, "Para avivar la esperanza del Pueblo de Dios," 7.

27. Oscar René Vargas, *Nicaragua entre el laberinto y la esperanza* (Managua: Ediciones Nicarao, 1993), 58.

28. Author's interview, Managua, July 7, 1994.

29. *Barricada*, December 15, 1993.

30. Author's interview, Managua, June 1994.

31. For a discussion of church-state relations in the first year after the 1990 elections, see Philip J. Williams, "The Limits of Religious Influence: The Progressive Church in Nicaragua," in *Competition and Conflict: The Latin American Church in a Changing Environment*, ed. Edward L. Cleary and Hannah Stewart-Gambino (Boulder, CO: Lynne Rienner, 1992).

32. Conferencia Episcopal de Nicaragua, "Sobre los principios que rigen la actividad política de toda la Iglesia como tal" (Managua: CEN, March 12, 1972), 2.

33. Author's interview, Managua, July 7, 1994.

15

The Economic Elite

Rose J. Spalding

It is sometimes alleged that the Chamorro administration was a government of and for the economic elite.[1] In fact, however, the Nicaraguan business elite was hardly so uniform or uncritical in its views of Chamorro-era officials. Just as it had felt a mixture of sentiments about the Sandinista government,[2] so, too, it divided in its assessment of the Chamorro administration. The economic elite did not, as a whole, prosper during those years. Although some self-exiled elites returned to Nicaragua after 1990 and the general economic framework shifted to favor them, the neoliberal transition overseen by the Chamorro government presented serious challenges, even to this privileged stratum of society.

Tension between governments undertaking economic restructuring and the business elite has been observed in numerous settings in Latin America. Stephan Haggard and Robert Kaufman note business opposition to the austerity measures and technocratic decision-making style adopted by economic reformers in Argentina under the military government in 1981 and 1982.[3] Charles Gillespie describes how a wide array of business elites became disaffected in the early 1980s with the Uruguayan military's orthodox economic policy reforms.[4] Elite opposition to privatization throughout Latin America is chronicled in William Glade's analysis.[5] As Haggard and Kaufman note in their discussion of economic restructuring in Bolivia, Brazil, and Peru, "notwithstanding our emphasis on labor, the absence of business support for the government's adjustment efforts was also a hallmark of these crisis cases."[6] Although some business sectors obviously benefited from economic reform, others were seriously undercut by this transition. Conflicting assessments of the consequences of reform led to sharp intra-elite conflicts in countries as varied as Chile, Peru, and Mexico.[7]

In the Nicaraguan case, important sectors of the elite claimed that the Chamorro government contributed to stagnation and decline with its overly rigid implementation of neoliberal economic policy. Elite hostility was exacerbated by the stylistic propensities of the Higher Council on Private

Enterprise (Consejo Superior de la Empresa Privada, or COSEP), the major private-sector organization. This association had assumed a forceful antistate perspective during the Sandinista years and found it hard to abandon this rhetoric, even in less inclement times. Elite disenchantment was also sparked by lingering questions about governmental propriety and contested property rights that the administration was unable to resolve.

The Chamorro government did, of course, have elite allies. Coming on the heels of the Sandinista revolution, when the traditional elite as a whole experienced a sharp social and economic decline, the Chamorro years provided a welcome change of pace for this group. A small but economically important sector gave persistent support to the Chamorro government and its principal architect, Minister of the Presidency Antonio Lacayo. Unlike much of the elite, that group was able, because of its members' connections and market savvy, to grasp the opportunities that the transition offered: they acquired state resources with privatization, they could attract investment capital, and they could compete in the international market. This small group, however, was not enough to rebuild a national economy. To achieve this goal, the Nicaraguan government would need to find a way to expand opportunities for others, including the new business sectors under workers, cooperatives, and small producers.

The Historical Legacy

The Nicaraguan elite has long been characterized by its lack of unity. Regional polarization fed the deep liberal-conservative divide that plunged the country repeatedly into war in the nineteenth and early twentieth centuries. Economic interests diverged when no one product was able to dominate the national economy. Through the twentieth century different economic activities (coffee, cotton, cattle, industry, commerce) competed for capital and concessionary treatment. As a 1994 Nitlapán review of rural stratification concludes, "[The agrarian elite] is a very heterogeneous sector in terms of its economic activities, size, and social origins."[8]

Given this variation, the business class found it difficult to unite on a common political project. It took repeated and fundamental political crises to bring the elite together. The initial version of COSEP, Nicaragua's first "business peak association,"[9] only emerged in 1972. The deepening corruption and acquisitiveness of the Somoza regime in the early 1970s[10] prompted economic elites to present their first cross-sectoral challenge to the dynasty at a national conference in March 1974.[11] This effort soon fizzled, as Anastasio Somoza skillfully divided the elite again through strategic bargaining, but it reignited at the end of the decade during the FSLN-led insurrection. COSEP provided the organizational mechanism through which the elite struggled for unification and pushed for change.

Political consolidation of the economic elite only really occurred, however, with the Sandinista revolution. Driven initially by the strong, antibourgeoisie rhetoric used by some in the FSLN leadership,[12] elite fears of the revolution deepened after 1981 with the second wave of expropriations. The first-wave confiscations, which focused on the properties of the Somoza family and a loose array of Somocistas, were not highly controversial, even among those economic elites who remained in the country. When subsequent legislation was approved allowing the government to expropriate other properties, however, they became increasingly alarmed.

Since land could be taken for a range of loosely defined reasons (decapitalization, the owner's absence from the country, or for "public utility"), many in the elite feared that their whole social class was being targeted for extermination. The recurring surges in expropriations, which peaked in 1982 and again in 1986,[13] contributed to a generalized perception of threat. The maze of regulations limiting the sectors of the economy that were open for private investment and controlling the production and distribution processes led even elites who were not expropriated to define themselves as a merely "administrative" bourgeoisie. More than any single factor, a palpable fear of class dissolution fostered widespread elite hostility.[14]

During the 1980s, COSEP became a forceful critic of the FSLN. In 1981 its leaders publicly denounced the Sandinista government for its "Marxist-Leninist" and "totalitarian" tendencies.[15] For distributing this denunciation to the international media, the top COSEP leaders were found guilty of violating national security laws in 1981, and several were sent to prison.[16] From that point onward, COSEP functioned as an archrival of the FSLN government.

Not all economic elites were equally hostile, however; indeed, a modest, though not insignificant, number came to support the regime. For them, the Sandinistas' commitment to a "mixed economy" gave adequate space to the private sector. Indeed, some elites who initially opposed the FSLN got closer to the regime at the end of the decade, when the Sandinistas began a series of more orthodox economic adjustments and attempted a reconciliation. Sandinista-sponsored organizations such as the National Union of Farmers and Cattlemen (Unión Nacional de Agricultores y Ganaderos, or UNAG) recruited among medium- and large-sized agricultural producers, hoping to link the less intransigent elements of the agricultural bourgeoisie to this process of social change.[17] The FSLN even convinced a small number of economic elites, such as Juan Diego López, a wealthy landowner and president of the national dairy association, to run as candidates on the party's electoral slate in 1990.

In general, however, the relationship between economic elites and the Sandinista government was adversarial. The tension was softened somewhat by family ties, which linked some of the FSLN leadership to prominent families,[18] by special subsidies and support provided by the government,[19] and by the pragmatic recognition of mutual dependence. But opposition to the FSLN government among the business elite was both generalized and clear. According to one postelection survey, 90 percent of those who classified themselves as "owners and proprietors" voted against the FSLN in 1990.[20]

For most business elites, the election of UNO candidate Violeta Barrios de Chamorro was greeted with enthusiasm. Although mildly disgruntled that former COSEP president Enrique Bolaños lost his bid for a position on the UNO ticket, COSEP leaders supported Chamorro's candidacy. They organized logistical support during the voter registration process, and top business people such as COSEP president Gilberto Cuadra joined Chamorro's advisory team. Her election was perceived, in many circles, as a victory of the Nicaraguan elite, which had come to reclaim political power.

The Chamorro Transition: The Government's Push for Alliance

The Chamorro administration made major efforts to build linkages to Nicaragua's business elite. Business leaders figured prominently in the "transition teams" set up by the incoming administration in each key policy area. Three COSEP officials (Enrique Dreyfus, an early COSEP president; Gilberto Cuadra, then president of the organization; and coffee association president Jaime Cuadra) were nominated for cabinet positions. All state enterprises were reorganized into a series of corporations to prepare for their privatization, and many of the country's most prominent business leaders were named to their boards of directors.[21]

As part of its overall commitment to a neoliberal economic transition,[22] the Chamorro administration moved quickly to divest itself of state enterprises. Indeed, according to the 1995 report by the National Corporation of State Enterprises (CORNAP) on the privatization process, of the 1,237 acts of "disincorporation" of state assets that had taken place in the 1990–1994 period, 544 (44 percent) involved the return of properties to former owners.[23] Those who could not be given back their properties were issued bonds which could be used for various purposes, including to purchase state enterprises, as collateral for bank loans, and, under certain circumstances, to pay taxes.

In addition to those who had their property returned by the Chamorro administration, private business people were the beneficiaries of another 246 privatization agreements, mostly in the form of purchases of farms, firms, equipment, or livestock from the state.[24] State corporations were sold at modest prices, in part because of the low demand for them.[25] In some cases, entrepreneurs who bought state enterprises did so simply by assuming some or all of a firm's debt. Private entrepreneurs were even given loans, at times, with which to make these purchases. Easy terms allowed investment-oriented elites to acquire extensive additional resources. In all, private business owners benefited, either through property returns or purchases of state property, from over one-half (52 percent) of the privatization agreements.[26]

Whole sectors of the economy were reopened to private investment shortly after Chamorro was inaugurated. In spite of constitutional prohibitions, private banks were reauthorized and private firms were again permitted to engage in foreign trade. Eleven banks had been authorized by mid-1995[27]; by the end of 1994 private banks held 57 percent of all bank deposits.[28] Private exporters returned rapidly; some 105 export firms had been licensed by the end of 1991.[29] New ventures developed as well, most notably a stock and bond market which offered the elite additional investment opportunities and sources of capital.[30]

Access to bank credit went overwhelmingly to the elite. Not only did private banks lend almost exclusively to this sector, but so also did the state banks. The latter dropped most of their smaller clients after 1988; the number of bank clients fell from 80,511 in 1988 to 10,815 in 1993.[31] Whereas small producers lost access to bank credit, the real amount of credit for large private producers remained fairly stable.[32] In analyzing the *córdoba* loans of the state banks for 1994, for example, the pattern of concentration is clear. Eighty percent of the state banks' loans went to the top 11 percent of the institutions' clients—that is, those borrowing more than 100,000 *córdobas* (U.S. $14,225).[33]

Although borrowers were required to use their properties as collateral, the banks were slow to foreclose on unpaid loans. Only very large unpaid debts, which threatened the future of the state bank system, prompted the state banks to mount a campaign among elites for repayment. After months of unproductive requests for payment in 1994, for example, the state banks released information about the unpaid debts of Roberto Rondón, the Chamorro administration's first minister of Agriculture and Livestock, and Ramiro Gurdián, former president of COSEP.[34] But in sector after sector, bad loans to economic elites were restructured and concessionary terms offered. In spite of the elite's weak performance, the state bank system was slow to apply punitive measures.

In addition to these actions, the administration used its extensive decree powers to create new legislation that bolstered business interests. Driven by the belief that the elite's investments served the common good, not simply the interests of this small sector, the government offered a series of concessions to investors, particularly those in nontraditional areas. The Decree Law on the Promotion of Exports and its by-laws offered tax exemptions on both imports and locally produced materials used in exports and included a five-year tax reduction on earnings from nontraditional exports. The Industrial Free Zones Law reestablished free-trade zones in 1991, and this sector expanded quickly. Foreign investment, including returning flight capital, was offered remittance guarantees and protection against expropriation.

Not all of the Chamorro government's policies were, strictly speaking, orthodox expressions of neoliberalism. Faced with complaints from industrialists that free trade would destroy Nicaragua's industrial sector, for example, the government requested asymmetrical terms for its participation in the revived Central American trade agreement. The Temporary Protection Tariff (Arancel Temporal de Protección, or ATP) imposed duties of 5 to 15 percent on approximately nine hundred imports beginning in 1994. Although the ATP was to be phased out by 1999, it offered special assistance to industrialists during the transition process.[35]

In sum, the government attempted to work closely with private-sector organizations in policy development and review. In both of the *concertación* processes in 1990 and 1991, business organizations were invited to send representatives to negotiate agreements with the Chamorro administration and organized labor about how the new economic model was to be implemented. The government repeatedly requested the assessment by business organizations of proposed economic changes including, for example, the consumer and labor code negotiations and emerging industrial policy.[36] Private-sector organizations were given positions on the boards of economic agencies and commissions such as the USAID-financed Exports and Investments Center (Centro de Exportaciones e Inversiones, or CEI) and the National Agricultural Commission (Comisión Nacional Agropecuaria, or CONAGRO). As a result, the economic transition won the backing of important sectors of the elite, particularly in the pockets of the economy that benefited most under the new rules. Support for the reforms was most visible in the financial sector, larger commercial operations, and among nontraditional exporters.

Allowed to reopen and given a relatively free hand by the administration, private bankers expanded rapidly. Although these bankers carefully avoided a narrow political alliance with the Chamorro government, they applauded the general economic outlines that the administration pursued.[37] Moreover, many business people in larger commercial establishments also prospered following deregulation and trade liberalization. Both the American Chamber of Commerce in Nicaragua (AMCHAM) under its president Carlos Reynaldo Lacayo and the national Chamber of Commerce under its president Roberto Terán publicly emphasized their cooperative relations with the government.[38]

Producers of nontraditional exports, who benefited from Nicaragua's postrevolution entry into the Caribbean Basin Initiative, also tended to endorse the broad outlines of the economic transition. Large producers who wanted to expand into nontraditional products formed a new group, the Nicaraguan Association of Producers and Exporters of Nontraditional Products (Asociación Nicaragüense de Productores y Exportadores de Productos No-

Tradicionales, or APENN) in 1990; over time this organization expanded and, with support from USAID, even extended some services to cooperatives and small producers.[39]

Interpersonal bonds linked some economic elites to top government officials,[40] and others were wooed with prospects of gain. In terms of their political orientation, beneficiaries were quite diverse, although most might be loosely classified as "moderates" and "pragmatists." Not surprisingly, they included some of the country's most prominent and durable business leaders[41]; they also included elites who had been affiliated with the Sandinista government. The FSLN, after all, had initiated the structural adjustment process in 1988 and 1989. Some sectors in the party regarded a reorientation toward the market as positive; others concluded simply that it was inevitable.[42] Although adversaries of the Chamorro government in a formal sense, these party activists, disparagingly labeled the "new Sandinista bourgeoisie" by their critics, had economic interests that bound them to the regime.[43]

State-Elite Tensions in the Chamorro Years

In spite of regime efforts, the state-elite relationship remained brittle. Friction was particularly evident between the government and leaders of COSEP, two of whom (Gilberto Cuadra and Jaime Cuadra), nominated for cabinet positions during the transition period, withdrew on the day that Chamorro was inaugurated to signal their opposition to the retention of Humberto Ortega as head of the armed forces. Although COSEP representatives did agree to participate in the two *concertación* processes, they refused to sign any of the agreements produced by these meetings and persuaded representatives of their affiliates to do likewise.

COSEP also supported the position of the Association of Confiscated Property Owners when it demanded the immediate return of all expropriated property. One COSEP affiliate, the Nicaraguan Union of Agricultural Producers (Unión de Productores Agropecuarios de Nicaragua, or UPANIC), endorsed the 1992 suspension of U.S. aid orchestrated by Republican Senator Jesse Helms, even though this aid included $50 million in credit for Nicaraguan businesses.[44]

More important than these signals of organizational opposition, economic elites indicated their hesitancy about the transition through their resistance to investment. Nicaraguan business people entered the 1990s with low investment rates. Annual private investment levels, which had fallen to 2.8 percent of GDP between 1979 and 1989, reportedly rose to only 6.5 percent in the 1990–1993 period, far below the traditional 1966–1978 average of 10.2 percent.[45] Worse still, new private investment peaked at the beginning of President Chamorro's term and declined thereafter.[46] Although more

willing to risk investment under Chamorro than it had been under the
Sandinistas, the elite remained cautious. These modest investment levels,
running around an annual average of U.S. $119 million between 1990 and
1993, fell far short of replacing the estimated U.S. $2.2 billion that had left
the country in capital flight between 1970 and 1990.[47] With private investment remaining low and public investment dropping from 16.4 percent of
GDP in the 1979–1989 period to 6.9 percent in 1990–1993,[48] overall investment levels were insufficient to reactivate the economy.

We are left, then, with an anomaly. On the one hand, the Chamorro
government made substantial efforts to stimulate elite economic recovery;
on the other, much of the private sector remained skeptical and withdrawn.
Four elements help us puzzle through this apparent contradiction. First, an-
tigovernment sentiment was a legacy of the private-sector organizational
development during the two previous decades. COSEP, the principal elite
association, had been forged during the conflict with the Somoza regime
and tempered during the struggle with the Sandinista revolution. During
those hard years of political struggle, it had developed an antistate ideology
and a penchant for confrontation.[49] These experiences molded the organization and led to a certain political ossification. Its president, Gilberto Cuadra,
phrased it metaphorically: "As in nature, the shape of our tree is determined
by the winds that we have encountered."[50] Having developed an adversarial
relationship with the government in previous years, COSEP found it difficult to shift to a more conciliatory style.

Second, elite dissatisfaction was exacerbated by lingering uncertainties about property rights. Pressure from old owners for the return of expropriated properties, and the failure of the Sandinista government to issue
clear titles to new owners, created a morass of intractable claims and coun-
terclaims that the Chamorro government was forced to adjudicate.[51] In addition to past claimants, workers in state industrial enterprises had also been
guaranteed the opportunity to acquire 25 percent of the complexes in which
they had worked,[52] and former soldiers and Resistance fighters had also
been promised land as part of their demobilization agreements. Beyond the
legal uncertainties about who owned what, economic elites faced the prospect of strikes or land invasions by disgruntled sectors, further compromising property security.

Third, some business leaders alleged that the regime was rife with favoritism and corruption, giving unfair advantage to family members or political allies of top government leaders.[53] According to these elites, the
Chamorro administration continued a long tradition of blurring the line between state and private interests. Rumors flew during the Chamorro years
about government leaders' purported business dealings with the FSLN and
the military and about favoritism toward industries in which these officials
reportedly had investments. For those who adopted this perspective, a cen-

tral issue was government ethics and accountability. Their suspicions were fed both by Nicaragua's long history of governmental corruption and opportunism and by the absence of effective regulations limiting the ability of high officials to profit from political connections.

Fourth, perhaps the most important source of tension flowed from the neoliberal model itself. The government's contraction and inactivity in the face of continuing economic collapse became a source of considerable controversy within the elite. During the Sandinista era, economic elites had generally opposed the "mixed economy" model and pushed for a shift toward a market-based economy. This stance was particularly prevalent among national-level leaders in COSEP,[54] but a pro-market sentiment was common in the private sector. The reality of a market transition, however, was much harsher than these elites anticipated. In spite of government actions to support and buffer the business sector, many producers had difficulties in meeting the challenges of neoliberal reform.

A survey of private producers undertaken in 1992 by COSEP, the Central American Institute of Business Administration (Instituto Centroamericano de Administración de Empresas, or INCAE), and the Ministry of Economy and Development (Ministerio de Economía y Desarrollo, or MEDE) captured emerging elite ambivalence about the model.[55] The 413 respondents who attended COSEP-organized seminars generally approved of trade liberalization and the stable exchange rate, but they were less enthusiastic about the sharp reduction in credit and the high interest rates that accompanied the contraction of the state bank system. Reeling from this adjustment, 90 percent of the respondents described Nicaragua's interest rates as either "very high" (53 percent) or "high" (37 percent).

This survey indicated not only that neoliberal economics had several undesirable costs, but also that producers wanted at least some forms of government help. Eighty percent of the respondents stated that they would expect their productivity to increase "much" if there were technological development programs in place. A substantial group of producers used this survey to call for pump priming, cheaper credit, and technical assistance.

A study of private-sector investment patterns by the International Foundation for the Global Economic Challenge (Fundación Internacional para el Desafío Económico Global, or FIDEG) found similar results.[56] Based on 1993 interviews with leaders of all the major private-sector organizations and survey responses from over thirty of the country's major firms, this analysis concluded that one of the main factors negatively affecting investment decisions was the economic passivity of the Chamorro regime. Although the range of factors mentioned was quite extensive, this study highlighted problems such as the "lack of comprehensive production programs and of programs facilitating technological change," "deteriorated infrastructure" (ports, roads, energy, and basic public services), and "the lack of a vision through which to incentivize production and investment through tax policy."[57]

As with the COSEP-INCAE-MEDE survey, respondents in the FIDEG study expressed considerable ambivalence about the character and role of the state. One theme that emerged from these interviews concerned state corruption and inherent untrustworthiness.[58] At the same time, respondents called on the state for increased assistance, pushing for the creation of a development institute to stimulate investment and state action to improve infrastructure.

The sense that proactive government participation in development was necessary, if problematic, fed directly into private-sector recommendations to the government.[59] At a forum on "Economic Prospects for 1994/96" in September 1993, the presidents of major private-sector organizations called on the government to design and implement a national development plan.[60] In the following year, leaders of both UNAG and UPANIC organized meetings with top government officials and presented formal plans calling for development programs, lower interest charges, debt relief for producers, and fuller access for agricultural producers to their own hard currency earnings.[61] Cattle ranchers, who suffered from declining international prices and recurring drought, were particularly insistent in their demands for assistance. Borrowing from the organizational tactics of labor and political dissidents, renegade ranchers rejected demands for repayment of bank loans and organized roadblocks, forcibly halting the flow of milk and cattle from Matagalpa, Boaco, and Chontales in early 1995.[62]

The elite's challenges to the government often centered on its implementation of structural adjustment agreements signed with international financial institutions. For many in the private sector, these agreements needed to be rethought and further modified based on local conditions. COSEP president Gilberto Cuadra, for example, concluded in early 1995 that "the ESAF [Enhanced Structural Adjustment Facility] is not the solution to our problems," and he called for "a change to the Southeast Asian model of development," with more extensive state support.[63] Former COSEP president Ramiro Gurdián concluded: "If I were president [of Nicaragua], the first thing I would do would be to tell the IMF [International Monetary Fund] to leave."[64] Private elites called on the government to recapitalize the state banks and put more resources into credit for production. These comments, made repeatedly in public and private forums, suggested the intensity of business objections to the Chamorro administration's neoliberal shift.

In some ways, state-elite tension between 1990 and 1995 was not surprising. As we saw above, elite ambivalence about neoliberal adjustments was observed in much of Latin America. The conflict in Nicaragua highlights the difficulties of implementing economic restructuring that not only exacerbates the social problems of the poor but also undermines the investment and growth prospects of the elite.

Conclusion

Public linkages between the Chamorro government and prominent private elites should not overshadow the fact that the core of the elite encountered serious difficulties throughout this period. In spite of the proliferation of imported vehicles, freshly painted homes and businesses, and the opening of new restaurants and shops, members of the Nicaraguan elite faced major problems in identifying a new niche in the international economy. The first flush of enthusiasm and return migration after the inauguration of President Chamorro soon gave way to the challenge of producing without adequate infrastructure, learning to deal with global competition, and confronting their own limitations as entrepreneurs and managers.

The elites' push for more state assistance in meeting this challenge opened them to criticism. As one consultant's report for USAID on the private sector concluded: "There is confusion between the concepts of 'private enterprise' and 'free enterprise.' The private sector is constantly seeking advantage, but not always through an opening of the market."[65] Yet, as of 1995, state support for managerial retraining and technological innovation appeared necessary in order to facilitate an economic transition and promote general prosperity. Such a program would need to be carefully defined and delineated to reduce the room for discretionary implementation and favoritism. It would also need to be extended, not only to traditional elites but also to other private producers, including small- and medium-sized producers, cooperatives, and the new workers' enterprises. Identifying a more inclusive new development model that would serve both new and old producers would be the task of Chamorro's successors.

Notes

1. Defining the "economic elite" is difficult because of the multifaceted nature of elite status and the limited nature of the data on the distribution of resources in Nicaragua. Clearly, however, the country's elite is composed of a relatively small number of people. The distribution of bank resources is suggestive. Data on all bank loans (private and state) for 1994 indicate that a total of only 3,039 clients had *córdoba* loans totaling 250,000 or more (U.S. $35,562 at the December 1994 rate of exchange). See Superintendencia de Bancos y Otras Instituciones, *Informe anual del sistema financiero, Año 1994* (Managua: República de Nicaragua, 1995), 29.

2. See Rose J. Spalding, *Capitalists and Revolution in Nicaragua: Opposition and Accommodation, 1979–1993* (Chapel Hill: University of North Carolina Press, 1994).

3. Stephan Haggard and Robert R. Kaufman, *The Political Economy of Democratic Transitions* (Princeton: Princeton University Press, 1995), 57–60.

4. Charles G. Gillespie, "Uruguay's Transition from Collegial Military-Technocratic Rule," in *Transitions from Authoritarian Rule: Latin America*, ed. Guillermo O'Donnell, Philippe C. Schmitter, and Lawrence Whitehead (Baltimore: Johns Hopkins University Press, 1986), 179–80.

5. William Glade, ed., *Privatization of Public Enterprises in Latin America* (San Francisco: ICS Press, 1991), 1–17.

6. Haggard and Kaufman, *Democratic Transitions*, 198.

7. This division within the business class on the question of neoliberal reform is chronicled in some detail by Guillermo Campero, *Los gremios empresariales en el período 1970–1983* (Santiago, Chile: Instituto Latinoamericano de Estudios Transnacionales, 1984); Francisco Durand, *Business and Politics in Peru* (Boulder, CO: Westview Press, 1994); and Matilde Luna, Ricardo Tirado, and Francisco Valdes, "Businessmen and Politics in Mexico, 1982–1986," in *Government and Private Sector in Contemporary Mexico*, ed. Sylvia Maxfield and Ricardo Anzaldúa Montoya (La Jolla: Center for U.S.-Mexico Studies, University of California, San Diego, 1987), 13–43.

8. Nitlapán, *El campesino-finquero y el potencial económico del campesinado nicaragüense*, Vol. 1, *Tipología y regionalización agrosocio-económica de los sistemas de producción y los sectores sociales en el agro nicaragüense* (Managua: Nitlapán, Universidad Centroamericana, 1994), 112.

9. For a fuller discussion of business peak associations in Latin America, see Francisco Durand and Eduardo Silva, eds., *Business Peak Associations and Political Change in Latin America* (forthcoming).

10. See Instituto Histórico Centroamericano, "Imperio económico de la familia Somoza," in *Nicaragua: Reforma o revolución*, Vol. 1, App. 2 (N.p.: December 1978), 319–24.

11. For a report on that conference, see Consejo Superior de la Iniciativa Privada, *Conclusiones sobre el tema: Estrategia de desarrollo socio-económico para la década de los 70* (Managua: mimeo, 1974).

12. At the first national meeting of the FSLN party members after Somoza's ouster, the "treasonous bourgeoisie" was labeled "the main instrument of the counterrevolution." See FSLN, "Análisis de la coyuntura y tareas de la Revolución Popular Sandinista," in *Sandinistas: Key Documents/Documentos Claves*, ed. Dennis Gilbert and David Block (Ithaca, NY: Latin American Studies Program, Cornell University, 1990), 90–91.

13. The number of land expropriations rose to 268 in 1982, dropped to 106 in 1984, and rose again to peak at 449 in 1986. See Centro de Investigaciones y Estudios de la Reforma Agraria (CIERA), *La reforma agraria en Nicaragua, 1979–1989* (Managua: CIERA, 1989), 9:40, table 2.

14. See Spalding, *Capitalists and Revolution*, 189–218, on the forces that shaped elite opposition to the Sandinista regime. This sense of threat was intensified by the escalating conflict between the United States and the Sandinista government, since many elites who were educated in the United States or had family members living there were strongly influenced by Washington's interpretations of the revolution. Elite fears of expropriation were not entirely misplaced. The Ministerio de Desarrollo Agrícola y Reforma Agraria (MIDINRA)'s 1983 economic plan, the "Marco Estratégico del Desarrollo Agropecuario," projected that only 6 percent of agricultural land would be held in large estates in the year 2000. See CIERA, *Reforma agraria*, 1:157, 161.

15. See COSEP letter to Daniel Ortega Saavedra, October 19, 1981.

16. See Dennis Gilbert, "The Bourgeoisie," in *Nicaragua: The First Five Years*, ed. Thomas W. Walker (New York: Praeger, 1985), 172–75.

17. See Daniel Núñez (interview), "The Producers of This Country Support Our Revolutionary Government," in *Nicaragua: The Sandinista People's Revolution*, ed. Bruce Marcus (New York: Pathfinder Press, 1985), 359–66.

18. See Carlos M. Vilas, "Family Affairs: Class, Lineage, and Politics in Contemporary Nicaragua," *Journal of Latin American Studies* 24, no. 2 (May 1992): 309–41.

19. For example, see Trevor Evans, "El algodón: Un cultivo de debate," *Cuadernos de Pensamiento Propio* (April 1987), on the hefty subsidy given to the cotton producers during the Sandinista revolution.

20. Paul Oquist, "Sociopolitical Dynamics of the 1990 Nicaraguan Elections," in *The 1990 Elections in Nicaragua and Their Aftermath*, ed. Vanessa Castro and Gary Prevost (Lanham, MD: Rowman and Littlefield, 1992), 14.

21. Prominent private-sector leaders named to the governing boards of these corporations included Carlos Pellas (Corporación Nicaragüense de la Agroindustria Azucarera), Alfredo Marín (Corporación Avícola Nicaragüense), Carlos Mántica (Corporación Comercial del Pueblo), Samuel Mansell (Corporación Agroindustrial del Valle de Sébaco), Ernesto Salazar (Corporación Nicaragüense de la Carne), Rafael Martínez (Sociedad de Empresas Pecuarias del APP), and Ramiro Gurdián and René Bequillard (Corporación Nicaragüense del Banano).

22. On Nicaragua's neoliberal transformation, see Trevor Evans, coord., *La transformación neoliberal del sector público* (Managua: CRIES, 1995), 179–261; and José Luis Medal Mendieta, *Nicaragua: Políticas de estabilización y ajuste* (Managua: Multiprint, 1993).

23. CORNAP, *Avance del proceso de privatización al 31 de diciembre de 1994* (Managua: República de Nicaragua, 1995), 45. Of the land transferred out of state enterprises in the cattle, cotton, and coffee sectors, former owners received 41 percent, 51 percent, and 35 percent, respectively (or 40 percent of the total). Ibid., 17, 19, 36. Much of the land that was not returned to former owners was property that had been confiscated from Somoza family members and their associates under Decrees No. 3 and No. 38. Although some Somocistas were subsequently compensated ("U.S. Prods Nicaragua on Seized Land," *New York Times*, July 25, 1995), their land was generally transferred on to state farm workers or demobilized army and Resistance forces.

24. CORNAP, *Avance del proceso de privatización*, 48.

25. For case-by-case information about the terms, cost, purchaser, and legal representative for each acquisition of state assets, see the appendix to ibid., 1995. For a critical appraisal of this report, see Mario de Franco, "Nicaragua: Experiencia de Privatización de Empresas Públicas," paper presented at a national seminar on privatization organized by the Economic Commission on Latin America, the Swedish Cooperation Agency, and the UN Development Program, Managua, June 12, 1995.

26. CORNAP, *Avance del proceso de privatización*, 48.

27. Former president of the Association of Private Banks, author's interview, Managua, June 27, 1995.

28. Superintendencia, *Informe anual del sistema financiero*, 21. In spite of pressure to the contrary, state bank loans continued to outpace deposits, while private banks tended to hold larger reserves than were legally required. See Comisión Económica para América Latina y el Caribe (CEPAL), *Nicaragua: Evolución económica durante 1994* (México, D.F.: CEPAL, 1995), 4. As a result, the weight of private banks measured in terms of lending was lower than that measured in terms of deposits. Loans made by private banks totaled only 38.2 percent at the end of 1994. Superintendencia, *Informe anual del sistema financiero*, 23.

29. Ernesto Pérez, "Comportamiento del comercio exterior de Nicaragua en 1991," *Revista de Economía Agrícola* 4 (March 1992): 4.

30. See Miguel Campos Marcenaro's interview with Carolina Solórzano, the general manager of the stock and bond market, "La bolsa de valores en Nicaragua," *La Tribuna*, June 16, 1995, supple. 2.

31. Nitlapán, "Evolución reciente del sector agropecuario en Nicaragua: Los efectos de las políticas de estabilización y ajuste estructural (1988–1993)," first draft, August 1994, 16.

32. Ibid., 17.

33. Superintendencia, *Informe anual del sistema financiero*, 42. Private bank loans were even more concentrated. Whereas 80 percent of the state bank *córdoba* loans went to borrowers of more than C100,000, 91 percent of private bank loans went to this stratum. Ibid., 72.

34. In 1994, when bank policy was changed to limit future state bank loans to the amount recuperated from past ones, large unpaid loans severely restricted the institutions' ability to continue functioning. Faced with the prospect of rapid shrinkage, the state banks began to pressure large borrowers for repayment. When quiet pressures failed, they moved to foreclose, first on Rondón, one of the country's largest cattle ranchers, whose total debt (only a modest portion of which was overdue) was C10.2 million (U.S. $1.4 million), and then on Gurdián, for C9.4 million (U.S. $1.3 million) from a 1992 package designed to rebuild the private banana sector. See "Embargo a Rondón por mora bancaria," *Barricada*, August 18, 1994; "BANADES: 'Un precedente,' " ibid., August 19, 1994; "Requerimiento de pago a Rondón vence hoy," *La Prensa*, August 19, 1994; "Presidenta condena actitud de Rondón," *Barricada*, September 15, 1994; "BANIC embarga a Gurdián," ibid., September 27, 1994; "¿En qué gastó Gurdián los 9 millones?" ibid., October 4, 1994; and "Gurdián 'se prepea' con el BANIC," ibid., October 5, 1994.

35. USAID/Nicaragua, "Trade, Industry, and Investment," draft report, March 1995, 1.

36. American Chamber of Commerce in Nicaragua official, author's interview, Managua, June 28, 1995; Chamber of Industry of Nicaragua (Cámara de Industrias de Nicaragua, or CADIN) official, author's interview, Managua, June 30, 1995.

37. See interviews with three bank managers/presidents—José Félix Padilla of Intercontinental Bank (Banco Intercontinental, or INTERBANK), Eduardo Montealegre of Central American Bank of Credit (Banco de Crédito Centroamericano, or BANCENTRO), and Gilberto Wong of Export Bank (Banco de la Exportación, or BANEXPO)—in "Se siente recuperación económica," *El País* 3, no. 30 (April 1995): 27–31.

38. See the interview with Carlos Reynaldo Lacayo in "Se siente recuperación," 29–30. See also the interview with Terán in "¿Qué liderazgo necesita el COSEP y el país?" *Barricada*, September 5, 1994. When asked about his "closeness to the government," Terán responded, "I'm pragmatic. I try to arrange things in a simple way. . . . My opinion is that in economic matters one should be close to the government because the solutions are there."

39. APENN, "¿APENN: Por que se funda APENN?" *Boletín Informativo* (November–December 1994): 14–20; USAID/Nicaragua, "Nicaragua 2000: A Vision for the Year 2000" (mimeo, March 1995); USAID/Nicaragua director George Carner, interview with Latin American Working Group delegation, March 13, 1995; former APENN president, author's interview, Managua, June 24, 1995.

40. Antonio Lacayo, as a former member of CADIN and general manager of a cooking oil-processing conglomerate, had organizational connections to many in the elite.

41. The privatization process substantially restored and in some cases even increased the assets held by major economic groups. The Pellas family, for ex-

ample, had one of its major assets, the San Antonio sugar mill complex (Ingenio San Antonio, or ISA), returned by the Chamorro government. Technically, the ISA had been sold by the family to the FSLN government for U.S. $12 million in 1989, but the sale took place under pressure following the Ingenio's expropriation in 1988. The Sandinista government failed to meet its payments for the property, and the Chamorro government returned the plant to the Pellas family after the transition rather than auctioning it off to the highest bidder. The family was required, however, to assume the Ingenio's C67.4-million debt. (Nicaragua Sugar Estates management official, author's interview, Managua, September 21, 1990; see also CORNAP, *Avance del proceso de privatización*, app.). Members of the family also opened a new bank, the Bank of Central America (Banco de América Central, or BAC) and mobilized capital through which a Central American consortium acquired stock in the Nicaraguan Brewery Company. See "Trabajadores defienden la venta de marca Victoria," *Barricada*, July 12, 1994.

42. See Alejandro Martínez Cuenca, *Nicaragua: Una década de retos* (Managua: Editorial Nueva Nicaragua, 1990), for a discussion of the Sandinista government's internal leadership debates about economic policy.

43. See the diagnosis and critique of this alliance presented by Sandinista leader Henry Ruíz in an interview with Jorge Katín, "Principal aliado de Lacayo es FSLN," *El Semanario*, June 29–July 5, 1995.

44. See UPANIC, "Comunicado," June 11, 1992, published in *La Prensa*, June 21, 1992.

45. Alejandro Martínez Cuenca, "El comportamiento inversionista en Nicaragua," *Materiales de Estudio y Trabajo* 13 (1994): 15.

46. UNAG, *Aporte para una agenda de desarrollo sostenible* (Managua: UNAG, 1995) 6, table 1.

47. Martínez Cuenca, "Comportamiento," 12, 54. Martínez Cuenca estimates capital flight from 1970 to 1979 at U.S. $1.2 billion, and for 1980 through 1990 at U.S. $1.1 billion.

48. Ibid., 15.

49. See Rose J. Spalding, "Revolution and the Hyperpoliticized BPA: Nicaragua and the Consejo Superior de la Empresa Privada (COSEP)," in Durand and Silva, *Business Peak Associations*; and CARANA Corporation, *Nicaragua's Political Economy: The Role of the Private Sector* (Arlington, VA: CARANA Corporation, July 1991), a consultant's report prepared for USAID/Nicaragua.

50. Author's interview, Managua, June 29, 1995.

51. According to a 1995 Carter Center report, 25 percent of the agricultural land was claimed by former owners. See Council of Freely Elected Heads of Government, "Report on a Property Issues Conference, Montelimar, Nicaragua, July 4–5, 1995," Carter Center of Emory University, *Working Papers Series* (1995): 3.

52. Gobierno de Nicaragua-Central Sandinista de Trabajadores, "Acuerdo," February 2, 1993.

53. On Nicaraguan private-sector distrust of politicians, see CARANA Corporation, *Nicaragua's Political Economy*, 8–9. This perspective was widespread in the society, not just a view held by oppositional elites. According to a national survey conducted by the Instituto de Estudios Nicaragüenses (IEN) in November–December 1994, 87 percent of the respondents agreed with the statement that there was corruption in the government. See IEN, "La gobernabilidad y el acuerdo nacional en Nicaragua" (Managua: unpublished report, January 1995), 9.

54. When I asked ninety-one private-sector leaders about their preferred economic model in 1990 and 1991, 50 percent of the national level leaders in COSEP's agricultural affiliate, UPANIC, stated a preference for a pure market system,

including full privatization of state enterprises. In contrast, only 29 percent of UPANIC's regional or sectoral leaders favored such an extreme pro-market approach. Private-sector leaders not affiliated with COSEP were even more critical of a market-based approach. Sixty-nine percent of the UNAG leaders favored either a "mixed economy" or "socialism." For details, see Spalding, "Hyperpoliticized BPA," in Durand and Silva, *Business Peak Associations*.

55. COSEP/INCAE/MEDE, "Encuesta nacional a empresarios privados: Algunos resultados preliminares," unpublished document, May-June 1992.

56. Martínez Cuenca, "Comportamiento," 25–50.

57. Ibid., 26–27, 29.

58. Ibid., 31–32.

59. See business leaders' comments in Armando Medrano Chávez, "Política crediticia y de tasa de interés," *Revista de Economía Agrícola* 7 (January 1994): 55–67.

60. See interviews with the heads of the Chamber of Construction, the Chamber of Commerce, and UPANIC in *Barricada*, September 13, 1993. See also CADIN, *Estrategia para la reactivación productiva*, unpublished document, July 1993.

61. See "UNAG plantea propuesta económica al gabinete," *Barricada*, August 30, 1994; and "Propuesta a fondo de productores," ibid., November 23, 1994. See also the "Carta de entendimiento de la misión agropecuaria que visito la República de Chile," published as the appendix to UNAG, *Aporte para una agenda*, 83–87. This proposal, which was written by participants in a high-level government-private sector delegation that toured Chile at the end of 1994, called for the creation of a state development institute that would establish a twenty-year sustainable development plan.

62. See "Anuncia paro de ganaderos," *Barricada*, January 10, 1995; "Día de tranques en Región Norte," ibid., February 7, 1995; "BANIC hará uso de la vía judicial," *La Prensa*, March 18, 1995; and "Acuerdos alcanzados en las reuniones entre CONAGAN y representantes del gobierno y de los bancos estatales de fechas 21, 23, 28, 29 de marzo y 6 de abril del año en curso," ibid., April 22, 1995.

63. See "G. Cuadra cree que 1995 podría ser un mejor año," *La Prensa*, January 3, 1995.

64. Author's interview, Managua, June 22, 1995.

65. CARANA Corporation, *Nicaragua's Political Economy*, 24.

16

The Urban Informal Economic Sector

John G. Speer

Political and economic changes during the first half of the 1990s brought new challenges for Nicaragua's urban informal economic sector, perhaps the most visible and least understood group in society. The visibility and importance of the informal economy derived from its size; by some estimates, one-half of employed city dwellers generated income from activities outside the formal economy.[1] Street vendors, taxi drivers, market sellers, and home-front grocers lent bustle to cities and towns where combined unemployment and underemployment surpassed 50 percent.[2]

The informal economy was a broad terrain for urban survival, yielding subsistence for some people and riches for a few; it was also a hub of political contestation with the numbers to swing an election or to barricade a city. Yet, because the large majority of informal sector workers remained unorganized at their workplaces, the neoliberal Chamorro government gave scant attention to their occupational needs. Despite its efforts to devise a "popular democracy," the revolutionary Sandinista government had failed to create many structures of representation within the urban informal economy.

Growth of the informal economy during the 1980s and 1990s made this sector crucial for the stability of political institutions. Authorities neglected informal workers at their own peril. Nicaragua's informal sector often was perceived by local observers to be overwhelmingly populated by critics of the revolutionary leadership,[3] but this perception was belied by research in the late 1980s and early 1990s.[4] Neoliberal politicians were ill advised to assume high levels of support. The informal sector was marked by an ideological diversity which matched the diversity of conditions faced by its members. Commonplace caricatures of the informal sector as a petit bourgeois marketplace of counterrevolutionary ideas failed to account for the variety of ways that this segment of the population interpreted its political environment.

Informal Employment and Urban Survival

Economic adjustment policies in the late 1980s and early 1990s meant severe austerity for most Nicaraguans. In the absence of sufficient foreign aid to pay for production incentives, maintain employment levels, and fund social programs, these economic policies translated into higher costs to consumers. Layoffs in the private and state sectors, shrinking real wages, and a rising consumer price index helped to keep purchasing power strikingly low, at about 2.5 percent of 1980 levels by the end of the decade.[5] Real salaries slipped 85 percent in 1988 alone.[6] Urban areas experienced unemployment and shrinking purchasing power most acutely. In-migrants arrived to cities with far too few jobs to employ even longtime city residents. Tens of thousands responded by entering the urban informal sector of the economy.

According to the somewhat restrictive classification criteria of the Regional Employment Office for Latin America and the Caribbean (PREALC), as much as 35 percent of the economically active population in Managua was employed primarily in informal activities by 1982.[7] Other agencies adopting more inclusive definitions estimated that either in Managua or in all Nicaragua 50 percent of the economically active population was engaged in informal activity by the early- to mid-1980s.[8] These estimates all seem to exclude what Alejandro Portes calls "hidden wage workers," or home workers employed by formal sector factories on a piecework basis but not covered by labor legislation and other regulations.[9] Nor do they count the continued growth of the informal sector during the late 1980s and early 1990s. It is entirely possible that by 1995 upwards of 50 percent of urban Nicaraguans earned most of their income in the informal sector.

It is not difficult to understand why the urban informal economy grew so rapidly. In the absence of adequate employment opportunities in the formal sector, people did what they could to make a living. Furthermore, those who were employed in the formal sector, but whose wages did not cover basic needs, often found it possible to supplement or even surpass their regular salaries with informal economic activities. Also, distortions in market equilibria caused by price policies created opportunities for commercial intermediaries.[10]

Unemployment stood at 32 percent of Nicaragua's economically active population when the FSLN came to power in 1979, according to PREALC estimates. Due largely to Sandinista employment policies, this figure fell to 19 percent by 1981.[11] Employment gains reversed, however, by 1984 and 1985. Official figures registered 21.1 percent unemployment in 1985 and 25.1 percent by 1987. As migration from the countryside to urban centers accelerated, rising unemployment was seen mostly in the cities, and exclusively in nonagricultural activities.[12] Business failures and state sector layoffs beginning in 1988 added to the pool of unemployed people. Indeed, more than ten thousand professionals entered the informal sector by the late 1980s.[13]

In the midst of high unemployment, low purchasing power, and periodic shortages of consumer goods, the existence of two consumer markets —one with official prices and distribution centers designed to guarantee access to basic goods, and the other unregulated—created opportunities for profit in the informal sector. During the 1980s the state itself became the main source for goods exchanged in parallel markets.[14]

All these factors created a highly competitive and overcrowded informal economy, already impoverished before the new influx of small merchants. Still, the worst difficulty for the informal sector caused by structural adjustment policies was not overcrowding so much as it was the restriction of demand, since salary constraint figured as a key element in the stabilization program.[15] Formal sector workers not only flowed into informal activities to supplement or replace lost income, but they also had far less disposable income to spend on goods and services. While formal sector workers who retained employment throughout the middle and late 1980s found some relief in expanding nonwage benefits, very few informal workers could count on being reached by supplementary programs such as workplace distributions of basic consumer goods, free lunches, or free transportation.

Revolutionary Power versus the Informal Sector

During the first years after 1979 the Sandinista government showed some interest in organizing informal sector workers into occupational associations. For most such groups, the lasting effects of these early organizational efforts were minimal, at best. By the mid-1980s official hostility toward the informal sector could be heard.[16] The FSLN launched a propaganda campaign against speculation that questioned the national loyalty of numerous informal sector workers. The highly publicized Iron Fist (*puño de hierro*) operation carried out in 1986 against "speculators" by the Ministry of Interior Commerce (MICOIN) tended to generalize an image of the informal sector as a center of speculation. Early attempts at cooperativization turned toward aggressive measures to license traders and service workers, collect taxes, interrupt illegal trade at highway roadblocks, and foster "vigilance" among consumers, encouraging them to report hoarding and speculation to the authorities.[17]

Public support for the Iron Fist and the similar July Victory (*victoria de julio*) campaigns were minimal. Still, by the time of the 1990 elections, the informal sector was perceived by many to be a center of opposition to the FSLN. The extent of this opposition was exaggerated. Hostility to the FSLN that did exist was only partially attributable to the negative impact of economic policies on this sector. The FSLN's aggressive pronouncements against hoarding and speculation may have been even more decisive than the impact of economic policies, which were varied. Official discourse which characterized the informal sector as unproductive and counterrevolutionary (or at least not revolutionary) may have alienated a crucial base of support.[18]

Regime Change and Economic Policy

The Chamorro government also did not perceive the informal sector as a crucial political base. To the contrary, analysts sympathetic to informal workers contended that economic policies in the early 1990s were designed, in part, to impoverish the informal sector in order to expand the supply of cheap labor.[19] Nevertheless, many traders experienced a moderate level of economic relief with the policies of the Chamorro government. For the majority, the economic environment remained harsh.

If Nicaraguans expected a quick recovery with the ascension to power of the Chamorro government, they hoped for too much. It was unlikely that anything short of massive infusions of foreign aid would pull the country out of economic crisis in the short or medium term. Such aid was not forthcoming during the early 1990s. For instance, even though Washington pledged $300 million for 1990, by April 1991 only $116 million had been released; and, of that amount, only $80 million was in the form of liquid capital.[20]

President Violeta Barrios de Chamorro responded to the economic crisis by deepening the structural adjustment policies that had been the mainstay of FSLN economic policy since 1988. The adjustment mirrored Sandinista policies in several respects: restrictive monetary and credit policy, the introduction of a new currency, tight-fisted investment policy, employment cuts in the public sector, cutbacks in subsidies, and salary controls.[21]

Other aspects of economic policy went beyond what the Sandinista government had been willing to do. State factories were clearly in disfavor, as the government decapitalized or privatized many such enterprises. At first, this policy was accompanied by a direct assault on organized labor, but that assault was moderated after July 1990. Rates for public services such as utilities and transportation were allowed to rise well beyond levels maintained by the FSLN.

Individuals on fixed incomes suffered dramatic declines in real wages. Totally disabled persons received U.S. $45 per month at the end of Sandinista rule; by September 1990 these pensioners were getting the equivalent of only U.S. $18 per month. Because the value of the currency was constantly adjusted downward during the first years of the Chamorro government, the Jesuit publication *Envío* figured that "even those earning a minimum wage equivalent to U.S. $50 [monthly] could only purchase some 30 percent of the basic fifty-three-product market basket."[22]

Very few of the unemployed found relief in job opportunities created by the new government. As unemployment climbed during Chamorro's first year, the administration's primary employment program (the Emergency Social Investment Fund) opened only a handful of jobs.[23] State jobs continued to be eliminated, in part through the Occupational Conversion Program, which paid state workers four months' severance pay and eight months' bank credit in exchange for leaving their jobs. Many of the several thousands of workers who took this option opened small businesses in the midst of a recession and an overabundance of retailers.

For the poorest informal sector workers, daily economic struggle got worse during the early 1990s, while the better-off stratum of the informal sector enjoyed a moderate level of relief. As a whole, the 1990 adjustment policies of the Chamorro government were probably less detrimental to the informal sector than the 1988 and 1989 adjustments of the Sandinistas. Commercial activities benefited from the government's policies while productive and service subsectors suffered.[24]

By early 1991 the increase in the number of Managuans involved in buying and selling was astounding to observe. Every neighborhood had innumerable home-front stores (*pulperías*), some very well stocked. In some neighborhoods every second or third house offered something for sale, be it cigarettes, ice, bags of chips, soup, bread, or clothing. Marketplaces grew rapidly; scores of new stalls were built at the city's largest market and at the Roberto Huembes Market to accommodate extra sellers. Vendors crowded busy intersections with cheap imported merchandise. In addition to the typical offerings of cigarettes, gum, parrots, and newspapers seen throughout the 1980s, vendors began to hawk television antennae, boom boxes, Miller beer, and other new imports.

Benefits accruing to the commercial sector were short-lived, however. Anti-inflationary measures announced in March 1991 caused a severe restriction of demand. The spark for commerce in 1990—formal sector salary increases and an overvalued currency—fizzled with the new economic measures. A 400 percent currency devaluation and the renewed slide of real wages dried up spending and investment capital in the informal sector. The boom of small-scale commercial activity slumped visibly during President Chamorro's second year in office. Although hyperinflation was reeled in eventually—down to 12.4 percent by 1994—small merchants joined artisans and other small producers as clear losers in the new economy. In 1993 alone, more than thirty thousand primitive industrial units and handicraft producers went under.[25]

Political Attitudes of Informal Sector Workers

Just as the impact of economic policies was felt differently by various subsegments of the informal sector, so, too, did their perceptions of the political environment vary. This ideological diversity should be no surprise. As Matos Mar indicates, the interests of all informal sector workers are not alike. Street vendors are most concerned with securing a hassle-free and profitable place to sell. Shop owners are hampered by red tape and paperwork required to formalize their enterprises. Workers in small shops lack job security and benefits. Taxi drivers face high costs of operation and want the government to reduce tariffs and gasoline prices.[26] In short, the vulnerabilities and interests of informal sector workers differ according to their specific occupation. Some Nicaraguan informal workers sought to deal with their occupational problems by entering cooperatives. Many more remained unorganized. Because the economic problems and organizational experiences of these workers are not alike, it is reasonable to expect that there would exist a great deal of ideological and partisan diversity among this part of the population. Survey research conducted in early 1991 confirmed this expectation.

Survey data were collected in January 1991 for a larger study on the motivational bases of political support among Nicaraguan informal sector workers. During a four-day period, 480 informal sector workers in the Managua area were interviewed by the professional research firm, ITZTANI-INOP. Eighty members from each of six occupational groups were selected: taxi drivers, market stallkeepers, street vendors, owners of *pulperías*, highly mechanized workshops, and less mechanized workshops.[27] Taxi drivers were interviewed at five different cooperatives, while market stallkeepers were interviewed at three Managua markets.[28] To select practitioners of the other neighborhood-based occupations, a random selection of twenty neighborhoods was generated by computer.[29] In each neighborhood, four members each of the remaining four occupational groups were sought out by interviewers traveling on foot. In order to qualify, a workshop or *pulpería* had to employ five or fewer workers.

Research results indicated a high degree of partisan and ideological polarization within Managua's informal sector in the early 1990s. Among workers willing to declare partisan sympathies, 62 percent favored UNO and 38 percent aligned with the FSLN. Support for the FSLN was three points off the percentage of all Nicaraguans voting for Sandinista candidates in the 1990 election. Based on this finding, the notion that the informal sector was a center of counterrevolutionary attitudes seems exaggerated, at best. In fact, informal workers rated policy performance by the FSLN more favorably than that by the Chamorro government in each of the nine areas of policy that they were asked to assess (compare Table 1 with Table 2).

They were especially pleased with FSLN efforts to provide police protection, public housing, school construction, health care, and neighborhood services: in each of these areas between 58 and 71 percent ranked FSLN performance as good or excellent. Informal workers were less charitable in ranking FSLN exertions in the areas of public transportation, jobs for the unemployed, aid for the self-employed, and narrowing the gap between social classes, where good or excellent ratings nevertheless reached between 37 and 47 percent.

Table 1. **Evaluations of Policy Performance by the FSLN**

Policy Area	Terrible	Bad	Good	Excellent
Public transportation	15.8%	37.4%	41.7%	5.0%*
Police protection	10.8	31.4	48.7	9.1
Public housing	6.7	29.3	57.7	6.5
School construction	8.0	20.9	62.7	8.5
Health care	8.9	31.1	54.1	5.9
Jobs for unemployed	13.8	41.2	42.6	2.4
Aid for self-employed	14.0	47.7	35.0	2.3
Neighborhood services	8.9	29.6	57.7	3.8
Narrowing gap between rich and poor	23.9	38.2	35.0	2.9

*Row totals may not add to 100 percent due to rounding error.

Clearly, informal workers were divided in their attitudes toward the legacy of the FSLN. The results are not surprising in such a highly polarized political setting. What is surprising is the extent to which informal sector workers rated Sandinista efforts favorably. These people mainly were an impoverished population in a daily struggle to meet survival needs, who belonged to an economic sector that was largely ignored by the major political factions in the country.

Table 2. **Evaluations of Policy Performance by the Chamorro Government**

Policy Area	Terrible	Bad	Good	Excellent
Public transportation	21.1%	35.5%	41.9%	1.4%*
Police protection	23.5	43.0	32.4	1.0
Public housing	23.8	49.8	25.1	1.3
School construction	22.1	52.4	25.1	0.3
Health care	30.3	40.5	28.8	0.5
Jobs for unemployed	37.1	53.8	9.1	0.0
Aid for self-employed	28.4	49.5	21.4	0.8
Neighborhood services	16.2	43.8	38.9	1.1
Narrowing gap between rich and poor	46.3	39.9	12.9	0.8

*Row totals may not add to 100 percent due to rounding error.

However, for representatives of what is often thought to be a conservative or reactionary sector of Nicaraguan society, most workers in the sample were anything but pleased with the initial policy performance by the neoliberal Chamorro government. Combined good and excellent ratings in no case totaled more that 43.3 percent (public transportation) and reached as low as 9.1 percent for job creation. Almost no one was willing to assign excellent marks to the Chamorro government in any of these nine areas of public policy.

Workers were also more likely to turn thumbs down on performance by the Chamorro government than on FSLN performance. Nearly all of the respondents who expressed an opinion said that President Chamorro's employment policy was bad or terrible. Unfavorable ratings for every other policy area ranged between 57 and 86 percent of the sample, while unfavorable evaluations of FSLN performance in no case totaled more than 62 percent of those polled.

Perhaps it is not astonishing that there existed less disagreement about the performance record of the Chamorro government than there did about the FSLN; it was, after all, the revolutionary process associated with the FSLN that so polarized the Nicaraguan political community. What is startling is that these workers, who might be seen as a natural constituency for the neoliberal Chamorro government, were so negatively disposed toward the performance of the new administration.

Support for a Transitional Political System

David Easton's seminal work on political support notes that troubled times might cause leaders and their programs to fall out of favor, but criticism could be "weathered out" by the political system provided that there existed a sufficient reservoir of diffuse support for the regime and for the political community.[30] Similarly, Gabriel Almond and Sidney Verba reason that positive feelings among the mass public about the political system were crucial for the development and survival of democratic institutions.[31]

Given the numerical significance of the informal sector workers, the cultivation of their support for the country's political institutions assumed vital importance in the 1990s. Unfortunately, none of Nicaragua's major political factions exerted much effort to ensure a voice for informal workers in the country's "dual transitions from authoritarian rule."[32] This marginalization helps to explain a high degree of alienation from the political system evident within the informal sector.

To examine levels of system support, six items were included in the survey: 1) Do you agree or disagree that the courts nearly always make fair judgments? 2) It is foolish to trust the government; 3) The basic rights of citizens have never been respected by the government; 4) The majority of the legislators comply with their duties; 5) The Constitution is not good, it should be changed; and 6) How proud does it make you feel to live in a country with a system of government like the one we have in Nicaragua? The items were measured on five-point scales. Table 3 shows the distribution of responses to these questions, with responses divided into two categories.

Table 3. Levels of System Support among Informal Workers

	High Support		Low Support	
	%	(N)	%	(N)
Courts	42.5	(147)	57.5	(199)
Trust in government	43.5	(171)	56.5	(222)
Human rights protection	39.0	(147)	61.0	(230)
Legislature	37.0	(113)	63.0	(192)
Constitution	38.0	(125)	62.0	(204)
Pride in system	63.0	(254)	37.0	(149)

Only in the case of pride in the system did the majority of respondents express high levels of support. The overall picture was one of political alienation. Not only did the majority of informal workers exhibit low support for the political system, but nonresponse rates were high, ranging from 16 to 37 percent. Political alienation may have been a cause for refusal to reply to some of these items; if so, system support was very low indeed in the early 1990s.

It would be a mistake to think of system support in Nicaragua as a single conceptual construct. A summative scale of the six items falls short of acceptable reliability standards (standardized Cronbach's alpha = .45). To better understand the structure of system support, the same six items were subjected to factor analysis. The results suggest that the political system was perceived by informal workers as consisting of diverse parts, not all of which were equally worthy of their support. Loadings for a three-factor solution are shown in Table 4.

Table 4. Three Dimensions of System Support in Nicaragua

Response Items	Social Contract	Governmental Institutions	Regime
Constitution	**.82085**	.20927	.02889
Human rights protection	**.81989**	-.19166	.10992
Legislature	-.15173	**.82706**	.05649
Courts	.16829	**.79490**	.06101
Pride in system	-.01607	.01504	**.82142**
Trust in government	.14050	.09230	**.74268**
Eigenvalue	1.6	1.4	1.1
% variance explained	27.1 +	22.9 +	17.8 = 67.8

Note: Entries are loadings for varimax rotated factor analysis.

Factor 1, containing support for human rights protection and for the Constitution, can be thought of as **support for the social contract of society**. Next, support for two institutions of government, the legislature and the courts, is construed in tandem by informal workers; thus, factor 2 can be conceived of as **support for governmental institutions**. The appearance of pride in the governmental system and trust in government together on the third factor might best be understood as representing generalized **support for the regime**. Three scales corresponding to the three dimensions of system support were created.[33]

Correlations reported in Table 5 show that system support is linked to partisan identification. Compared with FSLN partisans, UNO partisans exhibited significantly higher support for the regime (pride and trust) and for the country's political institutions (courts and legislature). Nicaragua's social contract (the Constitution and human rights protection) were evaluated more favorably by FSLN sympathizers than by UNO identifiers.

Table 5. Correlations between System Support and Partisan Identification

	Regime	Social Contract	Institutions
Party identification (strong UNO to strong FSLN)	-.36*	.11**	-.18*
Partisan identification with UNO	.28*	-.03	.12**
Partisan identification with FSLN	-.31*	.12**	-.13*

Note: Table entries are Pearson r coefficients.
*Significance LE .01; **Significance LE .05

Table 6 summarizes cross-tabulations between party preference and system support. These computations highlight differences between partisans and also differences between partisans and nonpartisans. The nonpartisans were divided into two groups: those saying openly that no party pleased

Table 6. Levels of System Support by Partisan Identification

Party	Regime			Social Contract			Institutions		
	High	Low	NR*	High	Low	NR*	High	Low	NR*
UNO (N=143)	60	38	2	22	68	9	34	50	15
FSLN (N=86)	20	80	0	33	67	0	15	79	6
No party (N=190)	37	54	9	17	66	17	30	54	16
No response (N=61)	43	31	26	18	49	33	20	39	41
Chi-square	88.27			41.92			47.85		
Signif.	.00			.00			.00		
Degrees of freedom	6			6			6		

Note: Table entries are percentages. For cross-tabulations, scales were dichotomized (low = 1 through 2.5, high = 3 through 4). Row totals may not add to 100 percent due to rounding error.
*NR = No response

them versus those declining to respond at all. The difference between UNO partisans and FSLN partisans was most stark in their evaluations of the political regime, with 80 percent of FSLN sympathizers critical of the regime and with a clear majority of UNO identifiers giving high support. Support for the social contract was highest among FSLN partisans, but criticism was equally high among this group, UNO identifiers, and those saying that they did not identify with any party. Criticism of the country's political institutions was very high among FSLN sympathizers (79 percent), but UNO identifiers were also not enthusiastic about this part of the system, with one-half giving low marks and only one-third declaring support.

Informal workers who replied that none of Nicaragua's parties pleased them were more openly critical of the political system than were those who declined to answer questions about party preference. Furthermore, the fact that nonresponse rates on the support scales were highly concentrated among nonresponders on the party identification measure suggests that this group of informal workers was more withdrawn from politics altogether than was the group which explicitly rejected all political parties.

Some interesting differences were found in levels of system support between occupational groups (Table 7). The most intriguing comparisons involved those cases where there existed a high level of agreement among practitioners of an occupation. The question becomes, "What causes this relative level of consensus?" Looking first at support for the regime, 60 percent of laborers in mechanized workshops agreed that the regime is not worthy of support. This answer makes sense, given that: 1) the regime tends to be associated with the new government; and 2) the economic policies of the new government created an unprecedented influx of manufactured goods to Nicaragua. While most groups experienced economic difficulties, mechanized workshops suffered problems that could be related directly to new economic policies instituted by the Chamorro government. Demand for the repair of decrepit consumer durables dropped precipitously.

Table 7. Levels of System Support by Occupational Group

Occupational Group (N @ 80)	Regime			Social Contract			Institutions		
	High	Low	NR*	High	Low	NR*	High	Low	NR*
Workshops (LM)	40	54	6	24	61	15	29	51	20
Workshops (M)	36	58	6	28	62	10	31	56	13
Pulpería owners	38	45	18	24	58	19	29	46	25
Taxi drivers	51	48	1	15	81	4	33	61	6
Market stallkeepers	43	51	6	19	66	15	15	70	15
Street vendors	41	51	8	19	63	19	26	49	25
Chi-square		19.67			18.36			24.00	
Signif.		.03			.04			.00	
Degrees of freedom		10			10			10	

Note: See Table 6 for explanation of scaling. (Workshops: LM = less mechanized; M = highly mechanized).
*NR = No Response

Taxi drivers stood out as the group with the most uniform opinions about the social contract, with 81 percent in the low support column. Why? At least two factors set taxi drivers apart from the other groups: they were all men, and they all belonged to cooperatives. While prior survey research in Nicaragua showed significant differences in the political opinions of men and women, these differences were not found in levels of support, but rather in determinants of support.[34] It seems more likely that the taxi cooperatives functioned as workshops of discontent, or places where common political views were forged through the discussion of political issues.

Market stallkeepers expressed the most uniform opinions about the political institutions of the country, with 70 percent in the low support category and only 15 percent voicing high support. These results probably reflected a reaction to the high degree of political division and turmoil present in Managua's markets during the early 1990s. Not only did the markets grow rapidly with the influx of marginal sellers, but crime in the markets also saw a dramatic rise.[35] While Managua's mayor, Arnoldo Alemán, worked to abolish commercial associations founded during the FSLN tenure, market sellers on both sides of the political landscape expressed feelings of abandonment by the government.[36]

Street vendors and *pulpería* owners were most likely to withhold opinions. What set these groups apart in the sample was their slight level of organization and workplace interaction with others engaged in the same economic pursuit. Thus, in contrast to taxi drivers, who gathered daily with others facing similar struggles, and in contrast to market stallkeepers, who found themselves immersed in relatively well-organized hubs of economic activity, street vendors and *pulpería* owners "went it alone." The absence of these experiences did not result in higher levels of support for the political system, but in lower levels of expressed alienation.

Conclusion

Violeta Chamorro's ascension to power was accompanied by hopes and promises of economic improvement. Most informal workers in the early 1990s were able to cite concrete ideas about what the government might do to make life better. Since progress toward greater equality and prosperity did not match the vision cultivated in revolutionary rhetoric, and since Nicaragua's change of government failed to bring much relief, there existed within the informal sector abundant raw material for the manufacture of discontent. Thus, discontent with the political system characterized a majority of Managua's informal sector workers.

It was also true, however, that under the transitional regime headed by Violeta Chamorro social goods were distributed differently than they were under the FSLN. Benefactors of either distributional scheme were apt to reward the government for success, even if they stopped short of identifying with the party in power—even, in fact, if they identified with an opposing political faction. Governments in Nicaragua were able to generate support for the larger system by distributing benefits to the population and by successfully managing the national economy.

Many informal workers, however, bore the brunt of the protracted economic crisis that began in the late 1980s and continued into the 1990s. Their suffering helped to explain why system support was so low among this part of the population. Economic management and the distribution of social goods were not themselves enough to ensure the existence of popular support for the system. Partisanship stood out among the most important orientations to politics among Nicaragua's informal workers. This symbolic orientation seemed to structure the very definition of the political system for the respondents. Partisanship correlated strongly with each dimension of system support. Nonpartisans were more withdrawn and alienated from the political system than were those who identified with one of the major political factions within the government. Partisans of each political stripe could find something to like in the prevailing system.

Thus, power sharing may have been crucial for the maintenance of political support. Cooperation between the FSLN and the Chamorro government in national dialogues may have been part of the glue that prevented even more dangerous erosion of support for the political system from developing among Nicaragua's urban poor. Although the country had been deeply polarized by political violence, Nicaraguans had also demonstrated a remarkable capacity to compromise and to build coalitions. The 1979 success of the revolution itself depended on the unification of three FSLN factions, and it depended as well on a broad front of opposition to the Somoza regime that included leaders from all sides in the current array of political forces in the country.

Holding together Nicaragua's sometimes explosive society hinged on the cooperation between contending partisan forces. When such cooperation faltered, political violence increased. But, as of 1995, it appeared that system stability would also depend on the ability of contending partisan forces to maintain vital bases of support for their particular organizations and leaders, lest alienation among the urban poor once again express itself as direct confrontation with political elites. For this reason, political groupings and candidates could ill afford to ignore the country's huge informal sector.

Notes

1. Economist Intelligence Unit, *Nicaragua, Honduras: Country Profile* (London: Economist Intelligence Unit, 1994), 36.
2. Ibid.
3. Oscar René Vargas, ¿*Adónde va Nicaragua? Perspectivas de una revolución latinoamericana* (Managua: Ediciones Nicarao, 1991); Roberto Pizarro, "The New Economic Policy: A Necessary Readjustment," in *The Political Economy of Revolutionary Nicaragua*, ed. Rose Spalding (Boston: Allen and Unwin, 1987), 224–25.
4. Amalia Chamorro et al., "El debate sobre el Sector Informal Urbano en Nicaragua," in *Informalidad urbana en Centroamérica: Evidencias e interrogantes*, ed.

Rafael Menjivar Larín and Juan Pablo Pérez Sainz (Guatemala City: Fundación Friedrich Ebert, 1989), 153–89.

5. Mario Arana et al., "Políticas de ajuste en Nicaragua: Reflexiones sobre sus implicaciones estratégicas," in *Cuadernos de Pensamiento Propio*, Essay Series #18 (Managua: CRIES, 1990), 49.

6. Daniel Pérez and José Somarriba, "Impacto de la reforma económica en la fuerza de trabajo," *Boletín Socioeconómico* (January/February 1989): 16. These data do not reflect nonwage benefits. Richard Stahler-Sholk, "Stabilization, Destabilization, and the Popular Classes in Nicaragua, 1979–1988," *Latin American Research Review* (Spring 1990): 71–72.

7. Roser Sola Monserrat. *Geografía y estructuras económicas de Nicaragua en el contexto centroamericano y de América Latina* (Managua: Universidad Centroamericana, 1989), 59.

8. Roger Aburto et al., *Problemas y contradicciones en el analisis del Sector Informal* (Managua: Universidad Centroamericana, 1987); Centro de Investigaciones y Estudios de la Reforma Agraria, *Managua es Nicaragua* (Managua: CIERA, 1984), 24.

9. Alejandro Portes et al., *The Informal Economy: Studies in Advanced and Less Developed Countries* (Boulder, CO: Westview Press), 18.

10. Political and economic change in Nicaragua took place against the backdrop of external aggression and economic embargo. Michael E. Conroy, "Economic Aggression as an Instrument of Low-Intensity Warfare," in *Reagan versus the Sandinistas: The Undeclared War on Nicaragua*, ed. Thomas W. Walker (Boulder, CO: Westview Press, 1987), 57–79.

11. Richard Stahler-Sholk, *Empleo, salarios y productividad en la Revolución Popular Sandinista* (Managua: CRIES, 1986), 1–2.

12. Sola Monserrat, *Geografía y estructuras*, 56.

13. Stahler-Sholk, "Stabilization, Destabilization, and the Popular Classes," 75.

14. Aburto et al., *Problemas y contradicciones*, 12.

15. Pérez and Somarriba, "Impacto de la reforma económica," 10–17.

16. Giovanni D'Ciofalo, *El Sector Informal Urbana en Managua* (Managua: Ediciones CENTRA, Ministerio de Trabajo, 1987).

17. "Crisis económica: Como sobrevive Managua," *Envío* (December 1986): 32–35; Aburto et al., *Problemas y contradicciones*, 14.

18. Stahler-Sholk, "Stabilization, Destabilization, and the Popular Classes," 76.

19. "How to Get Foreign Aid: Making the Poor Pay Isn't Enough," *Envío* (May 1991): 35.

20. Edwin Saballos, "Flexión de musculos," *Pensamiento Propio* (August 1990): 21–23; idem, "El retorno del AID," ibid. (September 1991): 33–35.

21. William Hupper, "Panel económico," *Boletín Socioeconómico* (May/June 1990): 15.

22. "Who Will Conquer the Chaos?" *Envío* (November 1990): 6.

23. "Economy," ibid. (July 1991): 14–15.

24. "The Rich Get Richer," ibid. (March 1991): 43.

25. Economist Intelligence Unit, *Country Report: Nicaragua and Honduras* (London: Economist Intelligence Unit, April 1994), 14. Inflation figure is from idem, *Country Report* (London: Economist Intelligence Unit, April 1995), 22.

26. Reviewed in Victor Tokman, "Policies for a Heterogeneous Informal Sector in Latin America," *World Development* (July 1989): 1074–75.

27. For the purposes of this chapter, there is no need to offer a full-blown justification of the sampling design. The sample represents a good deal of diversity within Managua's informal sector, but no claim is made to its representativeness of the sector as a whole.

28. The taxi drivers were interviewed at Cooperativa 2 de Agosto, Cooperativa 19 de Julio, Cooperativa Carlos Fonseca, Cooperativa Pedro Joaquín Chamorro, and Cooperativa Jorge Salazar. Forty market stallkeepers were interviewed at the oldest and largest Managua trading center, the Mercado Oriental; and twenty each at two peripheral markets built by the FSLN government in the city in the early 1980s, the Mercado Roberto Huembes and the Mercado Ivan Montenegro.

29. The neighborhoods selected were: Américas 4, Primero de Mayo, Villa Austria, 14 de Septiembre, Grenada, Centroamérica, Jorge Dimitrov, Maximo Jerez, Domitila Lugo, Unidad de Propósito, Santa Rosa, San Luis Norte, Ducauli, Christian Pérez, San Judas, Santa Ana, René Cisneros, Ciudad Sandino, Monseñor Lescano, and Batahola Norte.

30. David Easton, *A Systems Analysis of Political Life* (New York: Wiley, 1965).

31. Gabriel A. Almond and Sidney Verba, *The Civic Culture* (Princeton, NJ: Princeton University Press, 1963).

32. Philip J. Williams, "Dual Transitions from Authoritarian Rule: Popular and Electoral Democracy in Nicaragua," *Comparative Politics* 5, no. 2 (January 1994): 169–85.

33. Seven-point support scales were computed as MEAN.1 (V1,V2), meaning that only one valid observation was required to return a score.

34. Kenneth J. Mijeski et al., "Women and the FSLN: A Multivariate Analysis of the Female Vote in the 1990 Nicaraguan Elections," paper presented at the Annual Meeting of the Southeast Council of Latin American Studies, Charleston, South Carolina, April 2–4, 1992.

35. *Barricada*, June 30, 1990.

36. Ibid., June 8, 1990; *La Prensa*, July 7, 1990.

17

The Mass Media

Kent W. Norsworthy

Nicaragua is a "media intense" society. The communications media play a fundamental role in national affairs, in the formation and expression of elite as well as broader public opinion, in entertainment and culture, and in other forms of mass symbolic exchange. From the emergence of the first media enterprises over 150 years ago to this day, Nicaraguan journalism has been intricately bound up with the fierce political and ideological struggles that checker the country's history as an independent nation. Traditionally, political bosses who own the media use them, first and foremost, as a mouthpiece to bestow favors upon their political allies and to verbally tar and feather all those whom they perceive as adversaries.

Beginning in the mid-1970s, the media played an important role in successive transformations of the political and social landscape in this turbulent land. Their reach and influence grew even further as yet another round of changes swept the country after the 1990 elections. Following the transfer of state power from the Sandinista National Liberation Front (FSLN) to a coalition of conservative parties grouped in the National Opposition Union (UNO), for years Nicaragua remained immersed in the so-called triple transition: war to peace, a state-run to a market economy, and "democratic consolidation." The mass media were at the forefront of all three facets of this transition. In some instances, their role meant encouraging the transition, acting as the nation's public conscience, pointing to the directions in which the government should be headed, and presenting a vision for moving the country forward. In other instances, the media acted as a powerful brake on the transition and served as a sounding board for the most recalcitrant sectors, holding up to society a portrait of that which refused to be left behind.

Along with economic survival, perhaps the fundamental challenge that the media faced in the 1990s was the battle for political independence. The immediate imperative was to break with the legacy of the 1980s, when most media outlets were reduced to the role of propagandists for belligerents in the military conflict. From a broader perspective, however, the challenge was much more fundamental. A modern, politically independent media enterprise simply had no precedent in Nicaraguan history. During the 1990s, journalists, media workers, and directors who desired to break with this tradition had to stake out their own territory apart from, and for the most part in spite of, an imposing political class.

The Legacy of Media Reform

The Sandinista government promoted a far-reaching media reform project during its years in power (1979–1990)—one of the most comprehensive of its kind undertaken in Latin America.[1] By the end of the 1980s, several important elements of the "democratization of communications" project could be clearly discerned. First, through a far-reaching redistribution of media enterprises, the Sandinistas achieved a reasonable balance in ownership of the mass media, involving the coexistence of private, mixed, state, and cooperative ventures. Second, media content (with the exception of television, monopolized by the Sandinista state) exhibited an impressive political and ideological pluralism, ranging from positions far to the left of the governing FSLN across to the extreme right, which had no qualms about using its outlets to openly advocate the government's overthrow.[2]

Third, efforts were undertaken, mostly in the state-supported media, to foster popular participation and criticism in the media.[3] Fourth, through control over the state and FSLN-supported media outlets, and to a lesser degree through legislation, the Sandinistas attempted to replace the commercial and advertising-driven structures that generally undergird media systems in capitalist economies with socialist- and social democratic-inspired philosophies of mobilization, public service, and social responsibility.[4] And fifth, even though it did not develop an explicit media policy, the Sandinista government did use policy, legislation, and other instruments as part of its effort to synchronize media changes with national reconstruction and development goals.

Between 1979 and the mid-1980s the government implemented media changes gradually, alongside other initiatives such as the national literacy crusade, agrarian reform, and the creation of a popular army. At the ideological level, a far-reaching project of "cultural democratization" was in the forefront of efforts to build an effective counterhegemony. The pace and scope of change in all these areas, however, were increasingly constrained as the decade advanced by escalating defense needs in the face of Washington's all-sided destabilization campaign. By 1985 the army was absorbing a huge chunk of the national budget, and militarization had put many of the revolution's civilian-inspired transformations on the back burner.

The August 1987 signing of the Esquipulas Peace Accords held out the promise of bringing an end to the war and opened a new period that culminated with the transfer of power in April 1990. The dramatic political changes of the Esquipulas process also involved important modifications in the media.[5] The government, committed to seeking the broadest possible participation in the 1990 elections, opened the political system. This political opening and concomitant decline in military tensions found its corollary in the media with the reopening of suspended outlets and the elimination of prior censorship, on the books since the declaration of a State of Emergency in March 1982.

Foreshadowing post-1990 developments, a plethora of perspectives inundated the media (particularly the electronic media) as the electoral campaign unfolded in 1989. Substantial modifications to the media and electoral laws paved the way for broad opposition access to the air waves, further diversifying radio, and for the first time introducing opposition points of view on television. But the media became engulfed in the extreme polarization that characterized the electoral process. With the wounds of nearly a decade-long military conflict still fresh, the campaign largely degenerated into a verbal mud-slinging contest. In this battle the media, and especially the press, were literally in the vanguard.

Economic developments also fundamentally impacted on the media during this period. In 1988 the Sandinista government launched the first in a series of far-reaching austerity programs in an effort to confront the deepening economic crisis. These programs marked a transition away from the state-centered development model, and the class alliances that underpinned it, toward a very different regime—one that privileged market mechanisms, prioritized the provision of incentives to capitalist producers, and transferred the burden of economic adjustment to the poorest sectors. For many media enterprises, the redefinition of the role of the state and the reintroduction of the logic of the market meant struggling for survival without the government subsidies to which they had become accustomed.

In sum, the Sandinista reform project had brought about important structural changes in the media, but the model depended on a strong, dynamic, and economically solid state. When we examine developments in the post-1990 period, therefore, it is important to keep in mind that the Sandinista model had by the late 1980s become unsustainable. It had already entered into crisis and was in the midst of profound transformation even before the FSLN left office.[6] In this sense, the trends described below, particularly in the case of radio and television, were less the product of new policies resulting from the change in government (indeed, the Chamorro government had no policy in this area) than changes that were inevitable given the country's evolving political and economic situation. In turn, this evolving situation was itself part of much larger changes bound up with Nicaragua's relationship to the global system.

The Media during the Chamorro Government

If the Sandinista government's approach to media reform emphasized a strong role for the state in strategic developments in the country's mass media, the point of departure for the government that followed it could not have been more diametrically opposed. It was symbolically captured in the Chamorro administration's familiar refrain: "The best media policy is no media policy at all."

This laissez-faire approach and essentially unrestricted press freedom contributed to an impressive expansion in the number of media enterprises operating in the country. But one must exercise caution when moving to a qualitative assessment.[7] Contradictory tendencies were at work during the Chamorro period: on the one hand, an expansion and consolidation of the democratization of communications initiated during the previous decade continued while, on the other hand, a virtual counterreform took place through imposition of the logic of the market, undermining some of the most important advances made during the 1980s.

Practically all institutions in Nicaragua were transformed through the neoliberal program imposed on the country beginning in 1990, including in a very distinct manner the mass media. Indeed, by the middle of the decade, the media were unrecognizable in comparison to the pre-1990 period, both quantitatively and qualitatively. Underlying this change was a fundamental reorientation of the very logic that drives the national media system. What had once been a thriving Nicaraguan advertising industry had all but disappeared under the "social responsibility" ethic of the Sandinista period, and most commercial media enterprises either folded or sought a revenue base elsewhere. With the 1990 change in government, the country was ripe for a veritable boom in the advertising industry. Enterprising capitalists rushed to fill the void created by an explosion of commercial activity resulting from rapid trade liberalization and the absence of any regulatory framework.[8]

The boom proved to be somewhat artificial, reaching its zenith in 1992 as advertisers began to resign themselves to the fact that, although the effects of liberalization had not yet run their course and the number of new media outlets was still growing, the economic growth and recovery optimistically promised by the government was nowhere in sight.[9] Between 1990 and 1994 at least twenty-one new advertising agencies were launched where only one had existed before. With the drop in overall advertising expenditures beginning in 1993, however, there was a reconcentration in favor of the largest and strongest agencies, with the total number down to twelve in 1994. Prolonged high levels of unemployment and ever-increasing poverty blocked the development of a mass consumer base in the country. Advertisers had to accept the reality of selling to a tiny elite and, for the moment, limiting activities aimed at the majority to merely cultivating tastes and aspirations in hopes that someday the economy would turn around. This factor was perhaps the principal one responsible for a drop in advertising outlays each year between 1992 and 1995.

More important than the quantitative growth of the advertising industry were the deeper effects of the ongoing reorientation of the domestic media system on the basis of an advertising-driven model, resulting in intense competition at all levels of the media. The return of an advertising-based model also had profound ideological consequences, including the attendant glorification and reification of capitalist values, consumerism, and the promotion of a savage brand of individualism. Although reduced purchasing power kept the bulk of the population outside the circuit of mass consumption stimulated by advertising, the constant bombardment of advertisements had a profound effect on their desires and aspirations. The new advertising-based media model was the perfect ideological counterpart to the neoliberal restructuring taking place at the level of the economy and political society. Moreover, the advertising industry went far beyond simply peddling consumer goods and made serious inroads into the areas of public relations, political campaigns and political marketing, and persuasion.

The intense competition for audience share and for advertising revenues within the electronic media took many forms: between television and radio, between AM and FM, and between broadcast and cable television, among others. Increased competition resulted in ever more refined strategies of audience segmentation. Many of the new FM radio stations, for example, were explicitly and exclusively geared to a young audience, while over fifty specialty publications, plus dozens of radio and television programs and newspaper sections and supplements, carefully targeted audiences based on gender, sexual preference, ethnicity, and, of course, political tendency. Television and radio were engaged in an intense turf war aimed at altering the traditional patterns of segmentation via programming schedule, whereby television dominated during the evening prime-time hours while radio was strongest during the morning and afternoon. Intense competition also gave an impetus to modernization and professionalization. The appearance of new television and radio stations with the most advanced technologies forced existing broadcasting outlets to make significant investments in order to replace their outdated equipment.

Despite the electronic media's growing predominance, the daily newspapers still played the lead role in influencing debate among the elite. Even here, however, radio and television began, for the first time, to cut into the dominance of the press. Television executives were particularly adroit in this regard. As of the mid-1990s, all were broadcasting at least one weekly magazine-type show. Most combined the one-on-one interview format with live listener call-ins. Content was, for the most part, eminently political. Radio had less success in its attempts to employ this format, but it did achieve dominance in coverage of current and breaking news stories, including live on-site coverage during events of national significance.[10]

Modernization was not only technical but also referred increasingly to professionalization within the journalism trade, individual media enterprises, and the media as a social institution. Professionalization involved, above all, breaking with the Nicaraguan tradition that dictates that media outlets must be closely tied to political parties and projects. The pattern remained largely unbroken in the written press (notwithstanding *Barricada*'s 1990– 1994 experiment—see below), but the electronic media registered some success. Peacetime conditions and the imperatives of civic struggle contributed greatly to this professionalization. As the levels of military conflict gradually receded between 1988 and 1992, the deep polarization and adversarial relations that were the hallmark of the Nicaraguan media became more and more anachronistic.

In the ensuing years, journalists in particular came a long way toward putting aside their partisan differences and past rivalries, uniting around a mutual set of demands and positions specific to the profession.[11] Journalists from the traditionally rival Union of Nicaraguan Journalists (Unión de Periodistas de Nicaragua, or UPN) and Association of Nicaraguan Journalists (Asociación de Periodistas Nicaragüenses, or APN) were more often struggling together instead of against each other.

Democratization went hand in hand with modernization and professionalization. During the 1990s the Nicaraguan media increasingly provided new democratic spaces from within civil society and in relative independence from the realm of party politics—a significant advance for democratization when conceived in broad social terms, beyond the simple holding of periodic elections. Former director of *Barricada* and media researcher Carlos Fernando Chamorro evaluated the media's performance in this regard:

> I believe that the Nicaraguan media have made a very positive contribution in terms of democratization. In the first place, if we look at a democratic discourse, beyond the issue of elections and the simple alterability of political parties in power, and talk about a democratic discourse which incorporates pluralism, participation, and economic aspects, you will find that this is a practically universal discourse in the media. Nobody in this country is using the media to preach against democracy. . . . Second, there is a growing consensus throughout the media in terms of condemning violence as an alternative to democratic methods. These are big changes compared to the situation five years ago.[12]

The Press

Despite the advances noted above, the press faced a deep crisis in the 1990s, expressed above all in the precipitous drop in circulation faced by all four dailies. As of early 1995, combined daily sales were under 60,000,[13] perhaps half of what they were in 1990. Economic factors were largely responsible for the drop: on the one hand, the dramatic decline in the population's purchasing power, and on the other, the prohibitive cost of the dailies. With an average price per issue of about U.S. $0.40 each, on a per-page basis Nicaragua's daily newspapers were among the most expensive in the world.[14] Revenues had also declined as advertisers exhibited an increasing preference for the electronic media. *La Prensa* still typically covered 75 percent of the space of its weekday editions with advertising, but ad copy was comparatively sparse in the other three dailies.

Survey data indicate that Nicaraguans were turning less and less to the newspapers for news and information and more and more to radio and television. A 1991 nationwide poll showed that 43.2 percent of respondents identified radio, 31.1 percent newspapers, and 25.7 percent television as their principal source of news and information.[15] Four years later, a Managua poll produced these results: radio, 49.9 percent; television, 38.5 percent; and newspapers, only 10.1 percent.[16] Individual newspapers experienced significant, often abrupt, changes during this period, with only *El Nuevo Diario* maintaining a fairly even keel in terms of presentation, editorial line, and coverage.

The most interesting case was *Barricada*. During the short space of five years the daily went through a profound metamorphosis, from a shrill official party organ to the most serious, modern, and independent paper in the country, and then back again to its former self. The experience of *Barricada* during this period is at once a lesson in how the new vision of a modern media enterprise (in this case one born with the revolution) can be applied to the Nicaraguan reality, and in how the country's prevailing political culture can truncate such experiments.

As the official organ of the FSLN and the de facto paper of record for the government between 1979 and 1990, there was no question that *Barricada* would have to undergo transformations in the post-1990 period as the Sandinistas took up their role as opposition. The battle, both within the newspaper and within the party, was over what form those transformations would take. After months of work on an alternative, the FSLN National Directorate approved the paper's "New Editorial Profile" in December 1990.[17] In the document, director Chamorro argued that *Barricada* needed sufficient autonomy to allow those who write for the paper to "formulate alternatives that would nourish revolutionary thought," thus allowing them to become "leaders of public opinion." The idea was to convert the newspaper into a nonsectarian forum for criticism, debate, and even dissent, and thus to appeal to an audience beyond the ranks of convinced FSLN militants on the basis of credibility.[18]

In January 1991 the daily revamped its masthead, dropping the insurrectionary logo, the red and black background, and the "Official Organ" slogan. *Barricada* had become a paper "In the National Interest." For those at *Barricada* who promoted the new project, the changes turned out to be a double-edged sword. In the ensuing months and years they watched the project prosper: advertising revenues and circulation increased, and the paper began to develop a reputation as the country's most serious and professional newspaper. The editorial page became a vibrant space for debate over revolutionary alternatives, projecting the image of a party in renovation to sectors far beyond the FSLN rank and file while at the same time serving as a respected arena for nonpartisan discussions on important national issues.

During this same period, however, the FSLN was wracked by increasingly fractious internal divisions that would culminate in an open split and the formation in 1995 of the Sandinista Renovation Movement (MRS). Leaders from the "orthodox" camp increasingly interpreted "pluralism" on the pages of *Barricada*—defined as providing space to a multitude of viewpoints on the internal party crisis—as an unpermissible use of official party resources to champion the cause of the dissenters.

In the end, *Barricada* fell victim to the party's internal crisis when, in October 1994, the FSLN leadership ordered Chamorro's removal, triggering the resignation of the editorial board, deputy director, and the editor. Some 80 percent of the journalist staff resigned shortly after the arrival of the new leadership, headed by FSLN veteran Tomás Borge. Under Borge, the paper reverted to a shrill propaganda organ for the orthodox FSLN. Six months after the change, *Barricada*'s circulation had dropped by over one-third. The paper had lost most of the influence that it had gained outside the ranks of the FSLN.

La Prensa's experience was not altogether different from *Barricada*'s. The 1990 electoral results also meant that transformations would be inevitable at *La Prensa*. Overnight a newspaper which for sixty-four years had built its mystique as "bastion of the opposition" found itself in the awkward position of having its chief proprietor and director, Violeta Barrios de Chamorro, as President of the Republic.[19] In the ensuing period, modernization and professionalization were cut short by the heavy-handed imposition of political criteria, foreshadowing the experience across town at *Barricada*.

Following the elections, *La Prensa* launched modest efforts at professionalization and modernization under the leadership of editor Cristiana Chamorro, daughter of the president. But Cristiana's editorial leadership provoked a backlash among more conservative elements on the staff and editorial board. In January 1991 she was forced to resign her post as editor, and her mother was removed from the board of directors. For some, the changes were a welcome step toward recovering *La Prensa*'s much-heralded independence, but others lamented the abandonment of the modernization project with Cristiana's departure and attributed her removal to the tenacity of anti-Sandinismo among the staff. According to this view, Cristiana was forced out not because she had converted *La Prensa* into a pro-government daily, but because she had failed to adopt a sufficiently critical stance toward the government's policy of national reconciliation, seen by the Right as an unnecessary concession to the Sandinistas.

La Prensa was able to weather the crisis in the ensuing years by achieving a degree of success in two areas. First, it managed to retain a large part of its traditional readership by perpetuating the image of "bastion of the opposition." And second, *La Prensa* had far more success than the other three dailies at consolidating an advertising-based revenue stream, allowing the enterprise to continue to thrive even while circulation dropped.

The country's fourth daily, *La Tribuna*, began circulation in July 1993. Publicity surrounding the long-delayed inauguration trumpeted *La Tribuna* as a new experiment in "independent journalism." The paper's modern visual presentation, based on extensive use of color, a clean and relaxed layout, and the sophisticated use of graphics, helped to generate widespread expectations that *La Tribuna* would follow in the footsteps of *Barricada* in aspiring to become a modern paper independent of any particular political party or project. Despite initial optimism that *La Tribuna* would indeed embark upon such a path, the paper soon began to drop its mask and reveal its true nature as little more than a platform for the political views and presidential ambitions of its owner, Haroldo Montealegre, of the Liberal Constitutionalist Party (PLC).

Of the four dailies, *El Nuevo Diario* experienced the least change during this period. Structured as a worker-owned cooperative, the paper was one of only a handful in Latin America that continued to publish on the basis of revenues from advertising and newspaper sales alone. Like the weekly *El Semanario*, *El Nuevo Diario* was politically sympathetic to the MRS. It staked out its political claim on the basis of relentless criticism of the Violeta Chamorro government, but its essence continued to be sensationalist, often bizarre, coverage of crime, tales of the supernatural, and entertainment. Shunning the brand of professionalism briefly aspired to at the other three dailies, *El Nuevo Diario* over the years built a loyal following among readers who considered the others too political, too serious, and too dull.

Television

Television experienced the most profound changes and the most dynamic growth. In practically all indicators, television displaced the print media since 1990 while posing an increasingly powerful challenge to the traditional dominance of radio as the country's number-one truly mass medium. Audience surveys discussed earlier reinforce the conclusion that television was rapidly becoming the medium of choice among Nicaraguans. The explosion in television was propelled by rapid growth in the number of over-the-air channels and in the arrival and rapid diffusion of new delivery systems such as cable television. In 1990 there were only two broadcast television stations, Channels 2 and 6, run by the state as a monopoly network, and no cable television. By 1995 there were five VHF and two UHF broadcast stations, and a sixth VHF station was scheduled to begin broadcasting later that year.[20] Television's growing economic importance was indicated by its expanding share of advertising revenues. The medium accounted for just under one-third of all advertising outlays in 1992, for 40 percent in 1993, and for about 50 percent in 1994.[21]

As was typical throughout Latin America, prime time television was dominated by imported *telenovelas*. Several stations had taken to running daytime ones as well. The combined total of seventeen *telenovelas* on all channels accounted for over 25 percent of all broadcast time. Domestically produced programming became a thorny issue with the expansion in the number of stations and the ever-growing number of hours in the broadcast day on each station. Domestic programming as a percentage of the broadcast day plummeted in relation to the 1980s. For instance, during the period of the Sandinista television monopoly, Channel 6 averaged 26.5 percent domestic programming, while Channel 2 had 16.0 percent. In comparison, as of mid-1993, domestic programming on Channel 6 was down to 14.7 percent, and Channel 2 to just 5.6 percent.[22] However, measured in absolute terms, there was a net increase in the total amount of domestically produced programming, and Channels 4, 2, and, to a lesser extent, 8 demonstrated their awareness of audience preferences for it.

A huge explosion took place in the combined length of the broadcast day. During the 1980s the two channels were on the air for a combined total of under twenty hours per day. As of mid-1995 the combined broadcast day for the five stations was over sixty hours. The only way to cheaply and quickly fill these hours was with imported programming, which typically costs a fraction of producing a domestic program. The biggest single programming area for domestic production was national news. Here again, the contrast with the 1980s, when there was only one television news show, was stark. Each of the five stations broadcast at least one nightly news program. In addition to their national programs, three of the stations also transmitted at least one international news program.

Cable television also expanded dramatically. From none in 1990 there were over thirty small cable companies nationwide in 1995, less than one-third of which were located in Managua. Although there were no hard data on the number of subscribers, survey results and programming trends on broadcast television pointed to the growing penetration and influence of cable television. Cable was prohibitively expensive for the majority of impoverished Nicaraguans, but the cost was low for those families with even a modest regular income. Rates varied depending on subscriber location and among the different cable companies, but monthly subscription rates started out at around the purchase price of one daily newspaper (about U.S. $10 per month).

Another phenomenon appearing for the first time in Nicaraguan television was an appeal to the local audience—a factor crucial in maintaining the popularity of radio. This trend was ironically spurred, in part, by cable television. Under existing legislation, cable enterprises had the right to fill one cable channel with their own programming. As a result, in several outlying municipalities, these companies launched short news programs, highlighting regional and local events—one factor that pushed national news programs to strive for better coverage of local events around the country.

Nicaragua belatedly entered the era of "telepolitics," a trend that emerged in other Latin American countries during the 1980s.[23] For the first time, television became an important forum for the debate of national issues and the projection of political figures, above all through several live-broadcast magazine-format programs—among them, Channel 8's "Porque Nicaragua Nos Importa" and "A Fondo," both directed by station owner Carlos Briceño, and Channel 2's ninety-minute morning program, "Buenos Días," anchored by Danilo Lacayo. Also on Channel 2 was the weekly newsmagazine "Esta Semana con Carlos Fernando," hosted by the former director of *Barricada*.

Radio

The 1990s was also a boom period for radio. Between 1990 and 1994 the government's telecommunications frequency authority, ANDER, assigned over one hundred frequencies. Of these, sixty were on the FM band, compared to only four FM stations that existed in 1990. Another forty-nine frequencies were assigned in AM. As of mid-1995, according to ANDER, a total of 114 radio stations were broadcasting in Nicaragua—66 on FM and 48 on AM—more than twice the number in existence five years earlier.[24] This growth can be attributed to one overarching factor: station start-up and maintenance costs were minimal, which allowed the entry of dozens of entrepreneurs (and aspiring politicians) who otherwise would never have had a chance of establishing themselves on the media landscape. Many new FM stations set up shop with tiny and inexpensive microtransmitters, and their programming was tailored to meet the needs of small local audiences.

Religious programming expanded dramatically. In 1990 there were only two church-oriented radio stations: Radio Católica and Ondas de Luz. By 1995 there were seven new religious stations on AM and FM, plus the evangelical Channel 21 on UHF, a development that ran parallel to the increased influence of the Catholic and Protestant churches.

In part, radio's continued success was due to its nature as a localized medium with enormous potential to appeal to local audience tastes and interests. There was at least one radio station in each of the country's seventeen departments, and most surveys indicated that these departmental stations had the highest audience share in rural communities and towns throughout the country.[25] Despite this fact, growth in the radio sector from 1990 through 1995 was disproportionately based in Managua: 46 of the 60 new FM stations launched since 1990 were in Managua, as were 23 of the 49 new AM stations. In contrast, there were only 3 AM stations in the country's vast Atlantic Coast region, which encompasses half of the national territory and was home to nearly one-tenth of the population.

Unlike television, radio presented a fairly diverse content spectrum. Imported music continued to predominate, but there was still a wide variety of domestically produced radio programming rooted in local and national culture and traditions. FM programming included a variety of music formats, news, and listener call-in shows, while AM programming often featured popular "Revistas Radiales" (a mixture of news, with music and opinion), traditional newscasts, music, radio dramas, humor shows, sports, and listener call-in shows.

Another major growth area was the "Radionoticieros," or independently produced radio news programs. A popular genre before 1979, during the State of Emergency in the 1980s these programs were banned outright. As of the mid-1990s listeners could chose from over eighty such programs. In most cases, they were one-person free-lance operations, with journalists renting air space from the station and selling advertising time on their own programs.

Overall, growth in the number of radio stations contributed to a reduction in the levels of polarization and politicization that have traditionally characterized the Nicaraguan airwaves. But here, too, old habits die hard: the polar extremes on the political spectrum, on the right Radio Corporación and on the left the FSLN's Radio Ya, consistently ranked among the top five stations in national audience surveys. During several tense political junctures, the physical installations of Corporación and Ya were attacked.

Conclusion

Writing in 1994, Guillermo Rothschuh Villanueva, dean of the Communications School at the Central American University in Managua, asserted that "despite everything, I continue to cast my lot with the media. I am very interested in the media's modernization. I insist on the need for the media to generate and to nurture a new culture, a culture of democracy, a culture of tolerance, a culture which will allow for the existence of opposition in this country, so that to disagree will no longer be a crime . . . a culture which will eliminate exclusion as a way of doing politics in Nicaragua."[26]

As Rothschuh Villanueva indicates, during the 1990s the mass media became increasingly active protagonists in the Nicaraguan transition. The process was characterized, above all, by the drive for political independence among individual journalists and media enterprises, alongside the increasing importance of the electronic media—especially television—as mediators of politics, culture, and ideology. In part a continuation of the democratization of communications begun during the 1980s, these trends marked an important break with the country's troubled political history and constituted a key aspect of Nicaragua's unique transition.

Notes

1. On media reform in Latin America, see Elizabeth Fox, ed., *Media and Politics in Latin America: The Struggle for Democracy* (London: Sage Publications, 1988); and in Nicaragua, Armand Mattelart, ed., *Communicating in Popular Nicaragua* (New York: International General, 1986).

2. Wartime censorship was exercised against the most vociferous anti-Sandinista media outlets, but in the larger picture censorship did not impede the use of radio and the press for diffusion of a wide variety of political and ideological viewpoints. Volumes have been written on Sandinista censorship, most of them superficial and overly ideological. Three good accounts are John Spicer Nichols, "The Media," in *Nicaragua: The First Five Years*, ed. Thomas W. Walker (New York: Praeger, 1985); Michael Massing, "Nicaragua's Free-Fire Journalism," *Columbia Journalism Review* (July–August 1988); and Penelope O'Donnell, *Dar la palabra al pueblo* (Mexico City: Universidad Iberoamericana, 1995).

3. On participatory radio, see Robbin Dale Crabtree, "Democratizing Radio Broadcasting in Nicaragua: A Case Study of Regional Community Radio, 1979–1989" (Ph.D. diss., University of Minnesota, 1992); and Robert A. White, "Participatory Radio in Sandinista Nicaragua," mimeograph, no date. An excellent analysis of the dilemnas faced by community radio after 1990 is José Ignacio López Vigil, "Community Media in Neoliberal Times," *Envío* (April 1993): 36–43.

4. On changes in advertising, see "The Media in Nicaragua: Breaking the Mold (Interview with Guillermo Rothschuh Villanueva)," *Barricada Internacional*, August 1988.

5. For more on the media during the 1987–1990 period, see Marvin Saballos Ramírez, "Procesos políticos, elecciones, y comunicación en Nicaragua," *Diá-logos de la Comunicación* 29 (March 1991): 16–23.

6. An excellent study which examines this dynamic in the case of participatory radio is Clemencia Rodríguez, "The Rise and Fall of the Popular Correspondents' Movement in Revolutionary Nicaragua, 1982–1990," *Media, Culture, and Society* 16, no. 3 (July 1994): 509–20.

7. The case of "policy" regarding the assignation of new frequencies in the electronic media is instructive. Under Chamorro, the predominate view was that pluralism consists of simply admitting as many new voices (transmitters) as possible. In the absence of a guiding political framework, this view translated into a series of imbalances, such as in the geographic distribution of media outlets and of access to media consumption.

8. The Sandinista Media Law, which included advertising regulations, was abolished by the FSLN administration in 1990. The Chamorro government never promulgated any law or regulations to replace it.

9. Advertising expenditures jumped from U.S. $1 million in 1990 to U.S. $20 million in 1991 and then peaked at U.S. $35 million in 1992. Expenditures dropped by almost U.S. $5 million in each of the following two years. Fatima Cruz, spokesperson for the Nicaraguan Organization of Advertising Agencies (ONAP), interview with author, Managua, June 29, 1995.

10. The most graphic example was the role that radio played during the 1993 hostage drama. See "Entrevista al Dr. Guillermo Rothschuh Villanueva: La radio barrió a los otros medios," *Periodistas* 7 (September–October 1993): 29–32; and Guillermo Rothschuh Villanueva, *La otra cultura: Propuestas para el cambio* (Managua: Universidad Centroamericana, 1994), 54–58.

11. Material on this theme can be found in most issues of *Periodistas*, a monthly magazine of and for Nicaraguan journalists of all political persuasions, edited by Guillermo Cortés.

12. Carlos Fernando Chamorro, interview with author, Managua, July 6, 1995.

13. In Nicaragua, there are no independently audited circulation figures. While the circulation figures claimed by each daily for itself vary widely, there is general agreement on the combined total for all four. This particular figure is cited in Guillermo Rothschuh Villanueva and Carlos Fernando Chamorro, *Los medios y la política en Nicaragua* (Managua: Friedrich Ebert Stiftung, 1995), 48.

14. Published length varies. *La Prensa* consistently published the longest editions, reaching as much as thirty-two pages per day. The other three papers typically published editions averaging sixteen pages.

15. The poll, conducted by Costa Rica-based Borge y Asociados in March 1991, was cited in Elberth Durán Hidalgo, "Periodismo nica frente a las puertas del cambio," *Pulso del Periodismo* (April–June 1993): 22.

16. Rothschuh Villanueva and Chamorro, *Los medios y la política*, 80.

17. The changes at *Barricada* actually trace back to 1987, when, spurred on by the post-Esquipulas political opening, the paper began to professionalize. It sought a degree of autonomy from the FSLN in order to produce a newspaper that could appeal to a broader audience. The experiment was cut short, however, with the arrival of the elections, and during 1989–90 *Barricada* was fully at the service of the FSLN campaign. Two good accounts of the changes implemented at *Barricada* are Adam Jones, "Beyond the Barricades: The Sandinista Press and Political Transition in Nicaragua," *New Political Science* 23 (Fall 1992): 63–90; and Carlos Fernando Chamorro, "Medios para la democracia," *Tendencias* (December 1993/January 1994).

18. See "El nuevo perfíl editorial," an internal *Barricada* document cited extensively by Jones in "Beyond the Barricades."

19. On the history of *La Prensa*, see Patricia Taylor Edmisten, *Nicaragua Divided: La Prensa and the Chamorro Legacy* (Gainesville: University Presses of Florida, 1990).

20. The UHF stations have not managed to pose much of a challenge to VHF. Channel 21, which broadcast evangelical programming twelve hours per day, went on the air in August 1992, while Channel 23 broadcast twenty-four hours per day of music videos beginning in November 1993.

21. These figures are from M & R Consultores, Managua, "Inversión Publicitaria," 1993 and 1994; and from Rothschuh Villanueva and Chamorro, *Los medios y la política*, 44.

22. Elmer Fabián Medina Sánchez, "Historia y diagnóstico actual de la infraestructura de los medios masivos de comunicación en Nicaragua" (Managua: Universidad Centroamericana, 1993), 23.

23. Two good starting points for the literature on politics and television in Latin America are Thomas E. Skidmore, ed., *Television, Politics, and the Transition to Democracy in Latin America* (Washington, DC: Woodrow Wilson Center Press, 1993); and the March 1991 issue of *Diá-logos de la Comunicación*.

24. Rothschuh Villanueva and Chamorro, *Los medios y la política*, 51.

25. Guillermo Rothschuh Villanueva, interview with author, Managua, July 4, 1995.

26. Rothschuh Villanueva, *La otra cultura*, 84–85.

Reflections

Thomas W. Walker

To have studied Nicaragua for the nearly three decades from the late 1960s to the mid-1990s is very humbling. The truly kaleidoscopic changes of that period frequently made a mockery of seemingly serious analyses and predictions. Accordingly, I am very reluctant to offer firm conclusions based on what transpired in the first six years following the 1990 election. Yet it does seem important at least to engage in some synthesizing reflections about the rich experiences of that short period. Perhaps the best way of doing so is to address a series of questions: Does it make sense to talk of "sovereignty" in reference to a small, intervened country such as Nicaragua? How does intervention such as that suffered by Nicaragua affect civic culture and the state of democracy in general? What did neoliberalism mean for that country in the 1990s? What was unique and what was universal about the Nicaraguan transition? Was it really a "democratic" transition? And finally, did the Nicaraguan revolution die in 1990?

Sovereignty

At first blush, the events of the 1980s and 1990s would lead one to conclude that "Nicaraguan sovereignty" is an oxymoron. If the Sandinista revolution was, above all, an attempt to assert sovereignty, then the U.S. response—the Contra war, economic aggression, active intervention in and manipulation of the 1990 election—seemed to prove that the dream of sovereignty for a microstate in the major hegemon's backyard was an illusion. Nor was U.S. behavior in the 1990s—the manipulation of Nicaraguan policy through bilateral and multilateral funding, the issuing of a five-year "Country Development Strategy" for its newly recovered client state—any more respectful of that country's sovereignty.

On closer examination, however, the picture may not be so clear-cut. After all, the Sandinista revolution had created a constitutional and institutional framework which, with some modifications that were negotiated in the 1990s, would continue as the cornerstone of Nicaraguan government and politics thereafter. In addition, many of the grass-roots organizations born in that revolution would survive the Sandinista fall from office (see

Chapter 11) and would, in the 1990s, serve frequently to restrain and blunt the most antipopular aspects of the international neoliberal agenda.

Finally, the Chamorro administration itself sometimes demonstrated that it had a will of its own and could defy external constraints in important instances. For example, as the Bush and early Clinton administrations pushed a polarizing agenda of de-Sandinization from 1990 through 1993, President Violeta de Chamorro insisted on a policy of reconciliation which allowed the FSLN, still the largest organized party in the country, legitimate space in the political system. Sandinista leaders were involved in important negotiation and pact-making, and Humberto Ortega was retained as the commander of the armed forces through early 1995. Although it met with strenuous objection from Washington, the retention of General Ortega proved to be a brilliant move. It assuaged Sandinista fears that the military might be employed to violently de-Sandinize Nicaragua in the fashion that Guatemala's military in the post-1954 period had been used to bloodily demobilize groups and individuals associated with that country's deposed mildly revolutionary, democratic government. As a result, the Sandinistas cooperated in the drastic and peaceful reduction of their armed forces. Thus, though events of the 1980s and 1990s had dramatically demonstrated serious limits on Nicaraguan sovereignty, they also showed that some "wiggle room" still existed.

Intervention and Democracy

It would appear, at least in the case of Nicaragua, that foreign intervention had been damaging to civic culture. It can be argued that U.S. interventions (initially against Zelaya, Zeledón, and Sandino, then on behalf of the Somozas, and finally against the Sandinistas), however successful they may have been in achieving Washington's short-term objectives, damaged Nicaraguan politics in at least two ways. First, they created a tendency on the part of some politicians to look to the gringos for solutions to their problems rather than to engage in negotiation and compromise, the essence of any democratic system. The Conservatives did this early in the century, the monied elite and opposition microparties continued this tradition in the 1980s, and the anti-Sandinista right took up the baton from 1990 onward. This tendency, in turn, led to frequent polarization, impasse, and violence. Second, by providing yet another dimension for disagreement and conflict, nationalist-collaborationist squabbling arising out of frequent interventions may well have been one of the major factors contributing to the extreme fragmentation of Nicaragua's party system as seen in the mid-1990s (see Chapter 10).

What about the argument that U.S. intervention was carried out in behalf of democracy? Although few would still maintain that the Yankee "big stick" policy did much to promote democracy during the seven decades following José Santos Zelaya's forced resignation in 1909, one often hears the argument that democracy returned to Nicaragua in 1990 as a result of U.S. pressure. To maintain this position, however, one has to ignore the 1984 elections, the drafting and promulgation of the 1987 Constitution, and the writing of election and party laws in 1988. The 1990 election was simply the latest in a sequence of steps taken by a temporarily sovereign Nicaraguan state to consolidate electoral democracy in the face of U.S. hostility and interference. Indeed, it might well be said that the most antidemocratic aspect of both the 1984 and 1990 elections was the role that the United States played in them.[1]

Was not all that left behind with the end of the Cold War? Perhaps. It is true that Washington's initial postelection policy of de-Sandinization eventually gave way to a more pragmatic decision to treat all political groups, including the FSLN, as legitimate actors.[2] But one wonders if 1990 was to be the last year in which the CIA, the National Endowment for Democracy, and the American embassy in Managua would be massively involved in engineering the outcome of a Nicaraguan election. And one also wonders with Lawrence Whitehead if, after "so many years of harassment and political warfare against the Sandinistas, . . . Washington [would] become a staunch defender of Nicaraguan democracy" in the (admittedly very) hypothetical case of an electoral return to power by "their old antagonists"?[3]

Neoliberalism

The issue of neoliberalism is an interesting one. Nicaragua's experience in the 1990s seems to add to the growing body of evidence from throughout Latin America that neoliberalism, like liberalism in the late nineteenth and first half of the twentieth centuries, can be both an effective stimulant to growth and a real threat to social justice. As Mario Arana shows in Chapter 5, the neoliberal structural adjustments begun in the last two years of the Sandinista period and intensified under the Chamorro administration did eventually result in sharp reductions in inflation and modest growth in gross domestic product. At the same time, however, these policies apparently inflicted severe suffering on many Nicaraguans. The losers included peasants, the huge informal economic sector, and other small- and medium-sized producers who found themselves with little or no access to credit; thousands of government employees who lost their jobs in downsizing; poor people in general who found the social services to which they had become accustomed during the revolutionary period drastically cut back; and even some Nicaraguan entrepreneurs who went bankrupt in the face of competition from cheap imported products.

By the mid-1990s the socially regressive aspect of neoliberalism had become apparent even to normally very conservative forces. For instance, both in Nicaragua and in Latin America in general, the Catholic Church, which by most measures had been moving ever rightward since the election of Pope John Paul II in 1979, had come to denounce the economic fad of the time. Nicaragua's Cardinal Miguel Obando y Bravo, in the 1994 interview cited by Andrew Stein (see Chapter 14), decried the growing gap between rich and poor and observed: "If not controlled, [the market] creates even greater inequality." Similarly, the 25th Ordinary Assembly of the Latin American Bishops' Council meeting the following year stated:

> We want to say out loud that we cannot remain indifferent [to] so many signs of death that appear everywhere: extreme poverty, growing unemployment, uncontained violence and the many forms of corruption and impunity that drive so many families into anguish and sorrow. . . . We denounce "economism" as one of the principal causes of such inequity, that is, the absolutizing of market forces and the power of money, forgetting that the economy is to be at the service of the people and not the other way around.[4]

Thus, neoliberalism, in that it appeared to cut two ways, posed a dilemma. On the one hand, it had the positive effect of stimulating growth and lowering inflation. At the same time, however, it was not at all clear that the social defects of neoliberalism as seen in the 1990s would be any more short-lived than those of Latin American liberalism a century earlier.

Thus, we come to a very important question: Is neoliberalism, with its income-concentrating and socially regressive characteristics, compatible with democracy? William Robinson argues that it is not (see Chapter 2); and there is compelling logic on his side. It certainly would seem that an economic system that generates badly distributed growth favoring a minority at the expense of the majority can only be perpetuated in the long run through less-than-democratic means.

Perhaps the only way for Nicaragua to escape from the dilemma would be for its governments to heed Arana's suggestion that economic policy be more fine-tuned to the country's social and economic reality. Pure neoliberalism is impossible: there is always some government involvement and manipulation. So the question was not whether there should be manipulation, but in whose behalf should that manipulation be done. Instead of placing near-absolute faith in the domestic elite and foreign investors, it seemed that Nicaraguan governments might have been better advised to have used limited credit and other resources to nurture the large "reformed sector" (workers who received privatized state properties in the 1990s), peasant cooperative and private farmers who received land during the Sandinista period, and small- and medium-sized urban entrepreneurs. Favoring those numerically important, potentially very productive sectors might have been good for both the economy and the future of democracy. Indeed, the logic of democracy seemed to predict such an outcome.

The Transition

Nicaragua's experience with regime transition was, in some senses, unique, and in others quite reminiscent of transition experiences elsewhere. As Philip J. Williams noted in the 1994 article cited at various points in this volume,[5] its uniqueness clearly lay in the fact that it involved a long two-phase process, which featured an emphasis on participatory democracy in the early 1980s followed by electoral democracy from 1984 onward. This process, in turn, left a legacy of grass-roots participation in the 1990s that made it difficult for elites totally to ignore the interests and wishes of the nation's poor. Nicaragua in the 1990s was different from Brazil, Argentina, Chile, and other states in the region. Since the transitions in those countries took place after demobilizing reigns of terror, elites were free to negotiate pacts and policy without being unduly concerned about the cowed and silent masses. Nicaraguan politics in the 1990s—with its strikes, demonstrations, takeovers, grass-roots participation in major bargaining concerning privatization, and so forth—was "messier," but in some senses more democratic, than posttransition politics in those other countries.

On the other hand, there were many aspects of the transition that were strikingly similar or analogous to aspects of transition elsewhere. As in many other countries, there was a long process of pact-making among elites. This process had actually begun under the Sandinistas in the late 1980s. In that period there had been many attempts at *concertación*, most of which had been frustrated by U.S. opposition to collaboration with the Sandinistas. From 1990 onward, however, as Shelley McConnell and Daniel Premo show in "Institutional Development" and the "The Redirection of the Armed Forces" (Chapters 3 and 4), there was a long series of negotiations and various pacts or agreements which led to a redefinition of the rules of the political game (the 1995 amendments to the 1987 Constitution) and of the role of the military in it (the 1994 Military Code). In order to reach these agreements, negotiators had to consent to limit their ability to threaten each other's vital interests and instead seek a common ground which a workable majority in the National Assembly could accept.

What was perhaps most interesting in all of this—and most instructive for future transitions in other countries—was the way in which the redirection of the military was handled. As in Chile at the same time but under very different political circumstances, the defeated and outgoing political force was allowed to retain control of the armed forces for a period of time after the 1990 change in government. The United States, which had raised no major objection to Augusto Pinochet retaining control of the Chilean army after that country's transition to democracy, decried President Chamorro's retention of Ortega as chief of Nicaragua's army. But, as noted above, her decision appears to have been a wise one in that, in allaying legitimate Sandinista fears, it allowed important issues such as the reduction and depoliticalization of the military to be addressed in a calmer atmosphere.

Indeed, it would seem that self-proclaimed advocates of democratic transition might learn a lot from the Nicaraguan and even the Chilean experiences. For instance, instead of continuing its rigid anti-Castro policy on Cuba, Washington might be well advised to pursue a more practical, humane, and flexible policy that would allow it eventually to accept a transition in which Fidel Castro and the revolutionary army would retain some role in the process. This policy would guarantee against a counterrevolutionary bloodbath and in doing so make change more palatable to the incumbents. Of course, much would depend on the willingness of Castro eventually to accept a transition. But it is interesting that this strategy is precisely the position held by Elizardo Sánchez, the bitterly anti-Castro head of the Cuban Commission for Human Rights and National Reconciliation.[6]

A "Democratic" Transition?

It is also useful to ponder whether or not the transition in Nicaragua, as of 1996, was truly democratic. I do not want to give a rigid definition of democracy. This subject has been debated extensively for many generations; and, as with many human phenomena, achievable reality often falls short of the ideal even when the latter can be defined. For practical purposes, let us say that democracy is something which involves: 1) universal suffrage; 2) clean, competitive elections held against good background conditions; and 3) a reasonably participatory civil society in which people of all classes feel free to organize into parties and groups to promote their interests vis-à-vis a relatively responsible and responsive government. This said, there was ample cause for both hope and worry in Nicaragua in the mid-1990s.

The negative side is articulated well by Robinson. He is probably correct in saying that the political form most compatible with neoliberalism is polyarchy, which, though it features regular elections, is dominated by a handful of elite groups who control governments that rule over a relatively docile and nonparticipatory population. At least as implemented under the Chamorro administration, structural adjustments did tend to favor the elite few and accentuate class differences. In addition, cutbacks in social spending made in the name of fiscal austerity meant a deterioration of the educational infrastructure which, in turn, impacted negatively on literacy. This impact was ominous, since an educated public is certainly important to real democracy.

On the other hand, there were positive signs. In the successful negotiations leading to the 1995 amendments to the 1987 Constitution and the issuing of the 1994 Military Code, a significant segment of Nicaragua's elites had demonstrated a capacity to compromise. In addition, the 1994 elections on the Atlantic Coast had showed that clean electoral procedures established in the 1980s could be respected in the 1990s. But, most important, the Sandinista revolution had created the rudiments of a "civil society," defined by an author in another setting as "social institutions such as . . . voluntary associations and a public sphere which are outside the direct control . . . of the state."[7] Alive and well in the 1990s, Sandinista-era grassroots organizations balanced associations representing the elite. Thus, the political "playing field" of the 1990s, though not without notable imperfections, was considerably more "level" than that of the 1970s.

Sandinista Revolution: Rest in Peace?

Finally, we can address the final question of whether or not the Sandinista revolution died with the change of government in 1990. I recall, at a roundtable on Nicaragua in California exactly a year after the election, that I observed in passing that the revolution was dead. After the session, Magda Enríquez, a friend on the panel who also happened to be an FSLN militant, expressed her dismay and disagreement with that comment. I also remember thinking that she was not facing reality.[8] After all, not only were the Sandinistas out of office, but they also were not likely to be allowed to make a comeback, even through free elections. But in retrospect it seems that I may have missed Magda's point. True, the FSLN was not likely soon to return to formal power, but the fact remains that many of the changes that they had brought to Nicaragua in the 1980s would be long-lasting, if not permanent.

Eric Selbin makes this point when he argues that the revolution continued after the 1990 change in government because, in the 1980s, "both institutionalization and some degree of consolidation" had taken place.[9] Much of the material in our volume confirms the validity of Selbin's argument. Obviously, since the Sandinistas lost the 1990 election, consolidation had been less than thoroughgoing. Nevertheless, it was clear, regardless of whether or not they identified with one or the other of the two Sandinista parties (or, for that matter, with neither) that many ordinary citizens had become more politically literate during the Sandinista revolution. Notably, they were now more inclined to work collectively through grass-roots organizations to protect and promote their legitimate interests. This cooperation was certain to have an impact on Nicaraguan politics for the foreseeable future.

At least as important, there had been very significant institutionalization. The Constitution of 1987, though amended in 1995, remained the basic law of the land after 1990. The Sandinista People's Army, though renamed and drastically reduced in size, survived as a guarantee against a bloody, anti-left demobilization of the type frequently carried out by U.S.-trained military establishments throughout Latin America in the previous four decades. The Atlantic Coast Autonomy Law of 1987, though sometimes violated by the Chamorro administration, remained essentially intact. The very respected fourth body of government, the Supreme Electoral Council created in the 1980s, survived the change in regime by guaranteeing clean elections, first on the Atlantic Coast in 1994 and probably nationwide into the indefinite future. And the various grass-roots organizations, born during the late 1970s and early 1980s, though weakened in the late 1980s, bounced back to play an important role in the 1990s. Thus, even if the Sandinistas themselves never returned to power, the Sandinista revolution had not died.

Notes

1. John Oakes makes that point in reference to the 1984 election, as does Lawrence Whitehead concerning both elections. See John B. Oakes, " 'Fraud' in Nicaragua," *New York Times*, November 15, 1984, Op-ed page; and Lawrence Whitehead, "The Imposition of Democracy," in *Exporting Democracy: The United States and Latin America, Case Studies*, ed., Abraham F. Lowenthal (Baltimore, MD: Johns Hopkins University Press, 1991), 131–36.

2. Indeed, Ambassador John Maisto (appointed in 1993) commented to the 1994 Latin American Studies Association Research Seminar in Nicaragua (of which I was coordinator) that it was time to leave behind the "hang-ups of the Cold War." Interview, Managua, June 27, 1994.

3. Whitehead, "The Imposition of Democracy," 235.

4. "Injustice Inherent in Neoliberal Capitalism," *Central America Report* 15, no. 3 (June 1995): 12. Since there are several periodicals with this title, we should stress that this one is published by the Religious Task Force on Central America in Washington, DC.

5. See note 36 in my Introduction to this volume.

6. In a March 25, 1995, interview in his apartment in Havana, Sánchez argued that "anti-Castro fundamentalism" in the United States was actually serving Castro's interests by providing an external enemy, diverting attention from problems at home, and thus delaying the onset of the inevitable process of political transition. He asserted that, if it really wanted change, Washington should renew normal trade and diplomatic relations with Havana, which would permit a greater exchange of people and ideas. Once these relations were restored, the United States should then support "an evolutionary process of transition in which the current government plays a role." He pointed to the transition in Chile as a good example. (I was visiting Cuba with William Watts, top aide to National Security Adviser Henry Kissinger during the Nixon administration, and Wayne Smith, the former U.S. Interest Section Chief in Havana in the late 1970s and early 1980s. Due to Smith's status as a former U.S. diplomat concerned with human rights but very critical of American policy toward Cuba, we were given great freedom in interviewing people of various points of view, including Sánchez.)

7. Victor M. Pérez-Díaz, *The Return of Civil Society: The Emergence of Democratic Spain* (Cambridge, MA: Harvard University Press, 1993), 57.

8. The panel was held at Stanford University on March 25, 1991.

9. Eric Selbin, *Modern Latin American Revolutions* (Boulder, CO: Westview Press, 1993), 142.

Epilogue
The 1996 National Elections

On October 20, 1996, an impressive 86 percent of the Nicaraguan electorate went to the polls to vote in the first national elections in over six years.[1] According to "provisional" final results announced on November 8, Liberal Alliance candidate Arnoldo Alemán won the presidency with 51 percent of the vote, followed by FSLN candidate Daniel Ortega with 37.7 percent. Nineteen other candidates split the remaining 11.3 percent. In the National Assembly, Liberals took 42 seats, followed by the FSLN with 36 and nine other parties with a total of 15. Liberals won mayoral races in ten of the nation's 16 departmental seats (including Managua), while the FSLN took the other six. Ironically, even as international observer groups rushed to praise the elections less than a day after the polls had closed,[2] evidence was mounting that the vote count and transmission process were badly flawed. The FSLN and various other parties quickly decried fraud, and it eventually took the Supreme Electoral Council several weeks to make dubious sense of a very imperfect tally.

Thus, several key questions may be asked: What type of man was President-elect Alemán? Why did he and the Liberals score such a decisive victory? Were the elections really clean? And what impact might they have on the consolidation of democracy in Nicaragua?

Arnoldo Alemán

The fifty-year-old lawyer/farmer whom Nicaraguans had just chosen as president was a very talented politician. As a student, Alemán had distinguished himself in both secondary and law school. A Liberal by political tradition, he later developed an intense hatred for the Sandinistas who, in 1979, nationalized the BANIC banking conglomerate for which he worked as a lawyer and then in 1989 (as his wife was dying of brain cancer) seized his agricultural properties and put him under house arrest. Entering politics in that same year, he became mayor of Managua in 1990.

As mayor, Alemán made a national reputation as a sort of right-wing populist. One of the leading figures in a group of vehemently anti-Sandinista politicians, he allied himself with the conservative Catholic Church hierarchy and surrounded himself with returning Miami exiles. Calling for the restoration of properties confiscated under the Sandinistas, the revamping of public school curricula to reflect Catholic values, and the resignation of General Humberto Ortega from his position as head of the Sandinista People's Army, Alemán was a thorn in the side of the defeated Sandinistas. In fact, he even ordered the destruction of revolutionary murals throughout Managua and the extinguishing of the "eternal flame" at the grave of Sandinista hero Carlos Fonseca Amador. At the same time, the mayor was completely at home in the role of "man of the people," drinking and eating in popular restaurants, employing large numbers of the poor in highly visible public works projects, and frequently expressing concern for the plight of the disadvantaged.

Why the Liberal Victory?

Alemán's victory appeared to have been the result of several factors. First, he ran a very effective campaign, which began practically from the moment that he became mayor. Fortified with USAID funds directed toward municipal governments—in particular, Managua—where the people had elected non-Sandinista mayors, Alemán repaired roads, erected street signs, constructed traffic circles, built parks, and awarded patronage to the politically faithful. At the same time, he reconstructed a Liberal Party infrastructure throughout the country, which paid dividends in the impressive Liberal vote in the Atlantic Coast elections of 1994. After he resigned as mayor in 1995 in order to run for the presidency, he began to move toward the center of the political spectrum, toning down his harsh anti-Sandinista rhetoric and stressing the need for credit for small farmers. As a populist, he still tended to use different—and often contradictory—rhetoric when appealing to different groups, but, overall, his image became more centrist.

The FSLN, on the other hand, had the problem of trying to overcome the legacy of economic decline and war in the 1980s and the so-called *piñata* of 1990 as well as the internal divisions and the ultimate rupture of the party in 1995. Only in mid-1996 did it finally work out an effective campaign strategy, distancing itself from policies of the 1980s and reaching out to former adversaries (confiscated landholders, former Contras, and the Church hierarchy). In the weeks before the election, that strategy paid off in a narrowing of the gap between Alemán and Daniel Ortega in some of the polls to a statistical dead heat.

Ironically, the last-minute Sandinista surge apparently served to trigger anti-Sandinista behavior from conservative forces that had previously taken an ostensibly hands-off stance toward the election. The first of these forces was the U.S. government. On October 4, State Department spokesman Nicholas Burns remarked at a press briefing that he did not consider Daniel Ortega to be a democrat and added that "considering his actions against the United States in the past, I think we need to remember that." It is true that, when this and subsequent similar statements by Burns generated criticism that the Clinton administration had abandoned its neutrality, Burns did read a prepared statement on October 11 that contained the sentences: "The U.S. has not and will not take sides in Nicaragua's election. We are prepared to recognize and work with any candidate whom the Nicaraguan people choose as their president in democratic elections."[3] However, these formal remarks were immediately followed by more apparently off-the-cuff anti-Sandinista comments. To many observers, this was a case of having one's cake and eating it, too. The formal statement appeared designed to blunt U.S. and international criticism of Yankee meddling while the off-the-cuff remarks, covered widely in the Nicaraguan media, sent a clear warning to the people.

The second supposedly neutral force apparently moved by the narrowing poll figures into taking a clearly partisan position was the hierarchy of the Catholic Church. Just before the vote, Cardinal Miguel Obando y Bravo held a Mass in the National Cathedral ostensibly to honor the outgoing president, Violeta Chamorro. In fact, to many it appeared to be a thinly veiled Liberal campaign rally. Alemán and Roberto Cedeño, the Liberal candidate for mayor of Managua, were asked to read from the Bible. The Cardinal was dressed in a robe of white fringed with red (the color of the Liberal Party) rather than the green that is customary for that season in the religious calendar. More important, he read from an apparent parable in which a traveler takes a cold and dying viper to his breast in order to save its life.[4] When it revives, the snake bites and kills its kind but foolish benefactor. The intended lesson of this story must have been clear to even the simplest Nicaraguan citizen. On Election Day, all subscribers to the NICANET beeper service received the unauthorized message, "Kill the viper." At the same time, the front pages of both *La Prensa* and *La Tribuna* ran photos of Obando blessing Alemán, shown in a devout pose.[5] And on the day following the election, Alemán was heard to comment on at least one occasion that "the viper" was dead.[6]

The Character of the Elections

What of the charges that the Liberals had stolen the elections by outright fraud? Immediately after the "provisional" final results were announced on November 8, Guillermo Osorno, the Christian Road presidential candidate who placed third, had warned that "if the anomalies are not cleared up completely, there will be a legal but illegitimate government."[7] In a similar vein, Daniel Ortega (who had delivered a generous concession speech within twelve hours after the polls closed in the 1990 elections) declared on November 22, when the Supreme Electoral Council finally confirmed Alemán's victory, that "the Alemán government is not legitimate even if the elections are now legal."[8] Were these men simply poor losers? As of December 1996, it seemed impossible to make an absolute judgment. What was clear was that the 1996 elections were marred by far more anomalies and apparent cases of fraud than the national elections of 1984 or 1990 or the Atlantic Coast elections of 1994.

A large part of the blame for the poor quality of the 1996 elections can be attributed to the National Assembly. On the one hand, that body had delayed in approving the implementation of a national citizen's identification card system (which would be used to verify voters) until 1996. This delay meant that, at a time when it should have been focusing on preparing for the elections, the Supreme Electoral Council was forced to devote much of its energies to the issuing of these cards and, in twenty-six municipalities where violence made this complex process impossible, registering voters through the issuance of civic passes (*libretas cívicas*). On the other hand, in 1996 the Assembly made a number of changes in the electoral laws that were far more political than prudent. Some of the new rules were vague and contradictory; others had the effect of making the process much more complex and difficult. Furthermore, part of the changes mandated a sweeping replacement of electoral personnel, ostensibly for the purpose of reducing Sandinista influence.

There were other problems. First, the grossly underfunded Supreme Electoral Council, headed by Rosa Marina Zelaya, tended to approach its duties in what some people dubbed a "monoprogrammatic" fashion. In other words, it would devote most of its attention at any one point of time to one major problem, leaving others inadequately addressed. In addition, many new electoral officials—especially at the local level—lacked experience or adequate training. And, finally, the proliferation of parties (described in Chapter 10) and the fact that the election involved voting for six different types of office meant that electoral officials and voters alike were required to handle and understand six long, complicated ballots.[9]

All of these factors combined to produce a voting process that was marred by notable inefficiency and many seemingly innocent errors. Of the dozen or so voting places where I observed in the remote northern region of Yalí, few opened on time.[10] Some officials were agonizingly slow in servicing voters, and there were minor errors, such as in one place where voters' thumbs were not being fully inked (one of several measures taken to prevent multiple voting) or two places where local officials were reluctant to give international observers admission to the polls.

The greatest confusion and largest number of anomalies, however, occurred after the polls closed and throughout the next month. Clearly, a breakdown in the system did happen as electoral workers—many of whom had not eaten or slept for up to forty-eight hours—delivered tally sheets (*actas*) and marked and unused ballots to departmental electoral councils and transmitted unofficial results to the Supreme Electoral Council in Managua. In Managua near-riot conditions developed when the departmental electoral council proved to be very slow in processing tally sheets and ballots. As a result, much of this material was dumped in streets, gutters, and ditches by enraged poll workers.

It is during this period of confusion after the closing of voting places that attempts at fraud may have occurred. Certainly, that was the charge made by the FSLN and several other parties. The largest number of vote count and transmission anomalies seems to have taken place in three regions under electoral councils run by Liberal presidents—Managua, Jinotega, and Matagalpa. It was here also that the Supreme Electoral Council encountered the greatest resistance in its effort to carry out a recount. In the end, the tallies for hundreds of polling places in these departments—233 in Managua alone—were either lost or annulled for irregularities.[11] At the time of this writing, it was not clear how much of this problem could be attributed to the politically innocent mishandling of electoral material and how much was due to intentional attempts at fraud. Evidence pointing to the latter can be seen in the fact that the Liberal president of the electoral council of Matagalpa was actually found to have some thirty thousand unmarked ballots illegally in his possession. In all, 1996 had proved to be a disappointment for electoral observers such as myself as well as for many Nicaraguans who had grown accustomed to clean and efficiently run elections in their country.

Future Impact

In any democracy, especially an infant one such as that of Nicaragua, it is never a good sign when many of the losers question the legitimacy of electoral results. Whether the Sandinistas and other parties were fully justified in categorizing Alemán's victory as illegitimate is, perhaps, irrelevant. What counts is that the 1996 elections were marked by great inefficiency, widespread anomalies, and some clear attempts at fraud. The perception of these problems could not help but dampen the civic enthusiasm that had marked the participation of ordinary Nicaraguans in elections from 1984 onward.

One obvious hope was that many of the problems seen in 1996 could be corrected in subsequent elections. When announcing the final results, Council President Zelaya herself noted that the Electoral Law contained "grave deficiencies" that would have to be corrected in the future.[12] Certainly, the rewriting of the electoral laws would help a lot. In addition, no future elections would face the extra confusion that occurred in 1996 as the result of trying to issue citizen identification cards and carry out an election simultaneously. Similarly, because many parties failed to win enough votes to retain their status as legally registered entities, ballots in subsequent elections would surely be shorter and more user friendly.[13] Finally, voting in the future would be further simplified by the fact that not for another twenty years would elections for six different types of office take place simultaneously.

What about the new government? What would it be like, and would it be inclined to strengthen or weaken democratic institutions? At one level, speculation about these matters in the immediate wake of the elections seemed foolish. After all, the president-elect was a conservative populist—and populists of any stripe are difficult to predict because they have a tendency to make contradictory campaign appeals to different groups. However, a couple of very basic observations seemed safe.

The first was that Nicaragua's economic reality and international position would surely leave the new president with very little room to maneuver in making broad policy. Given that his country was economically strapped and heavily dependent on the U.S. $500 million in international aid that it received annually, Alemán would have to pay close attention to the will of the international donor community.[14] Concerned first and foremost with the implementation of the neoliberal economic model, international donor states and organizations would insist on stability as the basis for economic growth. Thus, regardless of personal inclinations, Alemán would be under tremendous pressure to continue President Chamorro's policy of reconciliation and healing rather than confrontation and revenge.

In addition, Alemán would face at least two constitutional and political constraints. One of these was self-imposed: on at least one occasion following his victory, he had rejected the idea of seeking reelection.[15] Although such a concession may seem superfluous, given the fact that the amended 1987 Constitution prohibits reelection, it takes on significance if one remembers that there is a Latin American tradition of popular presidents amending constitutions in order to allow for their own reelection (for example, Juan Perón in Argentina in the 1950s, Joaquín Balaguer in the Dominican Republic in the 1960s, and Carlos Menem of Argentina and Alberto Fujimori of Peru in the 1990s). The other constraint was the fact that the new president would face a National Assembly that had been strengthened by the constitutional amendments of 1995 and in which the Liberals would control only 45 percent of the votes. These domestic constraints, like the international ones mentioned above, would probably necessitate bargaining and compromise.

Conclusion

Although the elections themselves had not been as flawless as those to which Nicaraguans had become accustomed, there was still reason for optimism. Many of the problems that tarnished the 1996 elections were of a one-time nature or could easily be corrected. There was no clear proof that such fraud as did take place was anything more than ad hoc and essentially local. There was a good chance that international and domestic constraints indeed would promote government by negotiation and compromise rather than confrontation and conflict. And, for five years, the Liberals—angry and isolated since the late 1970s—would have their turn. If they did not abuse it, this fact, too, might prove healthy for Nicaragua's civic culture.

Notes

1. Remarkably, more than a month after the elections, there was still debate as to how many Nicaraguans had actually voted. The results at many polling places were lost or invalidated for anomalies. The Supreme Electoral Council (CSE) at that point was counting people who had voted in those places as having abstained. Using that strange logic, the turnout on Election Day was officially around 77 percent. However, when those individuals are counted as having voted, the turnout was about 86 percent—almost identical to that of 1990. See UCA-Nitlapán-*Envío* team, "How Nicaraguans Voted," *Envío* 15, no. 185–86 (December 1996–January 1997): 38.

2. For a well-informed critique of the work of the observers, see Judy Butler, "Observing the Observers," ibid., 50–61.

3. Statement by Nicholas Burns, spokesman, "Nicaragua: U.S. Delegation to Observe the Elections," Washington, DC: State Department Press Release, October 11, 1996.

4. In fact, the Bible contains no such parable.

5. UCA-Nitlapán-*Envío* team, "A New Period for the Nation," *Envío* 15, no. 185–86 (December 1996–January 1997): 7–8.

6. From Nicaraguan television coverage viewed by the author on October 23, 1996.

7. "Nicaragua: Official Election Results Formally Questioned," *Central America Report* 23, no. 44 (November 14, 1996): 4.

8. "Nicaragua: Alemán's Victory Confirmed," ibid., 23, no. 46 (November 28, 1996): 8.

9. For an excellent discussion of the mechanics and procedural problems of the 1996 elections, see Judy Butler, David R. Dye, and Jack Spence, *Democracy and Its Discontents: Nicaraguans Face the Election* (Cambridge, MA: Hemisphere Initiatives, October 1, 1996).

10. I was part of an invited observer team sent by Hemisphere Initiatives/Washington Office on Latin America.

11. UCA-Nitlapán-*Envío* team, "The Roots of the Electoral Crisis," *Envío* 15, no. 185–86 (December 1996–January 1997): 16–35.

12. "CSE oficializa a presidente electo," *Noticias de Nicaragua en Síntesis*, Managua, November 23, 1996, http://www.notifax.com.ni.

13. In Chapter 10, this volume, Coleman and Stuart argue that the number of parties would shrink if electoral legislation included a performance criterion for the survival of political parties. Such a criterion was adopted subsequent to the writing of their chapter.

14. This opinion, voiced by many observers in Nicaragua, was reiterated on the day after the election by Martin Stabile, chief of the Inter-American Development Bank mission in Managua, in an interview with the group I was with.

15. Toby Mailman, "New Nicaraguan Election Results Still Not Final," Nicaraguan Solidarity Network of New York, November 9, 1996, nicanetüblythe.org.

Index

Abortion: Church and, 241
ACRN. *See* Nicaraguan Resistance
  Civic Association
Advertising, 284–85, 289, 290
Afro-Nicaraguans, 179, 219. *See also*
  Creoles; Garífunas
Agrarian policy, 97–111
Agrarian reform: environmental
  aspects, 133; INRA institute, 101,
  214; peasantry and, 29; post-
  Sandinista, 100–102; reversed,
  197–98; Sandinista, 155, 206;
  socialists and, 177
Agricultural credit: structural
  adjustment, 104, 198
Agricultural extension services, 103
Agricultural Producers' Cooperative
  Enterprise (Empresa Cooperativa de
  Productores Agrícolas, or
  ECODEPA), 106
Agriculture: agribusiness sector, 35;
  labor unions and, 196–98;
  neoliberalism, 43; privatization,
  35; production, 104; recovery
  predicted, 87
AGROEXCO, 102–3
Agro-export economy: Chamorro
  administration and, 196–97; labor
  needs, 29; Sandinistas favor, 155;
  social costs, 5; Somozas and, 4;
  after World War II, 98
Agüero Rocha, Fernando, 172–73
Alemán, Arnoldo, 171–72, 190, 276,
  305–6, 307; reelection issue and,
  310
Alliance for Peace, 214
Alliance for Progress, 16
Altimirano, Eli, 174, 175
American Chamber of Commerce in
  Nicaragua (AMCHAM), 254
AMNLAE. *See* Women's Association

ANC. *See* Conservative National
  Action
ANDER (telecommunications
  frequency authority), 291
Anti-Somoza Popular Militias
  (MILPAS), 174
APC. See Popular Conservative
  Alliance
Arce, Bayardo, 154, 156
Area of People's Property (Area de
  Propiedad del Pueblo, or APP), 98,
  101
Area of Workers' Property (APT),
  102, 103, 196
Argüello, Miriam, 48, 173
Armed forces, 65–77
Asia, 38, 138, 258
Assimilationist policy, 223
Association of Confiscated Property
  Owners, 255
Association of Nicaraguan Journalists
  (Asociación de Periodistas
  Nicaragüenses, or APN), 286
Association of South East Asian
  Nations (ASEAN), 38
Atlantic Coast, 145, 219–33; Center
  for Research and Documentation
  (CIDCA), 137; elections, 178, 303;
  radio stations, 292; separatism, 221,
  223–24, 233
Austerity programs, 283
Authoritarian regimes: alternatives
  to, 57; globalization, 25–26, 28;
  transitions from, 15; U.S. domina-
  tion and, 28
Autonomous Regions of the Atlantic
  Coast, 219–33; counterrevolutionary appeal, 206–7; development
  institute, 230; elections (1994),
  178, 179; judiciary, 56; natural
  resources, 131, 140; PLC in

About the Contributors

MARIO ARANA is senior economic adviser for the United Nations Development Program in Managua. Previously, he was research director with the Regional Coordinating [Body] for Economic and Social Research (CRIES), also in Managua. He has published widely on the country's economy in the 1980s and advised the Nicaraguan government on macroeconomic policy and development strategies. He holds B.A. and M.A. degrees in economics from the University of New Orleans and is presently a Ph.D. candidate in the same discipline at the University of Texas, Austin.

ARIEL C. ARMONY is a Ph.D. candidate in political science at the University of Pittsburgh. He is the author of *Argentina, the United States, and the Anti-Communist Crusade in Central America, 1977–1984* (1997) and of scholarly articles on Latin American politics. His present research focus is on the association between civil society and democracy in newly democratized countries, primarily in Argentina. Armony holds a B.A. from the University of Buenos Aires and an M.A. from Ohio University.

JUDY BUTLER is editor of the English-language edition of *Envío*, a monthly magazine of regional current events analysis produced by the Central American Historical Institute (IHCA) at the Central American University in Managua. Editor of the *NACLA Report on the Americas* from 1976 to 1983, she then moved to Nicaragua and worked for the Center for Research and Documentation of the Atlantic Coast (CIDCA) before joining IHCA in 1985. Among many other works, she is coauthor with Sheryl Hirshon of *And Also Teach Them to Read* and author of an unpublished book manuscript, "A Nation Divided: Chronicle of Nicaragua's Atlantic Coast." Butler holds a B.A. from Boston University.

KENNETH M. COLEMAN is a consultant on international development projects, after having served twenty-five years as a faculty member in political science at the Universities of Kentucky, North Carolina (Chapel Hill), and New Mexico. Among his publications is a co-edited book, *Understanding the Central American Crisis* (2d ed., 1991). He was a Fulbright professor at the National Autonomous University of Nicaragua (UNAN) in 1994. In 1996 he did research in El Salvador (published in *Estudios Centroamericanos* and in *Realidad*) and consulted in Guatemala. Coleman earned his B.A. at Grinnell College and his Ph.D. at the University of North Carolina, Chapel Hill.

DESIRÉE ELIZONDO is director of the General Environmental Division of the Nicaraguan Ministry of the Environment and Natural Resources (MARENA). Previously, she had worked for the United Nations Food and Agriculture Organization (FAO) as director of the Nicaraguan National Soil Fertility project, and later for the Norwegian Agency for International Development (NORAD), where she drew up environmental, economic, and agronomic criteria for the assignment of development assistance funds in Central America. She is an ABD in agronomy and soil sciences from the University of California, Davis.

JON JONAKIN is assistant professor of economics at Tennessee Technological University in Cookeville. He has participated in a number of research projects implemented through the Department of Agricultural Economics at the National Autonomous University of Nicaragua (UNAN) that investigated issues related to Sandinista-era agrarian reform and the peasantry. Jonakin has published in *World Development,* the *Canadian Journal of Development Studies*, and the *Canadian Journal of Latin American and Caribbean Studies*. He holds a Ph.D. in economics from the University of Tennessee, Knoxville.

KAREN KAMPWIRTH is assistant professor of political science at Knox College in Galesburg, Illinois. She has published articles in *Latin American Perspectives* and *Social Politics* on gender politics in Nicaragua and is currently working on a study of guerrilla struggle and feminist organization in Nicaragua, El Salvador, and Chiapas, Mexico. Kampwirth holds a B.A. from Knox College and an M.A. and Ph.D. in political science from the University of California, Berkeley.

PIERRE LA RAMÉE is director of the North American Congress on Latin America (NACLA) in New York. He was previously an assistant professor of sociology and has written on the Nicaraguan revolution as well as on economic policy, agricultural development, and land distribution in North and Latin America. Much of his Nicaragua work has focused on grass-roots organizations. La Ramée holds a B.A. and M.A. from McGill University in Montreal and a Ph.D. from Cornell University.

SHELLEY A. MCCONNELL is assistant professor of political science at Bard College in Annandale, New York. In 1989–90 she was a member of the United Nations elections observer team in Nicaragua (ONUVEN), and for the 1996 elections she directed the Carter Center's Managua Office. Her publications include two articles on Nicaragua's Constitution and an assessment of the country's politics following Violeta Chamorro's inauguration. McConnell holds a B.A. from Wellesley College, an M.A. from Stanford University, and is currently completing her doctorate, also at Stanford, with a dissertation on "From Bullets to Ballots: Nicaragua's Revolutionary Transition to Democracy."

KENT W. NORSWORTHY is a Ph.D. candidate in radio/television/film at the University of Texas, Austin, and a research assistant with the Latin American Network Information Center (UT-LANIC). A former assistant editor of *Pensamiento Propio*, he is the author of *Nicaragua: A Country Guide* as well as coauthor of *David and Goliath: The U.S. War against Nicaragua* (with William I. Robinson) and *Inside Honduras* (with Tom Barry). He holds a B.A. from Friends World College and an M.A. from the University of Texas.

ERICA POLAKOFF is assistant professor of sociology at Bloomfield College in Bloomfield, New Jersey. She has published several articles on poverty and underdevelopment in Bolivia and on squatter settlements and neighborhood associations in Nicaragua. Polakoff holds a B.S., an M.A., and a Ph.D. from Cornell University.

DANIEL PREMO is chairman of the Department of Political Science and International Studies at Washington College and also the Louis L. Goldstein Professor of Public Affairs. He has traveled widely in Latin America and written articles on the military, insurgency movements, and U.S.-Latin American relations. Premo holds a Ph.D. in Latin American studies from the University of Texas, Austin. Before entering academia, he served with the U.S. Information Agency in Guatemala and Colombia.

GARY PREVOST is professor of government at St. John's University in Collegeville, Minnesota. He has written extensively on the politics of Spain, Central America, and the Caribbean. He is the coauthor of *Democracy and Socialism in Sandinista Nicaragua* and co-editor of *Politics and Change in Spain and Cuba: A Different America, The 1990 Elections in Nicaragua and Their Aftermath*, and *The Undermining of the Sandinista Revolution*. Prevost holds a B.A. from Union College and an M.A. and Ph.D. from the University of Minnesota.

WILLIAM I. ROBINSON is assistant professor of sociology at the University of Tennessee, Knoxville, and research associate at the Center for International Studies of the Central American University, Managua. His publications include *Promoting Polyarchy: Globalization, U.S. Intervention, and Hegemony*; *A Faustian Bargain: U.S. Intervention in the Nicaraguan Elections and American Foreign Policy in the Post-Cold War Era*; and (with Kent Norsworthy) *David and Goliath: The U.S. War against Nicaragua*. He holds a B.A. in journalism and international studies from Friends World College, and an M.A. in Latin American studies and a Ph.D. in sociology from the University of New Mexico.

Rose J. Spalding is professor of political science at DePaul University. Her fieldwork in Nicaragua, which began in 1980, has resulted in various publications including *Capitalists and Revolution in Nicaragua: Opposition and Accommodation, 1979–1993* and an edited book, *The Political Economy of Revolutionary Nicaragua*. She holds a B.A. from the University of Kentucky and a Ph.D. from the University of North Carolina, Chapel Hill.

John G. Speer is a faculty member at Southwest College in the Houston Community College System with research interest in politics among the urban poor in Latin America. He has conducted case study and survey research among urban informal sector workers in Managua and Masaya and has published in *Comparative Political Studies*. Speer holds a B.A. in political science and history from the University of Texas-Pan American and an M.A. with ABD from the University of Kentucky.

Andrew J. Stein is assistant professor of political science at Tennessee Technological University. In 1991 and 1993–94 he conducted fieldwork in Nicaragua for his dissertation, "The Prophetic Mission, the Catholic Church, and Politics: Nicaragua in the Context of Central America." He has also done research on political participation and elections in Central America. He holds degrees from Kenyon College (B.A.), New York University (M.A.), and the University of Pittsburgh (M.A., Ph.D.).

Douglas Stuart H., a Nicaraguan citizen, is a researcher at the National Autonomous University of Nicaragua (UNAN). An anthropologist by training, Stuart earned a B.A. at the University of the Pacific, did graduate study at Stanford University, and served as Vice Minister of Education in 1979 and 1980. He has written on critical poverty in Nicaragua as well as on issues of *mestizaje* and ethnicity.

Latin American Silhouettes
Studies in History and Culture

William H. Beezley and
Judith Ewell
Editors

Volumes Published

David G. LaFrance, *The Mexican
Revolution in Puebla, 1908–1913:
The Maderista Movement and the
Failure of Liberal Reform* (1989).
ISBN 0-8420-2293-7

Mark A. Burkholder, *Politics of a
Colonial Career: José Baquíjano and
the Audiencia of Lima*, 2d ed. (1990).
Cloth ISBN 0-8420-2353-4
Paper ISBN 0-8420-2352-6

Carlos B. Gil, ed., *Hope and Frustration:
Interviews with Leaders of Mexico's
Political Opposition* (1992).
Cloth ISBN 0-8420-2395-X
Paper ISBN 0-8420-2396-8

Heidi Zogbaum, *B. Traven: A Vision of
Mexico* (1992). ISBN 0-8420-2392-5

Jaime E. Rodríguez O., ed., *Patterns of
Contention in Mexican History*
(1992). ISBN 0-8420-2399-2

Louis A. Pérez, Jr., ed., *Slaves, Sugar,
and Colonial Society: Travel
Accounts of Cuba, 1801–1899* (1992).
Cloth ISBN 0-8420-2354-2
Paper ISBN 0-8420-2415-8

Peter Blanchard, *Slavery and Abolition in
Early Republican Peru* (1992).
Cloth ISBN 0-8420-2400-X
Paper ISBN 0-8420-2429-8

Paul J. Vanderwood, *Disorder and
Progress: Bandits, Police, and
Mexican Development.* Revised
and Enlarged Edition (1992).
Cloth ISBN 0-8420-2438-7
Paper ISBN 0-8420-2439-5

Sandra McGee Deutsch and Ronald H.
Dolkart, eds., *The Argentine Right:
Its History and Intellectual Origins,*

1910 to the Present (1993).
Cloth ISBN 0-8420-2418-2
Paper ISBN 0-8420-2419-0

Steve Ellner, *Organized Labor in
Venezuela, 1958–1991: Behavior and
Concerns in a Democratic Setting*
(1993). ISBN 0-8420-2443-3

Paul J. Dosal, *Doing Business with the
Dictators: A Political History of
United Fruit in Guatemala, 1899–
1944* (1993). Cloth ISBN 0-8420-
2475-1   Paper ISBN 0-8420-2590-1

Marquis James, *Merchant Adventurer:
The Story of W. R. Grace* (1993).
ISBN 0-8420-2444-1

John Charles Chasteen and Joseph S.
Tulchin, eds., *Problems in Modern
Latin American History: A Reader*
(1994). Cloth ISBN 0-8420-2327-5
Paper ISBN 0-8420-2328-3

Marguerite Guzmán Bouvard, *Revolu-
tionizing Motherhood: The Mothers
of the Plaza de Mayo* (1994).
Cloth ISBN 0-8420-2486-7
Paper ISBN 0-8420-2487-5

William H. Beezley, Cheryl English
Martin, and William E. French, eds.,
*Rituals of Rule, Rituals of Resistance:
Public Celebrations and Popular
Culture in Mexico* (1994).
Cloth ISBN 0-8420-2416-6
Paper ISBN 0-8420-2417-4

Stephen R. Niblo, *War, Diplomacy, and
Development: The United States
and Mexico, 1938–1954* (1995).
ISBN 0-8420-2550-2

G. Harvey Summ, ed., *Brazilian Mosaic:
Portraits of a Diverse People and*

Culture (1995). Cloth ISBN 0-8420-2491-3   Paper ISBN 0-8420-2492-1

N. Patrick Peritore and Ana Karina Galve-Peritore, eds., *Biotechnology in Latin America: Politics, Impacts, and Risks* (1995). Cloth ISBN 0-8420-2556-1   Paper ISBN 0-8420-2557-X

Silvia Marina Arrom and Servando Ortoll, eds., *Riots in the Cities: Popular Politics and the Urban Poor in Latin America, 1765–1910* (1996). Cloth ISBN 0-8420-2580-4 Paper ISBN 0-8420-2581-2

Roderic Ai Camp, ed., *Polling for Democracy: Public Opinion and Political Liberalization in Mexico* (1996). ISBN 0-8420-2583-9

Brian Loveman and Thomas M. Davies, Jr., eds., *The Politics of Antipolitics: The Military in Latin America*, 3d ed., revised and updated (1996). Cloth ISBN 0-8420-2609-6 Paper ISBN 0-8420-2611-8

Joseph S. Tulchin, Andrés Serbín, and Rafael Hernández, eds., *Cuba and the Caribbean: Regional Issues and Trends in the Post-Cold War Era* (1997). ISBN 0-8420-2652-5

Thomas W. Walker, ed., *Nicaragua without Illusions: Regime Transition and Structural Adjustment in the 1990s* (1997). Cloth ISBN 0-8420-2578-2   Paper ISBN 0-8420-2579-0

Dianne Walta Hart, *Undocumented in L.A.: An Immigrant's Story* (1997). Cloth ISBN 0-8420-2648-7 Paper ISBN 0-8420-2649-5

Jaime E. Rodríguez O. and Kathryn Vincent, eds., *Myths, Misdeeds, and Misunderstandings: The Roots of Conflict in U.S.-Mexican Relations* (1997). ISBN 0-8420-2662-2

Jaime E. Rodríguez O. and Kathryn Vincent, eds., *Common Border, Uncommon Paths: Race, Culture, and National Identity in U.S.-Mexican Relations* (1997). ISBN 0-8420-2673-8

William H. Beezley and Judith Ewell, eds., *The Human Tradition in Modern Latin America* (1997). Cloth ISBN 0-8420-2612-6 Paper ISBN 0-8420-2613-4

Donald F. Stevens, ed., *Based on a True Story: Latin American History at the Movies* (1997). ISBN 0-8420-2582-0

Adrian A. Bantjes, *As If Jesus Walked on Earth: Cardenismo, Sonora, and the Mexican Revolution* (1998). ISBN 0-8420-2653-3

Henry A. Dietz and Gil Shidlo, eds., *Urban Elections in Democratic Latin America* (1998). Cloth ISBN 0-8420-2627-4   Paper ISBN 0-8420-2628-2